LONGMAN LINGUISTICS LIBRARY

VERB AND NOUN NUMBER IN

Verb and Noun Number in English: A Functional Explanation

Wallis Reid

LONGMAN
LONDON AND NEW YORK

LONGMAN GROUP UK LIMITED
Longman House, Burnt Mill, Harlow
Essex CM20 2JE, England
and Associated Companies throughout the world.

*Published in the United State of America
by Longman Inc., New York*

© *Longman Group UK Limited 1991*

First published 1991

British Library Cataloguing in Publication Data
Reid, Wallis
    Verb and noun number in English : a fundamental explanation.
    1. English language. Verbs
    I. Title
    425

    ISBN 0–582–08616–7
    ISBN 0–582–29158–5 pbk

Library of Congress Cataloging-in-Publication Data
Reid, Wallis Hoch, 1941–
    Verb and noun number in English : a functional explanation / Wallis
    Reid.
        p.   cm. — (Longman linguistics library)
    Includes bibliographical references and index.
    ISBN 0–582–29158–5 (paper)
    1. English language—Number.   2. English language—Verb.
    3. English language—Noun.   I. Title.   II. Series.
    PE1216.R4   1991
    425—dc20   90–24333
                                                              CIP

Set in 10/11pt Linotron 202 Times

Produced by Longman Singapore Publishers (Pte) Ltd.
Printed in Singapore

Table of Contents

Preface

One of the most basic assumptions of linguistic thinking is that some linguistic elements are controlled by others. Verb number is a prototypical example. In the sentence *The boy walks through the field* the *-s* on *walks* appears to be a purely automatic and mechanical response to the singularity of *boy*.

Traditionally such determined elements are sharply distinguished from freely-chosen ones, such as *boy* and *walk*, because the two types must be explained in different ways. Freely-chosen elements are attributed to the communicative intent of the speaker, the aesthetic and social dimensions of which are explored by scholars in a variety of disciplines. Determined elements, on the other hand, are the special province of the linguist. They are explained by constraints that exist quite apart from speakers themselves, and which take the form of the syntactic rules of the language. Since such rules operate within the boundary of single sentences, the sentence has served as the starting point for both traditional and modern linguistic theory.

This book proposes a different understanding of verb number in English. Neither the grammatical number of the verb nor that of its subject determines the other. Each is chosen for its semantic value, and each independently contributes to the communication of the speaker's intended message. As a consequence, this analysis posits *no rule of verb agreement* for English.

The purpose of this analysis is two-fold: (1) to present an innovative account of the principles shaping the morphological form of the verb, the same principles that govern lexical choice; and, in the course of that account, (2) to illustrate the unique *explanatory power* of a framework for linguistic analysis in which the sentence plays no central role.

The framework proceeds from the view that the structure of language is fundamentally determined by its function as an instrument of human communication. This position breaks with sentence-based theory to return to the Saussurean conception of a language as an inventory of *signs*. However, it expands the programmatic Saussurean picture by emphasizing the pervasive influence of general human psychological characteristics on both linguistic structure and language use.

In contrast to sentence-based theory, sign-based theory contains no formal component of syntactic rules. Instead, the occurrence of lexical and grammatical signs is accounted for directly in *instrumental* terms, through a demonstration that their meanings individually contribute to the communication of the speaker's intended message. The co-occurrence of linguistic signs is then attributed to their *mutual* contribution to a common communicative goal rather than to a mechanical relation of formal determination.

In abandoning the sentence-based framework, sign-based analysis must recharacterize linguistic structure in functional, not syntactic, terms. This begins with the initial characterization of the signs themselves. Critical here are their precise semantic values, for these must mesh with the pragmatic principles of goal-directed behaviour that together explain their syntagmatic distribution.

This reanalysis ultimately involves a different range of primary phenomena as well as a broadened conception of what counts as a valid communicative function. Our larger purpose, then, is to argue for this radically functional framework through an analysis of a linguistic feature – the third-person -*s* of the English verb – that would seem particularly intractable to functional explanation.

This book is intended for both a general audience and the professional linguist. General readers may wish to skip sections 1.4–1.14 of Chapter 1, which address the concerns of a reader already familiar with the problems associated with functional explanations of syntax. The ideas therein are redeveloped in a more leisurely fashion in later chapters.

Chapters 4 and 7 offer statistical support for the generality of usage patterns presented in Chapters 3 and 6 respectively. Although both chapters were written with a reader lacking statistical background in mind, they are unavoidably complex. General readers are encouraged to rely upon the summarizing discussion and to skim those sections addressing issues of quantitative analysis with which they are unfamiliar.

Acknowledgements

My intellectual debt to William Diver is immeasurable. From him I learned ways of thinking about language that permeate this book so thoroughly they defy separate attribution.

This book is very much the result of a cooperative effort. I owe an initial debt of gratitude to Erica Garcia and James McCawley for steering me away from premature publication. Their incisive substantive critique of an initial version of the manuscript led me to discard it entirely and start afresh with a new data base.

The present version has benefited greatly from the comments of students and colleagues who, with generosity and good humour, have ploughed through earlier drafts in decidedly less reader-friendly states. I thank Angela Bodino, JoAnn Bouson, Janet Emig, Justina Gregory, Laura Holland, Carolyn Kirkpatrick, Robert Kirsner, Robert Parker, Betsy Rodriguez-Bachiller, Michael Wherrity and David Zubin. Janet Johnston of Holmdel High School and Marylu Coviello, formerly of Secaucus High School, permitted me to administer the animal questionnaire to their students. Martin White of Ramsey High School aided in the development of pilot versions. Without their cooperation, as well as that of their students, Chapter 4 would not have been possible. Special thanks go to Anne Bertin for her tabulation work appearing in Chapters 4 and 10, and to Alan Huffman for his close critical reading of numerous chapters.

The encouragement and guidance from my friend Ricardo Otheguy deserves separate mention. Over the past five years Ricardo has husbanded each chapter through countless revisions, invariably responding with a demand for greater simplicity of expression and clarity of organization. The book owes much to his uncompromising insistence that the interests of the reader must always come first.

Thanks are due as well to the forbearance of the editors of this series who, having accepted one version for publication, saw it and its author disappear for more than four years with little explanation and only the haziest assurance of a completion date.

To my family I owe thanks of a different kind. For the majority of their lives Angus, Colin and Simon have had to make do with a father who often seemed more like a boarder than a parent. My wife Cornelia, for her part, has had to bear many more responsibilities of family life than were her share as a working mother. Cornelia has proved to be my most sensitive reader as well. I learned to count on her to find infelicities of expression that had slipped past all previous readers.

The publishers are indebted to the Canadian Museum of Civilization for permission to reproduce an extract from *The Indians of Canada* by D Jenness, published as number 15 in the Anthropological Series, *Bulletin No. 65* by the National Museums of Canada in 1932.

To Cornelia

To Cornelia

Chapter 1

Sign-based linguistic theory

The goal of linguistics, like that of any science, is to discover the essential nature of its object of study. But since the phenomena of language are heterogeneous and diverse, this inquiry can proceed along more than one path. In practice, then, linguists are forced to make an initial guess about the nature of language in order to begin. That guess will define the problems to be solved, guide the subsequent theory-building, and, in the end, determine the kind of understanding that will emerge.

The question of the proper starting point for a science of language has remained open to debate because language seems to present two faces, each favouring a different strategy of investigation. Outwardly, language provides a means by which people communicate their thoughts and pursue larger goals. If language is studied as an instrument serving human ends, then the interests and abilities of its users will play a central theoretical role. The mode of explanation will be functional in character, drawing connections between the expressive units of language and the uses to which they are put.

The inward face of language is of a formal abstract object. Like mathematics, language has a structure that seems to stand quite apart from the utilitarian purposes of its speakers. If language is treated as an autonomous system, then the explanatory framework will be axiomatic in character. Linguistic units will be posited and described strictly with an eye to the problem of stating the rules that govern their concatenation rather than in terms of the functional value they may have for language users.

It is generally agreed that a comprehensive treatment of language must follow both routes. But there remains the question of where to draw the line. What areas should be dealt with in purely formal terms and what areas require an appeal to the language user? This book is intended as a contribution to that continuing debate, at the heart of which lie conflicting beliefs about the essential nature of language.

The linguistic framework developed in the present work draws the boundary line at a place that greatly reduces the formal component. Since its relocation marks a departure from the familiar conception of a language as a rule-governed combinatory system, it is useful to note where the line is usually drawn, and for what reason.

1.1 Sentence-Based Linguistic Theory

Although the question of the proper domain of formal explanation is still debated, a provisional answer underlies most linguistic thought and practice: the boundary line is the *grammatical sentence*. Within the sentence lie those phenomena that can be successfully dealt with in purely formal terms. Beyond the sentence lie such areas as pragmatics, stylistics, rhetoric and text linguistics; these areas of investigation introduce the language user and focus on the way human values, interests, beliefs and goals shape the way language is used.

The present work departs from this traditional division in that the domain of language open to rule-based analysis does not extend to encompass the sentence. We shall argue for this redefinition of domains through an analysis of verb number in English.

The sentence as basic unit

But why choose verb number as the vehicle for arguing such a foundational issue of linguistic theory? Our choice is due to the conclusion linguists draw from the existence of features such as verb number. Verb number is typically seen as strong *prima facie* support for rule-based sentence grammar.

To be sure, sentence grammar has more going for it than verb number. In modern times the case has rested on 'grammaticality' judgements, and the need to account for the formal and semantic relations between sentences. But such issues arise only *after* a sentence-based framework has been adopted and thus cannot really be appealed to if one is attempting a justification for the framework itself. There exist, however, features of language that do, in fact, argue strongly for rule-based sentence grammar.

To forestall the suspicion that we are about to set up a straw man, we should acknowledge that proponents of sentence grammar are well aware that not everything within the sentence is susceptible to formal treatment. The most obvious intrusion of non-formal factors at the sentence level is lexical choice; whether the word *apple* or *orange* appears as the subject of a sentence is entirely a matter of the expressive intent of the speaker. So, too, for certain grammatical categories; whether a noun occurs in the singular or the plural, or whether a verb occurs in the present or the past is likewise determined by the speaker's expressive intent.

While recognizing these points of free choice, sentence grammarians point instead to the fact that many lexical and grammatical choices appear to trigger automatic morphological responses unrelated to expressive intent. The relation between a verb in German and the case of its grammatical object, or the relation between the gender of a Spanish noun and its associated adjective are prime examples here. Since these 'determining' relations hold over many intervening words, they provide a justification for the sentence as the basic unit of linguistic analysis and serve as observational evidence – if any be needed – that a description of a language must contain a purely formal component of sentence grammar.

Relations of formal determination
As the preceding summary has made clear, sentence grammar rests crucially on the assumption that there exist in language what we will call *relations of formal determination*. In a relation of determination one element mechanically controls, or governs, the appearance of another, and hence can be stated in terms of a rule.

Such determining relations have been the province of *syntax*, and in English, verb number is an often-cited example. In the sentence *The boy walks through the field*, the *-s* on *walks* is seen as an automatic syntactic response to the singularity of *boy*. One feature – that of subject number – is freely chosen for its expressive value. But a second feature – the verb affix – is merely a consequence of the first; no meaning is ascribed to it, and it contributes nothing to the communication. In short, verb number seems to present a syntagmatic relation of formal determination in its classic and most simple form.

The evidential role of verb number
Verb number is an ideal choice for a critical re-examination of formal determination as that notion is exemplified in traditional grammar. The determining relations of traditional grammar generally hold between linguistic categories that are overtly

marked, and this makes their existence checkable through simple observation. In modern syntactic theory, however, this is no longer the case. Within the generative-transformational framework, relations of determination hold between covert, abstract categories of underlying structure and the overt morphology that actually appears.

Since generative theory envisions a highly complex, covert level of linguistic structure, it anticipates exceptions on the observational level. But the informal generalizations possible there are now interpreted as evidence of a greater regularity at a more abstract level. They are cited as confirmation that traditional grammar, while unsuccessful, was nevertheless on the right track; its deficiencies were merely due to the fact that earlier grammarians lacked the formal mechanisms to capture their basic insights (Chomsky 1965:8).

In the face of the caveat that relations of formal determination cannot be observed directly, the question of their existence cannot be resolved on purely empirical grounds. One is left with the more elusive target of suggestive evidence. Still, the feature of verb number in English certainly appears to serve in that capacity as well as any other. The predictive success of even a simple agreement rule suggests that a more sophisticated version – one employing covert categories – will resolve the few remaining problems (e.g., *the couple is* vs. *the couple are*). And the success that clearly appears within reach for this elementary feature gives promise that, with enough time and ingenuity, more complex areas will yield to syntactic explanation. While over the years views have vacillated about what phenomena do and do not fall within the scope of sentence grammar, 'verb agreement' has remained as proof that there is indeed a central core.

1.2 A Functional Account of Verb Number

This book argues for a different understanding of verb number in English. In this view neither the grammatical number of the verb nor that of its subject determines the other. Each is chosen for its semantic value, and each independently contributes to the communication of the speaker's intended message. As a consequence verb number will be accounted for directly in terms of its unique communicative function. Our immediate purpose is to present an account of verb number in terms of the same expressive principles that affect lexical choice. But in so doing we will be removing one classic example of formal determination that has seemed to argue for rule-based sentence grammar.

The explanatory deficiency of syntactic rules

In challenging a rule of verb agreement in English we are not denying the striking statistical correlation between the form of the verb and its grammatical subject. If verb agreement were regarded simply as a provisional statement of a typical co-occurrence pattern, it could not be faulted. But a linguistic rule is not commonly regarded in that light. It is conceived as a theoretical construct, and its formulation carries an ontological claim. Our challenge, then, is to an agreement rule as a theoretical link in an explanatory chain, not as a mere rough-and-ready descriptive generalization (Collin 1985:23).

To clarify our intent, let us consider how a grammatical rule accounts for data, taking, for purposes of discussion, a simplified version of the verb agreement rule (cf. Lyons 1968:148) and the -s on *walks* in example [1].

[1]   The boy walk*s* through the field.

The rule is in the form of an *if/then* conditional statement:

> For (present tense) sentences with third-person subjects, if the grammatical subject is singular, then the verb has an -s affix, and if the grammatical subject is plural, then the verb has no affix.

A linguistic rule states a relation between formal elements in an independently-defined abstract class. Its explanatory force hinges upon the relation between an abstract class and a particular instance, a relation of *type* to *token*. In the case at hand, the observation – the -s of *walks* – is explained by virtue of the fact that (1) the sentence in which *walks* occurs falls within a class defined by the rule, and (2) its formal features match what the rule predicts.

Such syntactic accounts of the verb -s affix have two shortcomings. First, the attempts to state in purely formal terms what count as singular and plural subjects for the purposes of verb agreement have not been successful. This will be illustrated by a large body of examples collected from observation of language use in which the verb does not in fact 'agree' with the number of its grammatical subject. For example.

[2]   An annoyance to me are people who don't answer the phone.
(Leonard Lopate, *New York and Company*, WNYC (New York city radio station))

[3]   The sex lives of Roman Catholic nuns does not, at first
blush, seem like promising material for a book.
                                                    (*Newsweek*)
[4]   Eggs with ham or bacon was the staple for breakfast.
(Philip Roth, 'Memories of a Fifties Education', *The Atlantic*)

These data cannot, in the end, be circumscribed in purely formal
terms, and thus cannot be distinguished structurally from the
examples in which the verb *does* 'agree'. Consequently, the latter
do not constitute a well-defined structural class, and no rule can
be stated for them.

Secondly, in so far as an agreement rule is successful it still
offers little insight beyond that inherent in economical descriptive
generality. Specifically, it does not tell us why it is singular
subjects rather than plural subjects that call for an *-s* on the verb,
nor why English verbs should 'agree' with their subjects in the
first place. Both facts are treated by an agreement rule as
arbitrary features of the linguistic structure of English.

A functional explanatory relation

The account to be offered here contains, to be sure, an arbitrary
component. But the arbitrariness does not take the form of a
descriptive statement of syntagmatic distribution. It resides,
instead, in the characterization of the verb *-s* suffix itself. The *-s*
suffix will be treated as a fully-fledged expressive unit with
inherent semantic value. From that characterization its deployment will be shown to follow in accordance with general
principles of purposeful human behaviour. Since we have already
discounted the possibility of a purely formal description of its
distribution, the account will involve no theoretical level of
structurally defined abstract classes or co-occurrence patterns.
Rather, the crucial explanatory relation will be the functional
connection between *means* and *ends*.

1.3 Sign-Based Linguistic Theory

The treatment outlined above proceeds from the theoretical
position that the structure of language is fundamentally determined by its function as an instrument of human communication.
This position – actually more in the way of an initial orienting
hypothesis – represents a return to the Saussurean conception of
a language as an inventory of *signs*. Through work done
principally by William Diver and his students at Columbia
University over the past twenty years, it has been expanded into

a comprehensive framework for linguistic analysis that has come to be known (somewhat unfortunately) by the opaque name of Form–Content Analysis (Diver 1975; Garcia 1975; Kirsner 1979a; Contini-Morava 1989; Huffman, forthcoming).[1] Without laying a proprietary claim to the term, we will refer to it simply as *sign-based theory* as a way of highlighting its central defining feature.

Sign-based theory departs from sentence-based theory on two basic points: the status of 'sentence meaning', and its mode of explanation of 'sentence-level' phenomena. Interestingly, sign-based theory takes a position on these two points similar to that of sentence-based theory regarding 'paragraph meaning' and 'paragraph phenomena'. And for the same reasons.

Sentence meaning
It is generally recognized that the notional import of a whole paragraph is greater than the sum of its individual sentences. The juxtaposition of sentences in connected discourse leads us to make inferences and draw conclusions that cannot truly be ascribed to any single sentence.

Sign-based theory comes to the same conclusion with respect to 'sentence meaning'. In the Form-Content framework, the semantic information encoded by lexical and grammatical signs does not mechanically determine the interpretation of the utterances in which they occur. Using the word 'meaning' non-technically for the moment, language *under-determines* meaning far more dramatically than is usually recognized (Sperber and Wilson 1986:9–11). In particular, it determines nothing of propositional value.

This position amounts to a rejection of two conventional metaphors that have long guided linguistic theory-building: that of language as a *conduit* of meaning (Reddy 1979); and that of language as a *container* of meaning (Moore and Carling 1982). Both these guiding metaphors have supported the *compositional* view of meaning, in which words embody discrete semantic fractions of the whole, and the whole, in turn, is the straight-forward sum of those fractions (Ruhl 1989).

If meaning is not contained in utterances themselves, then its source must be outside language itself. That source is language users. Language users participate actively in the communicative act. They are not passive decoders, but *creators* of meaning. Language merely acts as a guide. In this creative act people bring to bear their entire store of world knowledge and experience, together with a finely-honed sense of what constitutes a plausible communication.

The central problems of linguistic analysis within the Form–
Content framework are (1) determining precisely what
information is encoded by language itself, as distinguished from
what language users create, and (2) establishing the way in which
this linguistic information facilitates the communicative process.
Work along this line has shown that the semantic values of lexical
and grammatical signs function more often as prompts, clues and
directions to the creation of meaning than as discrete conceptual
fractions.

The conduit and container metaphors also underlie the modern
conception of language as a *representational* system, so in
abandoning the former we also abandon the latter. (Here we
break with Sperber and Wilson.) Thus, in establishing the
contribution of linguistic information to the communicative
process we will fall short of accounting for 'sentence meaning' in
the fashion normally attempted. Specifically, no formal mapping,
or deductive steps, will be posited between linguistic signs and
what we will now call the *message*. This is for the principled
reason that the relation between linguistic information and a
message – the 'meaning' people create – is contributory, not
determining.

Goal-directed choice
We turn now to the second point of divergence from sentence-
based theory, the explanation of 'sentence level' phenomena. As
noted, sign-based theory posits no linguistic level of syntactic
rules. This would suggest that utterance construction is left
unaddressed, an open field of free choice. But 'free choice' is
itself a part of the rule-governed view, the term for the analytical
residue it invariably leaves.

The real alternative to the rule-governed view of language is
not free choice but *goal-directed* choice, selection motivated by a
specific communicative goal. Treating utterance construction in
terms of goal-directed choice means that language users are
operating at the micro-level of individual lexical and grammatical
signs according to the same principles generally acknowledged to
be at work at the discourse level, where individual sentences and
paragraphs are crafted so as to effect the aesthetic or rhetorical
intent of the text as a whole. In short, language users are being
accorded the same active role on the productive side of language
use as on the receptive side. But rather than as a creator of
messages, the language user is now functioning as an inventive
solver of communicative problems.

Clearly this goal-directed tack requires that each lexical and grammatical sign make some independent contribution to the communicative process. For if this were not so, then utterance construction could not be dealt with in purely instrumental terms. Linguistic formatives accounted for by relations of formal determination within sentence-based theory must now be dealt with in a very different way. None can be there by mere linguistic fiat; each must be fulfilling some functional purpose that contributes in one way or another to the intended communicative goal.

An illustration of goal-directed explanation
The active, creative role of the language user is so central a feature of the present framework, and has so profound an effect on its mode of linguistic explanation, that it deserves, we believe, a preliminary but non-trivial illustration at the outset before turning to the subject of grammatical number.

The English auxiliary *do* is an ideal vehicle for such preliminary illustration. It, too, is often cited as an instance of purely formal, syntactic determination in language; and, unlike verb number, it offers the opportunity to address the question of word order. Moreover, this morphological feature of English has a distinguished place in linguistic argumentation, having been chosen by Chomsky to illustrate the explanatory potential of generative theory in its seminal form (Chomsky 1957). For the reader familiar with that earlier treatment, the present analysis offers a striking example of the differing analytical consequences of sentence-based and sign-based theory.

A definitive treatment of *do* would require a comprehensive examination of its position within the entire English verbal system, particularly its relation to the modal auxiliaries. Since our purpose now is simply to illustrate sign-based functional explanation, only selected features of that larger picture (adapted from Diver 1984) will be presented.[2] Specifically, the discussion aims to provide answers to the following questions:

1. How can discourse principles explain grammatical phenomena within a sentence?
2. Why must this explanation involve goal-directed choice?
3. What kind of grammatical meanings are required for this mode of explanation?
4. What is the predictive power of such explanations, and how are they tested empirically?
5. How does sign-based theory handle facts of word order? And, most important,

6.   What is wrong *in principle* with syntactic rules as a mode of linguistic explanation?

1.4 Auxiliary *Do* in English

The picture Form–Content Analysis paints of utterance construction as a series of goal-directed choices recalls the traditional notion *constructio ad sensum*, 'expression according to meaning'. The grammars of the classical languages sometimes invoked this notion to explain why the ancient texts occasionally broke grammatical rules; their authors were simply saying what they intended rather than adhering to the syntax of the language. Putting it somewhat simplistically, the present framework adopts *constructio ad sensum* as its primary mode of explanation, not just as a fall-back measure in those places where another mode fails. That is, it aims to show that *all* collocations of linguistic signs are cases of *constructio ad sensum*.

While attractive in principle, *constructio ad sensum* would appear to have only limited application. Clearly it applies when Spanish, for instance, adds *no* to *Los niños juegan al fútbol* to form the negative statement *Los niños no juegan al fútbol*. The simple addition of *no* is recognized as a direct and logical way of saying what you want to say. But when English adds *do not* to [5], the English equivalent of the Spanish, to form its corresponding negative [6], the *do* is regarded (like verb number) as a semantically-empty, mechanical contrivance that makes no independent contribution to the speaker's intended message.

[5]   The boys play soccer.
[6]   The boys *do* not play soccer.

(Chomsky, to recall, analysed the *do* in [6] as a meaningless formative mechanically inserted as 'the "bearer" of an unaffixed affix', Chomsky 1957:62).

Constructio ad sensum appears inapplicable to *do* in [6] if it is understood to mean expression according to language-universal, logical principles of the kind that might be employed in designing a computer language. Construed in that narrow way, Spanish appears to be operating *ad sensum* while English does not.

Absent in that line of thinking is any consideration of the actual contexts in which speakers make negative statements. Negative statements do not pop up out of the blue. They arise when the possibility of the event has been raised in some way. A denial, then, is always a response to an implied possibility (Givon 1979:104).

When we turn to an examination of contexts which raise the possibility of an event, we find *do* appearing there as well.

[7] The boys *do* play soccer.
[8] *Do* the boys play soccer?

Both the strongly affirmative [7] and the interrogative [8] are typically found in contexts which have already raised in the mind of the speaker the possibility of the boys playing soccer. In all three semantic environments, we propose, *do* is alerting the hearer that the speaker is reacting to *a contextually-implied possibility*.

Emphatic *do*
The notion of *do* as a marker of contextually-implied possibility accords well with the use of the so-called 'emphatic' *do* in [7]. Speakers usually employ 'emphatic' *do* to affirm an event whose occurrence runs counter to an expectation established by the preceding context. I used it precisely for this purpose, for instance, in my discussion of sentence grammar above, when I wrote:

[9] But such issues [of 'grammaticality' and sentence rela-
     tions] arise only *after* a sentence-based framework has
     been adopted and thus cannot really be appealed to if one
     is attempting a justification of the framework itself. There
     exist, however, features of language that *do*, in fact, argue
     strongly for rule-based sentence grammar.

The sentence containing *do* affirms the existence of observational evidence for sentence grammar, something momentarily cast in doubt by the preceding sentence. The words *however* and *in fact* provide additional evidence that a message of contrastive affirmation is intended.

The following example, also drawn from the previous text, shows that the contextual feature responsible for 'emphatic' *do* can lie at some distance.

[10] These data cannot, in the end, be circumscribed in
      purely formal terms, and thus cannot be distinguished
      structurally from the examples in which the verb *does*
      'agree'.

Does underscores the fact that the event being affirmed parallels a denial [11] in the previous paragraph:

[11]   This will be illustrated by a large body of examples . . .
       in which the verb *does not* in fact 'agree' with . . . its
       grammatical subject.

In addition, *thus* in [10] marks the following material (containing
does) as a thematically important consequence of what preceded.
   As can be seen, the choice of 'emphatic' *do* is often due to
factors external to the sentence in which it appears. Because of
the importance of the surrounding context, I will continue to
draw examples from the present chapter. While this practice
would, of course, normally be unacceptable, it has the advantage
here (where the focus is primarily methodological) of illustrating,
through both qualitative and quantitative techniques of analysis,
the consistent application of a single communicative strategy in a
text available to the reader in its entirety. (All but [23] and [24]
were drafted a year before this discussion of *do* was envisioned
and with no conscious thought at the time to its manipulation.)
   Still to come is example [12].

[12]   The discussion so far has stressed the ways sign-based
       theory departs from basic assumptions about the nature
       of linguistic structure. However, the framework *does*
       share some links with current trends in the field.

The word *however* and the antonymous pair *depart/share* both
point toward an affirmation in the face of an implication to the
contrary in the previous sentence.

Statistical confirmation
By appealing to contextual features associated with 'emphatic'
do, we were able to substantiate our claim about its discourse
value in a way that goes beyond self-report or introspection. The
expressions of thematic highlighting *however*, *in fact*, and *thus*
provide evidence, independent of the presence of *do* itself, that
[9], [10] and [12] involve affirmations of contextually-implied
possibilities.
   This evidence is susceptible to quantification in the form of a
demonstration that such words occur *more frequently* with
'emphatic' *do* than with finite verbs lacking 'emphatic' *do*.
Sticking to the data at hand, the entire text of Chapter 1 will
serve as the corpus for this demonstration. Table 1.1 compares
how often such highlighting connectives introduce clauses containing 'emphatic' *do* with how often they introduce clauses
containing simple present and past tense verbs (excluding *be*)

TABLE 1.1 Occurrence of highlighting connectives with 'emphatic' *do* and with simple present and past tense verbs (excluding *be*)[3]

	+ *do*	− *do*	
+ Highlighting connectives	6 (86%)	31 (8%)	
− Highlighting connectives	1 (14%)	364 (92%)	$\chi^2 = 49.90$
			$p < 0.001$

Highlighting connectives = *but, though, while* (non-temporal), *in fact, however, thus, consequently, specifically, in particular*

lacking 'emphatic' *do*.

Table 1.1 reveals that expressions of explicit contrast or highlighting introduce clauses containing 'emphatic' *do* 86 per cent of the time, while introducing clauses in tenses with which 'emphatic' *do* was an (unchosen) option only 8 per cent of the time. According to a χ^2 test of significance the skewing in Table 1.1 would occur by chance less than once in a thousand.

Of course neither 'emphatic' *do* nor a highlighting connective actually mandates the other; each is chosen independently on slightly different grounds. But the fact that both contribute in their separate ways to a message of thematic prominence favours their joint selection more frequently than chance alone would predict. To anticipate our treatment of verb number, we will be arguing that the same holds there too. While subject and verb number are in principle independent choices, their closely-related semantic values favour certain combinations over others.

1.5 The Linguistic Status of *Do*

The discussion so far has proceeded informally, merely noting a consistent correlation between the morphological formative *do* and a certain kind of message. It is now time to characterize *do* more precisely in sign-based terms; and to see how its discourse value follows from its status within the grammar of English.

Do is one part of the unit *do Verb*, an independently chosen grammatical sign of English.[4] Its hypothesized semantic value is essentially that apparent in [9], [11] and [12], namely, the affirmation of an event whose possibility has been raised in the context. This complex semantic value will henceforth be called IMPLIED POSSIBILITY, AFFIRMED. (In Diver's analysis, *do Verb* stands at the top of a scale of implied possibility, with the modals *must*, *shall*, *may*, and *can* indicating decreasing degrees of likelihood.)

Once *do Verb* is characterized as a fully-fledged linguistic sign with inherent semantic value, one component being AFFIRMED, its use for affirmative emphasis follows straightforwardly. The appearance of *do Verb* in the examples above, as well as its regular co-occurrence with highlighting connectives, are all the result of a language user's selecting that linguistic signal because its meaning – IMPLIED POSSIBILITY, AFFIRMED – contributes semantically to the messages being communicated.

Emphatic do = negative do = interrogative do
A semantic treatment of 'emphatic' *do* is uncontroversial since, as a meaning-bearing element (a stress-bearer according to Chomsky), it is plausibly open to expressive manipulation. Not so, however, for the so-called 'negative' *do* in [6] and the 'interrogative' *do* in [8]. We now argue, however, that the *do Verb* of contrastive affirmation (to which the meaning IMPLIED POSSIBILITY, AFFIRMED has been assigned) is the same *do Verb* that appears in negation and interrogation.

This equation of the three *do*'s appears problematic because it has the effect of restructuring the correspondence relations among the sentences. *The boys do not play soccer* becomes the negative of *The boys do play soccer*, not the negative of *The boys play soccer*. But with *do Verb* now characterized as a sign marking the affirmation of a contextually-implied possibility, this is not unreasonable. To negate a proposition stated in its most positively assertive form is, after all, to make the most pointed denial.

Similarly, *Do the boys play soccer?* now becomes the interrogative of *The boys do play soccer*, not that of *The boys play soccer*. But again, questioning a proposition stated in its most positively assertive form produces the most pointed interrogation. The result, to be seen shortly, is that the *do Verbs* in negatives and interrogatives become cases of *constructio ad sensum* no different in principle from those in contrastive affirmation.

1.6 *Do* Negation

In extending the analysis of *do Verb* to negation the first issue is that of automaticity. Hasn't the addition of *do* become an automatic step in a single linguistic process of verbal negation?

The apparent automaticity of *do Verb* is, to a considerable extent, a product of the descriptive strategy of syntactic analysis. In keeping with its basic conception of a language as a rule-governed combinatory system, it partitions the various occurrences of *do Verb* into three logic-based categories (emphasis, negation and interrogation) so that *do Verb* itself can be portrayed as the mechanical consequence of some other element. In the case of *do Verb* in denials, the category is described as simple verbal negation and nothing more. *Do Verb* can then be treated as a mechanical insertion in the context of *not*, the morphological feature responsible for the logical negation of the verb.

In portraying *do Verb* as an independently-chosen expressive unit, the opposite analytical strategy must be employed. Its various occurrences must now be described in such a way as to include a feature for which *do Verb* alone is responsible. This means that: (1) the denials employing *do Verb* must be described as something more than simple verbal negation; (2) the contextual correlates of this additional feature will not be easily statable in purely formal terms (since *do Verb* is now chosen on independent grounds); and (3) one must be willing to search for this feature beyond the confines of individual sentences.

The hypothesized meaning for *do Verb* tells us what to look for: evidence that IMPLIED POSSIBILITY, AFFIRMED is an independent factor in a language user's choice of a *do*-negative from among the various expressive options available. Specifically, we should look for evidence that *do*-negatives are selectively employed just where the speaker or writer wishes to remind an interlocutor that the possibility of the (denied) event has been raised in the preceding context.

An examination of the contexts in which *do*-negatives are employed, *and avoided*, yields such evidence. For example, the Preface of this book contains six instances of negation, none of them employing *do Verb*:

[13]   a. *Neither* the grammatical number of the verb
       b. *nor* that of its subject determines the other.
       c. This analysis . . . posits *no* rule of verb agreement for English.
       d. To illustrate the . . . *explanatory power* of a framework . . . in which the sentence plays *no* central role.
       e. Sign-based analysis contains *no* formal component of syntactic rules.
       f. Sign-based analysis must recharacterize linguistic structure in functional, *not* syntactic, terms.

In a Preface of less than two pages, the texture must be sparse and lean. The subtly anaphoric nuance of a *do*-negative would have introduced an undesirable complexity, braking the forward momentum of the exposition. Negative messages were therefore communicated in other ways.

Following the brief overview of the Preface, Chapter 1 could afford to be more richly structured; now the momentary backward reference of a *do*-negative can help to create a more resonant text. The first instance of a *do*-negative is the following:

[14]   The present work departs from this traditional division in that the domain of language open to rule-based analysis *does not extend* to encompass the sentence.

The IMPLIED POSSIBILITY component of *do Verb* in [14] reminds the reader that the possibility of rule-based sentence analysis was raised two paragraphs back in [15].

[15]   The linguistic framework developed in the present work draws the boundary line at a place that greatly reduces the formal component. Since its relocation marks a departure from the familiar conception of a language as a rule-governed combinatory system, it is useful to note where the line is usually drawn, and for what reason.

The second occurrence of a *do*-negative argues more forcefully for its identity as 'emphatic' *do* by contrasting the former with the latter in a single phrase:

[16]   And the success that clearly appears within reach [for the verb *-s*] gives promise that, with enough time and ingenuity, more complex areas will yield to formal explanation. While over the years views have vacillated about what phenomena *do* and *do not fall* within the scope of syntax, 'verb agreement' has remained proof that there is indeed a central core.

As before, the event has been implicitly alluded to, here in the immediately preceding sentence. In addition, the initial *while* (in the sense of 'although') suggests a reversal of expectation between the *do*-negative and the following material.

The third occurrence of a *do*-negative elaborates a negation first expressed in general terms by the previous sentence.

[17] Such syntactic accounts of the verb -*s* have two
      shortcomings. First, the attempts to state in purely
      formal terms what count as singular and plural subjects
      for the purposes of verb agreement have not been
      successful. This will be illustrated by a large body of
      examples collected from observation of language use in
      which the verb *does not* in fact '*agree*' with the
      morphological number of its grammatical subject.

Note that the initial verbal negation is only minimally
foreshadowed (by *shortcomings*) and, significantly, it is worded
so as not to employ *do Verb* (*have not been successful*); the
do-negative appears in the development that follows, heavily
underscored with the adverbial phrase *in fact*.

Statistical confirmation
The discourse value of *do*-negatives as thematically important
denials of contextually-implied possibilities can be demonstrated
in the same way as was done for 'emphatic' *do*. Table 1.2 shows
how often the same highlighting connectives favouring 'emphatic'
do introduce clauses containing *do*-negatives compared to how
often they introduce non-verbal negation (i.e., nominal and
prepositional phrases) with *no, not, neither, nor* and *none*.

Table 1.2 shows that expressions of thematic highlighting
introduce clauses negated with *do Verb* 67 per cent of the time,
while introducing clauses containing non-verbal negation only 22
per cent of the time. This skewing supports the claim that
negation with *do Verb* implies thematic contrast more strongly
than does (non-verbal) negation without *do Verb*.

From a discourse perspective, the apparent choice this writer
was unconsciously making was between different degrees of

TABLE 1.2 Occurrence of highlight connectives with *do*-negatives and
           with non-verbal negation

	do-negative	*non-verbal negation*	
+ Highlighting connectives	10 (67%)	18 (22%)	
− Highlighting connectives	5 (33%)	62 (78%)	$\chi^2 = 11.85$
			$p < 0.001$

Highlighting connectives = *but, though, while* (non-temporal), *in fact,
however, thus, consequently, specifically, in
particular*

thematic contrast, not between the abstract structural categories of verbal and non-verbal negation.

Do verb **and** *be*

The analytical focus will now be narrowed just to verbal processes. With *do Verb* accorded inherent semantic content it is possible to offer a rationale for its restricted deployment with the verb *be*. The AFFIRMED component of the meaning of *do Verb* functions to focus attention on the associated event. *Be*, however, offers so little in the way of substantive semantic content there is scarcely any event upon which to concentrate. When an underscoring of a *be* clause is desired, it must be accomplished with words whose scope encompasses the predication as a whole.

[18a]   They are cited as confirmation that traditional grammar, while unsuccessful, was *nevertheless* on the right track.

[18b]   While over the years views have vacillated about what phenomena do and do not fall within the scope of syntax, 'verb agreement' has remained proof that there is *indeed* a central core.

The absence of *do Verb* in *be*-negatives follows a similar rationale. *Be* carries so little semantic information it offers scarcely anything of a substantive nature to deny; the intended denial is usually of the associated predicate complement.

[19]   [Language users] are not passive decoders, but *creators* of meaning.

In [19] the denial is of the particular state of being 'passive coders', not a blanket denial of existence. The position of *not* adjacent to both *are* and *passive decoders* reflects this expanded negative scope.

These considerations of semantic coherence are too delicate, however, to have a categorical effect. The peremptory, and event-centred nature of imperatives can supply the focus lacking in *be* itself, and the alternatives with and without *do Verb* are both in currency: *Do be quiet* vs. *Be quiet*. The somewhat exasperated tone of the former comes from the fact the speaker is implicitly acknowledging, through his use of *do Verb*, that his command runs counter to the present state of affairs.[5]

Elsewhere *do Verb* in the imperative has a different effect, but still one accountable for in terms of its hypothesized meaning. For instance, the more genteel tone of *Do sit down* over *Sit down* comes from the fact that *do Verb*, in alluding to a possibility raised by the (extra-linguistic) context, acknowledges the interlocutor's courtesy in refraining from sitting down until invited to do so. Without such acknowledgement of the interlocutor's freedom of choice, the effect is a bald command.

Structural gaps in the verbal system

The restricted deployment of *do Verb* with *be* has been dealt with entirely in speaker-centred, rhetorical terms (i.e., *constructio ad sensum*). Not all combinatory restrictions are open to such pragmatic explanation; sometimes they must be built into the structure of the linguistic code itself. A comparable state of affairs exists in the pronominal system, where the categories of sex and number combine with THIRD PERSON (*he, she, it*), but not with SECOND PERSON (*you*). This is an inherent, hard-wired feature of the linguistic code itself: English lacks a sign combining the categories of sex and number with SECOND PERSON.

Yet the locus of this paradigmatic gap is not altogether anomalous. The lack of sex and number information is a less serious omission in the second person, where the real-world referent is usually present, than in the third, where it is not, and where the identification of the referent thus gets a welcome assist from the additional information.

A similar paradigmatic gap exists in the verbal system. English lacks a sign combining the meaning IMPLIED POSSIBILITY, AFFIRMED with that of the subjunctive; a sign whose signal in the third person would be *do Ø Verb*.

[20a]   I recommend that he *not work* alone. (not: that he *don't work* alone)

vs.

[20b]   I know that he *doesn't work* alone.

But with *do Verb* accorded inherent semantic value, something can now be said about the locus of this structural gap in the signalling apparatus. Messages about events expressed with the subjunctive usually concern their possibility not their actuality, and the AFFIRMED component of *do Verb* would give them too much of an Indicative flavour.

The compound tenses
Other combinatorial gaps are harder to rationalize. The impossibility of combining IMPLIED POSSIBILITY, AFFIRMED with the progressive and perfect tenses – that is, the absence of *does (not) have gone* – seems to be a purely arbitrary fact about the signs available. Yet the inability of English speakers to combine the meaning IMPLIED POSSIBILITY, AFFIRMED with certain tenses ought to have some semantic (and hence distributional) consequence; the logic of the present analysis predicts it. What this consequence could be is suggested by examples [21] and [22].

[21]   The account to be offered contains, to be sure, an arbitrary element, *but* the arbitrariness *does not take* the form of a descriptive statement of syntagmatic distribution.

[22]   In challenging a rule of verb agreement in English we *are not denying* the striking statistical correlation between the morphology of the verb and its grammatical subject.

In [21] an explicit word of contrast, *but*, introduces the clause containing the negation with *do Verb*, while [22] contains no such word. The presence of *but* argues that [21] is intended to be slightly more pointedly contrastive than [22], just the effect motivating the choice of *do Verb* for affirmative emphasis. Example [17], as noted above, illustrates the same contrast: a *do*-negative, underscored with the phrase *in fact*, confirms and amplifies a denial first introduced (without *do Verb*) in general terms by the preceding sentence.

Statistical confirmation
This claim requires further substantiation because the difference in nuance between verbal negation with and without *do Verb* is hard to perceive when contemplated in isolation. Are [17], [21] and [22] merely well-chosen examples, or do they reflect a general distributional tendency? Only a statistical analysis can answer that question. Table 1.3 compares how often the same highlighting connectives introduce verbs negated with *do Verb* in this chapter with how often they introduce finite verbs negated without *do Verb* (e.g., *is not possible*; *have not proved*).

Table 1.3 reveals that expressions of explicit contrast or highlighting introduce 67 per cent of the clauses containing verbs negated with *do Verb* while introducing only 20 per cent of the verbs negated without *do Verb*. These results (a surprise when discovered) support the claim that *do Verb* is associated with

TABLE 1.3 *Do Verb* and highlighting connectives in verbal negation

	+ *do Verb*	− *do Verb*	
+ Highlighting connectives	10 (67%)	8 (20%)	
− Highlighting connectives	5 (33%)	33 (80%)	$\chi^2 = 11.20$
			p < 0.001

more pointly contrastive negation in comparison with verbal
negation without *do Verb* at a confidence level of 0.001.

Table 1.3 includes *be* negatives with simple predicate complements (e.g., *are not passive decoders*). Since it was noted that the
denial in such *be*-negatives is not centred on *be* itself, it might be
suspected the skewing in Table 1.3 is produced by them alone.
Yet when these are excluded from the count, the degree of
skewing remains nearly the same. Table 1.4 compares only
traditional compound tense negatives – progressives (e.g., *are not
denying*), perfects (e.g., *have not proved*), modals (e.g., *cannot
take*) and passives (e.g., *is not employed*) – with the *do*-negatives.

TABLE 1.4 *Do Verb* and highlighting connectives in verbal negation
(*be*-negatives with predicate complements omitted)

	+ *do Verb*	− *do Verb*	
+ Highlighting adverbs	10 (67%)	5 (21%)	
− Highlighting adverbs	5 (33%)	19 (79%)	$\chi^2 = 6.37$
			p < 0.02

The value of non-categorical data
The skewings in Tables 1.1–1.4 are less than 100 per cent because
the decision to employ both *do Verb* and a highlighting
connective in a single sentence is affected by other factors than its
relation to the immediately preceding sentence. In a text that has
undergone revision, the decision may be affected by the
subsequent material as well. In passage [23] the second sentence,
a *do*-negative, might well have been introduced by *but*. Instead,
that word was reserved to introduce the third sentence (also a *do*-
negative), thematically the most important of the paragraph.

[23] In the case of both *do Verb* and *Inversion* the critical
        distributional facts supporting the analysis were to be

found in connected discourse. This concern with discourse *does not come* from any vested interest in textual analysis per se; our focus has remained on the intrasentential problem of *do* and *Inversion*. *But* we *did not assume* that the solution necessarily lay within the boundaries of an individual sentence.

Since the various highlighting connectives reflect thematic importance in more finely-shaded ways than does *do Verb*, some *do*-negatives will inevitably escape our attempt to demonstrate their anaphoric nuance through mechanical distributional analysis. Yet it is still there; the first sentence of [23] suggests an interest in textual analysis which the following *do*-negative then denies. As can be seen, when multiple factors are at work, objective confirmation of such subtle nuances as claimed for *do Verb* must necessarily be in the form of non-categorical skewings of the kind illustrated in Tables 1.1–1.4.

1.7 *Do Verb* in Questions

We turn now to a briefer look at the use of *do Verb* in questions. As noted earlier, a question is a response to an implied possibility, so the IMPLIED POSSIBILITY component of the meaning of *do Verb* is always appropriate. The contextual environment of questions is evident even when they are rhetorical, the kind typically found in a written text. In example [24] the possibility of the examples being unrepresentative is raised in the preceding sentence.

[24] Our claim here requires further substantiation because the difference in nuance between verbal negation with and without *do Verb* is hard to perceive when contemplated in isolation. Are [17], [21] and [22] merely well-chosen examples, or *do* they *reflect* a general distributional tendency?

The AFFIRMED component of *do Verb*, as argued earlier, most appropriately applies to verbs with appreciable semantic content, not to the impoverished *be*. Thus *do Verb* is employed in the question *do they reflect . . .* but not in the preceding question *are [they] merely well-chosen examples*.

1.8 Sign-based vs. Sentence-based Analysis

The sign-based analysis of *do Verb* sketched above presents a rather different picture from that in the typical sentence-based treatment. This, we submit, is because each begins with a different conception of language and hence with different questions in mind. For sign-based theory *do* must be either a sign itself or a fraction of a sign (as proved to be the case). The analytical problem is to establish the identity of that sign, both formally and semantically; and then to account for its use as a creative exploitation of its systemic value.

In pursuing this tack we first established a working hypothesis for *do Verb* based on occurrences where its semantic value is most transparent (i.e., its use for affirmative emphasis). We then extended that hypothesis for testing in contexts where its application was initially less apparent. The contexts themselves were of no particular theoretical interest, since the rationale for the occurrence of *do Verb* in all three proved to be exactly the same.

A sentence-based approach begins instead with the question of the role of *do* in a variety of sentence types that enjoy a quasi-universal status; verbal negation and interrogation in the case at hand. *Do* itself is of interest only as it relates to those processes; so instances of *do* are parcelled out among them for separate treatment, preferably in terms of formal determination. No attempt is made at finding a common semantic core for *do* because finding one would add nothing to the picture of rule-governed automaticity. Generality at the systemic level is sought in the global processes of sentence formation not in a putative semantic value of an individual morphological formative.

1.9 Inversion

Turning farther afield now, what does sign-based theory make of the two instances of inversion in [24]? Isn't the inversion of subject and tensed verb in questions an arbitrary syntactic fact of English? Yes and no. Yes, if it is treated in purely formal terms as one step in a single linguistic process; and no, if it can be treated as an autonomous linguistic signal. Treating selected features of word-order as unitary signals, while clearly a departure from the Saussurean conception of atomic morphological units, adheres to its spirit as long as an invariant semantic value can be posited.

The possibility of assigning meaning to word-order may appear moot for inversion since it is employed for a variety of messages other than questions. But that suggests we should try to think of question messages in broader terms as was done with negation.[6]

Whenever one asks a question one implies ignorance of the answer. There is, then, always an element of doubt surrounding the event named in question. Once our attention shifts from 'question formation' to an examination of contexts in which the event is in doubt, we find inversion there as well.

[25]   *Should he* finish by three o'clock he can leave.
[26]   Rarely *is he* finished before three.

In [25] the finishing is in doubt since it is hypothetical. Similarly, in [26] the finishing is in considerable doubt on any given occasion since it occurs only infrequently. A reasonable working hypothesis, then, is that *Inversion*[7] in English is a linguistic signal whose meaning is DOUBT about the occurrence of the associated event. (See Penhallurick 1987:109–14, for a more detailed articulation of this rationale for *Inversion* with initial negative expressions as in [26].)

When *do Verb* and *Inversion* are each treated as independently-chosen signs, their joint use for questions becomes more in the way of a rhetorical strategy. When a speaker combines *do Verb*, signalling IMPLIED POSSIBILITY, AFFIRMED with *Inversion*, signalling DOUBT, the effect is to imply the speaker's lack of knowledge concerning the certainty of an event. The reasonable inference is that the speaker is seeking confirmation or denial, asking a question. Again, *constructio ad sensum*, though not along logical lines.

Linguistic categories
A critical point here is the differing theoretical status of the notions 'doubt' and 'question'. Doubt is a *bona fide* semantic category of the language – the linguistic meaning DOUBT – because it has a fixed morphological realization, *Inversion*. The notion question, on the other hand, is a contextually-dependent inference that is not invariantly associated with any single linguistic signal. So too, for the notion of hypothetical event (e.g., [25]). These aspects of messages are pragmatic extrapolations drawn by the hearer, not reified semantic features explicitly signalled by the language itself. It is in this sense that language users create 'meaning' from a text.

Strategic avoidance

This under-determination of the message by the meanings provides the explanation for certain familiar restrictions on the use of *Inversion*. *Inversion* is employed with strongly negative adverbs such as *rarely* and *seldom* only when these words occur initially. When they occur elsewhere *Inversion* is not employed.

[27] He is only rarely finished by three.

Similarly, *Inversion* is employed for hypothetical events in conjunction with only certain modals such as *should* and *could*. Elsewhere *if* is employed.

[28] If he finishes by three he can leave.

In view of the fact that the meaning DOUBT of *Inversion* is imprecise – open to various interpretations – the hearer must rely on additional semantic clues to decide how to interpret it on a given occasion. Since DOUBT is most frequently used for questions, that becomes the normal interpretation. But when the message departs from the norm, the hearer must be warned. This is the function of the initial adverbs and modals. Occurring initially, they can steer the hearer away from the statistically predominant inference of a question (Garcia 1979:35). But in the absence of such early warning, DOUBT is too likely to be momentarily misinterpreted as evidence of a question.[8]

To summarize, treating *Inversion* as a linguistic signal with a single invariant meaning accomplishes more than simply permitting a generalization about its semantic environments. It serves as the basis for explaining the 'constraints' on its use within those environments as well. Or, to put it in less mechanistic terms, as an explanation for its *strategic avoidance*.[9]

But how do we know that *do Verb* and *Inversion* have not, over time, become purely formal components in a single process of question formation? As before, the answer lies in examining instances where that combination of linguistic signs is avoided. When speakers wish to raise only a mild query without injecting an explicit element of doubt they do so without *do Verb* and *Inversion*.

[29] (You) mind if I join you?

Raising the voice slightly – intonational lack of closure – is enough to indicate uncertainty. Yet it falls short of acknowledging appreciable evidence to the contrary, the implication of the alternative *Do you mind if I join you*, due to the presence of the meanings IMPLIED POSSIBILITY, AFFIRMED and DOUBT.

1.10 Goal-Directed Explanation

We have seen how *Inversion* implies more to the hearer than its purely systemic value of DOUBT: interrogation in one context and hypotheticality in another. In choosing a linguistic meaning the speaker is counting on the hearer to make these inferential leaps. He chooses DOUBT precisely because he knows it will imply a question on a given occasion.

Yet question, as noted, is not a category internal to the linguistic code itself. It follows, then, that the explanatory connection between such communicative objectives and semantic categories cannot be stated in the mechanical terms suitable for elements within an autonomous axiomatic system. If the notion question is to be invoked – as surely it must – it must be as a communicative *goal* having, as its locus, the speaker alone.

This is why the present line of analysis requires explanation in the goal-directed terms of *means* and *ends*: the crucial explanatory connection hinges on the implicatory link between DOUBT – a fixed, systemic category of the linguistic code – and question – a notion arising only in the context of language use. This cognitive connection suggests an interpretive possibility that the hearer can then weigh directly in terms of its coherence with the text as a whole. The fact that interpretation is a holistic judgement of contextual plausibility, rather than a mechanical computation, is what enables it to proceed even when the structural configuration of the immediate context may, on occasion, be entirely novel.

A discourse perspective

In the case of both *do Verb* and *Inversion* the critical distributional facts supporting the analysis were to be found in connected discourse. This concern with discourse does not come from any vested interest in textual analysis per se; our focus has remained on the intra-sentential problem of *do* and *Inversion*. But we did not assume that the solution necessarily lay within the boundaries of an individual sentence.

Refraining from that assumption in the case of *do* proved strikingly fruitful. By looking at how *do*-negatives relate to the larger context, we recognized they were something more than simple negation at the outset. And that fact was the key to the solution of two distributional problems at a single stroke: the frequent co-occurrence *do Verb* and *not*, as well as the strategic deployment of that combination in extended discourse.

One defect of sentence grammar is its restriction of analytical scope. In attempting to simplify the problem of linguistic analysis by breaking it down into autonomous levels, each susceptible to self-contained analysis, sentence grammar deprives itself of the very data that provide a solution to its intra-sentential problem. And lacking a true explanation for why *do Verb* co-occurs with *not*, it can do no more than offer an economical statement of that problem: a syntactic rule.

1.11 The Abandonment of Syntax

But has our sign-based analysis really abandoned the notion of syntax? Might it not be countered that the rules of utterance construction are simply being redubbed rhetorical strategies in recognition of the fact that they no longer appear to be completely unmotivated? We argue that showing the principles of utterance construction to be less than completely arbitrary forces a shift in their epistemological status.

Two kinds of knowledge

Gilbert Ryle (1949) introduced a distinction we find particularly telling when applied to linguistic knowledge. Ryle distinguished between knowledge of the 'knowing that' variety and knowledge of the 'knowing how' variety. Knowing *that* a bicycle has two wheels, for example, is quite a different kind of knowledge from knowing *how* to ride one. The former can be said to have truth value, by virtue of being amenable to statement in propositional form, while the latter does not.

As long as the principles of utterance construction remain purely arbitrary, one is assured that knowing them is knowledge of the 'knowing that' variety (since they follow from nothing else the speaker knows). And this, in turn, assures us that the knowledge can, in principle, be reduced to an optimally economical statement in terms of discrete, rule-like propositions. This must be so, since a human being can only know a finite number of arbitrary facts.

But once those principles are shown to be less than completely arbitrary, one loses assurance of their finiteness. Drawing on their stock of 'knowing that' knowledge, people can be continually creating non-arbitrary 'how to' knowledge as the need arises. There is no end to it.

'How to' knowledge can be endlessly generated because its creation is essentially a form of problem-solving, and people are very good at solving problems. Confronted by the problem of communicating message A, they must fashion a solution from semantic tools x, y and z, (the meaning of the linguistic signs of their language).

But since any message poses a communicative problem that is unique in detail, people will adjust their solution accordingly. The pervasive theme of contrast and divergence running throughout the present chapter, for instance, may have inspired ways of deploying *do Verb* and highlighting connectives that are not in evidence in other texts.[10] Just such expressively-motivated 'creativity' is responsible for the difficulty encountered by analysts in reducing even so simple a choice as verb number in English to a fixed and finite set of rules.

To be sure, many of these communicative solutions have become routine, requiring no conscious reflection. But one is on a slippery slope here. The knowledge of rhetorical routines (e.g., how to ask questions) slides off into expressively-inspired innovation with no clear demarcation of when one has passed over into the domain of idiosyncratic creativity.

Establishing a boundary line
Rather than attempting to draw the line on speakers' often conflicting reports about what they believe their language compels them to do – judgements of 'grammaticality' – sign-based theory chooses to draw the line on the basis of an analytical judgement of arbitrariness. All that is purely arbitrary – all that has no motivation in terms of a speaker's communicative goal – is treated as knowledge of the 'knowing that' variety, amenable to statement in propositional form. Clearly the knowledge that English possesses a sign whose semantic value is IMPLIED POSSIBILITY, AFFIRMED falls into this category, for there is no reason why English should necessarily have such a meaning, nor any (synchronic) reason why it should be borne by *do Verb* rather than some other morphology.

On the other hand, all knowledge of the functional utility of that linguistic tool for communication, no matter how polished and routine, is treated as 'how to' knowledge and dealt with instrumentally in terms of the facilitating relation between means and ends. Thus our knowledge of how to produce a forceful denial by combining *not* with *do Verb* (in evidence at the sentence level) stands on a par with our knowledge of the open-ended number of reasons for when and where to do so (in evidence at the discourse level).

Statement of this knowledge cannot take propositional form because its validity lies not in its truth, but in its *efficacy*. As a mode of expression, linguistic rules are defective on two counts here: they are descriptively inadequate in being unable to express explicitly a relation of communicative efficacy; while being, in another sense, *too powerful*, for they allow the statement of arbitrary relationships as easily as systemically motivated ones (Zwicky 1968:99).

Relations of communicative efficacy must necessarily be stated discursively, since one is attempting to elucidate a novel conceptual connection, not codify an observable state of affairs. The reason the modern linguistic enterprise of axiomatizing linguistic knowledge has proven to be an ever-receding goal stems, in our opinion, from the erroneous assumption that 'knowing how' knowledge can, through a suitable idealization, be transformed into 'knowing that' knowledge.

1.12 Pragmatic Explanation

The discussion so far has stressed the ways sign-based theory departs from basic assumptions about the nature of linguistic structure. However, the framework does share some links with current trends in the field. To round out the picture we need to acknowledge its points of convergence and divergence with two areas of contemporary research, those of pragmatics and functionalism. (General readers may wish to proceed directly to 1.15.)

The ideas sketched above echo themes appearing in the pragmatic literature, and it is useful to place the Columbia School in the ongoing dispute over the proper domain of pragmatics. Pragmatics has emerged through the recognition of the discrepancy between the meaning of a sentence considered as an abstract linguistic object, and the meaning it has for language users. Indeed, pragmatics is often described as providing a link between the *sense* of a sentence – its literal meaning as a formal linguistic object – and its *force* – the meaning it conveys to a hearer when employed in an actual communicative context.

Leech (1983) sketches the history of the field as a play between the two radical positions of Semanticism and Pragmaticism. The former attempts to assimilate pragmatics within a formal, rule-governed semantics, while the latter attempts to assimilate (sentence) semantics within a non-formal, principle-governed pragmatics.[11] Leech himself advocates what he calls a *complementarist* view in which the study of language use is distinct from, but complementary to, the study of language itself as a formal system.

In developing this position Leech proposes that language use be viewed as problem-solving. The speaker has to solve the problem of finding the best way to bring about such-and-such a result in the hearer's consciousness; while the hearer has the problem of figuring out what the speaker intends him to understand. Human beings, with all their knowledge and abilities, must be placed centre-stage in the communicative process.

While innovative, Leech's position still preserves the sentence as the boundary line between the domains of formal and non-formal explanation. Non-formal pragmatic principles affect the speaker's choice of the specific sentence with which to produce a desired effect, but they play no role in shaping the linguistic features of the sentence itself. Those are still assigned to the formal component of sentence grammar.

The Columbia School shares with pragmatics a focus on language use and a reliance on non-formal principles of human behaviour and interaction: in particular, the goal-directed, problem-solving perspective of Leech. But it diverges from Leech's complementarist view by shifting the point at which pragmatic principles enter the picture. Goal-directed choice underlies the process of utterance construction in all its morphological detail (as was seen with *do Verb* and *Inversion*). As a result, pragmatic explanation advances into the central core of phenomena traditionally reserved for sentence grammar.

In terms of Leech's dichotomy it would appear that the Columbia School is an instance of Pragmaticism, since the domain traditionally assigned to syntax and semantics is entirely taken over by pragmatic explanation. But while it does not operate with a sentence syntax or semantics, it does postulate a level of arbitrary linguistic structure akin to Saussure's *langue*. So the Columbia School actually still qualifies in Leech's schema as a complementarist position, albeit by the skin of its teeth. Its restricted area of purely arbitrary linguistic structure consists of (1) the statement of the *signals* that comprise the morphology of a language, (2) the fixed and arbitrary (i.e., rule-governed) link between each signal and its invariant linguistic *meaning*, and (3) the paradigmatic semantic relations among these meanings. Admittedly, the formalist would find little of interest within this reduced area. But it does preserve the traditional picture of language as both a self-contained system of relationally defined units, and a functional instrument serving human needs.

1.13 Functional Explanation

The Columbia School might better be characterized as an instance of *radical functionalism*. The structure of language as an inventory of linguistic signs is motivated by the communicative function of language; and the deployment of those signs by speakers is accounted for by the contribution their meanings individually make to the communication of a specific message.

The viability of functional approaches to language has been heatedly contested in recent years, and on the whole we agree with generative critics that functional approaches have not proved entirely successful. Since the Columbia School is essentially functional in orientation, it would be useful to make clear how it manages to avoid some of the common pitfalls.

Syntax-based functional explanation

In a general critique of functional approaches to grammar, Newmeyer characterizes the usual research strategy as 'an attempt to show that the generativists' syntactic rules and constraints are nothing more than the reflexes of the exigencies of discourse or reflections of principles facilitating perception' (Newmeyer 1983:9). For reasons we are about to examine, the results of this approach are, in Newmeyer's judgement, less than convincing.

> Each purported 'explanation' of linguistic form in terms of
> communicative function that has come to my attention is one of two
> types. The first type attributes whatever structural property is being
> discussed to informally described human states, drives, needs,
> abilities, and such that have no basis in any existing formalized theory
> of human behavior or cognition. The other type simply proclaims that
> a phenomenon has been 'explained' if it is shown to correlate,
> however loosely, with some discourse function.
>
> (Newmeyer 1983:112)

Both types begin, as noted, with a provisionally-stated syntactic account and then attempt to develop functional explanations for the particular rules, categories and constraints that figure in it. In other words, they aim to provide a higher-level, functional explanation for constructs that already possess a measure of (formal) explanatory power in their own right.

Applied to the problem of verb number, this analytical strategy consists of two steps. An agreement rule is first posited on purely formal grounds with no initial concern for its possible communicative function. The question is then asked: 'What functional

purpose is served by such a rule?' Note that following this mode
of explanation the rule must be retained, even in the face of its
successful functional explanation, because the rule is the only
direct link to linguistic data. The functional explanation, as a
higher level component, can have no independent access.

The dualism of this approach puts the whole enterprise at a
distinct disadvantage. Consider again the path being taken. The
analytical objective is to establish an explanatory link between
linguistic structure and communicative function; yet the version
of linguistic structure serving as the starting point incorporates
the assumption that *no such link exists*! The syntactic framework
assumes the existence of a purely formal component of language,
and the categories and constructs of modern syntactic theory
have all been designed to facilitate the description of that self-
contained axiomatic system. Links and dependencies to things
outside itself have been deliberately cut. *Do*-negation, for
example, is characterized in sentence-bound, logical terms – no
more than the addition of a negative operator – rather than in
terms of how *do*-negation relates to the larger context.

Naturally it is then difficult to re-establish a bridge between *do*-
negation and sentence-external factors. When the problem of its
discourse value is finally addressed, there is, at that point, *no
basis for explaining it*; for *do* itself has already been characterized
as a meaningless formal contrivance. Not surprisingly, the result
is often the loose and unconvincing correlation between 'form'
and 'function' that Newmeyer finds. (In Catch-22 fashion, this
very failure is then cited as proof of the existence of an
autonomous sentence grammar.)

Description before explanation?

The idea that the syntactic version of linguistic structure could be
an obstacle to functional explanation runs counter to a long-
standing piece of conventional linguistic wisdom. Linguistic description and linguistic explanation – especially of the functional
variety – have been traditionally regarded as two separate and
logically distinct enterprises. As Bever argues, the description of
a language must be both independent of, and prior to, functional
explanation.

> The description of what language is must proceed independent of
> particular functional explanations of why it is that way. At a practical
> level, we cannot know what to explain until we have isolated and
> described it.
>
> (Bever 1975:585)

As support for this procedure Bever cites a home-shop drill press, a tool that, he says, can be satisfactorily described quite independent of the relation between its structure and its function.

Bever may be right about the feasibility of neutral description in the case of a drill press, an object whose physical structure is apparent through mere observation. But his analogy to language is inappropriate because language is not a discrete physical object. Language confronts us at the outset with two non-discrete phenomenological continua, those of sound and 'sense'. Description here necessarily involves the imposition of categories to yield discrete units, and this inevitably creates a discontinuity between the observable phenomenological continua and the descriptive categories; there will necessarily be some cutting and trimming in order to achieve a satisfactory fit. Moreover, the categories themselves are inevitably chosen with some particular kind of explanatory mechanism in mind.

At the theoretical level the separation of descriptive and explanatory concerns has been defended on the grounds that it is the only way to assure a fair test of the hypothesis that 'form follows function'; if linguistic 'form' is characterized in functional terms at the outset then the question is being begged (Comrie 1976:10). But this is to apply a stringency in theory-building that would be rejected as unfeasible if imposed in other domains. Consider, for instance, the reaction of a chemist if he were told he must describe the behaviour of matter with the primitives of alchemy – earth, air, fire and water – in order to ensure he was not begging the question of its molecular explanation.

The upshot is that a rule of verb agreement *cannot* be regarded as a purely descriptive statement neutrally summarizing the facts for possible later functional explanation (as Bever would have it); it is a principled description, one involving an idealization that already reflects a decision about what factors will and will not be relevant to the ultimate explanation. To put it in stark terms, any scientific theory creates, selects and describes its own facts (Popper 1959: 107n). It follows, then, that if functional explanation is the goal, a functional perspective must guide the enterprise from the outset.

The union of form and content

One corollary of adopting an initial functional perspective has already been examined. In taking the linguistic sign as the basic structural unit of language, we are implicitly rejecting the conception of linguistic structure as having a purely formal side. For the linguistic sign is a construct that unites 'form' and

'content' in a way that makes an independent analysis of
linguistic 'form' impossible; any statement of the behaviour of
linguistic signs (e.g., the regular co-occurrence of *do Verb* and
not) is at once a statement about both 'form' and 'content'.

This unity of 'form' and 'content' at the level of linguistic
structure means that the path to functional explanation will not
be the well-trodden one. In the introduction to a recent collection
of functionally-oriented articles John Haiman writes:

> All of the papers collected here explore one kind of functional
> explanation for various aspects of linguistic form: that linguistic forms
> are frequently the way they are because, like diagrams, they resemble
> the conceptual structures they are used to convey; or, that linguistic
> structures resemble each other because the different conceptual
> domains they represent are thought of in the same way.
>
> (Haiman 1985:1)

On an intuitive level such ideas have an undeniable appeal.
But one would be hard put to argue their correctness with
someone who was not sympathetic to begin with. Why, precisely,
should there be any consistent and reliable connection between
linguistic form and conceptual structure? They reside, after all, in
substantively distinct domains. And for every example that can
be offered in favour of a parallelism, an alternative one can be
offered arguing the contrary. The would-be functionalist is on
shaky ground here.

In the present framework, the functionally-motivated connections obtain not between linguistic form and conceptual substance;
those links are all conceded to be arbitrary, following the
Saussurean dictum of the arbitrariness of the sign. They obtain,
rather, between the inherent conceptual substance of linguistic
signs and people's larger communicative goals.

The conceptual categories of a language and people's communicative goals are partitioned into separate domains in
accordance with the traditional idealization of a language as a
discrete and self-contained object of knowledge. Yet they clearly
partake of the same cognitive substance. And this makes it
possible to establish motivated connections between the two.
One need no longer argue in terms of *a priori* notions about how
language ought to be structured, but in terms of an analytically-
negotiable, conceptual link between two points on a single
cognitive tapestry.

This imposes a control upon the analytical procedure that is
lacking when iconic connections between pure form and communicative function are claimed. The content side of the

linguistic sign constrains the link that can be posited: there must always be a recognizable conceptual connection between the fixed and inherent semantic value of a linguistic sign and its various communicative functions.

Just such a link exists between the meaning DOUBT (about the occurrence of the associated event) signalled by *Inversion*, and messages of interrogation, hypothetical events, and infrequently-occurring events. As a consequence, the sequences of verb-subject in examples [8], [24], [25] and [26] are described as instances of that linguistic sign. But no such link can be claimed between the meaning DOUBT and the messages expressed by [30] and [31].

[30] There was a large bookcase in the corner.
[31] It's a beautiful day, said John.

Consequently, the order of the subject and the verb in [30] and [31] cannot be described as instances of that same linguistic sign, despite the formal similarity. The upshot is that the analysis of linguistic form is not, strictly speaking, truly formal, since the identification of the signals is guided and controlled by a complementary analysis of their linguistic content.

1.14 The Data of Linguistic Analysis

The discussion of negation with *do* illustrated how sentence grammar, by excluding discourse phenomena as outside its purview, denies itself the data crucial to the explanation of the intra-sentential phenomena for which it does assume responsibility. Not mentioned yet is its equally debilitating exclusion of sentence-level data, namely, the exclusion of the structurally 'deviant' sentences that frequently occur in actual language use.

While the significance of excluding the latter will only become apparent in Chapters 2–8, it is important to lay the groundwork for this argument because much of the data to come are of the type that (in the syntactic framework for linguistic analysis) would normally be discarded as 'ungrammatical' or reflecting the intrusion of 'performance factors'.

The issue here, of course, is what constitutes legitimate data. In our view there is no neutral, pre-theoretical way to decide the question, for it involves the explanatory scope of a linguistic theory, and to a considerable extent any scientific theory defines its own scope of responsibility. 'Legitimate data' is thus a theory-internal notion; what one theory must account for a competing theory can reasonably exclude.

Within the generative literature this issue arose with the introduction of the competence/performance distinction (Chomsky 1965). The competence/performance distinction was an attempt to delimit the responsibility of the axiomatic components of language by providing a principled basis for excluding certain data as outside its scope. Since Chomsky's rationale was in terms of the role of idealization in scientific theory-construction, it is appropriate to continue the discussion along those lines.

The role of idealization
No scientific theory attempts to account for observable reality in all its heterogeneous complexity and detail. Instead, it selects those features that seem to reflect the essential nature of its object of study, focusing on them and ignoring others. (This is the stage where initial assumptions about the nature of one's object of study play a critical role.) Through this process of selection and abstraction an idealized body of facts emerges that serves as the basis for hypothesis testing.

A syntax-based approach to functional explanation is only feasible if its syntactic and functional subcomponents require the same idealizational framework; in that case the two accounts would be addressing the same facts from two different perspectives. But if the two accounts require *different* idealizations, they will no longer be addressing the same facts, and a successful 'modular' account (to use Newmeyer's term) is not possible. This, we argue, is the case with the attempt to offer functional explanations for syntactic rules. To see why this is so, we must examine the idealization that each requires.[12]

The syntactic idealization
The syntactic approach to linguistic structure puts a premium on those facts that seem to reflect the operation of purely formal rules. Since the domain of these rules is taken to be the sentence, sentence-level facts are the primary focus of interest; namely, what morphological sequences count as well-formed (i.e., grammatical), and their inherent, linguistic meaning. Since the formal rules must operate autonomously, data that appear to reflect the intrusion of non-formal factors are set aside as extraneous to the focus of investigation. Those data include sentences whose grammaticality is problematic or whose interpretation depends upon a specialized context.

Because data obtained from actual language use present a

rather messy picture, such data are often eschewed in favour of speaker judgements (usually those of the analyst himself). In fact, reflective judgements are commonly regarded as more reliable evidence than observations of language use because they are less likely to be affected by extraneous (i.e., non-axiomatic) factors. Accordingly, statistical tendencies of usage are idealized into categorical facts of 'grammaticality'. The result is a body of facts well suited to treatment in purely formal terms.[13]

The functional idealization
By contrast, a functional approach to linguistic structure puts a premium on those facts that seem to reflect pragmatic, functional principles. Since the domain of these principles is not yet known, the sentence can serve as neither the upper nor the lower limit of investigation.

Of paramount importance here is the relation between a speaker's communicative intent and his linguistic behaviour. Since communicative motivation is strongest under the conditions of actual language use, data drawn from that source take primacy over people's reflections about what they might say. And 'grammaticality' judgements – judgements about what the language 'permits' – are of little relevance; at least when they conflict with what people actually do.

Examples that may strike speakers as problematic or that may require a specialized context to interpret are of particular value because they often illustrate combinatory possibilities of the language that cannot be imagined apart from the communicative pressures that produce them. Data reflecting statistical tendencies (such as those presented in Tables 1.1–1.4) are preferred to categorical facts because the interplay of competing principles is best illustrated in that form. The result is a body of facts well suited to treatment in terms of multiple, competing and often conflicting principles of goal-directed human behaviour (DuBois 1985).

Analytical consequences
How, then, does this idealizational conflict bear on the present analysis? While its full import will only become apparent in Chapters 5–8, our discussion to date has offered a preview. The empirical evidence against verb agreement in English, to recall, is the frequent occurrence of verbs that do not, in fact, 'agree' with the number of their grammatical subjects.

[2]   An annoyance to me are people who don't answer the
      phone.
[3]   The sex lives of Roman Catholic nuns does not, at first
      blush, seem like promising material for a book.
[4]   Eggs with ham or bacon was the staple for breakfast.

Naturally enough we would protest the attempt to exclude such
data from consideration on the grounds of their 'ungrammaticality'
since that notion does not figure in the idealization framework of
the functional approach being pursued.

In support of our own analysis of verb number as an
independently-manipulated expressive tool we will be citing
examples such as [32] in which a single writer employs contrasting
verb number with the same overt subject in a single sentence.

[32] According to university officials *the average salary* of the
      striking employees *is* $16,500 and *range* from $10,896 for
      the beginning employees to $25,110 for those at the top
      of the line.
                                   (Alfonso Narvaez, *The New York Times*)

If examples like [32] were to be dismissed as 'rule-breaking' for
stylistic effect, our analysis would be deprived of important
evidence in its favour.

Also cited will be examples in which different writers employ
contrasting verb number with the same head noun as subject.

[33a] By the time *New York's maze* of underground and
       underwater subways *was completed*, the railway era was
       ending and the age of the automobile had dawned.
                                   (Donald Dale Jackson, *Smithsonian*)
[33b] I had the opportunity to visit Denon in Tokyo, where *a
       maze* of studios large and small *share* space with the
       company's offices.
                                   (Gerald Seligman, *Stereo Review*)

If such data were to be dismissed as illustrating nothing more
than ideolectal differences (involving the grammatical status of an
individual lexical item), our analysis would again be denied
important data in its favour.

A syntax-based approach to functional explanation is problematic, we have argued, because it is hampered by the ground rules
within which it must operate. To remain truly modular, it must
restrict itself to those facts supporting the syntactic account. But

the way these have been culled and cooked makes success unlikely. To be convincing it really needs to appeal to facts of language use *that are not available to it*, data discarded in the process of creating an idealization suitable for a formal, syntactic account.

It might be imagined that a modular account could take an alternate divide-and-conquer form. This would be possible if the functional sub-component addressed only those facts that had been set aside by the syntactic sub-component. However the present analysis yields no such neat partitioning; the functional account applies *equally well* to those data usually attributed to a syntactic rule of verb agreement (e.g., [1]) as well as to the data the syntactic treatment often excludes (e.g., [2], [3], [4], [32] and [33]). It would appear then that the functional account should get the nod on the basis of its greater generality. In short, we will argue that there is no rule of verb agreement in English because there is no empirical justification for it; the distribution of the verb -*s* is already accounted for by more general principles.

Summary

If syntactic facts were susceptible to functional explanation, the enterprise could be postponed as one of low priority with no harm done. But adopting the framework of syntactic description precludes subsequent functional explanation. As the examination of English *do* illustrated, functional explanation must directly address facts of language use in all their contextual complexity, not features of an alternative, and competing (formal) explanation. If one accepts the definition of the problem of English *do* in purely formal, syntactic terms – *how* English speakers form negative sentences – nothing can surpass Chomsky's ingenious and elegant treatment of thirty years ago. But that treatment is an obstacle to accounting in a principled and consistent way for *where*, *when* and *why* they do so. Like the Maine farmer who put it to the city motorist asking directions, 'You can't get there from here', we concur (with Newmeyer) that you cannot get from syntactic description to functional explanation.

1.15 A Functional Framework

Unable to rely on the syntactic version of linguistic structure, functional explanation must develop a version of its own, one constructed from the outset with functional explanation as its goal. This reconceptualization must inevitably involve both a different range of primary phenomena and a broadened conception of what counts as a legitimate communicative function.

The analysis of verb number will provide a specific example of what language looks like approached from this radically functional perspective. The picture that will emerge involves the following features, listed here briefly, and developed in turn in the chapters to follow.

1. The view of language as a representational system is rejected in favour of a view of language as a *communicative instrument*.
2. The sentence is replaced as the basic structural and analytical unit of language in favour of the *linguistic sign*.
3. The conception of a language as an infinite set of sentences is replaced by the conception of a language as a *finite set of signs*.
4. The *intersection* of linguistic structure and language use is shifted from a point between sentence and utterance, to one between linguistic sign and utterance.
5. The immediate *object of explanation* is the speaker's choice of linguistic signs in the communication of messages, not 'sentence meaning' or 'grammaticality'.
6. The status of lexical and grammatical meanings as semantic components of the message is rejected in favour of the instrumental view of meanings as *hints* and *clues*.
7. Linguistic meanings are conceived as *distinguishing* tools rather than encoding tools.
8. Mapping relations between linguistic meanings and messages are replaced by *means-ends relations*.
9. The relation of *truth* between linguistic meanings and messages is replaced by a relation of *communicative efficacy*.
10. The view of utterance formation as rule-governed is rejected in favour of a view of utterance formation as *goal-directed*.
11. The *creative* aspect of language is reassigned to its human users, rather than to formal characteristics of linguistic structure.

All of the above are consequences of shifting the line of demarcation between the formal and the non-formal from the level of the sentence back to the level of the linguistic sign.

Strategy of presentation
While the linguistic sign is the fundamental explanatory construct

in this treatment of verb number, signs can explain nothing by themselves. They must be coupled with the goal-directed principles that guide the way people actually employ signs in the communication of messages. Equally important is the generality of these principles. They must be shown to operate elsewhere in English so that they have independent motivation.

This requirement can be met in a second area of English, that of noun number. Here can be found in an easily recognizable form all the principles relevant to our account of verb number. For this reason, the presentation begins with three chapters devoted to the number system for English nouns.

Certainly noun number appears to be a more promising area for functional explanation than verb number. The semantic value of the singular/plural distinction for nouns is clear, and much of the time the choice seems directly motivated by the message being communicated. Our focus of interest, however, will be on the problem areas of noun number – mass nouns, *pluralia tantum* nouns, Bloomfield's *wheat* and *oats*, and so-called 'zero plurals' like *sheep*. It is in the context of these problem areas that we will introduce the principles later to figure in the analysis of verb number.

The basic outline of these two analyses I owe to William Diver. They are presented briefly in Diver (1975), as well as in other work done within the Form–Content framework: Garcia (1975) for Spanish and Kirsner (1979a) for Dutch. The presentation, details and data, however, are my own.

The present work incorporates a revised conception of the role of quantitative data in hypothesis-testing. In earlier Form–Content research, (e.g., Reid 1977) statistical data had been implicitly regarded as a direct testing of the meanings on the basis of their mutual 'compatibility' or speakers' preference for redundancy. Following Kirsner (1985), the present analysis presents quantitative data as tests of hypothesized strategies of use. The analysis also draws on Halliday and Hasan's (1976) notion of *cohesion* and develops its application at the intra-sentential level of grammatical relations. This extension involves the role semantic 'redundancy' plays in perception and is crucial to our functional account of verb number.

While the tone of this introduction has necessarily been one of advocacy, the intent of the book is to provide a careful and consistent analysis illustrating the analytical consequences of fundamentally different conceptions of the nature of language. Since those of the sentence-based framework are already familiar to readers, we will proceed directly with our sign-based analysis, developing points of contrast only as they help to clarify the presentation.

Chapters 2–4 present the number system for nouns. The system for verbs appears in Chapters 5–7. Chapter 8 develops a broadened conception of functional explanation based on the notion of *textual resonance* inspired by Halliday and Hasan. Chapter 9 addresses the possibility of synthesizing our functional account of verb number with a syntactic account (required for the representational view of language), a possibility we reject because of the conflicting idealizational framework each requires. Chapter 10 completes the picture of sign-based linguistic theory by exploring the question of the ultimate phenomena it attempts to address.

Notes

1. Nascent features of the Columbia School appear in Diver's work on the English verbal system (Diver 1963, 1964). The first fully-fledged examples are Diver's analysis of Greek aspect (1969) and Kirsner's analysis of the Dutch verbal auxiliary *zullen* (1969). Programmatic discussions are to be found in Reid (1974) and Diver (1975, 1976). Diver *et al.* (1980, 1982) offer theoretical introductions coupled with short illustrative analyses of grammatical features in several languages. Diver (1981) compares the sentence-based framework of traditional grammar with sign-based theory by way of contrasting analyses of the Latin case system. Garcia (1977) offers a similar comparison with generative-transformational theory by way of contrasting analyses of distributional constraints on Spanish clitic pronouns.

   The most comprehensive work to appear is Garcia (1975), an analysis of the pronominal system of Spanish. Other full-length works address: presentative sentences in Dutch (Kirsner 1979a); Spanish gender (Otheguy 1977a); the German case system (Zubin 1978); the French clitics *le* and *lui* (Huffman 1985, also 1983); subject inversion in French (Gildin 1985, also 1979); negation and tense-aspect in Swahili (Contini-Morava 1989). Second-language acquisition studies examine: lexical meaning (Rodriguez-Bachiller 1985); the English verbal system (Bouson 1988); the English articles (Gorokhova 1990).

   Examples of lesser scope have examined: *wa* and *ga* in Japanese (Aoyama 1983); Swahili locatives (Contini-Morava 1976); Swahili tense (Contini-Morava 1983); Swahili *e*, *ka* and *nge* (Leonard 1980); Old English case (Penhallurick 1975); Old English word order (Garcia 1979); verbs of double government in Serbo-Croatian (Gorup 1987); Dutch demonstratives (Kirsner 1979b); *el/la* vs. *lo* in Spanish (Otheguy 1977b); Spanish *si* (Garcia 1983); the position of Spanish adjectives (Klein-Andreu 1983); French aspect (Reid

1977); the discourse use of German case (Zubin 1979); German gender (Zubin 1984, Zubin and Köpcke 1986); Hebrew existentials (Tobin 1982); Hebrew particles (Tobin 1989). A complete Columbia School bibliography appears in *Columbia University Working Papers in Linguistics* 10. Back issues of CUWPL are available by mail: Linguistics Department, 510 Casa Italiana, Columbia University, New York, NY, 10027.

2. Bolinger (1978) sketches an analysis of auxiliary *do* that essentially parallels Diver's unpublished version upon which we have relied. The Columbia School incorporates many of the views that Bolinger has argued so strongly over the past thirty years (e.g., Bolinger 1977). It owes him a greater intellectual debt than we have been able to acknowledge in this book.

3. Also omitted are present and past tense sentences containing any constituent negated with *no, not, neither* and *nor*, since the negativity introduces an additional factor favouring the highlighting connectives not present in sentences employing 'emphatic' *do*. These sentences containing a negative constituent have been reserved for comparison with *do*-negatives in Table 1.2.

    Some of the highlighting connectives occur only in sentences lacking 'emphatic' *do*. They are included because they are semantically equivalent to the connectives which do occur with 'emphatic' *do* in the present text.

4. The fact that tense and number information is borne by *do* as in [12] rather than *share* is the reason why *does share* must be treated as a single, morphologically-complex unit – *do Verb* – rather than as two independent ones.

5. Further support for the lexical content factor is to be found in the variation among speakers of English (to a considerable extent along British vs. American lines) involving the use of *do Verb* with lexical *have*. Negation of *have* is effected both with and without *do Verb: I don't have a clue*, vs. *I haven't a clue*. This variation supports the dearth-of-lexical-content rationale because it occurs with a verb just marginally greater in lexical specification than *be*. It is not, then, a fact we would wish to idealize away by partitioning British and American usage (with respect to *have* at any rate) for separate treatment.

6. The discussion of *Inversion* is based on Diver (1984) and Penhallurick (1987). Penhallurick, diverging from Diver on some details, presents a far more comprehensive analysis than space permits us here. Gildin (1985) offers a treatment of *Inversion* in French which parallels that proposed by Diver for English. See Klein-Andreu (1983) for another Columbia School analysis that posits a word-order signal (for the position of the adjective in Spanish).

7. The term *Inversion* implies a transformational process. Since a hearer never actually perceives such a process, this is not a satisfactory characterization of the signal. *Inversion* is being

employed informally here as a cover-term for a set of sequences in which the Entity in Focus (defined in Chapter 5) follows a lexical stem or auxiliary marked for tense.

8. Only modals and adverbs with a strongly negative or hypothetical flavour can serve in this function. In Diver's analysis of the English Modal System *should* and *could* – originally past tense forms of *shall* and *can* – downgrade the degree of likelihood implied by the latter.

9. The converse of strategic avoidance is strategic exploitation, the consistent deployment of a particular combination of meanings as the solution to a repeatedly arising communicative problem. A prime example here is the regular deployment of *do Verb* + *not* with the simple present and past tenses whenever a pointed denial of the event is intended. Only when the denial is more diffuse is *do Verb* avoided (e.g., 'In the present framework, the functionally motivated connections *obtain not* between linguistic form and conceptual substance. . .').

10. Student research papers have found the same associations between highlighting connectives and *do Verb* in other texts as found here. Had that not proved to be the case, different contextual correlates would have to be found that confirmed (or disconfirmed) the meaning IMPLIED POSSIBILITY, AFFIRMED posited for *do Verb*.

11. According to Leech, Ross's (1970) Performative Hypothesis represents Semanticism. Ross proposed to build into the semantic representation of a sentence the communicative value it has when actually employed by a speaker. Searle's (1969) Speech Act theory represents Pragmaticism. Searle 'views the theory of meaning (and in fact the whole of language) as a sub-part of a theory of action; meaning is defined in terms of what speech acts speakers perform relative to hearers' (Leech 1983:7).

12. This discussion owes much to Moore and Carling (1982) whose cogent critique of the idealizational framework underlying generative-tranformational grammar has clarified our own thinking on the issue. While Moore and Carling aim to underscore the reasons generative theory has failed when judged on its own terms, we have refrained from pushing the discussion in that direction.

13. See Givon (1979:22–43) for a scathing attack on this aspect of the generative framework, a feature he calls 'gutting of the data base'.

Chapter 2

The entity number system

The suffixes /-z/, /-s/ and /-əz/ on *boys, books* and *boxes* are known collectively as 'the plural -*s*'. The term plural carries semantic overtones and the -*s* suffix is clearly meaningful in some way. Since we will not be according this suffix semantic value by the usual syntactic route, it is useful to clarify, by way of introduction, how our treatment will diverge from the conventional one.

Though sentence-based theory accords the plural -*s* semantic value, it does so in a way that distinguishes it from the lexical stems to which it is attached. The lexical stem *boy* bears intrinsic semantic content whereas the -*s* has notional value only indirectly, by virtue of being the formal reflex of the underlying syntactic category 'plural noun'. This means that whenever a noun is interpreted differently in the singular and the plural, that difference must be ascribed to differing semantic values of the noun itself. So, for instance, the differing interpretations of *people* and *peoples* (the *people* arrived vs. the *peoples* of Southeast Asia) reflect different 'senses' of the lexical stem *people* alone.

By contrast, the present analysis will treat the -*s* suffix as a fully-fledged linguistic sign, a unit composed of a *signal* paired with a *meaning*. This places the -*s* on a par with a lexical stem: an expressive unit that directly contributes to the communication of messages through its intrinsic semantic content. The analytical possibility then arises of treating the interpretation of a noun in context as a semantic synthesis of two meaning-bearing units. In the case of *people* we will maintain a single semantic value for the stem, while attributing its shifted interpretation in the plural to a user-mediated interaction between it and the meaning of the -*s*.

2.1 The Entity Number System

The -*s* differs from a lexical stem, however, in that it is one member of a closed semantic system. This system consists of two linguistic signs, an -*s* signalling the meaning MORE THAN ONE, and the absence of an -*s*, a zero signal, signalling the meaning ONE. Together, they form a system in the Saussurean sense of a set of relationally defined units. On the morphological side the -*0* is defined in terms of -*s*. On the conceptual side the meaning MORE THAN ONE is defined in terms of the meaning ONE.

FIGURE 2.1   The English Entity Number System

	meaning		*signal*
NUMBER OF	ONE	=	*Entity* -*0*
ENTITIES	MORE THAN ONE	=	*Entity* -*s* (*s* = /s/, /z/, /əz/)

The meanings ONE and MORE THAN ONE relate to the number of entities designated by the attached lexical stem, which by itself is indeterminate as to number. 'NUMBER OF ENTITIES (designated by the attached lexical stem)' is thus the semantic domain of this system, the conceptual field sub-categorized by the two meanings.

The non-morphological component of signals

Two features of the signals deserve comment. First, they are not purely morphological. The -*s* and -*0* must be attached to a lexical stem that designates an *entity*. Since such words are normally regarded as belonging to the grammatical category 'noun', the number signals might have been defined more conventionally as *Noun* -*0* and *Noun* -*s*. But that would be misleading, for it suggests hearers could depend on the -*0* and -*s* to occur only with a fixed class of words known to them in advance. It is a familiar fact of English, however, that few words serve solely as the name of persons places or things.

[1]   The glass was full of *water*.
[2]   He *watered* the plants.

The inherent semantic content of the word *water* would seem to be the name of a physical substance as in [1]; yet this semantic value does not preclude its deployment in a different capacity, as in [2].

A functional grouping of words yields no neater results. The predominant use of a word like *up* would seem to put it in the class of prepositions.

[3] He walked *up* the hill.

Yet it is employed in the manner of an adverb, a verb, an adjective, and a noun as well.

[4] He looked the number *up*.
[5] They *upped* the price.
[6] The *up* escalator was not in service.
[7] The *ups* and downs of the stock market.

The point is that since most words can be pressed into service as nouns in the appropriate context, they do not constitute a fixed class. Noun status is imposed upon a word by the context rather than being an inherent linguistic property of the word itself. 'Nouns' are identified by language users on the spot, relying on contextual clues such as articles and position.

In view of the fact that the term 'noun' is well established within sentence-based theory as the name of a fixed syntactic class, it seems pointless to redefine it in an idiosyncratic fashion here. Better to dispense with the term altogether in favour of one that suggests what is really at issue: the interpretation of a lexical stem in context. The term *entity* then, as we intend it, designates the conceptual status of a word on an individual occasion, not a fixed class of words. By including this term in the definition of the number signals we are explicitly acknowledging the boot-strap element involved in their identification; one component of the signals is, in fact, a product of the comprehension process. It will be seen that the perceptual problem inherent in the recognition of these two signals, so defined, influences their deployment.

A second feature to be noted is that the two signals include a configurational component. The fact that the -*s* and -*0* directly follow the lexical stem has been made an integral, defining feature of each signal. Their position, then, is not a fact of syntagmatic distribution but one of signal identity. As such, it falls within the domain of the purely arbitrary, and no attempt will be made to offer a synchronic functional explanation.

2.2 Analytical Principles

Two basic principles underlie our approach to grammatical number, one relating to the nature of language itself and the other to the nature of language use. Of the two, the first is the more firmly established: linguistic signs constitute a language-specific system of semantic classification (Saussure 1916, Whorf 1962, Lakoff 1987).

This fact is well recognized in the area of lexical meaning. The word *chez* has no single-word equivalent in English. *Chez* encodes a concept unique to French. Admittedly it seems, at times, functionally equivalent to the English word *home*: *chez moi* = 'my home'. But not always. Nothing in English can match the compressed elegance of *chez Flaubert* (roughly 'in the work of Flaubert').

The notion of a language as a system of semantic classification holds for grammatical signs as well. The distinction made in French by the two past tenses the *passe simple* and the *imparfait* has no consistent counterpart in English and is often lost entirely in translation (Reid 1977, 1979; Reid and Gildin 1979). Similarly, Chapter 1 showed that *do Verb* allows English speakers to make distinctions that are not so easily made in Spanish, which lacks a direct equivalent.

The analytical consequence of this fact is that neither external reference nor a language-universal semantics can serve as the starting point for understanding the deployment of linguistic signs. Since linguistic meanings form a language-specific conceptual scheme, the explanation must be in terms of that system itself.

The second principle, while seeming to follow from the first, is less well recognized. Deployment of the categories of a language necessitates creative problem-solving on the part of both speaker and hearer. This is because of the *discrepancy* between the conceptual categories and the message being communicated. The speaker must operate with expressive units that often do not neatly match the message he or she wishes to convey; and the hearer, in turn, must bridge the gap between the language-specific categories and the intended message.

In other words, rather than developing a Whorfian picture of speakers entrapped by the conceptual categories of their language, we see speakers successfully surmounting these constraints to express messages for which the categories are not ideally suited. But in so doing, they exhibit an ingenuity and creativity that cannot, in the end, be captured in axiomatic terms. Hence the necessity of the problem-solving perspective in coming to an understanding of how people communicate through language.

Chapter 1 offered an example of both these principles applied to the problem of *Inversion*. *Inversion* was characterized as a signal of the semantic category DOUBT. In positing DOUBT as the meaning of *Inversion*, we created a discrepancy between its systemic linguistic value and its predominant use in the communication of messages of interrogation. Bridging that gap requires the problem-solving skills of language users who must attend to contextual clues to decide if a question is actually intended. But that discrepancy was an analytically useful one, for it enabled us to explain why *Inversion* is also employed in the communication of messages about hypothetical and infrequently-occurring events, as well as its restricted use for such messages.

It is important to recognize that the problem-solving perspective is at odds with the generally accepted conception of language as a representational system. When language is conceived as a system that directly represents thought, there does not seem to be much call for creative problem-solving in rendering our thoughts in words; we select words whose semantic values exactly match conceptual components of our thought and then arrange those words according to the fixed syntactic rules of the language. But this representational view erases the very discrepancy between thought and language responsible, we argue, for much of what otherwise appears arbitrary and unmotivated. The problem-solving tack requires highlighting the obstacles in communicating with language rather than extolling its success.

We have already laid the groundwork for an important mismatch between linguistic categories and communicative goals in the area of number. In refraining from positing 'noun' as an inherent category of English we have created a discrepancy between the organization of the lexicon and the messages people wish to convey. Clearly English messages contain conceptual components that fit the traditional definition of nouns as the names of persons, places and things. Yet the English lexicon does not appear to be organized in such a way as to neatly reflect that fact.

However, this discrepancy helps to explain the existence of a rich inventory of determiners that can compensate for the absence of fixed lexical classes by telling the hearer how to construe the associated lexical stem on a given occasion. The traditional picture of articles and quantifiers as mechanical responses to covert semantic features of the 'noun' has the tail wagging the dog. The grammatical signs impose an interpretation on lexical stems that by themselves are often conceptually and functionally indeterminate.

In this chapter and the next we will develop these two

principles in detail through their application to the problem of grammatical number in English.

2.3 Referential vs. Conceptual Number

Textbook examples of grammatical number in English often portray it as a direct reflection of referential number.

[8] The *boy0* walked down the street.
[9] The *boys* walked down the street.

Disappointment ensues, of course, if such usage is taken to be the rule.

[10] The *team0* scored three goals during the final minutes of the game.
[11] The *players* scored three goals during the final minutes of the game.

The objective referential reality described by examples [10] and [11] could well be exactly the same. What differs is how that reality is described. In [10] the human beings on the field are categorized as a 'team' while in [11] they are categorized as 'players'.

Once the lexical stem is recognized as a crucial ingredient in the choice of grammatical number the problem of [10] and [11] is quickly resolved. The lexical stem imposes a categorization in terms of which the counting is then carried out. [10] and [11] now become the textbook examples of grammatical number because they most effectively highlight the importance of the categorization imposed by the lexical stem. [8] and [9] are simply cases where referential and conceptual number happen to coincide.

Counting and categories

The importance of lexical categorization follows from a simple but fundamental fact about counting. Before counting can begin, one must settle on *what* is being counted, and this makes the act of counting inextricably tied to conceptual categories. How you categorize what is being counted affects the results. Consider, for example, attempting to count an array of produce from an apple tree and an orange tree; one arrives at one figure if it is all regarded as 'fruit' and two separate figures if it is regarded as 'apples' and 'oranges'.

Frege, citing Spinoza, makes the same point[1]:

we only think of things in terms of number after they have first been reduced to a common genus. For example, a man who holds in his hand a sesterce and a dollar will not think of the number two unless he can cover his sesterce and his dollar with one and the same name. viz., a piece of silver or coin; then he can affirm that he has two pieces of silver, or two coins; since he designates by that name piece of silver or coin not only the sesterce but also the dollar.

(Frege 1950:62)

According to this line of reasoning, whereas the act of enumeration by itself is mechanical and objective, the categorization which makes enumeration possible is imposed by the observer. Strictly speaking, then, one cannot speak of discrepancies (or, indeed, matches) between conceptual and referential number because the latter is not an objectively-assessable feature of external reality. One can observe that a particular language offers alternative categories in terms of which the counting can proceed; and argue that one is more suitable than another in a particular context. But no report of number has a greater claim to objective truth than any other. Each constitutes an observer-dependent act of interpretation.

In appealing to the categorization imposed by the lexical stem we have shifted the problem of the choice of grammatical number to that of the meanings of words. The semantic value of lexical stems must now be characterized in such a way that the accompanying number choice follows in a straightforward fashion.

This is easy enough for *team* and *player*. The meaning of *team* is not just 'aggregate of players'; the players must be functioning cooperatively in some kind of group activity. This unity of purpose, present in *team* but absent in *player*, is what enables physically discrete referents to be conceptualized as a single thing.

2.4 The Appeal of Reference

The limitation of referential number is widely acknowledged in principle. Yet referential number is so appealing a benchmark against which to test the proposition that grammatical distinctions are fundamentally semantic that it reasserts itself whenever the situation is less transparent than the one above.

It is easy enough to show that grammatical distinctions are not semantic ones by indicating the many cases where there is not a one-to-one correspondence. An often quoted example is that of *oats* and

wheat. The former is clearly plural and the latter singular. . . Further
examples are to be found in *foliage* vs. *leaves*, in English *hair*, which is
singular vs. French *cheveux*, plural. These distinctions are grammatical
and do not directly correspond to any categories of meaning.

                                                        (Palmer 1978:34–5)

Oats and *wheat* are a problem in anyone's book. But surely not
foliage and *leaves*. Palmer is certainly aware that these words are
employed in different situations to communicate different kinds
of messages.

[12] John raked *leaves* all morning.
[13] The fall *foliage* was breathtaking this year.

The difference between *leaf* and *foliage* is simply a slightly more
subtle version of that between *player* and *team*. *Leaf* designates a
particular feature of botanical morphology, while *foliage* designates large aggregates of such things. The former (in the plural)
is employed to suggest that the individual components are still
discernible as separate countable objects, as in the activity of
raking; while the latter is employed in reference to a visual array
that is often at too great a distance for its individual components
to be separately perceived.

In saying that 'grammatical distinctions are not semantic ones'
Palmer shows that for him 'semantic' pertains exclusively to an
external reality. And his phrase 'categories of meaning' cannot be
understood in language-specific terms, for then *hair* and *cheveux*
are poorly chosen examples. French *cheveux* ('hair *en masse*')
stands in contrast with *poil* ('a single strand of hair') while
English *hair* must do double duty. Systemically speaking, then,
they are not comparable; only referentially (and in translation)
do they appear equivalent.

The same hard-nosed, objectivist stance is evident in philosophically oriented treatments.

Turning now to why it is that words sometimes have count occurrences
and sometimes mass occurrences, we are immediately faced with the
problem of a tremendous amount of variation that appears to be
unnecessary and inexplicable. . . There is a count/mass difference
between *fruit* and *vegetable* but they apply to things that for all
accounts and purposes seem to be alike. Nor can I see anything that
would explain the count/mass difference between *footwear* and *shoe*,
clothing and *clothes*, *shit* and *turd* or *fuzz* and *cop*.

                                                        (Ware 1972:22)

Here, of course, Ware is pointing to the fact that *fruit* is usually employed in the singular for a referential plurality (we bought some *fruit*) while *vegetable* is always put in the plural (we bought some *vegetables*). But the account of fruits and vegetables examined by Ware must have been that of a dietician, for even a sober botanical description would have registered an important difference between the two types of produce. The most common fruits share three readily apparent physical characteristics; they are roughly spherical in shape, brightly coloured, and sweet to the taste. Included here are apples, oranges, tangerines, grape-fruit, peaches, pears, plums, pineapples, cherries, strawberries, raspberries, blueberries, and grapes.

These exemplars establish our prototypical conception of fruit, from which there can then be minor departures.[2] Bananas diverge from the prototype in their shape but are still brightly coloured and sweet. Lemons and limes diverge in their taste yet are still brightly coloured and spherical. Kiwis are dull in colour but are still spherical and sweet. Together they form a class of objects (botanically, all ripened ovaries) sufficiently alike that they can be grouped together and referred to as a collective mass.

By comparison, an array of the most common vegetables presents a much greater morphological and botanical diversity. There we have a collection of subclasses: roots (potatoes, carrots, turnips); bulbs (onions, garlic); stems (broccoli, cauliflower, celery, asparagus); fungus stems (mushrooms); immature leaves (cabbage, Brussels sprouts) mature leaves (lettuce, watercress, parsley); seeds (corn, peas, beans); as well as what is technically a 'fruit' (bell peppers, squash, tomatoes). But no one subclass predominates so as to establish a prototypical conception of a vegetable. A carrot is no more or less typically a vegetable than a cabbage. Understandably, then, speakers find it difficult to ignore this heterogeneity. They categorize them as a single thing lexically with the word *vegetable* (perhaps best defined as an edible, botanic non-'fruit' in the layman's sense) while acknowledging their heterogeneity in the choice of grammatical number.

As for Ware's other examples of inexplicableness, some clearly contrast in the same way as do *player* vs. *team* and *leaf* vs. *foliage*.

[14] The press made great sport of Imelda Marcos' large collection of *shoes*.

[15] Low-priced *footwear* from third-world countries has greatly damaged the domestic industry.

Language as a mirror of nature

In view of the fact that the perspective of language users is clearly the key to understanding the differing grammatical behaviour of pairs like *leaf* and *foliage*, *shoe* and *footwear*, why did Palmer and Ware ignore the obvious differences between these words and focus instead on their referential equivalence?

The answer lies in the traditional conception of language as a mirror of nature, a vehicle for the expression of objective truth. In that view the referential function of language is taken to be primary. Words are mere labels for pre-existing features of an external, objective reality. The perspective and biases of speakers can have no place, for if they were included the truths expressed would be tainted by a subjectivity that robs them of their philosophical (and scientific) interest.[3]

To be sure, the notion of a language as a speaker-centred conceptual scheme can accommodate a concern with reference so long as linguistic categories stand in a stable relation with the external world. But when the same external reality can be first one thing (*shoes*) and then another (*footwear*), the question arises whether the referential function of words is a fruitful one from which to begin semantic analysis. Both Palmer and Ware implicitly concede it is not.

2.5 Communicative Function

If the semantic categories of language do not reflect the objective structure of an external reality, just what do they reflect? Saussure's answer is that they reflect the exigencies of communication. Linguistic categories are conceptual tools for structuring and interpreting messages about an experiential reality that by itself is open to multiple characterizations.

The analytical consequence of this position is that semantic analysis must focus on the *communicative* function of words, not their referential function. The analyst is no longer simply matching words to 'things' established in advance; he is searching for the conceptual distinctions inherent in the language.

A focus on communicative function was evident in the discussion of *leaves* and *foliage*. These two words allow speakers to indicate the relative salience of individual components of aggregates on a particular occasion, aggregates that are only botanically the 'same' things. It is worth noting in passing that the vantage point from which Ware examined *shoe* and *footwear* is a hybrid that consistently adheres neither to an observer-independent reality nor to the picture of that reality as structured and interpreted by human beings. A shoe, after all, is objectively an assembly of objects – a sole, a heel, an upper, a tongue and a lace. What makes them all a single 'thing' is their functional utility to people as an article of clothing. So if subjectivity is to be eschewed, it must be at the outset; once accepted as legitimate in principle (implicit in Ware's acceptence of *shoe* as referentially 'singular'), it cannot be rejected out of hand for *footwear*.

Linguistic meanings as explanatory constructs
If semantic categories are not provided by an external reality, then they must be created by the analyst. This makes them theoretical constructs, and like all theoretical constructs they must be justified ultimately in terms of their explanatory power. So far, we have only shown how the meaning of a lexical stem can be formulated in a way that facilitates an explanation of the choice of Entity Number. But as explanatory constructs they must have some other justification than the choice of number, or else the treatment amounts to no more than a variant of a formal one, in which the grammatical properties of words are couched non-technically as an integral part of their definition.

That justification lies in the context of their use. If *leaves* and *foliage* are to be accorded different semantic values (so as to account for their differing grammatical number), those differing values must find confirmation in the ways people employ these words *quite apart from the choice of grammatical number*. Specifically, the same semantic values that account for the differing number choice for *leaves* and *foliage* must also account for the choice of one word over the other in different contexts. This means that instead of focusing on data illustrating the occasional equivalence of these terms, one will focus on data that reveal how they subtly differ.

While few would disagree in principle with the proposition that the semantic values of words should reflect their use, investigations of lexical meaning often bypass an examination of actual language use in favour of two methodological shortcuts: intropection and fabricated examples. Both can be effective at times. When words contrast as markedly as do *player* and *team*, their meanings can be identified out of context on the basis of an introspective examination alone. With more closely-related words like *foliage* and *leaves*, sentences constructed by the analyst may effectively establish the difference between them. But with pairs such as *fuzz* and *cop*, *shit* and *turd* (Ware's other examples of apparent grammatical arbitrariness), these analytical techniques are inadequate. Examples constructed by the analyst appear *ad hoc*, and a reader feels free to construct his own counter-examples. If, then, a difference in their semantic values is to be claimed, that difference must be supported by appeal to the practice of the linguistic community as a whole; that is, through a careful examination of their actual use in a variety of spoken and written texts.

2.6 *Persons* vs. *People*: A Case Study

To illustrate the kind of lexical investigation required to explain the choice of grammatical number, we offer now a detailed case study of *persons* and *people*. These two words pose the same analytical problem as Palmer's and Ware's examples. Like *leaves* and *foliage*, *persons* and *people* both apply to a plurality of referents; yet one occurs with *Entity -s* and the other with *Entity -0*.

These two words differ significantly enough in their meaning that an introspective examination provides an initial working hypothesis. *Person* means HUMAN BEING and *people* means AGGREGATE OF HUMAN BEINGS. HUMAN BEING must be construed here not solely as an instance of a biological species, but as a member of a social and moral order. (Note the use of *person* to include God in [19].)[4]

When these two lexical stems combine with the number meaning ONE their referential contrast clearly supports the hypothesized meanings.

[16] The *person0* who blocked my car in must have been in a hurry.

[17] The *people0* who blocked my car in must have been in a hurry.

However when *person* combines with MORE THAN ONE the referential contrast is lost.

[18] The *persons* who blocked my car in must have been in a hurry.

The difference in Entity Number suggests a conceptual distinction between *persons* and *people0*; but no support for that claim is provided by [17] and [18] other than the number choice itself. At this point data from actual language use become relevant. Can evidence for the semantic difference posited above between these two words be found in the context of their normal use in communication?

Integrating the Entity Number meanings with those of the lexical stems, the hypothesized semantic value of *persons* is 'more than one human being' while that of *people0* is 'one aggregate of human beings'. The systemic difference between them lies, then, in the extent to which the human beings are conceived as an aggregate. This leads to the prediction that with *persons* we should find a greater degree of individualization of the human beings involved than with *people0* (henceforth *people*).

[19] Ministers themselves often set the stage for the dream, referring to sexual intimacy that 'could never be complete without the three *persons* – man, woman, and God.'
(B. Ehrenreich, E. Hess, and G. Jacobs, *Mother Jones*)

[20] Looking out from the stage the night before, Durst had seen a sea of young well-scrubbed faces . . . The *people* in the club were young enough, he reasoned, that they might not have been able to identify with his memories of grade-school civil defense exercises, and for tonight he has broomed the segment.
(Casey McCabe, *Mother Jones*)

In [19] the referents of *persons* are individually identified, while in [20] the referents of *people* are characterized as 'a sea of . . . faces'. In addition, the *persons* in [19] have different roles to play whereas the *people* in [20] are functioning collectively as an audience. (See Addendum p. 85.)

[21] Only when two *persons* each carrying the same recessive gene mate is there a chance that their offspring will have the condition.
(Jerry Adler, *Newsweek*)

[22] Serious criminal acts have been committed. *People* who commit such acts must expect to face the consequences.
(Margaret Thatcher, *Newsweek*)

In [21] the referents of *persons* are individualized with the word *each* while in [22] there is no such individualization.

When extended passages are examined, extra-sentential evidence can support the hypothesized semantic contrast. Example [23], from a legal memo, concerns the definition of two contractual terms.

[23] Proposed Rule 202–1 would exempt from the definition of "investment advisor" a person controlling a registered investment advisor and *persons* affiliated with such controlling person, provided: (i) . . . The proposed amendment of Paragraph (12) of Rule 204–2 (which sets forth entities and *persons* who are covered by certain recordkeeping requirements) provides that the term "advisory representatives" includes any person who obtains information about the advisor's securities recommendations and who is in a control relationship to the advisor, an affiliated person of such controlling person or an affiliated person of such affiliated person.
(Matthew P. Fink, legal memo)

[23] concerns the legal status of individuals. The referents of *persons* are described with the same precision as those of the seven instances of *person∅* elsewhere in the passage; they are a plurality of individuals, not a group. The effect of *people* in place of *persons* (e.g., 'which sets forth entities and *people* who are covered by certain recordkeeping requirements') would be to diffuse the high level of definition maintained throughout the passage, a precision striven for in the specification of rules and laws.

Contrast this treatment of a plurality of human beings as separate individuals with their treatment as a group in the following example, the opening paragraph of an article about the construction of retirement communities.

[24] In recent years builders, developers and many others have been tantalized by visions of an aging America with plenty of money to spend. Though a fifth of the population sixty-five and older is poor or near poor, most elderly *people* have a considerably more comfortable style of life. The average after-tax income of the elderly is actually nine per cent higher than the rest of the U.S. population, according to Real Estate Research Corporation . . . In addition, nearly three quarters of retirement-age *people* own their own homes.
(Philip Langdon, *The Atlantic*)

In deciding to construct a retirement community the crucial consideration is the number of potential occupants. The circumstance and wealth of individuals is relevant only in so far as they arc typical of the class as a whole (cf., 'the average after-tax income'). And this class is set in contrast with another, the poor. From the point of view of a developer then, retirement communities are built for collectives, not individuals. Appropriately, the potential occupants are described with a word that categorizes them as an aggregate, *people*.

The larger context provides additional evidence of the writer's point of view. The four other references to possible occupants are also to groups: an ageing America; a fifth of the population; the elderly; the rest of the population. Significantly, they, too, are grammatically singular; the singularity of *people* is thus consistent with the other expressive choices in the paragraph. Put another way, those four expressions provide independent support for the claim that the word *people* contains an element of conceptual 'singularity', an element favouring its choice in passage [24] and disfavouring its choice in passage [23].

Unmentioned as yet is the grammatical number of the verb. Since verb number is the topic of Chapters 5–8, we will not attempt a comprehensive treatment here. Still, a brief discussion is in order since our case for the conceptual singularity of *people* would seem to predict the choice of a singular verb as well.

The first point to note is that *people* does occur with singular verbs.

[25]   But polygamy presents an almost insurmountable barrier
        to Catholic evangelization in Africa . . . 'Every *people*
        has its manner of marriage and forming families,' says
        Cardinal Joseph Malula of Kinshasa.

                                                       (*Newsweek*)

At the same time, the verb number of [25] cannot be due to the meaning of *people* alone, since *people* regularly occurs with plural verbs (e.g., [24]). Unlike *leaf* and *foliage* then, the meaning posited for *people* must be one that is equally compatible semantically with both options (for plural reference).

In this, our working hypothesis falls somewhat short of the mark. By defining *people* as AGGREGATE OF HUMAN BEINGS we highlighted the feature of its meaning that motivates the choice of Entity Number (at the expense of the choice of verb number). But the meaning of *people* could equally well have been phrased HUMAN BEINGS IN AGGREGATE, in which case its co-occurrence with plural verbs would not be an anomaly. The actual systemic value of *people* lies midway between these two formulations, making it difficult to express in English. It contains one component of inherent plurality, HUMAN

BEINGS, equally balanced with another whose number is unspecified, AGGREGATE.

The speaker then makes two independent choices of grammatical number. In choosing Entity Number the speaker specifies the number of aggregates. In chosing verb number, on the other hand, the speaker tips the balance in favour of one component or the other (of the meaning of *people*) depending on how salient the delineation of the aggregate is in the particular message being expressed. (Note that in [25] *people* is understood as referring to human beings who share a common cultural identity.)

As this brief discussion implies, the interpretation of *people* is always a semantic synthesis of lexical and grammatical meanings. Each choice of grammatical number independently contributes to its contextualized interpretation; each shapes an aspect left unspecifed by the inherent semantic value of the word.

Jack Abramowitz (1986) develops the present analysis of *person* and *people* with additional examples. [26], drawn from a news report about defendants charged with food poisoning, illustrates the two conceptual components in the meaning of *people* in more or less equal balance.

[26]   Thirty-eight *people* are on trial and are facing a total of 106,000 years in prison.

                                                    (*Newsday*)

The number *thirty-eight* applies to the component HUMAN BEINGS (as does the plurality of *are*); at the same time, the phrase *a total of 106,000 years* (as well as the *Entity -∅* of *people*) applies to the component AGGREGATE. The possible prison sentence of each individual is not worthy of separate note; instead, they are pooled to yield a single figure for the group as a whole.

By contrast, a greater focus on the individuality of the referents is responsible for the choice of *persons* in [27].

[27]   Psychoactive drug technology has a high potential for misuse by *persons*, medical staff, hospital systems and the society.

                            (H. Lennard, psychoactive drug seminar)

[27] sets up a progression through which we see drugs poisoning a culture first through individuals, then a group, then an institution, and finally society at large. With each step one draws away from the human beings as separate individuals to see them as part

of a larger social structure. This four-fold progression begins with the initial contrast between *persons* and *staff*, a contrast between a plurality of human beings and a professionally defined aggregate. Note that if the sequence had been *people, medical staff, . . . , medical staff* would seem to be a narrowing of referential scope rather than an expansion.

Illustrations of the contrast between *persons* and *people* become more effective as extraneous contextual variables are eliminated to leave just the one relevant to the lexical choice. Abramowitz offers several striking pairs.

[28] Our father, Jacob, went down to Egypt with seventy *persons* and there G-d made him number as the stars in Heaven. And he became a great nation. . .
(English translation of Passover Haggadah)

[29] Blessed is the One who keeps His promise to His *people* Israel.
(English translation of Passover Haggadah)

[28] concerns how one family, each member presumably worthy of note, enters a strange land and becomes a mighty and distinct nation. Abramowitz supports his claim about the focus on individuals in [28] with the observation that *persons* is a translation of *Nefesh*, meaning 'soul'. By contrast [29] refers to the descendants of those original settlers, now having become a cohesive social unit, a *people*.

[30] Bids by *persons* at an auction are simply offers to buy at that price and are not binding.
(*Chadman's Cyclopedia of Law*)

[31] [Regarding a painting which sold at auction for 39 million dollars.] We expected around fifteen million dollars, but when two *people* who are extremely rich and determined bid against each other, this can happen.
(*Newsday*)

Both [30] and [31] are generic statements about auctions. But [30] concerns the personal liability of the participants while [31] concerns the factors affecting the price of sale. As a consequence they differ in the salience of the individuality of the human beings involved. [30] holds across the board for each and every instance of a bid at an auction, and hence each and every participant; a single case of a binding bid would falsify the statement. [31], on the other hand, is a statement of general tendency (*this can happen*) that is not falsified by a single counter-instance. Appropriately, [30] refers to human beings with a word that maintains a focus on their individuality while [31] employs a word that subordinates their status as individuals.

A comparable referential context is again maintained in [32] and [33].

[32]   NOTICE: The subscriber forbids all *persons* from giving credit to Mrs. Sophie Provost on his account as he will pay no debts whatever she may contract.

([signed] Benjamin Jewell)

[33]   On Memorial Day weekend, signs will be posted at major entrances to the village, in the municipal parking lots, and in shop windows notifying *people* that they must help keep Southampton's business district beautiful: no bathing suits, much less anything of lesser clothing.

(*Newsday*)

Both [32] and [33] concern public notices, but the audience in one case is *persons* and in the other *people*. Abramowitz argues these lexical choices reflect the nature of the problem to which each is a response. The problem for Mr Jewell is the financial claims of individuals who have granted credit to Mrs Provost. Each and every claim is a significant problem for him, demanding a letter of refusal and carrying the possibility of legal action. Moreover, the problem itself arises at the individual level. Mrs Provost seeks credit from one person here, one person there, not from large groups of people at any one time. Thus, he addresses his notice to individuals, *persons*.

On the other hand, the village of Southampton has a problem of a different order. Apparently, the village has had difficulty in getting the crowds of visitors it receives each summer to remain properly dressed when they leave the beaches and enter the business areas. 'This becomes a problem worth dealing with only when it happens many times over', says Abramowitz. 'They wouldn't go to these great lengths to make their town rules known if they had only one or two isolated incidents each summer.' The description of the audience of the second public notice reflects, then, the dimension of the problem it addresses: the behaviour of crowds of visiting *people*.

Statistical confirmation

While the examples all support the hypothesized distinction between *people* and *person*, the question remains whether they accurately reflect a general distributional tendency. Chapter 1 maintained such a question can only be resolved by statistical evidence. Abramowitz provides such evidence in the form of a demonstration that *persons* is favoured over *people* in discourse where the individuality of the referents is consistently more germane. Abramowitz examined approximately 5000 words of newspaper text (*Newsday* and *The New York Times*) and 5000 words of legal writing (*Chadman's Cyclopedia of Law*) counting the instances of *persons* and *people* in each.

TABLE 2.1 Frequency of *People0* and *Persons* in Newspaper and Legal Texts

	Newspaper	*Legal text*	
people0	25	2	
persons	0	35	$\chi^2 = 54.20$
			$p < 0.001$

These results support the meanings posited for *person* and *people* because a generalization can be made about how the content of legal discourse differs from that of newspapers. Legal discourse is concerned principally with the promulgation of laws and regulations that apply to individuals; rarely does one find a statement about groups of human beings that does not apply categorically to each and every member. At the same time, the specific identity of the human beings is not known in advance, so they cannot be identified by name. If, as hypothesized, *persons* maintains a focus on the individuality of its referents, many occasions for its use will arise in legal discourse.

In newspaper discourse there is also frequent call to underscore the individual identities of a plurality of human beings. But in those situations they can usually be identified by name, since most newspaper reports concern particular events. Only rarely, then, do occasions arise for the use of *persons*.

On the other hand, newspaper reporters also have frequent call to refer to a plurality of human beings whose individual identities are irrelevant. If, as hypothesized, *people* subordinates the individuality of its referents, many occasions for its use will arise in newspaper discourse.

Table 2.1 confirms the predicted favouring of *persons* over *people* in legal discourse and the reverse favouring in newspaper discourse. And since these predictions derive from the meanings posited for the two words (as they relate to different communicative goals), the observed skewings are empirical support for the hypothesized semantic distinction.

Stylistic difference

Table 2.1 shows that *people0* did occur twice in legal discourse. And while Abramowitz found no instances of *persons* in his newspaper corpus, [19] and [21] provide examples of *persons* in news journals. Neither favouring is categorical. This is a useful fact because it serves to discredit an alternative account of the difference between *person* and *people* as purely one of genres: *person* carries the stylistic value 'legalese' while *people* carries the stylistic value of 'journalese'. If that were the case, then the skewing should be 100 per cent.

Instead, the systemic opposition between *person* and *people* is still evident within each genre. When *people* occasionally occurs in legal discourse, its appearance is motivated by the same semantic factor as that motivating the occasional appearance of *person* in journalistic discourse.

> [34] These *persons* argued that the *people* were generally ignorant and easily misled.
>
> (*Chadman's Cyclopedia of Law*)

Persons and *people* cannot, then, be treated as stylistically-conditioned, lexical variants. Their statistical skewing with respect to genres is simply the consequence of their systemic contrast (evident in individual examples) being exploited many times over in the same direction in response to a global difference in content.

Unity of phenomena

In this case study correlations between the words *persons* and *people* and contrasting communicative content were illustrated within contexts of different scopes. In reverse order these were:

1. contrasting genres
2. contrasting topics of paragraphs
3. contrasting messages of individual sentences

In each case the explanation was in terms of the meanings of *person* and *people* and their suitability for differing communicative goals.

Recall now that this excursion into the subtleties of lexical choice began as a search for an explanation for the different

Entity Number of *persons* and *people* (both referring to an observable plurality). We can now return to that question. The differing Entity Number is due to the differing meanings posited for these two words. The ONE of *people($\emptyset$)* specifies the number of aggregates referred to by its meaning AGGREGATE OF HUMAN BEINGS/HUMAN BEINGS IN AGGREGATE while the MORE THAN ONE of *persons* specifies the number of human beings referred to by its meaning HUMAN BEING. Thus the same systemic factor responsible for the correlations observed in 1, 2 and 3 above is also responsible for the choice of Entity Number.

At the same time the choice of Entity Number is not mechanical and automatic given the lexical choice, since both *person$\emptyset$* and *peoples* occur as well. It appears mechanically determined only if referential equivalence is to be maintained. But the goal of the present analysis is to account for speakers' choice of Entity Number, not the notion 'referential equivalence'.

To the list 1–3 above can now be added a fourth correlation between the two words and contextual factors.

4. contrasting Entity Number signals

This fourth correlation appears to differ from the first three because it involves a grammatical choice while the others involve a lexical choice. But that difference is simply an artefact of the analyst's perspective, who, for discussion purposes, treats some contextual features as 'given' and others 'chosen'. In actuality, no linguistic choice can be regarded as logically prior to any other: in constructing a text, a language user is making a series of interrelated choices all aiming at a common communicative goal.

That being the case, one is free to recast the differing choice of Entity Number in the context of *person* and *people* as a differing choice of *lexical stem* in the context of the meanings ONE and MORE THAN ONE (in such a way as to effect the same message contrast as in data sets 1–3). The result is that 1–4 now differ only in the scope of the 'determining' context examined. Correlations 1–4 are all observations of essentially the same linguistic fact – albeit from different perspectives – because all are explained by the same constellation of systemic and communicative factors interacting in the same way.

This case study has been an initial test of the Entity Number System, and in addition has served to illustrate the basic analytical strategy. The hypothesis claims that a speaker's choice of *Entity -$\emptyset$* or -*s* can be explained in terms of their meanings as they relate to the message. For *person* and *people* the explanation involved the interaction of the number meanings with that of the lexical stem. This meant that we first had to posit a semantic value for each stem and then test the two constructs on data drawn from natural language use.

After having established independent empirical support for the semantic distinction between the two stems, we returned to the initial problem. The choice of Entity Number was explained in terms of (1) slightly different communicative goals (as evidenced by the presence of either *people* or *person* and the larger context), and (2) the coherent semantic contribution of the meanings ONE or MORE THAN ONE (in conjunction with the lexical stem) to the intended message. The authors of the various examples were shown to be constructing their texts *ad sensum* according to the systemic values of the lexical and grammatical signs of English.

2.7 Problem Areas of Entity Number

A far greater obstacle to a semantic account of grammatical number than *persons* and *people* is the area of mass reference. In extending the present analysis in this direction we will draw heavily on the work of Anna Wierzbicka (1985), though her treatment differs in one significant way from our own. Wierzbicka sees the central problem to be that of legitimizing 'mass noun' as a non-arbitrary, conceptual category of English. Since the present framework does not recognize 'noun' as an inherent grammatical category (for English, at any rate), it naturally does not recognize subdivisions of that category. But for the moment we will postpone discussion of this issue until Chapter 3, focusing instead on the places Wierzbicka's analysis complements our own. Her work has succeeded in cracking a number of problems that had, for us, remained unresolved.

Wierzbicka follows essentially the same analytical strategy as we did with *person* and *people*, claiming subtly different semantic values for lexical stems of comparable referential value. In the following sections we summarize her treatment of four traditional problem areas for grammatical number in English, expanding her discussion where she does not seem to do her basic insights full justice. These problem areas are:

1. words like *sand* and *pebbles* that both refer to a plurality of physically discrete referents but which differ in grammatical number;

2. words like *butter* that are employed as mass nouns though their referents would suggest they should behave like count nouns since the referents have discrete physical boundaries;
3. words like *furniture* that occur only in the singular;
4. words like *scissors* that occur only in the plural.

Of primary importance here are the general psychological principles underlying the numerical categorization of entities. One of these principles will prove to be crucial in our later account of verb number. Since her treatment is more programmatic than definitive, that one principle will be subjected to additional quantitative testing in Chapter 4.

As noted, Wierzbicka sets out to establish that 'mass noun' is a genuine semantic category of English with a coherent conceptual core. While an alternative treatment of the theoretical status of the mass/count distinction will be offered in Chapter 3, we have preserved Wierzbicka's terminology in summarizing her work for ease of presentation.

Size and presentation
Wierzbicka begins by examining how the physical characteristics of objects affect the way they are categorized linguistically. Size is one important consideration.

> Other things being equal, stuffs consisting of bigger, more conspicuous individual entities are more likely to be viewed as 'multiplicities' and designated by plural nouns than stuffs consisting of smaller, less conspicuous entities.
>
> (Wierzbicka 1985:313)

This principle is clearly illustrated by *sand* and *pebbles*. Both words refer to multiplicities of discrete objects composed of the same physical substance. But the individual grains of sand on a beach are so small as to be scarcely perceptible from a standing position, while individual pebbles are clearly discernible as separate objects.

The size factor is still evident when the objects differ in material substance. So, for instance, *peas* and *noodles* are viewed as 'multiplicities' while *rice*, *sugar* and *salt* are viewed as an unstructured mass.

People's assessment of relative size is often affected by the circumstances of perception. Close up one perceives 'leaves', while from a distance one sees 'foliage'. Things which are

objectively the same size may, then, be categorized differently if
they are typically encountered under different circumstances.
Wierzbicka's example is *chives* and *grass*. The blades of each are
nearly identical in size. But chives are typically encountered
either as individual flecks of green in one's food or as a hand-
sized bunch of blades in the supermarket; while grass is typically
encountered as an expanse of verdant carpet whose individual
components rarely come to our attention.

Even in their agricultural setting chives and grass differ. 'If we
grow chives ourselves, again the area occupied with the chives is
usually much smaller and much more circumscript than an area
occupied with grass' (p. 331).

A more subtle difference in presentation involves the way
various foods are prepared and consumed. Olives and radishes
are eaten individually, one by one, whereas garlic is chopped up
and used as an additive to other foods. It is not surprising then
that we speak of olives and radishes as a plurality of individual
objects, while referring to garlic as a non-countable substance
(despite the fact that in its natural state a clove of garlic is
approximately the size of an olive).

Continuing in the food vein, the manner of presentation
overrides the consideration of size in the case of Brussels sprouts
and cabbage. While a cabbage is much larger than a Brussels
sprout, it is usually sliced for eating, and hence loses its
characteristic appearance. At the table (sliced) cabbage is a
shapeless mass. Yet in the garden, cabbage is as countable as
Brussels sprouts.

> [35]   Mr. McGregor was on his hands and knees planting out
> young *cabbages*, but he jumped up and ran after Peter,
> waving a rake and calling out, 'Stop, thief!'.
>
> (Beatrix Potter, *The Tale of Peter Rabbit*)

Salience of shape to category membership
After this preliminary discussion Wierzbicka turns to the heart of
the problem, the conceptual difference between so-called mass
nouns and count nouns. The traditional definition of a mass noun
is a word which refers to 'homogeneous continua without implied
boundaries' (Whorf 1962:140). According to this definition the
archetypical examples would be words such as *air*, *water*, *rain*,
sunlight, whose referents do, in fact, lack discrete boundaries.
Yet many mass nouns have referents that are physically quite
discrete: *butter*, *meat*, *milk*, *cloth*. Hence the common conclusion
that the mass/count distinction in English is by and large an

arbitrary one having no independent cognitive motivation.

But the difficulty may well be in the original definition of mass nouns. Mass nouns like *air*, *water*, *butter*, and *meat*, are correlated not with 'unboundedness' but rather with 'arbitrary divisibility'.

> If you take some water or some butter and divide it into parts, each of the resulting parts will be water, or butter: but if you take a bottle or a chair and divide it into parts the resulting parts will not be bottles or chairs. Words such as *bottle* or *chair*, referring to objects which cannot be divided, are normally countable, words such as *water* or *butter*, referring to 'stuffs' which can be divided at will, are normally mass nouns.
>
> (Wierzbicka 1985:315)

Butter and meat are 'unbounded' in the sense that there is no fixed position of the parts within any given portion, while the parts of a table or chair have fixed structural relations. As a result, the physical outlines of these objects relate in different ways to the meanings of the words that refer to them. The shape of a mass of butter on a plate is irrelevant to its being an instance of 'butter', while the shape of a chair is cognitively salient to its being a 'chair'.

If the crucial conceptual distinction here involves the cognitive salience of boundaries rather than their objective existence, one might expect this factor to vary for a given word in different situations. Wierzbicka's example is *chocolate*, which, she says, belongs to a class of nouns that can be either countable (a candy) or uncountable (a substance). On the cognitive salience of the physical boundary of *chocolate*, the candy, Wierzbicka is eloquent:

> They have a filling made of something other than chocolate: more importantly they have a definite size, which is important to the conceptualization: a (countable) chocolate is thought of as neither too big nor too small to be put into the mouth and eaten as a single entity. In addition to size, the texture of a chocolate matters, too: the filling may be soft and sticky, but the surface of a chocolate must be firm, so that one can pick it up with one's fingers and put it into the mouth without dirtying the fingers. Moreover, a chocolate must be attractive to look at. For all these reasons, half a chocolate is not a chocolate: divided into parts, a chocolate loses some of its defining characteristics ('mouthsize', clean surface, attractive symmetrical form).
>
> (Wierzbicka 1985:317)

On the other hand the physical discreteness and clear definition of (unsweetened) baking chocolate is irrelevant to its use as an ingredient in cooking. Though coming in individually wrapped squares somewhat larger than a chocolate, it is melted down and combined with other ingredients in the course of making cakes and brownies.

Wierzbicka offers a reason why the class of words that can be both count and non-count does not contain any designating liquids, powders or other substances which assume the shape of their containers. '[T]he double conceptualization – "stuff" or separate things – is possible only for substances which can occur as self-contained entities i.e., for substances which are hard or at least firm' (p. 318).

Despite her attempt to explain why certain words fall into this class and not others, the mere existence of such a class raises the question of the legitimacy of 'count' and 'non-count' as grammatical categories. For the *chocolate* class actually constitutes those words whose grammatical behaviour fails to confirm the expectations established by positing 'count' and 'non-count' as (grammatically relevant) features of inherent lexical meaning.

If *chocolate* were an isolated example it could be ignored as reflecting the ultimately fuzzy nature of all conceptual categories. But, as we will argue shortly, most words occurring in non-count contexts occur in count contexts as well, making the distinction more honoured in the breach than the observance. The few true non-count words like *information* and *cash* (which never occur with *Entity -s*) are the true anomalies to an otherwise regular pattern.

Non-taxonomic categories

The words *crockery*, *furniture* and *cutlery* pose a problem for Wierzbicka's thesis that 'mass nouns' designate objects whose shapes are not cognitively salient. *Crockery*, *furniture* and *cutlery* all apply to aggregates of objects whose physical shapes are crucial to their functional identity. Why, then, are they not categorized as MORE THAN ONE? That is, why do they not normally appear as *crockeries*, *furnitures* and *cutleries*?

Wierzbicka turns salience of shape to her advantage by countering that while 'furniture' and 'crockery' do have cognitively salient boundaries, the referents are normally conceived as objects *of different kinds* and hence cannot be counted together. (Recall Frege's point quoted in 3.3 that in order for things to be counted together they must belong to a common genus.) This entails a claim that *furniture* and *crockery* do not designate any single genus of objects. The way the meanings of these words differ from others involves a distinction between 'taxonomic' and 'non-taxonomic' supercategories. *Bird* and *tree* are taxonomic in that they belong to hierarchies of kinds; when we count a swallow and an eagle as two, it is because we can think of them both as 'birds'. On the other hand, supercategories such as 'crockery', 'cutlery' and 'furniture' are not taxonomic because they group together things of different kinds, sharing no similarity of form and only a general similarity of purpose.

> 'Cutlery' is not a semantic common denominator included in the meaning of *spoon*, *knife* and *fork* in the way that 'bird' is the semantic common denominator included in the meaning of *swallow*, *magpie* and *eagle*. Words such as *cutlery*, *crockery* or *furniture* stand for collective supercategories each of which is thought of as including a variety of things which can be used together.
>
> (Wierzbicka 1985:322)

In support of this distinction, Wierzbicka points to the fact that taxonomic supercategories can be used to refer to items of one kind. One can say

[36]   Mary drew some trees/birds/flowers

even when the trees in question all look like oaks, when the birds all look like magpies and the flowers all look like tulips. But one doesn't say

[37]   Mary drew some cutlery/furniture/crockery

if Mary drew only spoons, or only chairs, or only cups.

But to characterize non-taxonomic supercategories in terms of a restriction, as Wierzbicka does, harks back to the conception of language as combinatory system. More to the point is the positive utility of non-taxonomic supercategories in communication. Their communicative value lies in the fact that they allow objects with cognitively salient boundaries to be spoken of in a highly *imprecise* way, divorced from their specific and idiosyncratic functions. One speaks of buying and selling furniture, storing furniture in the attic, or furniture of a particular historical style. The functional identity of these objects is being suppressed here because it is not relevant to the particular messages being conveyed. On the other hand, one does not tell guests to draw up some furniture and sit down, or that the dinner is on the furniture, because the chairs and tables are now being conceptualized more precisely in terms of their normal functions. This is not so much a restriction on the use of the word *furniture* as simply the reverse side of its positive utility.

The proposal that imprecision can, on occasion, be a virtue makes no sense when the referential function of language is taken to be primary but is quite reasonable in terms of communicative function. The descriptive imprecision built into the meaning of *furniture* is exploited to nice polemical effect in [38]. Example [38] occurred in a student newspaper editorial protesting the university administration's withdrawal of official recognition of a fraternity because it refused to remove a bar (for the serving of alcoholic beverages) from its house.

[38]   From the standpoint of ADE [Alpha Delta Epsilon], however, a very different story unfolds. One fraternity, out of the numerous houses on campus, decided not to cave in or plead for mercy and instead told the University where it could shove its coasters. Claiming [the administration] has no right to tell it what kind of *furniture* it can have in its own home, ADE had the guts to ignore the directive and decided to cross the bridge of derecognition when it came.

                     (*The Daily Targum*, Rutgers University)

The administration had ordered the removal of the bar following the death of a fraternity member from intoxication. By using the word *furniture* the writer is suppressing the way a bar differs from a chair or table, a distinction highly relevant to the administration's action. And this, in turn, contributes to the writer's (amply-evidenced) rhetorical objective of portraying the administration's directive as intrusive and capricious.

Returning now to the choice of Entity Number, the fact that *furniture* co-occurs only with *Entity -0*, even for a referential plurality, can now be explained in terms of the same communicative goal responsible for the choice of *furniture* itself, namely, a desire for *imprecision* (cf., the rationale for *people0* vs. *persons*). When one chooses to refer to a mixed aggregate of tables and chairs with the non-specific word *furniture* – 'large-sized room equipment' – one is choosing to ignore their physical and functional heterogeneity. But then their status as discrete physical objects is likewise suppressed, and it makes sense to be imprecise grammatically as well. Counting them as ONE, an amorphous aggregate, is thus consistent with the cognitive perspective imposed by the stem. If referential precision had been desired, one would not have made the lexical choice of *furniture* to begin with.

Scale of relative similarity

With the introduction of non-taxonomic supercategories an interesting scalar phenomenon emerges that highlights the importance of relative similarity in the act of counting. The word *rice* designates objects that are identical in appearance and so small that their objective discreteness is ignored; they become an unstructured mass. On the other hand, *vegetable* designates objects that, while sharing the status of 'non-fruit produce' are sufficiently distinct from one another that aggregates are always treated grammatically as MORE THAN ONE.

Fruit stands midway between *rice* and *vegetable* with respect to countability. *Fruit* designates objects large enough to be easily counted, but similar in appearance, taste and function so that their separate identities can be ignored if one wishes. Accordingly, an aggregate can be counted as either ONE or MORE THAN ONE (i.e., *fruit∅* or *fruits*).

Finally, *furniture* designates objects so heterogeneous that in referring to them with this single cover-term one has moved to such a level of imprecision as to lose sight of their separate identities altogether; the result is that they can no longer be counted as multiple instances *of any single thing*; they are always a ONE.

The principle is clear: in order for counting to take place, objects must be sufficiently similar as to be regarded as instances of the same thing, yet dissimilar and discrete enough to permit enumeration. If they are either too similar (e.g., individual grains of rice), or too dissimilar (e.g., a table and a chair) they cease to be a plurality.

Pluralia tantum words

Another traditional obstacle to a semantic account of grammatical number has been words like *scissors* and *trousers*, which supposedly never occur with *Entity -∅*. Before exploring why this is so, it is worthwhile to examine what these words have in common, and why they should create a problem for the system of Entity Number. We depart for a moment from Wierzbicka's account to introduce a notion originated by Diver that is useful here.

2.8 The Spanned Opposition

Sometimes a given state of affairs may be described in more than
one way with equal accuracy; a glass can be either 'half empty' or
'half full', and a transaction in the marketplace can be either one
of 'buying' or 'selling'. Experiential reality is open to multiple
conceptual categorizations, each defensible in its own way.

When it comes to entities, some can be counted in more than
one way. Trousers, a wag observed, are plural from the cuffs to
the crotch, and singular from the crotch to the waist. In
characterizing this class of *pluralia tantum* words Allan
(1980:559) observes: 'scissors, braces/suspenders, glasses/spec-
tacles, pants, nutcrackers, pliers, scales, tights, tongs and
tweezers . . . all . . . have referents perceived as two moveable
leg-like members pinioned to a bridge at one end, so as to cross
each other'.

But at the same time, these objects each function as a unitary
instrument; a scissor blade cannot, by itself, scissor. The
referents of these words, then, all possess characteristics that
would support a categorization as either a single entity or a
plurality of entities. In short, the semantic opposition between
the meanings ONE and MORE THAN ONE is *spanned* by these
objects.

The occasional encountering of a message that spans a
grammatical opposition is not an analytical failure, but simply a
consequence of the fact that all of experiential and cognitive
reality does not neatly divide itself up along the lines of the
semantic distinctions of individual languages. The important
point is that the Entity Number System hypothesis correctly
predicts its own area of indeterminacy.

That being said, the problem remains as to why the choice of
Entity Number goes in the direction it does for a particular word.
While the grammatical resolution of spanned oppositions is
inevitably idiosyncratic, the principles underlying the resolution
are not. In the case of *scissors* and *trousers*, three previously-
established principles are at work.

1. a discrete referent is countable if its physical outline is
    critical to its category membership;
2. counting is carried out in terms of the meaning of the
    lexical stem;
3. things are counted together if they are alike.

First to be settled is the meanings of these words. One
possibility is to define the lexical stems as explicitly designating

only the component parts of the objects to which they refer in the plural. But if their meanings were formulated that way, they should be employed with the number meaning ONE to refer to a single component part (i.e., a 'scissor blade' or 'trouser leg'). In point of fact, speakers never do that; when these lexical stems occasionally do occur in the singular (*a scissor0*, *a trouser0*) they still refer to the composite objects.

This fact argues that *scissor* and *trouser* should be defined in the manner of *people*. The meaning of *scissor* lies mid-way between 'a cutting instrument composed of two blades pinioned at the middle' and 'two blades pinioned at the middle so as to form a cutting instrument'. The way in which these objects span the opposition of number is thus explicitly built into the lexical meaning of the stem.

Turning now to the number choice, Wierzbicka has argued that so-called count nouns are distinguished by the fact that the physical outline of their referents is critical to their category membership. Clearly the shape of a pair of *scissors* is crucial to its functional identity. Equally important is the fact that it is composed of two nearly identical parts. This means that unlike the legs, back, seat and rungs that make up a chair, the component parts of scissors are sufficiently alike to be counted together; with the result that the same consideration that makes it 'countable' at all, makes it countable as MORE THAN ONE. The case of *scissors* is, then, the converse of *furniture*: the same principle of relative similarity blocking enumeration beyond ONE with *furniture*, favours enumeration beyond ONE with *scissors*.

2.9 The Choice of Entity Number for Mass Reference

This concludes the summary of Wierzbicka's work. As noted earlier, Wierzbicka sees the central problem in this area to be that of legitimizing 'mass noun' as a non-arbitrary, conceptual category of the language. Our focus, however, is on the deployment of the Entity Number System. And while Wierzbicka's line of analysis is of invaluable help in explaining why words like *foliage* and *sand* do not normally occur with *Entity -s*, it does not directly address the question of what does occur, and for what reason.

Two analytical options are open. Either 'mass nouns' are not marked for Entity Number (that is, the lexical stem is followed by *nothing*, just like adjectives); or they are marked as ONE by virtue of being followed by a *-0*.

The first option amounts to claiming that speakers occasionally abandon the Entity Number System when its semantic opposition is not relevant to the message being communicated. Both the meanings ONE and MORE THAN ONE imply countability, and countability, it could be argued, is exactly what one wishes to avoid suggesting in getting across the idea of an unstructured mass.

That would be a plausible line of analysis if it were the case that English contained a large fixed class of words that were employed exclusively for reference to things conceived *en masse*; that is, they would all be like *cash* and *information*. Under those circumstances, hearers could recognize that a mass message was intended purely on the basis of the lexical stem alone. Furthermore, one would argue that since the signal for ONE was defined as the absence of *Entity -s*, and that signal never occurs with these words, positing the presence of *Entity -0* would imply a grammatical opposition that would never actually be exploited.

But in point of fact, English is not like this. As Jespersen observed, practically all 'mass nouns' are employed as 'count nouns' as well.

> The distinction between thing-words (countables) and mass-words (uncountables) is easy enough if we look at the idea that is expressed in each instance. But in practical language the distinction is not carried through in such a way that one and the same word stands always for one and the same idea. On the contrary, a great many words may in one connexion stand for something countable and in another for something uncountable, see, for instance:

Count		Mass
I saw a *chicken*	–	I ate *chicken*
a tall *oak*	–	a table made of *oak*
many *cakes*	–	much *cake*
various *noises*	–	a good deal of *noise*
have a long *talk*	–	much *talk*
have many *experiences*	–	have much *experience*
		(Jespersen 1933/1966:207)

Clearly these lexical stems do co-occur with *Entity -s*; so there is no formal obstacle (i.e., lack of formal opposition) to positing the presence of *Entity -0* when they are used in a mass sense. Yet there remains the problem of the semantic appropriateness of the meaning ONE for such messages. In what way is the number opposition relevant to a message about things *en masse*?

The answer lies in the interpretive problem these words pose for hearers. Since most are employed in both a 'mass' and a 'count' sense, their morphological identity does not resolve their interpretation; it must be resolved by the context. Exploitation of the number opposition of the Entity Number System furthers the communication of mass messages in the following way.

The meaning MORE THAN ONE implies several entities, each with discrete boundaries; for enumeration beyond one requires the recognition of points at which one entity leaves off and another begins. The meaning ONE, on the other hand, does not necessarily entail a referent with discrete boundaries. A mass referent can be regarded as ONE merely by virtue of being an unstructured whole, like the unbounded but singular surface of a sphere. Thus the meaning ONE, though not ideal, is not altogether inappropriate, as it does not oblige the hearer to interpret the lexical stem in the way compelled by its systemic opposite, MORE THAN ONE, with which it also occurs.

2.10 The Zero Article in Mass Reference

Since the interpretation of a word in a mass sense cannot proceed solely on the basis of its exclusive membership in a fixed class, nor from the meaning ONE (which normally implies discreteness), additional contextual information must be contributing to the process. But from what source?[5]

One important contextual element is the zero article. However the zero article cannot itself be assigned the value 'mass referent' because it is employed for a wider range of messages. It is used:

A. for a physically discrete referent never identified:
  [39] He went to 0 bed0 early. (= went to sleep on whatever bed)
  [40] He attends 0 church0 regularly. (= worships regularly)

B. for a physically discrete referent that can be identified:
  [41] He went *0* home0. (= *his* home)
  [42] He went to 0 town0. (= the *nearest* town)
  [43] The captain dropped 0 anchor0. (= the *ship's* anchor)

C. with names (of physically discrete referents):
  [44] 0 Einstein0 died in 0 Princeton0. (= the one and only)

D. for reference to entities lacking (cognitively salient) boundaries:
  [45] 0 Water0 boils at 212 F. (= any and all water)
  [46] The table is made of 0 oak0. (= the substance of an oak tree)

[47] $\emptyset$ Courage$\emptyset$ is an admirable virtue. (= any and all courage)

While message types A–D appear quite diverse, a unity emerges when they are compared with the usage of the definite and indefinite articles. By and large, *a* and *the* are employed:

1. with lexical stems applicable to many possible referents, thus creating a potential interpretive problem, and
2. in contexts where the identification of referent (or lack thereof) is actually relevant to the message being communicated.

On the other hand, the $\emptyset$ article is employed when either condition 1 or 2, or both, do not obtain. For example, the words *bed* and *church* can each have many possible referents and so pose a potential problem. But identifying specific real-world referents for *bed* and *church* in [39] and [40] is not relevant to understanding an A type message; it doesn't matter what 'bed' or 'church' is involved because the communicative focus is really on the respective activities associated with these entities.

The words *home, town* and *anchor* can also have many possible referents; and in contrast to type A, their identification *is* relevant in a B type message. But their identification poses no real problem for the hearer; not, at any rate, a problem requiring scrutiny of the specific linguistic context. When a speaker says *I'm going to $\emptyset$ town$\emptyset$ this morning* he is referring to the nearest town, the one he and his interlocutor are most familiar with. Similarly, the anchor a captain drops is assumed to be the ship's own anchor, not one destined for a shipyard and dropped in a loading accident.

In message type C there is no problem of identification since the names involved each have a unique referent. (Note, however, names occasionally do pose an interpretive problem and in such cases occur with both *a* and *the*: '*A* Mr. Forsythe called while you were out;' '*The* Mr. Forsythe?'.[6])

Finally, in message type D, while the lexical item can have many possible referents, the speaker is not differentiating among them. Only a general statement is being made, one that applies to any and all instances.

While these various uses of the $\emptyset$ article are semantically diverse, the common motif for a hearer in the process of constructing an interpretation is that the lexical stem poses *no problem of differentiation*. In effect, the $\emptyset$ article tells the hearer 'Don't worry about this one'. Recapitulating, that can be because:

    A.   actual referential identity is unimportant to the message being conveyed;

    B.   referential identity is important but there is no possibility for confusion (it's the one you would expect);

    C.   there is only one possible referent; or

    D.   the speaker is not differentiating among various possible instances.

This largely negative value of the $\emptyset$ article for the hearer – essentially 'not *a*' and 'not *the*' – can be characterised as DIFFERENTIATION NOT REQUIRED.

While a full-scale analysis of the English Article System goes beyond the scope of this book, a sketch must be provided because the signals of the Entity Number System figure as components of those in the Article System, due to the fact that the $\emptyset$ article must be assigned a different value in the plural.

As implied above, *the* and *a* both indicate that a differentiation among potential referents is required. Furthermore, *the* indicates that the hearer has sufficient information for that process, while *a* indicates that he lacks sufficient information; in other words, the context allows a *complete* identification (for *the*) and an *incomplete* identification (for *a*). These values are represented in Figure 2.2.

FIGURE 2.2 The English Article System in the singular

$$
\text{DIFFERENTIATION}
\begin{cases}
\text{REQUIRED}
\begin{cases}
\text{COMPLETE} & = \textit{the} \\
\text{INCOMPLETE} & = \textit{a}
\end{cases} \\
\text{NOT REQUIRED} \quad\quad\quad = \quad \textit{$\emptyset$ Entity-$\emptyset$}
\end{cases}
$$

In interpreting Figure 2.2, the meaning of each signal is the concatenation of all the values in upper case in the path moving from left to right. Thus the meaning of *the* is DIFFEREN-TIATION REQUIRED, COMPLETE.

On the other hand, the system has the following structure in the plural.

FIGURE 2.3 The English Article System in the plural

$$
\text{DIFFERENTIATION}
\begin{cases}
\text{COMPLETE} & = \textit{the} \\
\text{INCOMPLETE} & = \textit{$\emptyset$ Entity -s}
\end{cases}
$$

According to Figures 2.2 and 2.3, *0 Entity -s* is equivalant to *a* apart from the distinction of number. The REQUIRED vs. NOT REQUIRED distinction is not preserved with *Entity -s* because with a plurality of referents differentiation is always an issue.

Returning now to the use of the Entity Number System for messages about things conceived *en masse*, *Entity -0* contributes to the communication of such messages in two ways. Semantically it blocks a message about a plurality while leaving open the possibility that reference is being made to something *without* internal structure (i.e., it may be a ONE by virtue of being an unstructured whole). Formally it contributes by virtue of being a component of the signal for DIFFERENTIATION NOT REQUIRED, the meaning which helps to counteract the implication of discreteness usually associated with the meaning ONE.[7]

Of course the meaning of the lexical stem must lend itself to a mass message, and the larger context must be conducive to it as well. But such an interpretation arises through the joint interaction of the lexical stem, the meaning ONE (of *Entity -0*), the meaning DIFFERENTIATION NOT REQUIRED (of *0 Entity -0*), and the larger context.

2.11 Morphological Pathology

The preceding section has argued that the Entity Number meaning ONE is sometimes employed *faute de mieux* to communicate messages for which it is not ideally suited. We turn now to an example of the meaning MORE THAN ONE employed in a similar fashion. At issue here are words such as *acoustics*, *politics*, *dynamics*, *economics*, *athletics*, *logistics*, *blues*, *greasies*, *grumpies*, *smarts*. Like *scissors* and *trousers* (with which they are often grouped on formal grounds), these words also span the opposition of number. The 'acoustics' of a hall, for instance, comprise a complex set of properties including its resonance pattern, the arrival time of the initial and subsequent reverberations, their density, and the time required to decay to −60 db. At the same time, these properties combine to give a single subjective impression to listeners.

Despite the formal and semantic similarity between *acoustics* and *scissors*, the earlier rationale does not apply here since these words do not have discrete physical referents. The critical factor with these words is not semantic but formal.

Without the *Entity -s* these words would normally be taken as adjectives and most are, in fact, regularly employed as such.

Most end in either *-ic* or *-y*, derivational affixes usually marking a word as functioning adjectivally; others, such as *blue* and *smart*, though morphologically unmarked, have base meanings that are clearly adjectival in character. Their use for reference to entities poses a modest interpretive problem, for either their form or their meaning momentarily steers hearers in the wrong direction. This interpretive problem accounts for the number choice in the following way.

Both ONE and MORE THAN ONE suggest countability, a prototypical property of entities. Either number meaning, then, would help hearers to construe these words as entities, and in the case of a word like *acoustics* there is no basis for preferring one over the other on semantic grounds alone.

But when we consider the signals that bear these meanings a preference emerges. The signal of ONE, *Entity -0*, lacks overt recognizable morphology. Identifying a lexical stem as an instance of *Entity -0* requires interpreting that stem as designating an entity in the message – the very problem for which help is needed. Due to its signal, the meaning ONE can be of no help here. By contrast, the signal for the meaning MORE THAN ONE includes fixed overt morphology. For its identification hearers need only eliminate the verb *-s* and genitive *-s* as possibilities, both of which are unlikely given the lexical content of these words.

To illustrate this rationale, consider the interpretive problem posed by the lexical stem *acoustic* in [48], and how the Entity Number System resolves it.

[48]   The acoustics influence design considerations.

While the stem *acoustic* itself can be employed in both an adjectival and a nominal capacity, here the meaning MORE THAN ONE forces *acoustic* to be construed nominally (as the subject), and *influence* as its verb. If ONE had been chosen for the lexical stem *acoustic*, the perceptual problem would be unresolved, for both *the acoustic influences* and *the acoustic influence* could momentarily be understood as either one or two constituents.

[49a]   The acoustic influences design considerations.
[49b]   The acoustic influence design considerations.

Thus the Entity Number System still accounts for the choice of grammatical number in [48]; not because of the greater semantic suitability of the meaning MORE THAN ONE over ONE (as was argued for *scissors*), but because of the greater perceptual salience of its signal.

With that local, perceptual problem solved by the meaning MORE THAN ONE, the choice of grammatical number occasionally goes a different way when speakers have a second opportunity to categorize these entities numerically.

> [50]   Tolerance is the essential condition of *a decent politics*. It is not, however, itself *a politics*. . . Humanism, too, is prior to politics. . . . When humanism considers itself sufficient for *a politics*, it produces only *a politics of sensibility, a politics for narrators and spectators*; impotence, and finally silence.
>
> (Leon Wieseltier, *The New Republic*)

The mixed grammatical number of *a politics* is possible because the feature of the message associated with the phrase spans the opposition of number. Politics encompasses a range of political activity, never a single policy. At the same time, the various policies and actions can form a loosely coherent and complementary set, making it possible to compare and distinguish one set from another. *A politics* is anomalous only for an analysis attempting to deal with certain number markings as mechanically generated copies of others. But when each instance of grammatical number is treated as independently chosen, the switch poses no problem so long as separate motivations for each choice can be identified.

2.12 The Number Meanings with Decimal Fractions

Hirtle (1982:44) cites examples of noun number with decimals which he calls a mystery:

    1 gram
    .5 grams   (Does the notion of '5' call for the -*s*?)
    .1 gram(s)   (Usage seems to vary.)
    0 grams

The use of *Entity -s* in .1 gram(s) and 0 grams definitely poses a problem if its meaning is MORE THAN ONE.

Diver (1975) resolves the problem of .1 grams and 0 grams quite neatly in his analysis of English number by positing

OTHER THAN ONE as the meaning for *Entity -s*. OTHER THAN ONE is, of course, applicable to numbers that are both more and less than one. But the meaning OTHER THAN ONE doesn't completely resolve the problem of decimals because, as Morgan (1984) points out, *1.0 voters* (read 'one point zero voters') also apparently occurs with *Entity -s*. Moreover, positing OTHER THAN ONE for *Entity -s* would weaken our rationale for the use of the meaning ONE for messages involving things taken *en masse*; in the case of mass reference it could be argued that OTHER THAN ONE is more appropriate than ONE.

So far as we can see, Hirtle's examples are the sole data that would argue in favour of OTHER THAN ONE for *Entity -s*. This means that for young children learning English these would be the data forcing them to revise their initial hypothesis of MORE THAN ONE – which otherwise fits English usage quite nicely – in favour of Diver's alternative. The question arises, then, whether children ever actually encounter Hirtle's data.

Aware of this question, I have been on the lookout for such examples. Over the past five years I have not encountered a single instance in spoken or written English of the use of *Entity -s* with the critical decimal values 0.1, 0.0 and 1.0. In spoken English, fractions are always employed for quantities less than one. Fractions, of course, create a dilemma for the speaker as well, since neither number meaning of the present analysis is really suitable for values less than one. But for fractions there is a way around the impasse. Speakers can ignore the fractional complexity and make their number choice on the basis of the numerator alone (e.g., one third, two thirds).

An investigation of the mathematics curriculum in the local school reveals that decimal fractions are not introduced until fourth grade, presumably a point in time when children have already settled on the systemic value of *Entity -s* in English. An examination of the textbook in use revealed no instances of the critical examples mentioned above.

Our conclusion is that Hirtle's and Morgan's data are instances of what Haiman (1985) calls Linguish, manufactured examples which do not occur outside the pages of theoretical journals. As such they have no consequence for the young child fashioning his theory of English based on the usage to which he is exposed. Whether or not some speakers, through their constant exposure to decimals, revise their Entity Number System as adults in favour of Diver's alternative analysis is open to further investigation.

Notes

1. We are indebted to Anna Wierzbicka (1985) for this reference as well as the ones from Palmer and Ware to follow. Her work on grammatical number is summarized in 2.7.

2. Lakoff (1987) has served for us as an introduction to the seminal work of Eleanor Rosch (e.g., Rosch 1977) in developing the notion of prototype as the basis for cognitive categories. Lakoff's book offers a comprehensive summary of the work done over the past fifteen years in the nature of cognitive categories.

3. Lakoff (1987) provides a detailed critique of this traditional position that ranges over its philosophical, psychological and linguistic dimensions. No summary here would do it justice, and we strongly commend it to the interested reader.

4. The frame of reference imposed by these two words is at the heart of the abortion issue. The debate about the morality of abortion hinges not on the question of whether a foetus is biologically 'human' or 'living', or, indeed, 'human life', which it undeniably is; but on whether it is a *person* – an entity that enjoys legal and moral rights.

5. The following discussion is adapted from Diver (1984). Kirsner (1979a) must serve for a presentation of Diver's analysis in print. Kirsner presents an analysis of the article system in Dutch whose systemic structure is identical to that proposed by Diver for English and whose strategies of use closely parallel those of the English system.

6. The following example is drawn from language use:

> Critics tend to be as suspicious of youthful prodigies as promoters are anxious to promote them and audiences eager to embrace them. All the more do we wonder when *a Joshua Bell* comes along, peering seductively from the CD's front.
>
> (Scott Cantrell, *Ovation*)

In this case the name Joshua Bell still poses a problem of identification, despite the fact it presumably has only a single referent, because [6] occurred in a review of Bell's debut recording in June 1988. By employing *a* (= DIFFERENTIATION RE-QUIRED, INCOMPLETE) the writer is assuring readers that he does not expect them to know who this newcomer is. Note that [6] is not to be construed as 'someone like Joshua Bell' (cf. *a Heifitz* = 'a violinist comparable to Heifitz') since Bell was, at the time, too new on the scene to serve as a type.

7. In Figures 2.2 and 2.3 *Entity -0* and *Entity -s* are posited as components of the article signals *0 Entity -0* and *0 Entity -s*, thus formalizing the contextual feature that usually distinguishes the signal of the meaning DIFFERENTIATION NOT REQUIRED from that of DIFFERENTIATION NOT COMPLETE. In actuality the status of *Entity -s* falls just short of the *de jure* role accorded it here. This is because with words such as *people* and *cattle* it is the 'plural' *0* (= DIFFERENTIATION NOT COMPLETE), not the

'singular' $\emptyset$ (= DIFFERENTIATION NOT REQUIRED) that occurs. This makes good communicative sense, since *people* and *cattle* always refer to a plurality of referents. But morphologically *people* and *cattle* are still instances of *Entity -$\emptyset$* not *Entity -s*.

ADDENDUM to *Persons* vs *People*: A Case Study

Shortly before this book went to press we encountered the following example in which a speaker displays a conscious awareness that the word *people* downplays the individuality of its referents. The speaker, King-Devine, is a theatrical director preparing a production of the play *The Diary of Anne Frank*. Note that for King-Devine *people* downplays individuality even when quantified numerically.

> To help everyone get a feel for the story, King-Devine said she began each rehearsal by reading aloud at least one entry from the diary. 'This play is not about six million people dying in the Holocaust,' she said she told the cast one evening after reading. 'Its about six million individuals – with lives and hopes and dreams – being murdered. . .'
>
> *Town Crier*, Greenfield Mass
> April 17, 1991 p. 2

Chapter 3

Communicative efficacy

Chapter 2 developed the various ways ONE and MORE THAN ONE are employed in the communication of messages. Beginning with their straightforward use for referential number, we argued these two meanings are also used in ways that, while no longer justifiable on referential grounds, can still be explained in terms of their greater suitability over their systemic opposite. This treatment of grammatical meaning rests on a parallel and complementary treatment of lexical meaning. Chapter 3 presents this treatment, illustrates how lexical and grammatical meanings interact in the communicative process, and develops the implications of that interaction for linguistic theory.

3.1 Lexical Monosemy

In discussing the use of ONE for mass reference we skirted the issue of the meaning of the lexical stem. It is common practice, of course, to set up separate mass and count senses for words used in these two ways. So, for example, *chicken* would have the sense of 'common domestic fowl' in *I saw a chicken* and the sense of 'meat from a common domestic fowl' in *I ordered chicken*.

But such usage does not compel a polysemous treatment of the lexical stem because these contrasting interpretations of *chicken* follow quite straightforwardly from the immediate context, in particular, the quantifiers and articles implying discrete or non-discrete referents. Whether it is more advantageous to make the base meaning of such dual-functioning words count-like or mass-like would require a careful study of each, and the solution may well differ from word to word. But it seems safe to say that whichever way one decided, the contrasting interpretation could be reached on the basis of the information supplied by the associated grammatical morphology.

This monosemic approach to lexical meaning has been argued most recently, and forcefully, by Charles Ruhl (1989) in his book *On Monosemy*. Ruhl's orientation shares important commonalities with the Columbia School, and we cannot improve on his cogent and detailed argumentation for the methodological wisdom of a monosemic bias in lexical analysis. However, a monosemic treatment of the mass/count distinction in English was proposed by Weinreich (1966/1980) more than twenty years ago within a generative framework (cf., McCawley 1979:172). Since Weinreich argues his position on formal grounds it will be of greater interest to present our treatment as a development and modification of his own.

According to Weinreich, nouns were to be marked in the lexicon as inherently count or non-count, but allowed to co-occur with determiners bearing a *contradictory* count feature. A separate set of Construal Rules comprising part of a Semantic Calculator would then construe an interpretation out of such contradictory strings.

> The calculator acts on inputs containing formatives with contradictory features by construing a new semantic entity with a more elaborate structure, in which the transferred feature is decisive, but the contradictory inherent feature can be accommodated.
>
> (Weinreich 1980:179)

The important theoretical consequence of Weinreich's proposal is that the interpretation of a sentence would no longer be a simple amalgamation of its semantic parts; it is a *calculation* from its semantic parts. The interaction of semantic features is, in this case, reminiscent of physical objects in motion. When a billiard ball strikes another going at the same velocity at a 90° angle, the course of the latter is deflected to a trajectory at a 45° angle to its initial course. This new path represents a resolution of its initial vector and the vector of the one that struck it, a *vector product*. The interpretation of a sentence is, for Weinreich then, a kind of semantic vector product calculated from its sometimes conflicting semantic parts.

Since our own thinking has been shaped by the same considerations, Weinreich's reasoning is worth summarizing here. Weinreich began by pointing out the shortcomings of Katz and Fodor's (1963) treatment in which nouns as well as determiners were subcategorized as inherently [+Count] or [−Count], and the lexical rule only allowed the selection of a noun whose count feature matched that of the determiner.

> This solution conforms in spirit to all work in generative grammar to date. It fails, however, to account for the ability of English words to be used as *either* count *or* mass nouns. After all, any [−Count] noun X, when used with the indefinite determiner *a*, functions as a [+Count] noun meaning 'a kind of X': *a water, a wine, a blood*. Moreover, any [+Count] noun Y used with the mass determiner Null [i.e., the ∅ article WR] amounts to a [−Count] noun signifying 'the substance Y': *I prefer brick*. This conversion becomes especially effective with the use of the partitive determiner *some* (unstressed), or with other quantifier expressions: *move over and give me some pillow*; *leave me a little piece of garden*; etc. Hence, the introduction of selectional conditions into the Lexical Rule cannot be the correct solution.
>
> (Weinreich 1980:146)

To achieve descriptive success within the Katz and Fodor framework many nouns would have to have dual entries in the lexicon (e.g., a [+Count] *chicken* and a [−Count] *chicken*). Weinreich judged this to be unsatisfactory because it doubled the size of the noun vocabulary.

> The theory [of Katz and Fodor (1963)], despite its recourse to processes, resembles an item-and-arrangement model of language in its requirement that the meaning of a sentence contain nothing which is not stored in its dictionary. . . Hence, if K and F were to be extended to deal more hospitably with anomalies than merely to identify and discard them, a gigantically inflated dictionary, with a relatively small 'normal' part and with an indefinitely large 'anomalous' part, would be required.
>
> (Weinreich 1980:189)

For us, a far more decisive consideration than formal economy is one that bears on the acquisition process. The mechanism for mass reference is more productive than Weinreich's semi-conventionalized examples suggest. Lexical stems whose meanings unquestionably designate referents with cognitively salient boundaries are nevertheless occasionally employed in a mass sense, especially in spoken English, where the normative pressure against novel usage is not so strong.

[1]   It smells like new *baby* here.

(Bonny Gildin, upon entering a car)

[2]   You and Angus cannot be in the tub together. That's too
      much *boy*.
                        (Cornelia Reid, admonishing two brothers in
                                                      the bathroom)

And as Jespersen observed, the converse occurs as well; words
whose apparent semantic value would lead one to expect them to
be used only in a mass sense are occasionally employed in a count
sense.

[3]   Oh, that's one of Angus's *dirts*.
          (Cornelia Reid, referring to a small brown plastic pellet
        simulating dirt for use in a toy conveyor-belt truck loader)
[4]   Some [sprouts] such as those of the Moso bamboo and the
      Henon bamboo, are somewhat bitter or acrid, but when
      this flavor is objectionable it may be removed by boiling
      in two *waters*.
            (R. Young and J. Haun, *Bamboo in the United States*)
[5]   As you know, DialAmerica contributes $12\frac{1}{2}$ per cent to
      us for every subscription ordered. These *monies* will help
      us defray the costs of our annual operating expenses.
                          (R. Kirkley, fund raising letter)

It seems implausible to claim that the word *dirt* has had a
second, count sense ('a plastic pellet') in addition to its mass
sense all along, and that *baby* and *boy* have had a second, mass
sense in addition to their count sense all along. If for no other
reason, it becomes a puzzle as to how speakers of English would
ever have *learned* of these contrasting 'senses', for examples
[1]–[4] struck this writer as completely novel.
      A more straightforward and plausible account, we argue with
Weinreich, is to attribute the count interpretation of *dirts* in [3]
directly to the word *one* and the *Entity -s* of *dirts*, each of which
forces *dirt* to be interpreted in a count way despite its inherent
mass-like meaning. Similarly, the mass interpretation of *boy* in
[2] is forced upon it by the quantifier *much* despite its inherent
count-like meaning.

The hearer's contribution
This treatment of [2] and [3] is still in the spirit of Weinreich's
proposal because both sentences contain an element bearing the
semantic feature dominating in the resulting interpretation. The
meaning of *boy* is inherently count-like, designating a (whole)
young male human being; but the meaning of *much* indicates a

large mass-like quantity. Together they yield a semantic product midway between: a mass comprised of countable young human males.

But Weinreich's Semantic Calculator could not interpret example [1], for in *It smells like Ø new babyØ here* no lexical or grammatical element bears a feature 'mass referent'. *Ø Entity -Ø*, to recall, simply means DIFFERENTIATION NOT RE-QUIRED, and mass reference is only one of several reasons why this could be so. Compare the interpretation of *Ø (new) babyØ* in [1] with its interpretation in [6], said of a shrieking infant.

[6] I don't believe *Ø babyØ* is happy.

Now the reason why the lexical stem *baby* does not require differentiation is that there is only one possible referent on the scene. This means that in interpreting [1] the hearer is himself supplying a crucial component, namely, the most likely reason why DIFFERENTIATION is NOT REQUIRED for *baby* on that particular occasion: in contrast to [6], in [1] no particular 'baby' is being referred to.

3.2 Interpretive Problem-solving

If people are supplying critical components themselves in interpreting sentences in context, the relation between linguistic meanings and the message they help to convey must be conceived in a new way. The relation the Columbia School has adopted is stated by Garcia (1975:41):

> The linguistic signs do but point in certain directions and – most important – exclude certain possibilities. What specific meaning is intended, however, is inferred by the intelligence of the hearer, who combines the meanings offered by the speaker with his knowledge of the context of the utterance, and figures out 'what the speaker must have meant'.

In a similar vein, Lakoff (1977:239) writes:

> The meanings of the parts constrain, but do not provide, the inter-pretation of the whole. The whole makes sense only because some aspect of the reader's experience has been evoked by the meanings of the parts.

It will be recognized that Garcia's and Lakoff's views roughly parallel the conception adopted by one wing of the pragmatic tradition regarding the relation between 'sentence meaning' and 'utterance meaning'.

> A speaker, *qua* communicator, has to solve the problem: 'Given that I want to bring about such-and-such a result in the hearer's consciousness, what is the best way to accomplish this aim by using language?' For the hearer, there is another kind of problem to solve: 'Given that the speaker said such-and-such, what did the speaker mean me to understand by that?' This conception of communication leads to a rhetorical approach to pragmatics, whereby the speaker is seen as trying to achieve his aims within the constraints imposed by principles and maxims of 'good communicative behaviour'.
>
> (Leech 1983:x)

But whereas Leech had in mind the way language users arrive at the communicative 'force' of a sentence from its 'sense' (conceived as an abstract, linguistic object with inherent propositional value) we introduce this problem-solving perspective at the 'sense' level, as it were. This has the effect of transposing the 'sense/force' distinction of sentence pragmatics to the word level. The notion 'mass referent' is an intent of the speaker, and a creation of the hearer, without, at the same time, being a feature of meaning linguistically encoded in the text itself; mass reference is effected through semantic *implication*.

Once this tack is taken for unusual examples such as [1]–[5] it is apparent the mechanism applies equally well to the regular cases, those cited by Jespersen in Chapter 2. If, for the sake of argument, we say that the meaning of *chicken* designates the whole (countable) animal, its mass interpretation in [7] represents a creative extrapolation from its inherent meaning merely prompted by the assurance DIFFERENTIATION NOT REQUIRED.

[7] We ordered *Ø chickenØ*.

Plausibility in context

The active participation of the hearer does not end with the conclusion that a message of mass reference is intended. Consider how the interpretations of *chicken* and *boy* differ slightly. *Chicken* in the context of the *Ø ————-Ø* suggests edible flesh from the animal with no necessity of there being the makings of a whole chicken; example [7] could refer to a platter of chicken legs.

On the other hand, *too much boyØ* would never be interpreted in the context of [2] as a mass of 'boy' parts (e.g., only legs or only arms). That alternative interpretation to which [2] is open is discounted by the hearer as an implausible communication. Similarly, *waters* in [4] is elsewhere employed to refer to *glasses* of water.

[8]   Could we please have three waters?

But that unlikely interpretation of *waters* is discounted in the context of [4].

Since hearers can be relied upon to discount implausible interpretations, the speaker need not block them linguistically so as to deflect the interpretation from such unlikely paths; only plausible unintended paths need be blocked. But then the interpretation of an utterance is predictable *only by human beings*, not purely on the basis of the semantic information encoded by the utterance itself.

This is the point on which we depart from Weinreich and his Semantic Calculator. Unlike the interaction of billiard balls, 'sentence meaning' is not predictable in a mechanical fashion amenable to formalization. The meanings of linguistic signs, taken collectively, still *under-determine* the message.

To summarize, in the analytical line we are advancing the interpretation of utterances is neither a simple amalgamation nor a mechanical computation, but a solution to a problem. The problem confronting the hearer is to invent a communicative motivation responsible for the speaker's juxtaposing the particular linguistic signs he or she did. The hearer's interpretation is that explanation. By imputing a covert communicative goal to the speaker, his overt linguistic behaviour becomes understandable and rational.

3.3 Communicative Efficacy

A major theme of this chapter and the last has been the frequent discrepancy between the systemic semantic value of a linguistic sign and the messages for which it is employed. Despite such discrepancies, the lexical and grammatical meanings did, in various ways, further the communication of the speaker's intended message. To recapitulate:

> in *That's one of Angus's dirts* the referents of *dirts*, while not 'dirt' themselves, did function as 'dirt' in a child's toy;
> in *It smells like new baby here* the referent, while not a particular discrete 'baby', is a baby's olfactory calling-card;

in *Water boils at 212 F* the ONE of *water∅*, though not ideal, functions
in conjunction with the meaning of the *∅* article (whose signal includes
Entity -∅) to imply a message of an unbounded referent;
in *the acoustics influence* the MORE THAN ONE of *acoustics* serves
to steer hearers towards an entity interpretation of the lexical stem
and is preferable to ONE by virtue of the perceptual salience of its
signal.

In each case the relation between a linguistic sign and its
associated message has been one of *communicative efficacy*.
Required now is deductive support for the relation of communicative efficacy. In what way does our basic orienting view of
language as a communicative instrument anticipate that the
relation between meaning and message will be one of efficacy
rather than truth?

From an instrumental perspective the semantic categories of a
language have the status of communicative *tools*. Crucial here is
the nature of the relation between a *tool* and the various *tasks* for
which it is employed. In probing this relation we will look
momentarily at the use of tools outside the realm of language
altogether.

The tool-task relation of functional efficacy

The tools of the home carpenter are optimally suited for certain
tasks. A hand saw is an ideal tool for cutting wood, a hammer an
ideal tool for driving and drawing out nails and a screwdriver for
driving screws. So long as these tools are employed for such
purposes there is a perfect match between tool-design and use.

It is a familiar fact, however, that the number of different tasks
people wish to accomplish often exceeds the number of tools
available, and under such circumstances people will employ tools
in ways for which they are not ideally suited. In addition to
driving screws the home carpenter may employ a screwdriver to
open a can of paint; lacking a chisel, he may press it into service
to chip out a piece of wood in mounting a hinge in soft wood; and
lacking a crowbar he may employ the claws of a hammer to pry
up a floorboard.

The way people adapt tools to such novel tasks is *not*,
however, arbitrary and inexplicable. If the object of explanation
is taken to be people's deployment of particular tools on
particular occasions, then the design of a screwdriver accounts
both for its use to drive screws *and* for its use to open paint cans;
the home carpenter does not, after all, choose a saw, hammer, or
drill. Given the available options, a screwdriver is still the *best
available* tool for opening paint cans, even though not ideal.[1]

And when a crowbar with its greater leverage is unavailable, the claw-end of a hammer is, by default, the most appropriate tool for prying up floor boards. (Note that for carpentry tools, at any rate, using them for such unconventional tasks does not result in any structural alteration in the tool itself.)

Clearly, then, when people are limited to a given number of tools with fixed natures, explaining why people choose one rather than another for a particular task requires appeal to its *relative* appropriateness – suitability in comparison to the available alternatives.

The tool-task relation of communicative efficacy

What is the linguistic analogy to the mismatch between tool and task in our carpentry analogy? The discussion of mass reference provides an example. For a few animals the English lexicon has special words that distinguish between the animal itself and its flesh for eating: *cow* and *beef*; *calf* and *veal*; *pig* and *pork*. Here there is a perfect match (i.e., truth) between semantic tool and communicative task.

But for other animals the English lexicon has only a single word: *chicken*, *turkey*, *tuna*. Here the relation between the lexical resources of the language and communicative tasks is less than ideal, and the same semantic tool must be pressed into service to accomplish a task for which it is only relatively appropriate. Using the word *chicken* to refer to meat thus stands on a par with opening paint cans and prying up floor boards in our carpentry analogy, a task accomplished with a serviceable (though not ideal) tool at one's disposal.

The same relation of relative appropriateness obtains in the use of grammatical meanings. The meaning ONE of *Entity -0* is suitable for mass reference only in comparison with the alternative MORE THAN ONE; while *0 Entity -0* simply says DIFFERENTIATION NOT REQUIRED, mass reference being only one of several alternative reasons. Clearly the semantic values of these two signs are less than ideal for mass reference in comparison with, say, the quantifier *much*.

Message and meaning

The *tool/task* distinction being drawn here was first introduced in Chapter 1 and is essentially the one noted by Jespersen: the distinction between what speakers convey on particular occasions – what he called 'the idea expressed in each single instance' – and, the semantic categories in the linguistic code itself.

We have adhered to the terminological convention established in previous Columbia School research by employing the words *message* and *meaning* as technical terms to capture it. A *message* is the intended and understood import of a communication, also called utterance meaning (Kempson 1977). It is, by and large, introspectively accessible to speakers of the language. The mass and count interpretations of *chicken* are examples of *message* characteristics.

A *meaning*, on the other hand, is a semantic category of the language, a notional constant paired with a particular *signal*. Examples of linguistic meanings in Chapters 1–3 have been: IMPLIED POSSIBILITY, AFFIRMED (*do Verb*); DOUBT (*Inversion*); ONE (*Entity -0*); MORE THAN ONE (*Entity -s*); DIFFERENTIATION NOT REQUIRED (*0 Entity -0*); HUMAN BEING (*person*); and WHOLE LIVE COMMON DOMESTIC FOWL (*chicken*).

As noted in Section 2.5 (p. 55), a *meaning* in this technical sense is a theoretical construct, one often not introspectively available; its postulation is justified by its ability to account for the deployment of its associated *signal* by speakers of the language in communicating messages.

Sentence meaning

Notable for its absence in this picture is anything corresponding to '(literal) sentence meaning'. Traditionally 'sentence meaning' has been conceived as a linguistic object of propositional value existing apart from language users and encoded in language itself. But such a construct could only have a place in the present scheme if it were a mechanical computation from the meanings of linguistic signals.

Clearly this is not the case. The notional value of collocations of linguistic signals is determined *only in part* by the meanings they bear. They serve more often as hints, or clues, to the intended message than as actual components. And as mere hints and clues, their interpretation requires the active, creative participation of the hearer, who draws on contextual information, encyclopaedic knowledge, and his or her own sense of what constitutes a plausible communication. The mass/count distinction, to repeat, is not a feature of inherent, linguistic 'sense' but one of contextually-determined, communicative 'force', a pragmatic extrapolation by the hearer from the clues actually provided.

Like creative problem-solving in other realms, these extrapolations are not, we believe, a process amenable to axiomatization. Coming to the same conclusion, Leech argues: 'Unlike the sense-sound mappings and the sound-sense mappings of grammar, these problem-solving procedures cannot be defined by algorithms. They involve general human intelligence assessing alternative probabilities on the basis of contextual evidence' (Leech 1983:36).

Language and language use

The active participation of the hearer in creating messages means that the *meaning/message* distinction becomes the boundary between the linguistic system and language use. Only linguistic meanings (and their associated signals) are *in* a language; they exist independent of both speaker and hearer. Once one or more signs are chosen to communicate a message, the boundary has been crossed into language use, with the consequence that a different mode of linguistic explanation is necessary. On one side lies the *rule-governed* aspect of language: the categorical relations between signals and meanings that form a theory of the linguistic code. On the other side lie user-mediated, tool-task relations of communicative efficacy: the *goal-directed* aspect of language.

3.4 The Relational Value of the Number Meanings

The reason for our extensive examination of Entity Number is that the psychological and communicative principles operative in this area are the same as those operative in verb number, the major focus of this study. Moreover, these two instances of grammatical number interact in ways that make discussion of the latter impossible without reference to the former. However the most important principle relevant to an understanding of grammatical number has not yet been introduced, a principle deriving from the Saussurean dictum that language is a form not a substance. After an initial presentation in schematic form here, it will be subjected to quantitative testing in Chapter 4 before its application to verb number in Chapter 6.

The principle relates to the interaction of the Entity Number meanings with those of lexical stems. To review the present analytical line, the meanings of some lexical stems will be count-like and others mass-like (with perhaps still others indifferent to the distinction). But they will not be grouped into classes reflecting this difference because the grammatical behaviour of the words within each class is essentially the same. *Chicken* and *boy*, with presumably count-like meanings, occasionally occur with $\emptyset$ *Entity* $-\emptyset$ and the quantifier *much* just like *water* and *dirt*; and the latter, with presumably mass-like meanings, occasionally occur with *a* and *many* just like *chicken* and *boy*. At best, only generalizations of statistical tendency would be possible about such lexical classes.

On the other hand, an important grammatical generalization is possible about the group as a whole: save for the handful of exceptions such as *furniture*, *information* and *cash*, all occur with both *Entity -0* and *Entity -s*; and the difference in message consistently correlates with the invariant grammatical meanings of these two signals.

[9a] The *boy0* walked through the field.
[9b] The *boys* walked through the field.
[10a] *Sugar0* is often put in coffee and tea.
[10b] Some *sugars* are better for you than others. (fructose vs. sucrose)

ONE and MORE THAN ONE hold for [9] and [10] because in both cases the *b* message involves more instances than the *a* message, as shown below.

FIGURE 3.1 The Entity Number System and *boy* and *sugar*

Single young human male	Plurality of young human males
boy0 ONE	boys MORE THAN ONE

unstructured mass of 'sugar'	varieties of 'sugar'
sugar0 ONE	sugars MORE THAN ONE

Substantive differences exist, to be sure, between the two *a* and the two *b* messages. But those differences reflect the base values of the lexical stems. Those substantive differences can be factored out so as to leave a relational constant because the present analysis provides a construct to which that constant can be attributed: the grammatical opposition between ONE and MORE THAN ONE.

The fact that these two meanings operate in terms of their relational opposition is underscored when their use is examined with respect to the full expressive range of a single lexical stem. *Sugar* can refer not only to loosely-defined unstructured masses of the substance, but to well-defined discrete exemplars, the cubes of sugar one puts in coffee and tea.

[11a]   George only takes one *sugar0*.
[11b]   George takes two *sugars*.

Figure 3.2 illustrates this wider expressive range.

FIGURE 3.2   The Entity Number System and *sugar*

unstructured mass	single discrete exemplar	plurality of discrete exemplars	varieties of substance
	<ONE vs. MORE THAN ONE>		
sugar0	sugar0 | sugars		sugars

Note the many-to-one relationship between tool and task expected with any general-purpose instrument. Both the lexical stem *sugar* and the two number meanings, separately and in combination, are employed for more than one kind of message. Some such doubling up must inevitably occur whenever the communicative goals of speakers exceed the number of semantic categories available.

The relation between meaning and message is, in each case, one of communicative efficacy. For the lexical stem *sugar* this takes a straightforward form. Its mass-like meaning of a sweet edible substance is descriptively true of all its referents; a sugar cube is, after all, still 'sugar'. The various physical forms sugar may take need not be built into the lexical stem as separate and discrete senses because speakers bring to their use of English a familiarity with sugar cubes and chemical varieties of sugar. This comprises part of the constantly-embroidered tapestry of encyclopaedic knowledge upon which language traces its distinctions.

Communicative efficacy takes a different form with the number meanings. The opposition between ONE and MORE THAN ONE intersects with the referential potential of *sugar* so as to partition it into two ranges that contrast in relative 'oneness'. In context, each number meaning functions to narrow down for the hearer the referential potential of the lexical stem without, at the same time, pinpointing the intended interpretation. Further refinement is provided by the associated determiners.

The case of *hair* resembles that of *sugar*. (See Figure 3.3.) *Hair* differs from *sugar*, however, in the analytical importance that must be accorded the speaker's point of view. Sugar comes in two objectively different forms, granulated crystals and small solid cubes; this referential difference alone would seem sufficient to account for the grammatical treatment of *sugar* as either 'an unstructured mass' or 'a plurality of discrete exemplars'. With

FIGURE 3.3   The Entity Number System and *hair*

unstructured mass	single discrete exemplar	plurality of discrete exemplars	varieties of substance
	<ONE vs. MORE THAN ONE>		
hair0	hair0 |	hairs	hairs

hair, however, these two treatments do not reflect any external difference in manifestation.

[12]   Her undulating red *hair0* framed her face.
[13]   Two red *hairs* protruded from the middle of his scalp.

The *hair0* in [12] is composed of a large number of entities that are physically identical to the *hairs* in [13]. Their differing grammatical treatment is entirely a reflection of the relevance of their individual identity to the message being communicated. The act of 'framing' in [12] is done by all the hairs acting in concert, whereas the act of 'protruding' in [13] is done by each hair individually. (The extent to which cognitive salience alone determines the choice of Entity Number, entirely independently of referential considerations, will be developed in more detail in Chapter 4.)

3.5 The Extension of Lexical Meanings

The present analysis has succeeded in isolating a single communicative function for the Entity Number meanings by portraying them as tools for partitioning the expressive potential of individual lexical stems. But success on that score has created an analytical problem that does not exist in the more conventional polysemous treatment of lexical meaning. When lexical meanings are allowed the leeway of application permitted here, the problem then arises of accounting for their varying expressive range. For if only a relation of relative appropriateness need hold between meaning and message, why are not all lexical stems employed for as wide a range as *sugar*? And why, indeed, is the phrase *one sugar0* not employed for a single grain of sugar in addition to a single cube of sugar?

Value relationships
One factor affecting the extension of a lexical meaning is the alternative expressive resources available in the language. As

argued earlier, *chicken* and *turkey* are employed for the meat from the animal as well as the animal itself because English lacks words whose meanings explicitly designate 'chicken meat' and 'turkey meat'. On the other hand, *pig* and *cow* are not employed in that way because such specialized words do exist, namely, *pork* and *beef*. By the same token, the latter are not normally pressed into service for reference to the associated animal because of the existence of *pig* and *cow*.

FIGURE 3.4   The Entity Number System with Animals

1	2	3
unstructured	single	plurality
mass	whole animal	of animals

	<ONE vs. MORE THAN ONE>	
chicken0	chicken0	chickens
(pork0)	pig0	pigs
(beef0)	cow0	cows

The differing extensions of *chicken* and *pig* are, in a way, built into the language. But not in the meanings of *chicken* and *pig* themselves; those do not differ substantively other than as to species. What differs is their value within the larger semantic field. Given the paradigmatic alternatives that structure the field, all that need be said is that speakers choose the most appropriate semantic tool from among the available options.

Novelty of message
A second factor influencing the extension of a lexical meaning is the relative novelty, and hence predictability, of the communicative goal. Most coffee and tea drinkers have frequent call to refer to sugar cubes but little call to refer explicitly to individual sugar grains. As a consequence they employ the relatively imprecise grammatical distinctions to suggest the former while employing the more precise lexical alternative *grain* (*of*) to designate the latter (DuBois 1985:363).

Similarly, on the infrequent occasions when speakers refer to different kinds or heads of hair, they usually employ those explicit lexical phrases. Yet reliance on the meaning MORE THAN ONE alone is still a possibility.

[14]   Both our *hairs* got old. (i.e., 'We both turned gray')
                              (Larry Storch to Johnny Carson, *Tonight*)

[15]   Get in and I'll get the shampoo and I'll wash your *hairs*.
       (Cornelia Reid, to two brothers in the bathroom)

People

These two factors interact with the Entity Number System in an
interesting way to shape the extension of the word *people*.
English has a rich inventory of lexical stems for reference to
human beings conceptualized in a variety of ways, words whose
interpretation is further refined by the general-purpose grammatical distinctions of the language.

FIGURE 3.5   Deployment of the Entity Number System with *people*

1	2	3	4	5	6
unstructured mass	single human being	plurality of human beings	single weakly defined aggregate	single well defined aggregate	plurality of aggregates

				<ONE vs MORE THAN ONE>	
			people0	people0 | peoples	
(humanity0) (public0)	(person0)	(persons)			

Chapter 2 characterized the meaning of *people* as lying midway
between AGGREGATE OF HUMAN BEINGS and HUMAN
BEINGS IN AGGREGATE. This makes it most suitable for
message types 4, 5 and 6 in Figure 3.5.

[16]   Serious criminal acts have been committed. *People* who
       commit such acts must expect to face the consequences.
       (Type 4)
                                     (Margaret Thatcher, *Newsweek*)
[17]   But polygamy presents an almost insurmountable barrier
       to Catholic evangelization in Africa . . . 'Every *people*
       has its manner of marriage and forming families,' says
       Cardinal Joseph Malula of Kinshasa. (Type 5)
                                                      (*Newsweek*)
[18]   There was an ugly edge on events: more and more it
       seemed that two *peoples* lived in England, not one –
       enemies, hating each other, who could not hear what the
       other said. (Type 6)
                                     (Doris Lessing, *The Fifth Child*)

Speakers do not usually press *people* into service for message types 1, 2 and 3 because of the availability of the more appropriate lexical alternatives *humanity*, *public* and *person* (as well as names). Yet such occasions do arise. In both [19] and [20] the MORE THAN ONE of *peoples* reinforces the plurality of the HUMAN BEINGS component of its meaning rather than quantifying the AGGREGATE component, as is usually the case.

[19] Hi, peoples.

(Leonard Zamore)

[19] was the morning greeting of a senior lawyer to two members of the office staff. The nuance of reference falls between points 3 and 4 on the continuum. By implying a lack of interest in the identities of the individuals addressed (through the choice of *people*) while acknowledging they are somewhat more than a faceless mass (through the choice of MORE THAN ONE), the speaker subtly enforces the power relationship of the workplace while maintaining a surface jocularity.[2]

[20] Let me put this in its starkest and ugliest light. I am not sure, but I believe, that if the choice were between the survival of Israel and that of the remaining 4 or 6 billion *peoples* of the world, I would choose the 4 million *people* of Israel.

(Jane DeLynn, *The New York Times Book Review*)

The phrase *4 or 6 billion peoples* refers to the totality of human beings that comprise the world's population, not a plurality of ethnic groups. On the other hand, *4 million people* does refer to a single ethnic group (hence ONE) despite the plural quantifier *4 million*.

[21] There's nine people here. No, seven people. No, one *people*.

(Christine Lorentzen, pointing to herself)

The referent of *people* is now at point 2 in [21]. The speaker is a 12 year-old pupil speaking out of turn who apparently wishes to avoid explicit reference to herself. Here the only aspect of *people* appropriate to her message is its implication of the diminished importance of referential identity. She counteracts the referential plurality built into the meaning of *people* by supplementing her communication with a gesture. (Recall here Weinreich's proposal of allowing elements bearing contradictory semantic features to combine so as to yield a kind of semantic vector product.)

Examples [19]–[21] show that speakers are always free to depart from common usage if they have some communicative motivation to do so. One should not, then, build Figure 3.5 into the structure of English itself, in the form of binding constraints. One should merely build in the systemic value relations that give rise to the common usage, relations that pressure but do not compel.

Within the range 4–6, for which the meaning of *people* is better suited, ONE and MORE THAN ONE are employed in a relativistic fashion to steer hearers in one direction or the other. While the entire range contains an element of conceptual plurality, type 6 contains an additional element not found in types 4 and 5; multiple aggregates of human beings are involved in 6 whereas only a single aggregate is involved in 4 and 5. The inherent plurality of the word *people* becomes the base-line from which the two number meanings are evaluated. ONE means, in effect, 'as one-like an interpretation as is possible given the meaning of the lexical stem'.

A polysemous analysis

The traditional dictionary treatment of *people* ascribes multiple values to the word so as to capture explicitly the difference between message types 4 and 5. According to that line of analysis *people* has two distinct senses: *a*. 'a weakly-defined aggregate of human beings', and *b*. 'a political or cultural group'.

Upon examination, however, these two senses differ primarily with respect to the cognitive prominence of the referents' boundaries, precisely the parameter along which the number meanings and determiners jointly produce distinctions. Surely it makes more analytical sense to ascribe to the lexical stem *people* what its two interpretations have in common – AGGREGATE OF HUMAN BEINGS/HUMAN BEINGS IN AGGREGATE – and attribute features in the message involving definition and countability to the articles and number meanings which produce those same distinctions everywhere else (Penhallurick 1987:104).

The one additional factor coming into play here is our knowledge that a shared political or cultural identity is a likely reason that an aggregate of human beings may be discretely bounded, knowledge that is integrated into the comprehension process to produce message types 5 and 6. But a shared ethnic or political identity is not the only reason individuals may seem to form a discrete group. In [22] a shared disease is the reason.

[22] At the beginning of the AIDS epidemic many Americans
      had little sympathy for people with AIDS. The feeling
      was that somehow certain groups 'deserved' their illness.
      Let us put those feelings behind us. We are fighting a
      disease, not a *people*.
      (Surgeon General C. Everett Koop, *The New Republic*)

Furthermore, it is not always possible to decide which putative
'sense' of *people* is intended.

[23] As these officials see it, Iran's recent battlefield losses
      combined with the growing war weariness of its *people*
      may make a new leadership more receptive to negotiat-
      ing an end to the war.
                                                    (*Newsweek*)

Once a polysemous treatment of *people* is adopted, it is hard to
see how one could justify stopping at merely two 'senses'.

Verb number
As noted in Chapter 2, the number of the verb plays a role as
well. When *people* is the grammatical subject, the verb number
can help to distinguish between message types 4 and 5. But the
effect of verb number is not decisive. *People0* occurs with both
singular and plural verbs in both its putative 'senses'. (24a-
c = 'weakly-defined aggregate'; 25a-c = 'ethnic or political
group'.)

[24a] In Avery Fisher Hall three or four hundred people
       looks very small.
                             (Jaime Laredo, re: the Mostly Mozart
                                                concerts, WNYC)
[24b] Seven million people out on the street *was* thought of as
       a social catastrophe.
                             (Michael Harrington, *Morning Edition*)
[24c] More than 3.3 million people *were* out of work.
                                                    (*Newsweek*)
[25a] Every people *has* its collective memory, its national
       myth.
                             (*New York Times Magazine*)
[25b] 'A people *does* not marry its government for an
       eternity, as in a church wedding,' the Mexican poet and
       essayist Octavio Paz scoffed. 'They are tied together in

a modern way that allows a change of relationship when
things do not work.'

(*New York Times*)

[25c]   But when a people *are* pounded night after night with
that kind of frantic, hysterical reporting, it naturally
shakes their confidence.

(Richard Nixon, press conference)

A conceptual gestalt

The varying interpretations of *people* in [16]–[25] illustrate how
grammatical meanings, lexical meanings and cultural knowledge
fuse to yield a whole that is *more* than the sum of its semantic
parts. The meaning of *people* always undergoes interaction with
articles, number meanings and other contextual information
before emerging in the message. Thus it can never be observed in
its pure form, in much the same way that certain chemical
elements are never found in their pure state in nature, always in
compounds.

A dictionary, with its multiple 'senses' for *people*, has assessed
its semantic value *after* it has interacted with various other
elements in different sentences. It lists the various interpretive
products to which the meaning of *people* contributes rather than
the invariant contribution of *people* itself. While the independence and identity of the parts can be demonstrated analytically,
their interaction in language use produces a conceptual gestalt.

3.6 Polysemy

In view of the wide latitude of use ascribed to a single lexical
meaning, the question arises when, if ever, a lexical stem is
polysemous. Does sign-based theory rigidly adhere to the
monosemic principle 'one form, one meaning'? or are their
circumstances in which it is necessary and legitimate to posit
multiple meanings for a lexical stem?

The answer lies in the function of lexical (and grammatical)
meanings in sign-based analysis. As stated in Section 3.3, 'a
meaning . . . is a theoretical construct . . . (whose) postulation is
justified by its ability to account for the deployment of its
associated *signal* by speakers of the language in communicating
messages'. Multiple meanings are ascribed to a lexical stem, then,
whenever a single-meaning analysis is incapable of accounting for
all occurrences of the form.

So far only monosemic analyses have been examined. For

chicken, *pig*, *sugar* and *people* a single meaning is sufficient to account for why speakers choose these words, along with certain grammatical signs, to communicate the full range of attested messages. At the same time, their meanings do not predict a wider range of use once the alternative expressive options are taken into consideration. By way of contrast we now examine cases where a single-meaning analysis is not possible.[3]

Clearly two separate and distinct meanings must be ascribed to the proverbial *bank*: BORDER OF A RIVER and FINANCIAL INSTITUTION. Distinct meanings must be posited because no single meaning can account for all occurrences of this form. *Bank* is the manifestation of two distinct linguistic signs whose signals happen to be phonologically identical.

The same principle holds even when the various uses of a form are linked together in a chain of associative relationships, since from the synchronic standpoint the analytical problem is exactly the same as that of *bank*. Consider the word *dial*. As the linguistic meaning of *dial*, let us posit a shortened version of its first entry in *The American Heritage Dictionary*.

dial = GRADUATED CIRCULAR FACE OR DISK ON WHICH SOME MEASUREMENT IS INDICATED BY A MOVING NEEDLE OR POINTER

The prototypical instance of *dial*, so defined, is the face of a clock or meter. But since English lacks a word specifically designating the rotary mechanism of a telephone, *dial* becomes a serviceable tool for referring to it as well, even though a telephone 'dial' lacks all the prototypical features built into *dial* as defined above. (This parallels the use of *chicken* to refer to a baked chicken breast even though that referent lacks all the prototypical features of a whole live chicken.)

Moreover, *dial*, in conjunction with finite verb morphology, becomes a serviceable tool for suggesting a typical activity associated with a 'dial' (Clark 1979).

[26] He *dialled* the number.

The use of *dial* in [26] parallels the use of *water* for a typical activity associated with that substance: 'he *watered* the plants'. So far, then, only a single *dial* need be posited, since a relation of communicative efficacy holds between the meaning of *dial* (as defined above) and the various messages for which that form is employed.

With the replacement of rotary mechanisms by numbered keys, however, the conceptual link between a message about entering a telephone number and the meaning of *dial* is broken, since a 'dial' is in no way involved. Yet people still speak of *dialing* a number on these modern phones rather than, say, borrowing from computer lingo and speaking of *keying in* a number. To account for this innovation a new linguistic sign must be posited.

$dial_1$ = GRADUATED CIRCULAR FACE OR DISK ON WHICH SOME MEASUREMENT IS INDICATED BY A MOVING NEEDLE OR POINTER
$dial_2$ = TO ENTER A NUMBER ON A TELEPHONE

Synchronically these two *dials* have the same status as the two *banks*. The traditional distinction between homonymy (the two *banks*) and polysemy (the two *dials*) derives from the unwarranted introduction of a metalinguistic fact about the words; namely, that the etymological history of the two *dials* is so recent it can still be reconstructed by the layman, while the etymological history of the two *banks* cannot.[4]

With the recent introduction of $dial_2$ into the language, it now becomes the optimal linguistic sign not only for communicating messages about touch-tone telephones *but for rotary telephones as well*. This means that the still-present conceptual connection invoked earlier between the meaning of $dial_1$ and a message about entering a number on a rotary phone now need no longer be appealed to; the use of the form *dial* for such a message can be accounted for more straightforwardly by identifying it as $dial_2$ (whose meaning now matches the message perfectly), even though such usage was not the analytical basis for positing $dial_2$.[5]

Bank and *dial* must each be analysed as two distinct signs, we have argued, because no single meaning can explain the extension of each word. Sometimes a word must be split even though a single meaning does encompass its extension. This occurs when a word acquires different value relations in different semantic fields. A case in point is the word *glass*. *Glass* requires analysis as two distinct signs despite the still-present conceptual connection among the various uses of this form.

An initial hypothesis is that *glass* names the substance itself, defined along the lines of a typical dictionary entry.

glass = HARD, BRITTLE, UNCRYSTALLIZED TRANSPARENT SUBSTANCE TYPICALLY BASED ON SILICON DIOXIDE

This meaning contrasts with the names of other substances: *plastic*, *wood*, *paper*, *metal* and *steel*. As such, it becomes a suitable general-purpose tool for referring to anything made of that substance: a mirror; a window pane; an eyeglass; a magnifying glass; and spectacles (in conjunction with MORE THAN ONE). This parallels the use of *sugar* for reference both to the substance itself and to discrete exemplars such as sugar cubes.

But at least one use of the form *glass* has broken away and become a new signal with a new meaning: *glass* the drinking container. The analytical basis is not simply the fact that a glass can now be made of plastic. More importantly, even when it is made of 'glass' it cannot always be called so. A glass teacup is no longer a *glass*; to be a *glass* it must have a particular shape (Labov 1973). Put in systemic terms, the word *glass* has entered into value relations with other words, *cup*, *mug*, *bowl*, *plate*, which cannot now be accounted for by the meaning HARD BRITTLE SUBSTANCE. . . On the basis of that meaning, *glass* should still be able to function as a cover-term for glass cups, mugs and bowls. Since it does not, a new meaning must be posited to account for this otherwise inexplicable specialization.[6]

Principled polysemy
According to the principle of lexical analysis advanced here, the innovative use of a word for a new kind of message does not necessarily call for its analytical partitioning into two separate signs with different meanings. For so long as there exists *some* connection between the original meaning and the novel message – no matter how tenuous – it is presumably strong enough to have inspired the initial innovation. The principles underlying such innovation – metaphor, metonymy, and similarity of form or function – are an integral part of the creative aspect of language use and are at work to some degree in every act of speech (Lakoff and Johnson 1980).

The need for partitioning comes about later, when the innovation settles into an expressive niche in the new semantic field, gradually becoming specialized in response to a new set of value relations. Analytically, then, new meanings will be posited as often in response to subsequent *reductions* of expressive potential (e.g., *glass*) as to expansions (e.g., *dial*). Note how a consideration of value relations cuts both ways analytically, sometimes arguing for systemic unity (in the case of the Entity Number System), and sometimes for systemic partition (in the case of *glass*).[7]

3.7 *Wheat* and *Oats*

We turn at last to the case of *wheat* and *oats*. No analysis claiming to offer a semantic account of grammatical number could avoid discussion of these two words. *Wheat* and *oats* has become the classic argument against semantic accounts of grammatical categories.[8] For Bloomfield, to whom the notoriety of these two words is due, *wheat* and *oats* was proof that grammatical categories such as number could not be dealt with directly in semantic terms. It is worthwhile to examine his argument now in light of the present analysis arguing the contrary.

> To describe the grammar of a language, we have to state the form-classes of each lexical form, and to determine what characteristics make the speakers assign it to these form-classes.
> The traditional answer to this question appears in our school grammars, which try to define the form-classes by the *class meaning* – by the feature of meaning that is common to all the lexical forms in the form class. . . Similarly, school grammar defines the class of plural nouns by its meaning 'more than one' (person, place or thing), but who could gather from this that *oats* is a plural while *wheat* is a singular? Class meanings, like all other meanings, elude the linguist's power of definition, and in general do not coincide with the meanings of strictly-defined technical terms. To accept definitions of meaning, which at best are makeshifts, in place of an identification in formal terms, is to abandon scientific discourse.
>
> (Bloomfield 1933:266)

Bloomfield takes it as given that grammatical distinctions create classes and that in English one such class is 'plural noun'. He observes that this class cannot be defined in semantic terms; that is, in terms of a *class meaning*. From this he concludes that a semantic account of noun number is not feasible; only a formal account can succeed.

While his logic cannot be faulted, his assumptions can. The case of *wheat* and *oats* can be seen as arguing for a different conclusion, namely, the inappropriateness of dealing with the grammatical category of number in terms of syntactic classes.

When Bloomfield contrasted *wheat* to *oats* he was, in effect, permuting two variables at once, both the lexical stem and the grammatical affix. What Bloomfield chose to ignore was the contrast in message effected by *Entity -$\emptyset$* and *-s* for an individual lexical stem. When the lexical stem is kept constant a consistent correlation emerges between the affixes and features of the message relating to number.

[27a]   I threw the *oat0* back into the bin.   (= a single grain)

[27b]   I threw the *oats* back into the bin.   (= a handful of grains)

[28a]   The *wheat0* filled the bin to the top.   (= individual grains)

[28b]   Several parasite-resistant *wheats* have been developed recently.
        (= different varieties of individual grains)

In both sets of examples the *b* message contrasts with the *a* message in that more exemplars are involved.

The real grammatical difference between *wheat* and *oat* lies not in a 'count' vs. 'non-count' distinction, but in the place where the number opposition is exploited, as illustrated in Figure 3.6.

FIGURE 3.6   The Entity Number System with *oat* and *wheat*

1	2	3
individual grain	massed aggregate; generic class	varieties of grain

<ONE vs. MORE THAN ONE>		
oat0 | oats		oats
	<ONE vs. MORE THAN ONE>	
(grain of wheat0)	wheat0 | wheats	

Columns 1, 2 and 3 represent three types of messages about grains arranged in order of increasing plurality of reference. Column 1 is a single grain; column 2 is an aggregate of Column 1 (on a particular occasion or as the representative of a generic class); column 3 is a multiplicity of column 2.

The number opposition establishes a line of demarcation within the referential potential of each lexical stem: with *oat* the opposition distinguishes between message types 1 and 2/3; while with *wheat* it distinguishes between message types 1/2 and 3. These two exploitations are equally consistent with the meanings ONE and MORE THAN ONE because in both cases their relational value is maintained. Note that the so-called 'uncountability' of *wheat* has its analogue in *oat*; with both words one objective difference of referential number is suppressed.

While the use of *Entity -0* and *-s* with *oat* and *wheat* is consistent with their posited semantic values, their locus of application clearly demands an explanation. Wierzbicka has argued that in counting aggregates composed of physically discrete components the relevant consideration is usually their size: when the components are clearly perceivable and highly noticeable they are counted as MORE THAN ONE, and when they are not they are counted as ONE. *Pebble* and *sand* were cited as examples of these two prototypical situations.

FIGURE 3.7   The Entity Number System with *pebble* and *sand*

smallest exemplar	massed aggregate; generic class	varieties of substance
<ONE vs. MORE THAN ONE>		
pebble0 |	pebbles	pebbles
	<ONE vs. MORE THAN ONE>	
(grain of sand0)	sand0 |	sands

But as objects decrease in size they will, at some point, strike speakers as falling on the borderline between an unstructured mass like sand and an aggregate like pebbles; they will still be visible but insignificant enough individually that their objective status as discrete particles need not be taken into account. In such cases the grammatical opposition of the Entity Number System is spanned. Here we may reasonably expect to find variability of treatment, and that is what we find. (See Fig. 3.8.)

An explanation for the cross-over point in Figure 3.8 begins with a simple botanical fact. A wheat plant has about fifty kernels all clustered tightly around the stem to form the wheat *head* (as do barley and rye). By contrast, the kernels of an oat plant hang in pairs of two from *spikelets*, delicate branches extending an inch or so from the stem. So oat kernels are readily distinguishable to the eye as separate objects whereas wheat kernels are not.

Another botanical fact is that, unlike wheat, oats are difficult to winnow. The cultural status of these two grains is therefore different.

This is about oats on the stem, about oats the most coarse of grains. The poor oat was scorned as human fare for centuries. Oats, said some Romans, are fit for eating only by mares and by Germans. (Burn-and-pillage Germans, we will remember, were less than admired by the Romans.) A millennium and a half later, Samuel Johnson used oats to insult the Scots, defining the grain as one 'which in England is generally given to horses, but in Scotland supports the people'. Like the Germans earlier, Scots were seen by the English neighbors as tending towards barbarism.

There were also practical reasons for shunning the oat. It lacks the protein needed to capture gases produced by yeast in rising bread, so

FIGURE 3.8   The Entity Number System with *pebble*, *sand* and edible
             particles

1 smallest exemplar	2 massed aggregate; generic class	3 varieties of substance
<ONE vs. MORE THAN ONE>		
pebble0	pebbles	pebbles
.	.	.
pea0	peas	peas
blueberry0	blueberries	blueberries
oat0	oats	oats
		<ONE vs. MORE THAN ONE>
(grain of wheat0)	wheat0	wheats
(grain of rye0)	rye0	ryes
(grain of barley0)	barley0	barleys
.	.	.
(grain of sand0)	sand0	sands

oat bread won't rise enough to suit. And oats are hard to de-hull,
making home processing just about impossible.

(Kaldenbach 1990:22)

Oats and wheat differ, then, in two important cultural respects.
Oats are mainly used as animal feed whereas wheat is a staple of
human consumption. Secondly, when oats serve as food they
have traditionally been consumed unmilled (e.g., as porridge)
whereas wheat is milled.

Consider now how these two differences relate to their
numerical categorization. When oats are used for animal feed,
they are either in their natural state (for horses) or are crimped
(for cattle). In both cases they preserve a semblance of their
whole-grain shape, i.e., border-line countability. By contrast, it is
generally wheat byproducts that are used for feed; and when the
grain itself is used it is ground.

This difference is maintained in the domestic setting. When
these two grains arrive in the kitchen, oats still appear as whole
(rolled) grains, called oat *groats*, for use in porridge and granola.
Wheat, on the other hand, does not arrive in the kitchen in its
natural state of whole grains. Wheat is always ground for use in
baking. (And when ground, it is never called *wheat*, always
flour.)

On the stem, in the stable, and in the kitchen, then, oats differ
from wheat just as chives differ from grass, namely, in the

manner they typically present themselves to human beings. So despite Bloomfield's attempt to portray *wheat* and *oats* as a Tweedledum/Tweedledee pair parallel in every respect (save number), the two grains exhibit consistently different appearances in actual communicative contexts that motivate their differing Entity Number categorization.

But what about a purely generic reference to the species? Don't we always say *wheat* but *oats*? This would seem to call for further research (and probable revision of Figure 3.8) in view of the two clear counter-examples in the passage above..

[29]   The poor *oat* was scorned as human fare for centuries.
[30]   There were also practical reasons for shunning the *oat*.

Note, moreover, that *oat∅* in [29] and [30] contrasts with *oats* occurring within the same paragraph in both cases.

[29a]   The poor *oat* was scorned as human fare for centuries.
[29b]   This is about *oats* on the stem, about *oats* the most coarse of grains.
[30a]   There are practical reasons for shunning the *oat*.
[30b]   And *oats* are hard to de-hull, making home processing just about impossible.

All four are generic statements about the species; but the physical properties of each grain are more salient in [29b] and [30b] than in [29a] and [30a]. This parallels the *hair∅* vs. *hairs* contrast of [12] and [13] and the *foliage∅* vs. *leaves* contrast in Chapter 2.

Synchronic motivation?
It might be argued that while the difference in grammatical categorization of *wheat* and *oat* once had a synchronic motivation, it currently does not because most speakers are not familiar with the differing characteristics of grains, that for modern speakers of English it is a purely arbitrary fact and must be treated as such by linguists.

Here we must insist upon the distinction between a normative or pedagogical grammar, and a scientific grammar. To be sure, in an ESL classroom students must be told to say *oats* (not *oat*) and *wheat* (not *wheats*) when speaking of these two grains in some seemingly comparable contexts. But the grammatical theorist looks at data not with an eye to prescriptive 'correctness' but with an eye to their relation to his hypotheses.[9] Do they support or falsify his analysis?

With respect to the Entity Number hypothesis the number decision for *oat* could well have gone the other way and hence is, in a sense, arbitrary. But in this case it is an arbitrariness whose existence is predicted by the hypothesis. Recall that a spanned opposition is a situation in which both meanings of a grammatical opposition are more or less equally appropriate. Instances of a spanned opposition will inevitably arise in the course of applying discrete conceptual categories to a phenomenological continuum. Under such circumstances, the actual decision will necessarily be *ad hoc* (in the non-pejorative sense of being resolved on purely local grounds that may not apply in exactly the same way anywhere else). But since both grammatical options possess a measure of descriptive legitimacy, the hypothesis cannot be falsified here. The case of *wheat* and *oats* loses much of the theoretical importance Bloomfield wished to accord it when understood in these terms.

To this austerely theoretical line of argumentation can be added one last fact supporting the case for synchronic motivation, a fact of avoidance. This writer has learned that some modern pantries do include unground wheat, a recent addition stemming from the renewed popularity of whole-grain breadmaking that arose in the 1960s. But, significantly, it is not called *wheat*. In its whole-grain form it is known as *wheat berries*! Thus both unground oat(s) and unground wheat, when they look more or less the same in the kitchen, are currently counted as MORE THAN ONE.

3.8 Meanings as Distinguishing Tools

The differing conclusions regarding the feasibility of a semantic account of grammatical number can be traced to a fundamental difference regarding the nature of grammatical structure. Central to Bloomfield's conception was the notion of syntactic class. Grammatical morphemes such as the plural *-s* were simply formal markers of these classes. It followed that if grammatical distinctions were to be accounted for in semantic terms it would have to be through a *notional abstraction* over the members of the class itself.

By contrast the present framework proceeds from a conception of grammatical structure based on the notion of semantic opposition. A semantic opposition exists between relationally-defined meanings exploited for communicative purposes in similar contexts. In the present analysis, then, the locus of grammatical number lies in the paradigmatic semantic opposition between the meanings ONE and MORE THAN ONE of *Entity* -*0* and -*s*, whereas the notion 'plural noun' *has no independent status as a grammatical category.*

The fact that grammatical meanings exist as purely relational constructs explains why Bloomfield's attempt to abstract across the putative class of plural nouns failed to yield a common semantic denominator. As can be seen in Figures 3.1–3.8, ONE and MORE THAN ONE function first and foremost as tools *for distinguishing between messages*, not as invariant notional fractions of classes of messages. A meaning helps to distinguish the intended message from unintended possibilities for which the given lexical stem is also employed.

The analytical consequence is that in testing the Entity Number System one is directly testing the opposition between its two meanings, not each meaning in turn. For any lexical stem, *Entity* -*0* and -*s* must distinguish messages that contrast in relative 'oneness'. How and where this opposition is exploited will reflect (1) the most common communicative tasks associated with the particular lexical stem, and (2) the alternative expressive resources available in the language.

Notes

1. The ideal tool for opening paint cans would be an instrument with a wide curved blade matching the curvature of a paint can, a tool the writer ran across in a hardware store. With this tool the top can be pried up without bending the lip as often happens when a screwdriver is employed.

2. *Persons* wouldn't fill the bill here because that would have implied actual ignorance of the addressees' identities, while names would have implied a greater familiarity than was desired.

3. The following discussion is not based on a full-scale analysis of the words examined. While programmatic discussion is always risky, we believe it is worthwhile here because the impression would otherwise be left that sign-based theory provides no principled basis for a synchronic semantic analysis of a word distinct from its etymological history.

4. The fact that speakers can, upon reflection, see a connection among all the uses of *dial* might seem to argue that the word embodies a legitimate cognitive category. But cognitive categories need not necessarily be isomorphic with linguistic categories. The word *dial* can still be legitimately partitioned into two synchronically distinct signs on the basis of analytical principles justified in terms of the role of language as an instrument of communication. The discrepancy

between (cognitive) message categories and (lexical) linguistic categories will prove to be crucial in the functional explanation of verb number offered in Chapter 8.

5. A different analysis of *dial* might be called for if speakers began to call the array of twelve keys on a touch-tone phone a *dial*. This would be evidence that people's conception of a prototypical 'dial' had changed to one that encompassed both the face of a clock and that of telephones of all sorts. Under those circumstances, a monosemic analysis of *dial* (in both its nominal and verbal uses) might still be possible.

6. Note that in the specialization of *glass* the drinking container stands in contrast to the word's unspecialized range of reference elsewhere. For example, *glass(es)* does not distinguish one kind of visual aid from another, i.e., bifocals from non-bifocals; nor a full-length mirror from a shaving mirror; nor single glazing from double glazing.

7. While a single example may suffice to document an innovative expansion, detecting new value relations requires an extensive study of the larger semantic field along the lines of that offered for *person* and *people* and Labov's (1973) investigation of *cup* and *mug*.

8. In acknowledgement, Wierzbicka entitles her article 'Oats and Wheat: The Fallacy of Arbitrariness'. But she does not, in the end, actually address these two words together as a contrasting pair. Our treatment follows Wierzbicka's in spirit, but, we hope, is somewhat more sharply focused.

9. In the case at hand, building prescriptive correctness into the grammar of English would amount to incorporating the interaction of encyclopaedic facts with linguistic structure (a conflation that destroys the systemic regularity of the latter) for speakers who, in all likelihood, never talk about these two grains.

Chapter 4

The precision strategy

Chapter 3 developed two principles that will prove critical to our later treatment of verb number:

1. the relation between a linguistic meaning and a message is one of communicative efficacy;
2. the meanings in a grammatical system are exploited in terms of their relational opposition.

The first principle derives from our basic instrumental view of a language as a communicative system rather than a representational system. The instrumental perspective says that speakers will use a linguistic meaning in *any* way that furthers the communication of their message. What counts is its effectiveness in getting the job done, not adherence to logical principles. The second principle is a specific instance of the first: by employing linguistic meanings in response to their relational value with other meanings, speakers extract the maximum communicative yield from the semantic resources available. In this chapter these two principles will be shown at work in their most striking and extreme form. The specific area of application is that of animal reference.

4.1 A Problem of Signal Identity

The word *buffalo* in [1] is traditionally analysed as an irregular plural.

[1] Three *buffalo* graze in the field.

Within an analytical framework where syntactic considerations are primary that is clearly the most reasonable conclusion. Treating *buffalo* as an irregular plural makes for unproblematic rules of quantifier use and verb agreement.

Within a sign-based framework for linguistic analysis, however, the grammatical status of *buffalo* is not so clear-cut. Its referential plurality argues for the same conclusion as that of sentence-based analysis. Yet *buffalo* does have the appearance of the singular; and the use of a singular for a referential plurality is a common phenomenon (e.g., *hair*, *furniture*).

The present chapter will show that *buffalo* in [1] is indeed best analysed as a 'singular' (more accurately, an instance of the signal for ONE); and, moreover, such usage is consistent with principles already established for the use of the Entity Number System.

The salience of individuality

Chapter 2 established that cognitive salience is a decisive factor in how components of an aggregate are categorized. When they are barely perceptible they are treated as a single unstructured mass, like *sand*; whereas when they are larger in size they are treated as a plurality of individual objects, like *pebbles*.

As objects increase in size and distinctiveness the context of reference increasingly plays a role; on one occasion a speaker may wish to downplay their individuality and on another occasion to highlight it. Pairs such as *foliage* and *leaves* allow speakers to do this through their choice of lexical stem. Here both the lexical stem and the accompanying choice of Entity Number combine to effect the intended perspective.

But what happens when no suitable lexical alternative exists? Chapter 3 has shown that speakers sometimes exploit the grammatical opposition alone, combining ONE and MORE THAN ONE with the same lexical stem, to imply this subjective difference of perspective.

[2]   Her cascading red *hair0* frames her face.
[3]   Two red *hairs* protrude from his chin.

The separate hairs in [2], as noted earlier, are of no individual importance to the communication while in [3] they are.

The *buffalo* example differs from the *hair* example, of course, in that the former includes the quantifier *three*, suggesting that the individuality of the animals is indeed relevant to the message.

Would a speaker specify a plurality numerically and downplay it grammatically at the same time? Consider example [4].

[4]   He bought three *foot* of rope.

In [4] the category of quantification bears no natural physical relation to the object being quantified. In terms of the measurement category there are three, while the actual object being measured is a single length. It would appear that speakers are responding to this subtle case of a spanned opposition with a kind of cognitive assimilation, anticipating the unity of the rope itself through the singularity of *foot*. Example [4] clearly establishes the formal precedent, at any rate, for the pairing of contradictory number signals and shows it does not necessarily produce incoherence.

Animate reference
The *hair* and *foot* examples both involved inanimates. When reference is made to human beings, the richer lexical resources in this area usually permit speakers to indicate the relative salience of their individuality through the choice of stem; *persons* vs. *people* was the example developed in Chapter 2. Occasionally, however, speakers follow the *hair* model, exploiting the number opposition alone with a single lexical stem.

[7]   What's more, the last Israeli general election, in July 1984, indicated that the *youth* have swung heavily to the right.

In the following paragraph the same author wrote:

[8]   On the other side of the coin, the Palestinian *youths* of the territories have known nothing but occupation all their lives.

                                (Hirsh Goodman, *The New Republic*)

The difference in message between *youth* in [7] and *youths* in [8] parallels that between the *people* vs. *persons*. In [7] the event being described, 'swinging', must necessarily be performed by a group. A single individual does not 'swing' when he votes, even if he is changing his party affiliation. Only groups of people 'swing', and they do so by acting in concert. By contrast, the event of 'knowing' in [8] is performed by single individuals. A group of people 'knows' only by virtue of its members individually 'knowing'.

Employing the Entity Number meaning ONE to downplay individuality as in [7] carries with it the danger of misinterpretation, for *the youth* can, with equal likelihood, refer to a single human being. In order for this communicative strategy to be successful with animate referents there must always be some other indication in the context of the actual number of entities involved. In [7] the plural verb serves this function. With inconsequential inanimates, on the other hand, such contextual clarification is usually unnecessary. A phrase like *her hair* is most plausibly interpreted as referring to an unindividualized aggregate since people rarely talk about a single strand of hair, the alternative interpretive possibility.

4.2 Animal Reference

Returning now to the area of animal reference, to what extent does this general line of analysis apply there? Consider first the expressive options available for bovines. Here English provides a variety of lexical stems for differentiating among different circumstances of reference, each employed in conjunction with the Entity Number System.

FIGURE 4.1   The Entity Number System and bovines

unstructured mass	single animal	unindividualized aggregate	plurality of individual animals
		<ONE vs. MORE THAN ONE>	
beef0	cow0	cattle0	cows

In addition, English has *bull*, *ox*, *steer*, *yearling*, *calf* and *veal*. This rich lexical inventory has developed over the animal's long history of domestication because, no doubt, of its important cultural role as a source of both milk and meat.

Of importance here is the expressive option available for reference to a plurality. The words *cows* and *cattle* contrast along the same parameter as *persons* and *people*. *Cows* categorizes them as a multiplicity of individual animals; it reflects the point of view of, say, a dairy farmer, who is aware of how his animals differ from one another with respect to milk production and temperament, and who occasionally even gives them names. *Cattle*, on the other hand, categorizes them as an unindividualized aggregate; it reflects the point of view of, say, a rancher, who typically encounters his animals in large herds on the range, and who only takes an interest in their individuality shortly before their trip to market.

Consider now the communicative problem that arises when a speaker wishes to make this same point-of-view distinction with respect to an animal such as the buffalo, for which no lexical specialization has developed. He may:

(1)   not make it at all, employing *buffaloes* indifferently;
(2)   contrast *buffaloes* with non-specialized words like *herd*;
(3)   exploit the Entity Number opposition with the lexical stem *buffalo* alone, on the model of *hair* and *youth*.

Figure 4.1a illustrates this third option, and its parallelism with the use of the Entity Number meanings shown in Figure 4.1.

FIGURE 4.1a   The Entity Number System with bovines and *buffalo*

unstructured mass	single animal	unindividualized aggregate	plurality of individual animals
		<ONE vs. MORE THAN ONE>	
beef0	cow0	cattle0	cows
buffalo0	buffalo0	buffalo0	buffaloes

An investigation of the extent to which speakers actually exploit the Entity Number System in this way is the topic of the present chapter.

4.3 The Entity Number System of Homeric Greek

The initial plausibility of this communicative strategy can be strengthened by a demonstration that using number meanings in such a purely subjective way is not unique to English, and, moreover, that it occurs under circumstances in which an alternative analysis involving irregular plural forms is not a viable option.

Diver (1987) provides such a demonstration in a study of the Entity Number System in Homeric Greek. Although his data do not involve the same direct conflict with referential number as will prove to be the case for English, he clearly establishes the role of cognitive salience as an independent variable in the choice of Entity Number.

The system Diver proposes for Homeric Greek is represented in Figure 4.2. Both substantives and verbs are inflected according to this system. Because of the allomorphic complexity of Greek, *Singular*, *Dual* and *Plural* are employed as cover-terms for the various morphological alternates that serve as signals of the three meanings in the system.

FIGURE 4.2   The Entity Number System of Homeric Greek

```
                 ⎧  ONE = Singular
   NUMBER OF     ⎨
   ENTITIES      ⎪                           ⎧  TWO = Dual
                 ⎩  OTHER THAN ONE = Plural  ⎨
                                             ⎩  – (other than ONE or TWO)
```

The Greek System resembles the English System in that both have the meanings ONE and OTHER/MORE THAN ONE. (Diver posits OTHER THAN ONE for the Greek *Plural* as he does for English, a difference that does not prove significant in the present context.) It differs in that it has a third meaning, TWO, whose semantic substance is *included* within that covered by the meaning OTHER THAN ONE. The consequence is that when reference is to be made to two entities, the user has an option unavailable in English. He may employ the relatively imprecise meaning OTHER THAN ONE, which covers any number from two to infinity, as in English; or he may employ the more precise meaning TWO.

The focus of Diver's study is the principle underlying the choice between these two meanings: when reference is to be made to two entities, what makes Homer choose TWO in one instance and OTHER THAN ONE in another?

Diver begins by showing that the answer offered by the classical grammars, namely, that the *Dual* is chosen for natural pairs, does not hold. Statistically, natural pairs such as eyes, hands and feet *disfavour* the *Dual*, both in absolute terms and in comparison to all other pairs; that is, natural pairs disfavour the *Dual* to a greater extent than do incidental pairs (e.g., heralds, horses). This is shown in Table 4.1.

He then argues through individual example that the choice of the *Dual* is not motivated by a need to specify that there are two of something rather than some larger number. When objective reference is at issue, numerals are employed (e.g., two heralds).

Discourse prominence

The principle of choice Diver proposes does involve the communicative utility of precision. But the greater precision of

TABLE 4.1   Use of the dual for natural pairs in comparison with its use
for incidental pairs

	Dual	Plural	
Natural Pairs (Iliad I–XXIV)	71 (13%)	467 (87%)	
Incidental Pairs (Iliad I–VI)	190 (36%)	334 (64%)	$\chi^2 = 76.17$ $p < 0.001$

TWO over OTHER THAN ONE is not, to repeat, invoked in the interest of referential clarity. Rather, it is invoked for its implication of discourse prominence. Diver begins his line of reasoning with an empirically-based principle about the use of linguistic precision in general.

Principle 1:   More information and more precise information is provided for those parts of messages in which the speaker has greater interest.

In support of this principle Diver points to several familiar facts. In Latin and Greek an author regularly uses finite forms of the verb for the more important actions, and infinitives for the less important, the 'complementary' actions. The finite forms of course, as parsing shows, provide more detailed information than does an infinitive: person, number and mood are not indicated by the latter.

So also, continues Diver, with the use of the pronoun as subject 'for emphasis' (in Latin and Greek and in other languages where 'the pronoun subject may be omitted'). The pronoun supplies more precise information than would be explicitly present if the pronoun were omitted, and it is used for more important actions.

From this general principle of the use of precision in language, Diver derives what becomes his thesis.

Principle 2:   The *Dual*, as an increment of precise information, is introduced into a passage, or on to a word, that the author wants to highlight.

Diver proceeds to test this principle by a demonstration that the *Dual* correlates with two linguistic features associated with heightened discourse prominence: the Nominative case and explicit mention of the subject.

The association of the Nominative with discourse prominence scarcely needs documentation. The Nominative is the case of the grammatical subject, and, as traditional grammar tells us, the subject is what the sentence is about. Diver puts this in the form of a third principle.

> Principle 3:   The poet organizes his narrative so that, within each episode, the principal character of that episode is kept in focus, that is, in the Nominative, as much as is feasible, keeping in mind that there are other demands on the Nominative, such as indicating the performer of the action.

Diver illustrates this principle through an examination of the episode in Iliad II in which Odysseus, the principal character in the episode, is dissuading the Achaians from departing in their ships.

TABLE 4.2   Correlation of principal character with the nominative and oblique cases (= dative, accusative, genitive)

	Odysseus	Other persons	Things
Nominative	11	4	0
Oblique	1	10	10

As can be seen, Odysseus is kept in focus (i.e., in the Nominative) more consistently than are other persons, and mere things don't get into focus at all in this passage. Conversely, Odysseus appears not in focus (i.e., in various Oblique cases) only once.

From Principles 2 and 3 Diver derives a prediction.

> Prediction 1:   If the Nominative is regularly used to pinpoint focus, and the precision of the *Dual* can be used for essentially the same purpose, we will expect these two to be used together, in coherent combination, an abnormally high number of times. In corollary, the Oblique will be used with the *Plural* an abnormally high number of times also, and the other two combinations will then be abnormally low, as indicated by the +

and − signs in the diagram.

	Dual	Plural
Nominative	+	−
Oblique	−	+

Diver tests this prediction on the first six books of the Iliad, comparing all instances of the *Dual* on nouns and pronouns with just those instances of the *Plural* on nouns and pronouns that refer to two of something.

TABLE 4.3 Relation of *dual* vs. *plural* with Nominative vs. Oblique for referential pairs

	Dual	Plural	
Nominative	(+32) 103 (53%)	(−32) 93 (47%)	
Oblique	(−32) 87 (27%)	(+32) 241 (73%)	$\chi^2 = 35.96$ $p < 0.001$

Data base: Iliad I–VI

Each cell of the table departs by +/− 32 from what would be expected if the difference between the *Dual* and the *Plural* bore no connection to the difference between the Nominative and the Oblique cases. Prediction 1 is thus confirmed at a confidence level of 0.001.

Next Diver makes a second prediction by combining Principle 2 with the observation that explicit mention of the subject by a noun or pronoun is sometimes made purely to (further) heighten the prominence of the subject in the message. This prediction applies to the choice of verb number.

Prediction 2:   The number on the verb-ending is more likely to be *Dual* rather than *Plural* in those instances where the subject is explicitly mentioned.

Diver tests Prediction 2 on the same six books of the Iliad. As Table 4.4 shows, Homer puts the verb in the *Dual* more than twice as often (46 per cent vs. 19 per cent) in conjunction with explicit mention of the subject as when the subject is omitted, thus supporting the thesis that discourse prominence is a significant factor in the choice of the *Dual* over the *Plural* for referential pairs.

TABLE 4.4   Relation of the *dual* vs. *plural* on the verb with explicit vs. implicit subject for referential pairs

	Dual verb	Plural verb	
Explicit subject	42 (46%)	50 (54%)	
Implicit subject	10 (19%)	44 (81%)	$\chi^2 = 10.92$
			$p < 0.001$

Data base: Iliad I–VI

Finally, Diver returns to the issue of natural pairs. Natural pairs disfavour the *Dual* more than do incidental pairs (see Table 4.1), he argues, because they are all body parts, and as such, tend to be of lesser interest than their possessors. The one exception is ὄσσε, 'eyes'. This word occurs forty-two times in the *Dual* and never in the *Plural* in the Iliad. The usage of this one word is apparently the basis of the notion that the *Dual* is employed for natural pairs.

It turns out, however, that there is a second word in Greek for 'eyes', ὀφθαλμοί, which occurs forty-seven times in the *Plural* and only twice in the *Dual* in the poem. After examining all instances of each, Diver reports that ὄσσε is never used as a mere instrument of seeing. Its two chief uses are:

1. as a symbol of life vs. death, an eclipse of the entire person ('. . . darkness enfolded him, the eyes'); and
2. as part of the description of someone in the grip of a powerful emotion.

Diver concludes that ὄσσε means not the eyes as mere organs of sight, but the eyes as 'windows of the soul'.

The second word for eyes, ὀφθαλμοί, which overwhelmingly prefers the *Plural*, is used 47 per cent of the time in phrases such as 'He saw with his eyes'. And on the rare instances it occurs in the *Dual*, it is used in the manner of ὄσσε (i.e., 1 and 2 above), but in reference to animals, *not to human beings*.

4.4 The Precision Strategy in English

Diver's findings about the use of number meanings in Homeric Greek parallel the line of analysis sketched earlier for English. In one place Greek has lexicalized a distinction that typically reflects the varying importance of the referents in the discourse: 'eyes' as mere organs of sight vs. 'eyes' as windows of the soul. (This is akin to the lexical specialization of *persons* vs. *people* and *cows* vs. *cattle* in English.) The discourse status of 'eyes' conceived in these two ways is then further underscored through the choice of number meanings: the pedestrian ὀφθαλμοί favours the imprecise MORE THAN ONE while the evocative ὄσσε favours the precise TWO.

With other referents, such as feet and heralds, Greek has no such lexical specialization, and their varying discourse status is reflected indirectly through the choice of number meanings alone: the greater precision of TWO implies more prominence than the lesser precision of MORE THAN ONE. This is akin to the proposed use of the English number meanings with *buffalo*, shown in Figure 4.1a. We return now to a more detailed development of this precision strategy as it applies to English.

Modification of the strategy

In predicting how speakers would apply the precision strategy of Homeric Greek to English we must make a critical adjustment because of the differing structure of the number systems in the two languages. The English Entity Number System lacks the TWO vs. MORE/OTHER THAN ONE contrast that Greek exploits in the circumscribed area of referential pairs: English has only a single meaning, MORE THAN ONE, that explicitly indicates a referential plurality. Its systemic opposite, ONE, if applied to a plurality of discrete, countable animals, represents imprecision to an extreme degree, for it momentarily collapses the actual number of animals to unity. (Recall here the discussion of numerical imprecision with respect to *furniture* in Chapter 2.)

This means that in applying the precision strategy to English, MORE THAN ONE will have the *opposite* pragmatic effect of that in Greek. For referential pluralities it is now the *more* precise meaning (in comparison to ONE), just as TWO is the more precise meaning (in comparison to MORE/OTHER THAN ONE) in Greek. The precision strategy predicts, then, that MORE THAN ONE (e.g., *buffaloes*) should be associated with greater discourse prominence, and ONE (e.g., *buffalo∅*) should be associated with lesser prominence.

Evidence of the precision strategy in English
Anecdotal evidence of such associations comes from Hirtle
(1982), a study of English noun number from a Guillaumist
perspective. Though Hirtle rejects the traditional numerical
values of ONE and MORE THAN ONE for grammatical
number in favour of more abstract values involving movement
within the conceptual substance of 'inner space', his line of
analysis roughly parallels that followed here. He too argues that
the use of *buffalo* (as in [1]) for a referential plurality is still to be
analysed as a 'singular', and observes that despite the strictures of
prescriptive grammars even the word *deer* is occasionally
employed with the regular plural *-s*. Hirtle offers two striking
examples of the alternation between *deer* vs. *deers* and *buffalo* vs.
buffaloes that can be interpreted as reflecting different levels of
discourse prominence.

Hirtle's first example is a narrative passage (Hirtle p. 21) which
we will summarize with the original material paraphrased. The
young protagonist is recalling the frequent trips he used to take
to the Museum of Natural History with a teacher. *Deer0* occurs
as part of a section describing the various exhibits. The deer
exhibit is initially mentioned only in passing. There are glass
cases *with deer inside them lapping at ground springs*. *Deers*
occurs as part of a re-examination of the exhibits but is
introduced with an evaluative comment about the best part. Here
the boy focuses on an aspect of the exhibits of personal interest
to him. When he returns to the deer exhibit, now counting them
as MORE THAN ONE, he elaborates his original description,
suggesting greater interest, and introduces the word *nice*:

[9]   the *deers . . . with their nice horns and their nice spindly
      legs.*

Hirtle regards his second example as 'eloquent on the
distinction between individuals seen as constituting a greater
whole (the herd) and individuals seen as separate entities'. It
contains nine instances of *buffalo0* (referring to a plurality of
animals), but only two instances of *buffaloes*. Since we will
comment on these, they have been marked A and B in the
margin. (Note the author's use of *buffalo0* and *herd* as discourse
equivalents.)

[10]   Young men are usually sent out to collect and bring in the *buffalo* – a tedious task which requires great patience, for the herd must be started by slow degrees. This is done by setting fire to dung or grass. Three young men will bring in a herd of several hundred from a great distance. When the wind is aft it is most favourable, as they can then direct the *buffalo* with great ease. Having come in sight of the ranges, they generally drive the herd faster, until it begins to enter the ranges, where a swift-footed person has been stationed with a buffalo robe over his head, to imitate that animal; but sometimes a

A   horse performs this business. When he sees *buffaloes* approaching, he moves slowly toward the pound until they appear to follow him; then he sets off at full speed, imitating a buffalo as well as he can, with the herd after him. The young men in the rear now discover themselves, and drive the herd on with all possible speed. There is always a sentinel on some elevated spot to notify the camp when the *buffalo* appear; and this intelligence is no sooner given than every man, woman, and child runs to the ranges that lead to the pound, to prevent the *buffalo* from taking a wrong direction. There they lie down between fascines and cross-sticks, and if the *buffalo* attempt to break through, the people wave their robes, which causes the herd to keep on, or turn to the opposite side, where other persons do the same. When the *buffalo* have been thus directed to the entrance of the pound, the Indian who leads them rushes into it and out at the other side, either by jumping over the enclosure or creeping through an opening left for that purpose. The *buffalo* tumble in pell-mell at his heels, almost exhausted, but keep moving around the enclosure from east to west, and never in a direction against the sun. What appeared extraordinary to me, on those occasions, was that when word was given to the camp of the near approach of the *buffalo*, the dogs would skulk away from the pound, and not approach until the herd entered.

B   Many *buffaloes* break their legs, and some their neck, in jumping into the pound, as the descent is generally six or eight feet and stumps are left standing there. The *buffalo* being caught, the men assemble at the enclosure, armed with bows and arrows; every arrow has a particular mark of the owner, and they fly until the whole herd is killed.

(Jenness 1955:57–8, cited in Hirtle 1982:22–3)

Buffalo vs. Buffaloes
— individuation

Both instances of *buffaloes* involve some kind of heightened awareness of the animals as separate creatures. In A, the animals are approaching a single individual who has stationed himself so as to attract the animals to him. Standing at ground level, he sees not a herd, but the individual lead animals, who loom more and more distinct. Categorizing them as MORE THAN ONE reflects the subjective perspective of the man in direct line of the animals' path. By contrast, the occurrence of *buffalo0* preceding A involves three men directing the animals from behind; and in the occurrence of *buffalo0* following A, the approach of the animals is observed by a sentinel 'from some elevated spot' well out of danger.

The second instance of *buffaloes*, B, describes the activity of subgroups of animals within the herd: some animals break their legs, others break their neck. By contrast, the two instances of *buffalo0* flanking B refer to the animals as collectively involved in a single event.

To Hirtle's literary examples can be added two personal anecdotal examples from spoken English. I spend much time in a rural section of New England where deer often graze in open fields. On one occasion I was making conversation with a local hunter during deer season: 'Did you get any *deer*?' As he answered I realized I did not really understand how one went about hunting deer. I then overheard myself say: 'Do you go to a place where the *deers* go by?'

On another occasion my wife was telling one child about coming downstairs during the night and looking out the window: 'I looked out and saw seven or eight *deer* standing out in the field.' A moment later she mused aloud: 'As I looked at the *deers* I thought about how nice it was they were safe on our land.'

In both cases the message for which *deers* was employed evinces slightly greater awareness of the individuality of the animals than the message for which *deer0* was employed. In the first instance the animals were portrayed as 'going by' rather than as quarry, while in the second instance a bond of sympathy with the animals was being expressed.

4.5 The Questionnaire

What remains to be established is that such semantically motivated alternation is productive for a significant number of speakers. Furthermore, the analysis must be extended to cover those speakers – the majority, in fact – who do not employ the number opposition for a particular animal in the manner of the examples above. These two objectives have been pursued through a questionnaire administered to five hundred speakers.

Design of questionnaire
Thirteen animals were selected which varied in their physical appeal (rabbit vs. possum), and their likelihood of falling within the direct experience of the subjects (squirrel vs. antelope).[1] The animals were the following: rabbit, squirrel, beaver, raccoon, skunk, ground hog, possum (the American opossum), bear, giraffe, antelope, bison, deer and sheep. We assumed all the animals were familiar to the subjects, but, as will be seen, the results suggest we erred in the case of ground hog.

For each of the thirteen animals three sentences were constructed. All three contain explicit indications of a referential plurality. However, the sentences differ in the amount of interest they imply in the individuality of the animals themselves. This was achieved through a variety of grammatical and lexical means, as listed below.

1. in one sentence the animal is the grammatical subject and in another it is not.
2. one sentence describes a unique occurrence of the kind typically found in a narrative, while another describes a habitual occurrence or a generic statement about the species.
3. one sentence quantifies the animals with a specific number (e.g., *three*) while another employs a non-specific quantification (e.g., *several*);
4. one sentence involves a first person participant while another involves a third person participant;
5. one sentence involves live animals and another involves dead animals;
6. one sentence portrays the animals functioning freely in a non-threatening situation, while in another the animals are quarry or prey;
7. in one sentence the animals act individually, while in another they act collectively;
8. one sentence imputs a human-like consciousness to the animals while another does not.

The set of sentences designed for the animal *possum* illustrates nearly all of these features. Sentences A and C represent the extremes of contextually highlighted individuality while sentence B falls somewhere between, containing features of each.

A. Although the smaller one kept its distance, the two adult
    _____ approached me cautiously as I stood motionless.
B. When Chuck arrived a few seconds later, he found that
    Duke had treed the three _____ and was barking
    furiously at the trunk.
C. Though their flesh is somewhat gamy, hunters regard
    _____ as valuable animals to trap.

In sentence A the possum(s) are the subject of the verb
approached, while in B and C they are the objects of the verbs
treed and *regard*. Sentences A and B describe unique events with
the kind of descriptive detail that suggests a narrative, while C is
a relatively colourless, generic statement about the animals.
Sentences A and B quantify the number of animals with a
numeral, while sentence C does not. Sentence A involves a first
person participant, while B involves a single third person
participant and C involves an unspecified number of third person
participants. Sentence A portrays the animals as interacting with
a person, while B and C both portray the animals as quarry.
Sentence A imputes a human-like consciousness to the animals
('approached me *cautiously*') while sentences B and C do not.

These eight contextual features reflect the cognitive salience of
individuality in basically three ways: grammatical focus; egocentricity; and precision. Each will be explicated in turn.

Grammatical focus
The grammatical subject, as noted, is traditionally regarded as
the entity about which the sentence makes a predication. The
connection between cognitive prominence and the grammatical
subject, illustrated by Diver for Greek, has been corroborated by
discourse studies in a variety of languages. Zubin (1979), for
example, found that in German narratives main characters occur
as subjects a greater percentage of the time than subsidiary
characters. (Both Diver and Zubin account for this affinity by
assigning the grammatical meaning IN FOCUS to the Nominative
case.) Making the animals the grammatical subject in the A-type
sentences but not in the B- and C-type sentences is thus one
grammatical means of making the animals more prominent in the
A sentences than in the B and C sentences.

Egocentricity
Our own thoughts and actions have first claim on our attention
whereas those of other people must compete for attention on
their merits. The first person vs. third person contrast between

sentence type A and types B and C is intended to evoke this natural egocentricity of the subjects.

A more subtle appeal to people's egocentricity are the features in the A sentences that lessen the psychological gap between human beings and animals, the perception of animals as other-than-self. Words such as *cautiously*, as well as scenes of non-threatening interaction, invite subjects to view the animals as fellow creatures with whom they share a common existence.

One consistent way all B sentences (and most of the C sentences) discourage such sympathy is that they describe situations in which the animals are quarry or prey. When one is engaged in trapping or killing animals one is likely to distance oneself psychologically by regarding them as indistinguishable instances of a species.

Precision

As Diver noted, language users tend to provide more information about the more salient features of their communication and less information about the less salient features. Keenan and Comrie's Accessibility Hierarchy (Keenan and Comrie 1977) provides more detailed evidence than Diver's sketchy observations of this connection between precision and interest. Keenan and Comrie found that if a language permitted relativisation of only one grammatical constituent of a clause, that constituent was always the subject; and if it permitted relativisation of more than one constituent, the subject was always included among the permitted ones. Since a relative clause is one means by which language users can provide additional information about an entity, one would expect the most suitable candidate to be the entity which the sentence is primarily about.

Several of the parameters of contrast capitalize on this connection between precision and interest. Specifying the exact number of animals involved (e.g., *three*) as opposed to being inexact (e.g., *several*) is one form of precision. Another manifestation is the specific vs. generic contrast. Sentences A and B both describe unique events in ways that have a narrative flavour, whereas the C sentences state a fact about the animals in general. Summarizing a number of specific experiences by a single generic statement implies the specific experiences are relevant only in so far as they give rise to the general statement.

Holistic contrasts

The eight contextual features were not combined in exactly the same way in all thirteen sets of sentences. The questionnaire

investigates subjects' exploitation of the Entity Number System
in response to holistic contrasts between messages, not to the
individual contextual features that create the contrasts. In other
words, the contextual features are not being treated as independent variables in a statistical sense. Rather, they are being treated
as unanalysed complexes which relate to each other only in terms
of a three-point scale of the relative cognitive salience of
individuality.[2]

Format of the questionnaire
In consideration of length, three separate versions of the
questionnaire were prepared. Version I contrasted sentence types
A and B; Version II contrasted sentence types B and C; Version
III contrasted sentence types A and C. Reducing the questionnaire to twenty-six items meant that any single subject saw only
two of the three sentence types for each animal.

Before each sentence appeared the name of an animal in
parentheses. The instructions said: 'Read each sentence to the
end, and then fill in the blank with the form of the word in
parentheses which you would use. Don't bother to think too
long; simply put what first comes to mind.' The variation between
'several buffalo' and 'several buffaloes' was mentioned, and the
subjects were assured that both were considered correct.

The twenty-six sentences on each version were scrambled so
that the predicted response for one sentence could not serve as
the model for the subsequent sentence. Each of the contrasting
sentences for a given animal was separated from its mate by
twelve intervening sentences. This minimized the effect of the
first choice upon the second.

Administration
All three versions of the questionnaire were administered to high
school students ranging in age from fourteen to eighteen in two
middle-class suburban towns in New Jersey, Secaucus and
Holmdel. Each class of students received a packet of questionnaires containing a mixture of all three versions. A higher
number of Versions I and II were administered in anticipation of
there being fewer subjects sensitive to the contrasts on Versions I
and II than on III. A total of 178 usable response sheets for
Version I, 180 sheets for Version II and 154 sheets for Version
III were obtained.[3]

Method of analysis
The discussion so far has examined the contextual contrasts that

may affect a speaker's decision to refer to a plurality of animals with *Entity -∅* or *-s*. A more significant factor, of course, is the identity of the animals themselves; certain animals (e.g., *sheep*) are generally referred to only with a form identical to its morphological 'singular', while others (e.g., *dog, cat*) always occur in the plural in reference to a plurality; still others (e.g., *buffalo*) exhibit variation. Clearly, the effect of the contextual factors and that of the identity of the particular animal must be examined separately since they may conflict.

The questionnaires were designed to make this possible. The inclusion of two sentences involving the same animal allows the identity of the animal to be controlled for. If a subject chooses differently for the two sentences, any statistical skewing in the results should be due to the contextual contrasts between them and not due to the animal itself, which is a constant. On the other hand, subjects who choose the same way for both sentences are ignoring the contextual differences between the A, B and C sentences and attending only to the identity of the animal. By combining the results from the three questionnaires of this latter group (in a manner to be described) the contextual contrasts among the A-, B- and C-type sentences are effectively eliminated, since they are now a constant; any statistical skewing in the results should be due solely to the identities of the animals.

Pilot versions of the questionnaire revealed that most subjects alternated between these two strategies. Accordingly, each subject's responses were initially partitioned into two data groups for separate analysis. The first group comprises all those response pairs of subjects who chose differently (e.g., *possum* and *possums*, or *possums* and *possum*); the second group comprises all those response pairs of subjects who chose the same way (i.e., *possum* and *possum*, or *possums* and *possums*). The number of response pairs in the latter group was much larger; nevertheless nearly all subjects chose differently for at least one animal. On average each subject responded differently for 1.9 of the 13 animals on Version I (A vs. B), for 3.5 of the 13 animals on Version II (B vs. C), and for 3.7 of the 13 animals on Version III (A vs. C).

To summarize the analytical procedure to follow, each body of data will be examined separately because each reflects the application of the precision strategy in a different way. Sometimes subjects chose Entity Number in response to the contrasting complexes of contextual features between the two sentences for a given animal (evidenced by the fact that they made different number choices). Elsewhere, the same subjects ignored the contextual contrasts (evidenced by their choice of the same Entity Number meaning both times) and chose, as will be seen, on the basis of their interest in the animal in general. Each analysis is presented in turn.

4.6 Effect of the Contextual Contrasts

The first prediction involves the contextual contrasts among the A-, B- and C-type sentences. (This means it applies only to the responses of those subjects who chose differently for the two sentences about a given animal.)

> Prediction 1. If a subject employs different number signals for a plurality of the same animal, he/she will choose *Entity -s* where the immediate context implies a greater interest in the animals and *Entity -0* where the context implies a lesser interest.

The questionnaire offers thirty-nine opportunities to test Prediction 1, one time for each of the thirteen animals on each of the three versions. Prediction 1 leads to the following expectations.

Since the A sentences are loaded most heavily with contextual features suggesting interest in the individuality of the animals, subjects should choose *Entity -s* on both Versions I and III (and *Entity -0* for the contrasting sentence, whether it be B or C). Shown below are the expected responses for the *possum* sentences on Versions I and III of the questionnaire.

Version I:
    A.   Although the smaller one kept its distance, the two adult *possums* approached me cautiously as I stood motionless.
    B.   When Chuck arrived a few seconds later, he found that Duke had treed the three *possum(0)* and was barking furiously at the trunk.

Version III:
    A.   Although the smaller one kept its distance, the two adult *possums* approached me cautiously as I stood motionless.
    C.   Though their flesh is somewhat gamy, hunters regard *possum(0)* as valuable animals to trap.

On Version II, on the other hand, those subjects who choose differently should choose *Entity -s* for B (and *Entity -0* for C), because the B sentences now contain more contextual features evincing interest in the individuality of the animals than do the C sentences.

B.   When Chuck arrived a few seconds later, he found that Duke had treed the three *possums* and was barking furiously at the trunk.

C.   Though their flesh is somewhat gamy, hunters regard *possum(0)* as valuable animals to trap.

Figure 4.3 summarizes how Prediction 1 applies to each version.

FIGURE 4.3   Predicted results for subjects who contrast number signals for a given animal

Version I (A vs. B)	Version II (B vs. C)	Version III (A vs. C)
A: *Entity -s*	B: *Entity -s*	A: *Entity -s*
B: *Entity -0*	C: *Entity -0*	C: *Entity -0*

Note that a different response for sentence B is predicted on Versions I and II. This is because the precision strategy involves a relational contrast between messages, not a substantive contrast. Substantively the B sentence is the same on both versions, but its relational value is different. This is why there would be no point in attempting to treat the contextual features that distinguish it from the A and C sentences as independent variables.

It is also evident why the questionnaire data call for analysis in terms of *response pairs*, not individual responses. Whether or not a subject's choice for a B-type sentence confirms Prediction 1 depends on what that subject is implicitly comparing it to. In comparison to an A-type message, a B-type message represents a *lesser* degree of interest in the individuality of the animals, and should thus favour ONE; while in comparison to a C-type message it represents a *greater* degree of interest and should thus favour MORE THAN ONE. The subject's second choice for the same animal allows us to say which comparison he was implicitly making in choosing Entity Number for B.

Of course the subject is not comparing the two contrasting sentences that actually appear on the questionnaire, since they are separated by twelve intervening sentences. Rather, he is making his choice on the basis of his sensitivity to such relational contrasts experienced at a prior time and their impact on his own idiosyncratic usage of the Entity Number System. The questionnaire merely allows us to observe what that usage is.

If Prediction 1 is confirmed on both Versions I and II, that would show that different speakers exploit the Entity Number opposition in different places. But the *way* they exploit it remains the same: MORE THAN ONE reflects a greater degree of interest in the individuality of the referents than does ONE (when applied to the same referential plurality).

Rabbit

Version I of the questionnaire presented the subjects with the following two sentences for the animal *rabbit* (separated by twelve intervening sentences).

A. Just as the sun set, three _____ cautiously entered the garden and began to nibble the lettuce.

B. Returning to the woody undergrowth, Jake found his traps had caught a half dozen _____, enough for his hungry companions back at the house.

As expected, most of the subjects chose *rabbits* for both A and B; their responses were set aside for separate analysis. However twenty-seven subjects responded differently for A and B (i.e., 27 out of 178). Table 4.5 reports their responses.

TABLE 4.5   *Rabbit*: A vs. B

	Rabbits	*Rabbit∅*
Sentence A	27 (100%)	0
Sentence B	0	27 (100%)
		$p < 0.001^4$

All twenty-seven subjects chose *rabbits* for sentence A and *rabbit∅* for sentence B. Since sentence A emphasizes the salience of the individual animals in comparison to sentence B, the results confirm Prediction 1.

Version II of the questionnaire contained the following two sentences (separated by twelve intervening sentences). Note that sentence B should now favour *rabbits* since it contains a greater number of contextual variables implying interest than does sentence C.

B. Returning to the woody undergrowth, Jake found his traps had caught a half dozen _____, enough for his

hungry companions back at the house.
C.   The settlers often trapped _____ that year, which
were their only source of fresh meat.

Table 4.6 presents the results. (Recall these are different
subjects from those reported in Table 4.5.)

TABLE 4.6   *Rabbit*: B vs. C

	Rabbits	*Rabbit0*
Sentence B	60 (90%)	7
Sentence C	7	60 (90%)
		p < 0.001

Of the sixty-seven subjects who chose differently on Version II
(i.e., 67 of 180), 90 per cent responded in the predicted direction.

Together, Tables 4.5 and 4.6 underscore the fact that what is
being investigated is not how speakers respond to a given set of
contextual variables in a single sentence; for if that were our
intent, the predicted response for sentence B would necessarily
be the same for both Versions I and II. Rather, the object of
investigation is *the way they exploit the grammatical opposition of
number*. The results so far show that speakers consistently exploit
the opposition to reflect the *relative* degree of interest evoked by
the context in the individuality of a referential plurality. They
choose either *rabbit0* or *rabbits* for sentence B depending on their
previous experience in talking about rabbits, and the decision
they have come to (different from speaker to speaker) as to how
contextually salient the individuality of the rabbits must be in
order to merit underscoring with the meaning MORE THAN
ONE.

Version III of the questionnaire contrasted sentences A and C
(see above).

TABLE 4.7   *Rabbit*: A vs. C

	Rabbits	*Rabbit0*
Sentence A	54 (100%)	0
Sentence C	0	54 (100%)
		p < 0.001

Of the fifty-four subjects who chose differently on Version III (i.e., 54 of 154), 100 per cent chose in the predicted direction. Combining the results from all three questionnaires, 95 per cent of the subjects chose in the predicted directions.

Since the data group upon which Prediction 1 is being tested comprises only those subjects who respond differently for the two sentences involving a given animal, the four-celled table will necessarily be symmetrical, the second row providing no additional information. The results can therefore be presented more economically as follows:

TABLE 4.7a   *Rabbit*: A vs. C

	Confirmed	Disconfirmed
Sentence A: *rabbits*		
Sentence C: *rabbit0*	54 (100%)	0
		$p < 0.001$

All subsequent tables will be in the form of Table 4.7a.

Deer
The word *deer* presents a severe test of Prediction 1 because along with *sheep* it is a word all school grammars cite as never occurring with the plural -s. (The word is described as having an irregular plural form that happens to be identical to its singular form.) Given such prescriptive pressure, few subjects are likely to exploit the number opposition with this word. Nevertheless, those subjects who did so, responded, by and large, in the predicted direction. Version I of the questionnaire presented the subjects with the following two sentences involving the animal *deer*.

A.   Close by, from behind the tree, I watched the doe nurse the new-born fawn while the buck stood watch nearby. Suddenly their ears pricked up and the _____ were off in a flash in different directions.
B.   Their footprints enabled the hunters to track the four _____ easily.

Sentence A takes pains to emphasize the high level of interest in the individuality of the animals by employing the semantically precise terms *doe*, *fawn* and *buck*. Such extreme loading of the context was deemed necessary in view of the strong prescriptive pressure not to exploit the number opposition with the word *deer*. Table 4.8 presents the results.

TABLE 4.8. *Deer*: A vs. B

	Confirmed	Disconfirmed
Sentence A: *deers*		
Sentence B: *deer∅*	10 (83%)	2
		p < 0.02

Version II of the questionnaire presented the subjects with the following two sentences involving the word *deer*, and Table 4.9 reports the results.

B. Their footprints enabled the hunters to track the four _____ easily.

C. Hunters can track _____ most easily in the spring snow.

TABLE 4.9   *Deer*: B vs. C

	Confirmed	Disconfirmed
Sentence B: *deers*		
Sentence C: *deer∅*	24 (100%)	0
		p < 0.001

Again, the subjects chose differently for the B sentence on the two versions of the questionnaire depending upon what they were implicitly comparing it to.

Version III of the questionnaire presented the subjects with sentences A and C (see above), with the following results.

TABLE 4.10   *Deer*: A vs. C

	Confirmed	Disconfirmed
Sentence A: *deers*		
Sentence C: *deer∅*	23 (85%)	4
		p < 0.001

Combining the results from all three questionnaires, 90 per cent of the subjects (who chose differently) responded in the predicted directions.

The results of the remaining thirty-three tests of Prediction 1 follow without commentary. They are grouped according to animal in order of descending rates of overall confirmation. In all, Prediction 1 was confirmed in thirty-two of the thirty-nine tests. In five of the remaining tests, the results were in the predicted direction but failed to reach a 0.05 level of significance. Of the two last cases, one showed no skewing (A vs. B for *sheep*), and the other showed a (non-significant) skewing in the wrong direction (A vs. B for *bison*). General readers may wish to proceed directly to Section 4.7.

Bear
A.   I pressed my head against the bars of the cage. Two _____ were nuzzling each other, while a third was warming himself in the sun.
B.   Late that night the park ranger sighted several _____ prowling near the garbage pile.
C.   Eskimos often hunt _____ by luring them out of their lairs with the carcass of a seal.

TABLE 4.11 *Bear*: A vs. B

	Confirmed	Disconfirmed
Sentence A: *bears*		
Sentence B: *bear∅*	14 (74%)	5
		$p < 0.05$

TABLE 4.12 *Bear*: B vs. C

	Confirmed	Disconfirmed
Sentence B: *bears*		
Sentence C: *bear∅*	42 (82%)	9
		$p < 0.001$

TABLE 4.13   *Bear*: A vs. C

	Confirmed	Disconfirmed
Sentence A: *bears*		
Sentence C: *bear0*	45 (98%)	1
		p < 0.001

Overall rate of confirmation: 87 per cent.

Ground Hog
- A.   Unaware of my presence, the two _____ were nibbling away at the peas.
- B.   The next morning Butch found two dead _____ in his trap.
- C.   Woodsmen sometimes trap _____ as well, for their thick pelts.

TABLE 4.14   *Ground Hog*: A vs. B

	Confirmed	Disconfirmed
Sentence A: *ground hogs*		
Sentence B: *ground hog0*	9 (60%)	6
		non-significant

TABLE 4.15   *Ground Hog*: B vs. C

	Confirmed	Disconfirmed
Sentence B: *ground hogs*		
Sentence C: *ground hog0*	37 (90%)	4
		p < 0.001

TABLE 4.16   *Ground Hog*: A vs. C

	Confirmed	Disconfirmed
Sentence A: *ground hogs*		
Sentence C: *ground hog0*	32 (94%)	2
		p < 0.001

Overall rate of confirmation: 87 per cent.

Squirrel
   A.   Outside my window four _____ were busy gathering
        acorns for the approaching winter.
   B.   With his new rifle, Pete bagged four _____ his first
        time out.
   C.   Furriers prefer skins of _____ taken during the winter
        months because their fur is thicker then.

TABLE 4.17   *Squirrel*: A vs. B

	Confirmed	Disconfirmed
Sentence A: *squirrels* Sentence B: *squirrel0*	13 (76%)	4
		p < 0.03

TABLE 4.18   *Squirrel*: B vs. C

	Confirmed	Disconfirmed
Sentence B: *squirrels* Sentence C: *squirrel0*	41 (82%)	9
		p < 0.001

TABLE 4.19   *Squirrel*: A vs. C

	Confirmed	Disconfirmed
Sentence A: *squirrels* Sentence C: *squirrel0*	45 (90%)	5
		p < 0.001

Overall rate of confirmation: 85 per cent.

Skunk
   A.   As I stepped forward, two bushy striped tails shot up and
        both _____ eyed me quizzically as if they were
        deciding whether to take further action.
   B.   Their unmistakable odor gave them away, and Vince
        quickly shot both _____ burying them behind the
        barn.
   C.   Though their skins are valuable, their overpowering odor
        discourages hunters from trapping _____ when other
        animals are available.

TABLE 4.20   *Skunk*: A vs. B

	Confirmed	Disconfirmed
Sentence A: *skunks* Sentence B: *skunk0*	21 (70%)	9
		p < 0.01

TABLE 4.21   *Skunk*: B vs. C

	Confirmed	Disconfirmed
Sentence B: *skunks* Sentence C: *skunk0*	52 (81%)	12
		p < 0.001

TABLE 4.22   *Skunk*: A vs. C

	Confirmed	Disconfirmed
Sentence A: *skunks* Sentence C: *skunk0*	58 (94%)	4
		p < 0.001

Overall rate of confirmation: 84 per cent.

Possum

A.   Although the babies kept their distance, the two adult _____ approached me cautiously as I stood motionless.

B.   When Chuck arrived a few seconds later, he found that Duke had treed the three _____ and was barking furiously at the trunk.

C.   Though their flesh is somewhat gamy, hunters regard _____ as valuable animals to trap.

TABLE 4.23   *Possum*: A vs. B

	Confirmed	Disconfirmed
Sentence A: *possums* Sentence B: *possum0*	33 (66%)	17
		p < 0.01

TABLE 4.24   *Possum*: B vs. C

	Confirmed	Disconfirmed
Sentence B: *possums*		
Sentence C: *possum0*	52 (83%)	11
		p < 0.001

TABLE 4.25   *Possum*: A vs. C

	Confirmed	Disconfirmed
Sentence A: *possums*		
Sentence C: *possum0*	51 (85%)	9
		p < 0.001

Overall rate of confirmation: 83 per cent.

Giraffe

  A. Since the baby could not reach the lower branches, the
      two taller _____ nudged them down for the little one
      to nibble.
  B. Selecting prey lagging behind the herd, the lions took off
      after the two straggling _____ and killed them within
      minutes.
  C. Lions often prey on _____, selecting stragglers lagging
      behind the herd.

TABLE 4.26   *Giraffe*: A vs. B

	Confirmed	Disconfirmed
Sentence A: *giraffes*		
Sentence B: *giraffe0*	24 (77%)	7
		p < 0.001

TABLE 4.27   *Giraffe*: B vs. C

	Confirmed	Disconfirmed
Sentence B: *giraffes*		
Sentence C: *giraffe0*	59 (79%)	16
		p < 0.001

TABLE 4.28   *Giraffe*: A vs. C

	Confirmed	Disconfirmed
Sentence A: *giraffes* Sentence C: *giraffe0*	57 (89%)	7
		$p < 0.001$

Overall rate of confirmation: 82 per cent.

Antelope
  A.   There are covered birthing stalls inaccessible to the males, where the four female _____ are able to retreat when their time comes.
  B.   Spotting the herd from the air, the men swooped down and felled the four largest _____ on a single pass.
  C.   It was favorite sport to chase _____ across the plains of north Texas.

TABLE 4.29   *Antelope* A vs. B

	Confirmed	Disconfirmed
Sentence A: *antelopes* Sentence B: *antelope0*	26 (60%)	17
		non-significant

TABLE 4.30   *Antelope*: B vs. C

	Confirmed	Disconfirmed
Sentence B: *antelopes* Sentence C: *antelope0*	35 (70%)	15
		$p < 0.001$

TABLE 4.31   *Antelope*: A vs. C

	Confirmed	Disconfirmed
Sentence A: *antelopes* Sentence C: *antelope0*	60 (88%)	8
		$p < 0.001$

Overall rate of confirmation: 75 per cent.

Beaver
- A. As I rose, the two _____ slapped their tails on the water and submerged.
- B. Rather than clubbing the two animals (which would mar their beautiful coats) the hunters drowned the _____ in the shallow pond.
- C. Canadian woodsmen slaughter thousands of _____ annually.

TABLE 4.32 *Beaver*: A vs. B

	Confirmed	Disconfirmed
Sentence A: *beavers*		
Sentence B: *beaver0*	31 (79%)	8
		$p < 0.001$

TABLE 4.33 *Beaver*: B vs. C

	Confirmed	Disconfirmed
Sentence B: *beavers*		
Sentence C: *beaver0*	32 (64%)	18
		$p < 0.02$

TABLE 4.34 *Beaver*: A vs. C

	Confirmed	Disconfirmed
Sentence A: *beavers*		
Sentence C: *beaver0*	26 (87%)	4
		$p < 0.001$

Overall rate of confirmation 75 per cent.

Raccoon
- A. When my light hit their eyes the three _____ froze for a second before they scurried off into the undergrowth.

B.   After making the kills, Luke gathered up the limp bodies of several _____ and threw them into the sack.

C.   To make a full-length coat a furrier needs nearly a dozen _____ .

TABLE 4.35   *Raccoon*: A vs. B

	Confirmed	Disconfirmed
Sentence A: *raccoons*		
Sentence B: *raccoon0*	24 (75%)	8
		p < 0.001

TABLE 4.36   *Raccoon*: B vs. C

	Confirmed	Disconfirmed
Sentence B: *racoons*		
Sentence C: *racoon0*	27 (60%)	18
		non-significant

TABLE 4.37   *Raccoon*: A vs. C

	Confirmed	Disconfirmed
Sentence A: *raccoons*		
Sentence C: *raccoon0*	26 (81%)	6
		p < 0.001

Overall rate of confirmation: 71 per cent

Bison[5]

A.   I watched the two huge animals circle each other cautiously, and then, after a while, both _____ retreated to opposite sides of the field.

B.   That afternoon the men slaughtered forty-six _____ while standing on the observation platform of the slowly moving train.

C.   A century ago, wealthy 'sportsmen' would shoot _____ from the observation platform of specially chartered trains.

TABLE 4.38   *Bison*: A vs. B

	Confirmed	Disconfirmed
Sentence A: *bisons*		
Sentence B: *bison0*	13 (46%)	15
		non-significant

TABLE 4.39   *Bison*: B vs. C

	Confirmed	Disconfirmed
Sentence B: *bisons*		
Sentence C: *bison0*	30 (79%)	8
		p < 0.001

TABLE 4.40   *Bison*: A vs. C

	Confirmed	Disconfirmed
Sentence A: *bisons*		
Sentence C: *bison0*	24 (75%)	8
		p. < 0.001

Overall rate of confirmation: 68 per cent.

Sheep

A.   Though the other animals moved together as a herd, Tommy's two prize-winning baby _____ were wandering off in search of their own grazing area.

B.   Up on the hill Tommy could see three _____ grazing near the fence.

C.   The wool supplied by _____ is their most valuable product.

TABLE 4.41   *Sheep*: A vs. B

	Confirmed	Disconfirmed
Sentence A: *sheeps*		
Sentence B: *sheep0*	2 (50%)	2
		non-significant

TABLE 4.42   *Sheep*: B vs. C

	Confirmed	Disconfirmed	
Sentence B: *sheeps* Sentence C: *sheep0*	8 (62%)	5	non-significant

TABLE 4.43   *Sheep*: A vs. C

	Confirmed	Disconfirmed	
Sentence A: *sheeps* Sentence C: *sheep0*	6 (67%)	3	non-significant

Overall rate of confirmation: 62 per cent.

4.7 Speaker Diversity and Systemic Unity

Tables 4.5–4.43 show that Prediction 1 is confirmed on thirty-two of the thirty-nine occasions for testing. This establishes that one contributing factor in determining how an aggregate of animals is counted is the interest implied by the immediate context in the individual animals.[6]

This confirmation of the precision strategy serves, in turn, as support for the Entity Number System itself. Since MORE THAN ONE implies greater interest than ONE through its greater precision (when applied to a referential plurality), the distribution of *Entity -0* and *-s* by this group of speakers is in accordance with their hypothesized systemic values.

The fact that the precision strategy makes opposite predictions for the B sentences, depending on what each subject chooses elsewhere on the questionnaire, underscores the fact that the systemic consistency being demonstrated is a *relational* one, not a substantive one. Considering the subjects' responses to the B-type sentences in isolation, one sees nothing but idiosyncratic variation of a kind irrelevant to grammatical analysis. But at the inter-sentential level, their varying choices are revealed to be motivated by something they all share, namely, the fixed and inherent grammatical structure of English.

4.8 Relative Strength of the Contrasts

While Prediction 1 is by and large confirmed, differences exist in the strength of confirmation among the three tests for each animal. Since the contrast between sentence types A and C is greater than those between either A and B or B and C, a higher percentage of subjects should respond in the predicted direction for the A vs. C contrast (Version III).

> Prediction 2:   The confirmation rate of Prediction 1 on Version III should be higher than that on Versions I or II for each animal.

Table 4.44, compiled from Tables 4.5−4.43, shows the percentage of subjects responding in the predicted direction on Versions I, II and III. Only *deer* and *bison* fail to confirm Prediction 2.

TABLE 4.44   Confirmation rate on Versions I, II and III

	I (A vs. B)	II (B vs. C)	III (A vs. C)
rabbit	100%	90%	*100%*
deer	83	100	85
bear	74	82	*98*
ground hog	60 non-sig.	90	*94*
squirrel	76	82	*90*
skunk	70	81	*94*
possum	66	83	*85*
giraffe	77	79	*89*
antelope	60 non-sig.	70	*88*
beaver	79	64	*87*
raccoon	75	60 non-sig.	*81*
bison	46 non-sig.	79	75
sheep	50 non-sig.	62 non-sig.	*67* non-sig.

For eleven of the thirteen animals, Version III of the questionnaire showed the highest percentage of confirmation.

4.9 The Continuum of Cognitive Salience

The results so far establish that contextually-implied cognitive salience can be a significant factor in determining the choice of

Entity Number for aggregates of a variety of animals. Yet the response pairs reported in Tables 4.5–4.43 represent only 23 per cent of the total obtained. For any one animal, the majority of subjects (77 per cent) ignored the contrasts among the A-, B- and C-type sentences and responded the same way both times. Does this mean that most of the time the precision strategy is not operative with any given animal?

That, we argue, is not the case. The questionnaire tested the precision strategy on only a portion of the message types to which it applies. To see its generality of application the full range must be examined.

Wierzbicka's rationale for the use of a 'mass noun' for a referential plurality is essentially a form of the precision strategy.

[11] We grilled *chicken∅* for six people last night.

When several animals are cut up into edible parts, as in [11], the salience of the animals' (original) shape – and hence individuality – to the intended message cannot be lower. Accordingly all English speakers suppress the actual plurality of reference by categorizing the aggregate as ONE.

Speakers continue to categorize a plurality of discrete animal carcasses as ONE if their status in the message is that of meat.

[12] Americans traditionally roast *turkey∅* on Thanksgiving.
[13] We grilled *trout∅* for the guests that evening.

[12] and [13] are one step away from [11] since the turkeys and trout(s) still preserve a semblance of their form as whole countable animals; be that as it may, their individuality is of minimal importance to the communication.

One step closer to the B and C sentences on the questionnaire is [14]. The word *rabbit∅* refers to a plurality of live animals in their natural state, but again under circumstances in which their individuality is of little relevance.

[14] The settlers often trapped *rabbit∅* that year.

(Note that [14] cannot be considered a reference to the species, for that interpretation requires the definite article: *The rabbit* is a herbivorous animal.)

From [14] it is a short step to [15], the actual C sentence for *rabbit* on Versions II and III of the questionnaire.

[15]   The settlers often trapped _____ that year, which
       were their only source of fresh meat.

[15] now includes explicit reference to a plurality of animals,
(*were* in the following relative clause). Yet 114 of the 121 subjects
(reported in Tables 4.6 and 4.7) chose *rabbit∅*.

As can be seen, the cognitive salience of individuality is not
dichotomous but scalar: various features of the context can
combine to produce an open-ended number of points on the
continuum. The questionnaire distinguished three points relevant
to the choice of Entity Number (for at least some speakers); to
these can be added the points mentioned above, yielding a six-
point scale of increasing salience of the individual components of
a referential plurality of animals.[7]

1. Implied plurality of dead animals cut up into parts
    (example [11]);
2. Implied plurality of whole animal carcasses considered as
    meat (examples [12] and [13]);
3. Implied plurality of live animals as quarry (example [14]);
4. Generic statement about an explicitly designated plurality
    of animals as quarry or prey (example [15] = sentence type
    C);
5. Explicitly designated plurality of specific animals as quarry
    or prey (sentence type B);
6. First person observation of, or interaction with, an
    explicitly designated plurality of specific animals in a non-
    threatening situation (sentence type A).

The speaker choosing Entity Number is thus confronted by a
mismatch between the dichotomous grammatical option and the
much greater number of message gradations potentially relevant
to the choice. The dilemma for the speaker of English is to
decide at what point on the continuum to switch from ONE to
MORE THAN ONE. All speakers of English employ ONE for
points 1 and 2; and most continue to do so (for game animals at
any rate) for point 3. But beyond 3, speakers differ markedly as
to how salient the separate identities of the animals must be
before shifting to MORE THAN ONE. Thus, some speakers
cross over between 3 and 4, others between 4 and 5, and still
others between 5 and 6. The three-part questionnaire was
designed to isolate just those speakers who cross over at the
latter two points.

In summary, the reason the majority of subjects did not exploit the number opposition in response to the A vs. B vs. C contrasts (for any one animal), is that they *already* exploit it below point 4 (or above point 6), and the dichotomous nature of the opposition permits it to be exploited in only once place.[8]

4.10 The Effect of the Animal

Since the questionnaire only tested the contrasts between points 4 and 5, and 5 and 6, it cannot provide direct evidence of subjects crossing over from ONE to MORE THAN ONE below point 4 (or above point 6, if such can be imagined). But it can offer the next best thing: evidence that cognitive salience is a decisive factor in determining the percentage of speakers who, for any given animal, *have already crossed over*. This demonstration involves the response pairs of all those subjects who answered the *same* way for both sentences. These are subjects who (for a given animal) either:

1. cross over from ONE to MORE THAN ONE *below* point 4 (sentence type C) on the scale of implied individuality; or
2. cross over between points 4 and 5, but could not demonstrate they do so because they received Version II of the questionnaire (offering contrasts between points 5 and 6); or
3. cross over between points 5 and 6 but could not demonstrate they do so because they received Version I of the questionnaire (offering contrasts between points 4 and 5); or
4. do not cross over to MORE THAN ONE at all, even at point 6 (sentence type A).

There were striking differences in the direction of these subjects' responses: for *rabbit* almost all responded both times with *rabbits*, while for *deer* and *sheep* almost all responded with *deer(∅)* and *sheep(∅)*; and for *possum* there was an even split. Clearly the identity of the animal is a critical factor in determining at what point speakers cross over.

If these subjects are still choosing Entity Number in response to cognitive salience, as the precision strategy claims, then the more strongly an animal engages their interest, the lower the crossover point will be. This yields the following prediction.

Prediction 3: The relative percentage of subjects employing *Entity -s* for an animal indifferently (i.e., for both sentences) should reflect the relative degree of interest the animal inherently evokes in the minds of the subjects.

Table 4.45 presents the results from each of the three versions of the questionnaire, arranged in descending order of the percentage of subjects choosing *Entity -s* for both sentences involving a given animal.[9]

TABLE 4.45   Percentage of subjects choosing *Entity -s* for both sentences involving a given animal

Version I		*Version II*		*Version III*	
rabbit	99.3%	ground hog	98.6%	ground hog	98.3%
ground hog	98.2	rabbit	93.7	rabbit	98.0
squirrel	96.9	squirrel	89.2	squirrel	95.2
bear	96.2	raccoon	88.1	beaver	95.1
beaver	94.2	beaver	87.6	raccoon	91.8
skunk	93.8	skunk	86.2	bear	90.6
raccoon	93.2	bear	82.0	skunk	84.3
giraffe	89.8	giraffe	71.4	giraffe	83.1
possum	55.9	possum	43.5	possum	51.1
antelope	37.8	antelope	33.1	antelope	38.1
bison	22.8	bison	10.6	bison	10.7
deer	6.7	deer	2.6	sheep	5.5
sheep	4.6	sheep	1.8	deer	4.7

Each version of the questionnaire yielded different percentages for a given animal and slightly different rank orders. These differences are presumably due to the fact that each questionnaire reports the answers of a different mix of subjects crossing over at either point 4 or 5 for a given animal in response to the contextual contrasts. Since the effect of the linguistic context has already been examined, we now want to factor it out as much as possible. Table 4.46 groups the animals into eight levels that represent those features of rank order consistent across all three versions of the questionnaire. (The percentages have been recalculated on the raw figures from all three versions combined.)

A problem of interpretation now arises. In the absence of any independent measure of the relative interest-evoking potential of these animals, one is hard put to say whether or not the ranking

TABLE 4.46 Consistencies of rank order in percentages of *Entity -s* across Versions I, II and III

I.	ground hog	98.3%; rabbit 97.2%
II.	squirrel	93.9
III.	beaver	92.3; raccoon 91.1; bear 90.1; skunk 88.9
IV.	giraffe	82.4
V.	possum	50.3
VI.	antelope	36.1
VII.	bison	15.1
VIII.	deer	4.7; sheep 3.9

in Table 4.46 accurately reflects it. But if relative familiarity can be taken as a factor in determining inherent interest, then the results make a certain amount of sense. Groups I and II are both animals frequently observed in a suburban setting. The animals in group III are, by comparison, less frequently observed.

The ranking below group III suggests that factors besides familiarity are at work. Giraffes, antelopes and bison do not inhabit the eastern United States and are thus outside the direct experience of the subjects. Not so, however, for deer. Deer(s) are occasionally to be seen leaping across wooded roads at dusk or standing in fields in the early morning. And sheep, though only to be found on farms, also presumably fall within the subjects' experience. Yet both are at the bottom of the ranking.

One additional factor may be the herd-like behaviour of antelope, bison, sheep and, to a lesser extent, giraffe and deer. If an animal is always thought of as appearing in a group, its individuality would presumably be diminished. Another anomaly is possum, which ranks below giraffe rather than along with beaver, raccoon and skunk. But then the American (o)possum, with its hairless rat-like tail and long snout, has a particularly unappealing appearance.

4.11 An Independent Measure of Speaker Interest

Pilot versions of the questionnaire yielded rankings closely duplicating those in Table 4.46. In constructing the final version it seemed necessary to move beyond post-hoc speculative interpretation. If, as the precision strategy claims, the ranking is due to the inherent interest these animals evoke in the subjects, then the ranking should correlate with independent measures of the animals' ability to evoke interest. This is an inevitable prediction of the hypothesis and thus one against which it should be tested.

Prediction 3a: The rank order of the percentage of subjects
consistently choosing *Entity -s* for pluralities
of a given animal will correlate with independent measures of the inherent interest the
animals evoke in the subjects.

To test Prediction 3a a second questionnaire was constructed.
This second questionnaire, appearing on the reverse side of
Versions I, II and III, asked the subjects (1) whether or not they
had observed each animal in a natural setting, and (2) whether or
not they found the animal interesting to watch.

The responses of the subjects were tallied separately for each
version of the questionnaire. Minor discrepancies of rank order
were found among the percentage of subjects responding YES to
the question 'Does this animal interest you?'. By treating the
results from Versions II and III as a test of replicability of the
ranking yielded by Version I, minor discrepancies due to
differences among the three sub-groups of subjects were
identified and collapsed.

Table 4.47 groups the animals into nine levels that represent
those features of rank order consistent across all three sub-groups
of subjects. (The percentages have been recalculated on the raw
figures from all three sub-groups combined.)

TABLE 4.47   Consistencies of rank order among all three sub-groups of
subjects responding YES to the question 'Does this animal
interest you?' (percentages)

I.	deer	81.1%		
II.	raccoon	72.8;	rabbit 69.8;	bear 66.7
III.	beaver	62.4		
IV.	squirrel	57.8		
V.	giraffe	49.1		
VI.	ground hog	40.6		
VII.	antelope	34.0;	skunk 33.5	
VIII.	possum	29.6;	sheep 24.2	
IX.	bison	20.5		

4.12 Parallelism of Rank Ordering

There are encouraging similarities between the order of the
animals in Tables 4.46 and 4.47. Five animals are within one rank
of each other: *rabbit, beaver, giraffe, antelope, sheep.* Another
four are within two ranks of each other: *raccoon, bear, possum,
bison.* The most striking discrepancies involve *deer* and *ground*

hog. (*Deer* ranks first on the *Interest* scale but falls at the bottom of the *Entity* -*s* scale; while *ground hog* ranks first on the *Entity* -*s* scale but ranks eight on the *Interest* scale.) There are, however, reasons to believe extraneous factors strongly influenced the subjects' choice of Entity Number for these two animals, factors which justify setting them aside before testing the correlation between the two rankings for statistical significance.

As noted earlier, *deer* and *sheep* are the two animals always cited in school grammars as words which have an irregular plural. Using *deer* and *sheep* for referential pluralities has become a deeply ingrained shibboleth of correct usage. It seems justified, then, to attribute the position of *deer* on the *Entity* -*s* scale to this strong prescriptive pressure.

The prescriptive pressure on *sheep* is not detrimental to Prediction 3a as it is for *deer*. *Sheep*, occurring at the bottom of the *Entity* -*s* scale, ranks penultimate on the *Interest* scale. It would appear that this animal's inherent ability to interest, together with the strong prescriptive pressure, combine to disfavour its categorization as MORE THAN ONE. Be that as it may, if *deer* is to be excluded from the test of Prediction 3a on the grounds of prescriptive pressure, then *sheep* must be excluded as well.

For *ground hog*, the evidence for extraneous factors is found in the subjects' answers to the second question they were asked about each of the thirteen animals: 'Which animals have you observed live in their natural habitat?' Table 4.48 reports their answers, again grouped into levels representing those features of rank order consistent across all three sub-groups of subjects.

We were puzzled why only 56 per cent of the subjects reported

TABLE 4.48 Consistences of rank order among the three sub-groups of subjects answering YES to the question 'Have you observed this animal live?' (percentages)

I.	rabbit	96.6%		
II.	squirrel	96.8		
III.	deer	86.1		
IV.	raccoon	82.4		
V.	sheep	72.5;	skunk	70.2
VI.	possum	62.9		
VII.	ground hog	56.2		
VIII.	beaver	48.3		
IX.	bear	30.6		
X.	giraffe	13.4		
XI.	antelope	10.4;	bison	10.3

having seen a ground hog when, in the writer's experience, they can often be seen on the grassy areas bordering local highways (far more often than, say, deer, reportedly observed by 86 per cent of the subjects). Through subsequent interviews it was discovered that *ground hog* is not the term many of the subjects employ for this animal. It also goes by another name, *woodchuck*.[10]

Michael Wherrity (personal communication) has noted an additional factor. This animal, when going by the name of *ground hog*, has a special cultural status. Groundhog Day, February 2, is the point that indicates an early or late spring. Supposedly the ground hog emerges from hibernation and hurries back to his burrow if it is sunny and he sees his own shadow, presaging prolonged winter weather. If February 2 happens to be uneventful, TV and print reporters will treat this as a news story, with front-page pictures and feature segments showing reporters standing around a ground hog presumably looking for his shadow. For many subjects, then, *ground hog* is only the name of that (singular) animal who once a year enjoys national attention, not the animal they occasionally see along the highway (which is, for them, a woodchuck). A plurality of such animals would thus merit individualization via *Entity -s*, which is what 98 per cent of the subjects chose to do.[11]

If there is legitimate reason to set aside *ground hog* and *deer* (and, for consistency, *sheep*) because of these extraneous factors, then the degree of parallelism between the two rankings increases. Table 4.49 juxtaposes the rankings presented in Tables 4.46 and 4.47 (excluding *deer*, *sheep* and *ground hog*).

TABLE 4.49 Comparison of *percentages of Entity -s* ranking and *Interest* ranking (excluding *deer*, *sheep* and *ground hog*)

Per cent of Entity -s	Per cent of Interest
I. rabbit 97.2	I. raccoon 72.8; rabbit 69.8; bear 66.7
II. squirrel 93.9	II. beaver 62.4
III. beaver 92.3; raccoon 91.1 bear 90.1; skunk 88.9	III. squirrel 57.8
IV. giraffe 82.4	IV. giraffe 49.1
V. possum 50.3	V. antelope 34.0; skunk 33.5
VI. antelope 36.1	VI. possum 29.6
VII. bison 15.1	VII. bison 20.5

Spearman Rank-Order Correlation r = 0.758; p < 0.02

The parallelism between the two rankings is now quite striking. Two animals, *rabbit*, and *bison*, rank the same on both scales. Three other animals, *beaver*, *possum* and *giraffe*, are within one position; and three more, *raccoon*, *bear* and *antelope*, are within two positions. This degree of agreement would occur by chance less than one time in fifty.

4.13 *Sheep* and *Deer*

Two problems remain: the linguistic status of *sheep* and *deer*. Both these terms were excluded from the previous correlation on the grounds of prescriptive pressure. This pressure is clearly evident on *sheep*, which proved to be the one animal for which the A vs. B vs. C contextual contrasts failed to show any significant effect. Yet, as noted earlier, the prescriptive pressure on *sheep* is not actually detrimental to the predicted correlation between *interest* and *Entity -s*, since this animal ranks at the bottom of both scales (Tables 4.46 and 4.47). In the case of *sheep*, then, the prescriptive pressure is not at odds with the purely systemic dynamics of the language itself; it merely pushes speakers to a categorical resolution of factors which by themselves are already strongly pointing in that direction.

Our conclusion is that despite the prescriptive pressure, the distributional facts do not conflict with the predictions of the precision strategy to the extent that *sheep* requires a morphological analysis different from that of the other animals; that is, the *sheep* of *two sheep* is still *Entity -0*.

The case of *deer* is more problematic. On the one hand, 63 subjects – 12 per cent of the total – contrasted *deer* with *deers* (Tables 4.8, 4.9 and 4.10) in conformity with Prediction 1 at an overall confirmation level of 90 per cent, the second highest for any animal. For those subjects, at any rate, *deer* is clearly an instance of *Entity -0* (= ONE). On the other hand, 95 per cent of the remaining subjects chose *deer* for both sentences, despite the fact that this animal rated highest on the scale of interest. For these subjects, *deer* demands a different morphological analysis.

But rather than positing an irregular 'plural' form for these subjects, we simply say they yield to the strong prescriptive pressure *not* to employ the Entity Number System with this word. For them, the word *deer* in both *A deer grazes* and *Three deer graze* is unmarked for Entity Number: a case of *deer*, not *deer0*.

The problem with hypothesizing an irregular 'plural' allomorph for *deer* is that it would stand in opposition to the formally identical *Entity -0* of the 'singular', thus creating a methodological problem for its testing. Once Entity Number is posited for *deer*, its deployment becomes subject to all the predictions about speakers' choice of number meanings applicable elsewhere. But these all require that the Entity Number categorization be independently established, which cannot be done. For example, neither Prediction 1 nor 3a could be tested on *deer* because both require establishing what percentage of the subjects categorize the animal as MORE THAN ONE as opposed to ONE. Yet with the introduction of a second *Entity -∅* signal, there is no way to determine which *deer∅* responses represented that irregular formal alternate (= MORE THAN ONE) and which were the regular *Entity -∅* (= ONE). In short, the data that would confirm that speakers exploit the number opposition in the conventional ways are observationally identical to the data that would disconfirm it, making Entity Number for *deer* an empirically untestable hypothesis.

4.14 Quantitative Data and Grammatical Theory

In testing the Entity Number System as applied to animal reference we have relied heavily on non-categorical, quantitative data. These kinds of data are widely accepted as germane in socio-linguistic and variationist studies, but their relevance to grammatical theory has been problematic. Returning now to this issue for a fuller discussion than in Chapter 1, we will be arguing for the relevance of quantitative data to grammatical theory, but not on the usual grounds.

This issue was first brought to a head by Chomsky in a passage that has become notorious. Chomsky states his position in terms of the idealization necessary for grammatical analysis.

> Linguistic theory is concerned primarily with an ideal speaker-listener, in a completely homogeneous speech-community, who knows its language perfectly and is unaffected by such grammatically irrelevant conditions as memory limitations, distractions, shifts of attention and interest, and errors (random or characteristic) in applying his knowledge of the language in actual performance. This seems to me to have been the position of the founders of modern general linguistics, and no cogent reason for modifying it has been offered. To study actual linguistic performance, we must consider the interaction of a variety of factors, of which the underlying competence of the speaker-hearer is only one. In this respect, study of language is no different from empirical investigation of other complex phenomena.
>
> (Chomsky 1965:3–4)

In rejecting the Chomskian position, critics have sometimes

argued that homogeneous speech communities do not exist; that speaker variation is so basic and inescapable a fact of language that it cannot be legitimately idealized away.

Criticism along those lines, we believe, misses the mark. The same points could be made about gravity and air resistance; yet, as Chomsky would surely argue, their presence does not prevent those factors from being legitimately set aside in formulating the Laws of Motion. Any idealization is, by definition, a departure from the observable complexity of experiential reality; that's the whole point. An idealization is justified insofar as the factors and phenomena it excludes are *external* to the immediate object of investigation (Katz and Bever 1976:21).

Yet there are grounds on which an idealization can be fairly attacked. One might argue that the idealization is not justified by the larger theoretical framework; alternatively, one might attack the validity of that framework itself.

The Chomskian idealization does not seem open to criticism on the first ground. Basic to the generative conception of language is the working assumption that language has, at its heart, an autonomous component of purely formal sentence grammar. Clearly this assumption justifies envisioning a community of speakers who all share one version of such a grammar and focusing on just those linguistic facts for which that grammar is responsible. Such communities may, in actuality, have extremely few members, but no matter. One need only add the caveat that the 'communities' are to be defined linguistically, not socially.

In constructing such a grammar, premature introduction of non-categorical facts of actual language use and speaker variation would only muddy the waters since the factors responsible for the variation must necessarily lie outside the grammar itself. Better to address them at some later time, once this axiomatic component of the language has been established.

The locus of homogeneity

If Chomsky's homogeneous speech community is to be faulted, then, the critique must focus on the conception of language and grammar that justifies it. The extent of our critique depends upon how his phrase 'a homogeneous speech community' is construed. Are the speakers homogeneous in that they all share a single linguistic system? or are they homogeneous in that they all speak in the same way? In other words, are they homogeneous at the *theoretical* or the *observational* level?

For Chomsky it doesn't matter which way the notion of a homogeneous speech community is construed because with a conception of linguistic structure as purely formal and mechanical each interpretation implies the other. On the other hand, within a sign-based conception of linguistic structure, a third possibility exists. A speech community may share a single linguistic system governed by the same psychological and communicative principles; yet these principles permit – indeed, oblige – speakers to choose where to exploit the expressive potential of the system to best advantage (as they see it).

In this case, the principles responsible for the observational diversity are *intrinsic* to the functioning of the system. They state, in general terms, the way the system is actually exploited, as opposed to other imaginable ways that would also be consistent with the system. They are thus the crucial link between the system and its use. Without them no empirical predictions whatsoever can be made by which the hypothesized system can be tested.[12]

Just such a situation exists in the present case. Our questionnaire subjects form a community of English speakers who (by hypothesis) all share the Entity Number System as one structural feature of their language. These speakers all exploit the opposition between its two meanings ONE and MORE THAN ONE according to the precision strategy to distinguish between different levels of contextually-implied individuality.

But since the gradations of individuality can be greater than the number of linguistic contrasts available, different speakers will exploit the opposition in different places; no one place is any more favoured (systemically) than any other. Only the *direction* of the exploitation is fixed: MORE THAN ONE indicates greater individuality than ONE (when applied to a referential plurality).

Here the observational diversity is not a complication. Indeed, the very heterogeneity among speakers at the observational level provides the most compelling evidence of their homogeneity at the systemic level. If all the speakers had, say, responded in the same way to the B-type sentences on the questionnaire, the purely relational deployment of the number meanings could not have been demonstrated so effectively. And it is the fact that speakers are all using the number meanings in ways that preserve their relational opposition that allows us to say they all share the same grammatical system, despite the observational heterogeneity.

Language variation

The irony of much of the contemporary work in language variation is that its practitioners undermine their claim about the theoretical centrality of the phenomenon by conceding to Chomsky the crucial point of the locus of its causal factors. They do this through their reliance on a conventional syntactic framework for describing the variation. Consider the present case. A typical syntactic analysis posits the grammatical categories of 'singular' and 'plural' for all English nouns. These underlying categories are identified on the grounds of selected facts of distribution, principally their co-occurrence with other grammatical categories (e.g., quantifiers and verb number). The various morphological reflexes of 'singular' and 'plural' are duly noted and grouped as allomorphs, one such being a -∅ alternate of the regular plural -s for words like *sheep* and *deer*.

At this point the morphological phase of the analysis is complete. The analyst may note the alternation between the -s and -∅ suffixes in the 'plural' (e.g., *buffalo*), and perhaps even suspect that some semantic factor plays a role. But he is unlikely to probe too deeply; he knows in advance that whatever combination of semantic, psychological or social factors are at work, they are irrelevant to his immediate concerns, since they operate on variants that have been dubbed grammatically equivalent.

The student of language variation taking the analytical conclusions of the syntactician as his starting point has his problem well defined: the investigation of the extra-grammatical factors responsible for the alternation between two grammatically equivalent units. Through attentive observation of language use he may well discover the same correlations found here between the -∅ and -s suffixes and individuality. But at that point he has no way of *explaining* such correlations; for the status of these suffixes as systemic alternates would predict a random association. He is forced to conclude that speakers regularly imbue structurally equivalent forms with semantic nuances unrelated to their systemic linguistic value.

The irony here is that the greater his success in describing such correlations, the more the variationist confirms the syntactician's belief in the irrelevance of facts of language variation to grammatical theory. As for the variationist, he is inclined to conclude the converse. The result is a stand off. The variationist feels a self-righteous superiority to the ivory-tower syntactician, secure in his belief that he has his fingers on the pulse of the language as it is actually spoken; while the syntactician cultivates an attitude of benign condescension, secure in his belief that he is part of a research programme that will one day unlock the mysteries of language with a capital L.

4.15 The Prerequisites for Grammatical Analysis

Sign-based linguistic theory avoids this dualism in two ways.

First, it does not begin by idealizing a special body of grammatical facts (i.e., relations of determination and grammaticality judgements) standing apart from language use as the proper domain of grammatical theory. Considerations of verb number and quantifier use have no *a priori* claim to primacy over the subtle contextual contrasts among the A-, B- and C-type sentences.

Secondly, sign-based theory operates with a conception of linguistic structure in which systemic homogeneity lies in the invariant value relationships among its components rather than in a consensus among speakers as to how to express a given type of message. Thus it does not require an initial idealization to produce a homogeneous data base at the observational level. It assumes that members of a (socially defined) speech community share the same linguistic system, and it attempts to characterize the structure of that system in a way compatible with the inevitable diversity.

Both these working hypotheses are likely to be revised in the course of particular analyses. A case in point is our acknowledgement of the (extra-systemic) constraining effect of prescriptive pressure on *sheep*. As for the assumed systemic homogeneity of a speech community, we ended up positing a minor instance of systemic heterogeneity in concluding that *deer* has a different linguistic value (marked and unmarked for number) for different groups of speakers.

The important point is that by adopting these two working hypotheses in their strongest form initially, we assure that the analysis of grammatical structure will be initially exposed to the widest range of linguistic data. Any later exclusion of data will then be on empirical rather than *a priori* grounds.[13]

Working from an enlarged data base, the sign-based analyst will inevitably diverge from the syntactician in his conclusions about the grammatical structure of the language. In the case at hand, *sheep*, *possum* and (for some speakers) *deer* are identified as instances of *Entity -0*, the regular signal of the meaning ONE, because this identification renders the observed distribution of those forms explainable in systemic terms via the precision strategy.

Our use of the term variation may now appear somewhat disingenuous. The questionnaire data constitute variation – the alternation of grammatically equivalent units – only when described in syntactic terms. In sign-based terms, the questionnaire data show speakers choosing different linguistic signs according to their contrasting systemic values for subtly different messages. As Popper reminds us, different theories produce different facts.

In view of the theory-dependent nature of linguistic fact, we cannot fault the Chomskian idealization on the basis of fact alone. In the end, the criticism must be couched in the more general terms of explanatory ambition. The Chomskian conception of an autonomous formal grammar – the conception which justifies the idealization of a speech community homogeneous at the observational level – is under-ambitious because it sets aside on *a priori* grounds data which, through analysis based on different explanatory principles, can be accounted for by the systemic grammatical structure of the language.

Notes

1. The selection was initially restricted to vertebrates, on the assumption that few speakers would make distinctions of relative contextual salience for animals of lower orders. It was later confined to mammals, since pilot versions of the questionnaire indicated the class of vertebrate was an additional factor that could not be accommodated in the final version. Household pets (e.g., dog and cat) were not included since it is already well-known that speakers always categorize a plurality of these animals as MORE THAN ONE (for reasons consistent with the hypothesized precision strategy).
2. Care was taken in the construction of the C-type sentences to prevent them from being interpreted as referring exclusively to the meat of the animal (for which *Entity -∅* is always employed). So, for instance, while the C sentence for *possum* speaks of the flesh of the animal, it includes two indications that a plurality of animals is still being referred to: *their* flesh; valuable *animals* to trap.
3. All questionnaires from students who indicated their first language was other than English were discarded. According to the teachers who administered the questionnaires, the classes did not have speakers of so-called Black English, the one version of American English to which the present hypothesis is believed not to apply (see note 13).
4. All probabilities were calculated using a one-tailed binomial test.
5. The less common (but scientifically correct) term *bison* was employed for the animal most Americans call *buffalo* because the latter term occurs in the lyrics of 'Home on the Range', a song all Americans know by heart. One line refers to pluralities of animals employing the singular for each: '. . . where the buffalo roam, where the deer and the antelope play'. Since *deer* and *antelope* appear on the questionnaire as well, any evidence of the precision strategy involving the term *buffalo* might be dismissed as adding nothing to that which might emerge with the terms *deer* and *antelope*.

6.   Prediction 1 was also confirmed for *duck, bear, buffalo* and *fish* on a pilot version of the questionnaire involving, for the most part, sentence types A and B.

7.   Reference to a single animal is not a point on the scale because the choice of ONE for such messages is not an instance of the precision strategy, which applies only to referential pluralities.

8.   The fact that the confirmation rates of Prediction 1 are less than 100 per cent on most of the tests suggests that some speakers have not had sufficient practice in applying the precision strategy for a given animal so as to have settled upon a cross-over point they can consistently apply on isolated occasions. (Recall that the contrasting sentences for a given animal were neither juxtaposed on the questionnaire, nor imbedded in coherent discourse, as were the *deer* and *buffalo* examples cited by Hirtle.)

9.   The Ns on which the percentages were calculated are different in each case because for each animal a different number of subjects ignored the contextual contrasts among the A-, B- and C-type sentences.

10. The choice of *ground hog* over *woodchuck* on the questionnaire was made on the basis of the preferred usage of several students in a private girls' school midway between Secaucus and Holmdel.

11. An additional fact favouring individualization is that *ground hog* is bi-morphemic, the only such term included. This introduces a feature of linguistic precision not present in the other animal terms. And that, in turn, would favour the choice of *Entity -s*, since the greater referential precision of its meaning MORE THAN ONE matches the greater precision of reference of the term *ground hog*.

12. These are analogous to what Katz and Bever (1976:24) call 'correspondence principles'. Both sign-based and sentence-based theory require mediating principles which allow their formal models of language proper to be tested empirically. Katz and Bever lament the virtual absence of such principles in generative theory.

13. For example, the questionnaires of any speakers of Black English would have been excluded from this study because there is strong reason to believe a systemic difference regarding entity number exists between the dialects of Black and Standard English. In Standard English, *Entity -s* stands in opposition to *Entity -0* which bears the meaning ONE. This obliges speakers of Standard English to employ *Entity -s* whenever they do not wish to signal the meaning ONE. We suspect, however, that Black English does not have the signal *Entity -0*, only *Entity -s*, which for Black English speakers is a free-floating sign outside a grammatical system, similar in status to the genitive *-s*. Consequently, Black English speakers feel free to 'omit' *Entity -s* (for any of a variety of reasons including phonological) because 'omitting' it does not result in the signal *Entity -0*, as it does in Standard English. Thus *book* in the phrases *one book* and *three book* is simply unmarked for grammatical number, as is the case with *deer* for the majority of Standard English speakers.

Chapter 5

The focus number system

Application of the precision strategy to the Chapter 4 data required describing *possum*, *rabbit* and *sheep* as instances of the regular *Entity -Ø* signal for ONE. Describing with an eye to subsequent explanation is standard procedure in theory-based inquiry. The molecular theory of matter is a classic example. In its descriptive capacity the theory posits a basic distinction between elements and compounds. Each element is described in terms of the number of protons and neutrons in its nucleus and the number of electrons in its outer valence ring. This chemical description of each element then functions as the basis for explaining a number of its measurable physical properties, such as its relative mass and its combinatory behaviour with other elements to form compounds.

The analysis of Entity Number in English has aspired to the same kind of convergence. It posits the linguistic signal *Entity -s* which, by hypothesis, bears the meaning MORE THAN ONE. In its descriptive capacity this construct serves to group and label various *-s*'s in English, distinguishing them from others with which they are observationally identical. In its explanatory capacity this construct provides the reason for its collocation with other linguistic signs in discourse: its meaning contributes to the message being communicated.

This mode of explanation parts company with the physical sciences, however, due to the fact that between the constructs of linguistic theory and the observations stands a human being. Unlike chemical elements, which combine all by themselves in accordance with their intrinsic nature, linguistic signs are combined by speakers, and speakers are doing so for some purpose. This has the effect of introducing an uncontrolled variable. The observations cannot be predicted directly by the theory because speakers' goals are, as Chomsky puts it, 'stimulus free'. And even when the communicative goal (and the linguistic means) can be controlled for, as on the questionnaire, the theory still cannot predict exactly how speakers will choose to express it. That is, we could not predict whether an individual speaker would employ the Entity Number System to distinguish a B-type message from an A-type or from a C-type message; or, alternatively, to comment upon his relative interest in the animal itself.

This fact alters the explanatory relation between theory and observation from a purely deductive one to a *mediational* one. The theory establishes a principled connection between the observations – linguistic discourse – and the communicative strategies and goals that together shape that discourse.

This same analytical path will be followed in our approach to another manifestation of grammatical number in English. The -*s* suffix appearing on English verbs will be characterized as the morphological component of a linguistic signal that bears a specific meaning in a grammatical system. The distribution of this linguistic sign in discourse – in particular, its combinatory behaviour with the signs of the Entity Number System – will be explained in terms of the unique contribution of its hypothesized meaning to the communication of messages.

The analysis consists of four parts, each presented in a separate chapter. The present chapter is essentially expositional, describing the Focus Number System and its relation to the other systems with which it intersects structurally. The Focus Number System hypothesis is then revised in response to preliminary testing and shown to be provisionally superior to the competing hypotheses of subject-verb agreement and speaker error.

The subsequent three chapters are devoted to empirical validation. Chapter 6 illustrates the deployment of the Focus Number System for expressive purposes through examples drawn from actual language use. Chapter 7 tests for the generality of such usage through quantitative analysis. Finally, Chapter 8 addresses the question of the communicative value of the system when it appears to be functioning redundantly.

5.1 The Focus Number System

The suffixes /s/, /z/ and /əz/ in [1]–[3] all figure in a grammatical system that resembles the Entity Number System in both form and substance.

[1]   Angus walks down the street.
[2]   Colin waters the lawn.
[3]   Simon watches television.

For ease of discussion we will collapse the phonologically determined alternation between /s/, /z/ and /əz/ and refer to them collectively as -s. With this simplification the system can be represented as composed of two linguistic signs. Both the signals and the meanings are nearly the same as in the Entity Number System, but the pairing is reversed; -s is now associated with the meaning ONE and the absence of -s with the meaning MORE THAN ONE.

FIGURE 5.1   The English Focus Number System

	meaning	signal
NUMBER OF ENTITIES IN FOCUS {	ONE	= *Occurrence* -s
	MORE THAN ONE	= *Occurrence* -∅

The meanings ONE and MORE THAN ONE indicate the number of entities upon which attention is being concentrated with respect to the Occurrence described by the associated lexical stem. This fact is built into the system as the name of the semantic substance they categorize: NUMBER OF ENTITIES IN FOCUS. The following sections explicate various formal and semantic features of this system in more detail.

Occurrence
Like the signals of the Entity Number System, *Occurrence* -s and *Occurrence* -∅ contain both a configurational and a message component. The configurational component takes the form of the fixed position of the -s and -∅ following a lexical stem; their status as suffixes is arbitrary and so is built into the signals as part of their definition. As for the message component, the two suffixes must be attached to a lexical stem that designates an *Occurrence*, either an action or state, in the specific message being communicated. Action-like and state-like Occurrences are unified linguistically by virtue of being categorized by other grammatical systems (to be elaborated shortly) in terms of time, probability, and the involvement of entities required for them to take place.

Occurrence vs. verb
Words designating Occurrences would normally be said to belong

to the syntactic category 'verb'. But as was argued for 'noun', in order for that category to play a role in the present analysis it would have to be the case that a word could be identified as a 'verb' purely on the basis of its membership in an exclusive lexical class definable in advance. The fact of the matter is most words that function as 'verbs' function in other capacities as well. For example *walk*, *water* and *watch* in [1]–[3] can also designate entities:

[1a]   He frequently took *walks* through the woods.
[2a]   The bony fish have managed to colonize all the *waters* of the world.
[3a]   His night-time duty consisted of several four-hour *watches* a week.

For such dual-functioning words as *walk* and *water*, their Entity and Occurrence interpretations are so closely related that only a single semantic value need be posited; their varying interpretations can be dealt with in the same way as the mass and count interpretations of *chicken* in Chapter 2. For others, such as *watch*, their Entity and Occurrence interpretations have specialized in ways that would seem to require separate semantic values (cf. *glass*).

In either case, however, their interpretation poses a problem. As far as language users are concerned, words that refer to Occurrences must be identified in context by their syntagmatic position and any overt grammatical signals that may be present (i.e., auxiliaries and suffixes). Construing a lexical stem as an Occurrence can happen in so many ways that it is not, we believe, a procedure amenable to characterization in purely formal terms. This fact is acknowledged in the way the signals of the Focus Number System have been defined; one component of their definition is a product of the comprehension process.

The entity in Focus
The semantic substance categorized by the two meanings ONE and MORE THAN ONE is NUMBER OF ENTITIES IN FOCUS. The entity in Focus is a grammatical category in its own right and is usually identical to the grammatical subject. Despite this referential identity, the two constructs are not equivalent. While the difference between them is not immediately critical here, the category 'subject' is so closely tied to sentence-based theory that our claim to be offering a sign-based account of verb number is bound to ring hollow if the impression were left that it

requires a construct that is inherently sentence-based. For this reason, the theoretical status of these two constructs will be contrasted in somewhat more detail than required by the analysis of Focus Number itself.

5.2 The Notion of Grammatical Subject

Within sentence-based theory 'subject' is a category established in advance of the analysis of any specific language. The *a priori* status of the notion subject is particularly clear in traditional grammar, which derives the category strictly through a logical analysis of thought. Traditional grammars typically include a brief introductory section which defines a sentence as the expression of a complete thought and then partitions it into two notional parts: what the sentence is about, the subject; and what is said about the subject, the predicate.

Early generative theory was more cautious in its approach. It effectively retained the category by preserving the initial split of the sentence into two component parts, while rejecting their traditional notional definitions. It offered, instead, the possibility that subject and predicate could eventually be defined configurationally in terms of their position in the structural description of a sentence (Chomsky 1965:69–74).

More recently, the problem of arriving at a general definition of the notion subject has been pursued through empirical investigation of the semantic and syntactic properties of subjects in a variety of languages. Through such investigation Keenan (1976) arrived at a comprehensive list of prototypical characteristics of subjects, only a fraction of which manifest themselves in any particular language.

In summary, sentence-based theory has always regarded the problem associated with the notion subject as one of definition rather than justification. And in modern times the responsibility for its definition has been assigned to a more general theory of universal grammar.

The advantage of an *a priori* category such as subject is that it can be employed in advance of a satisfactory definition. The working grammarian can take the category as given and proceed directly to investigate how it is realized in a particular language. Its disadvantage is that the category may not actually exist in the language under investigation, in which case the analyses that employ it will always fall short of empirical success.

Sign-based theory, by contrast, provides no inventory of *a priori* grammatical categories from which to draw. Its universal component confines itself to general principles of language – such as the rule-governed relation between signal and meaning, the central role of opposition in structuring grammatical systems, and the goal-directed relation between meaning and message – while leaving open to empirical investigation the actual grammatical categories in a specific language.

A category is justified in language-specific terms by a demonstration that its definition explains a range of distributional and semantic facts associated with some morphological feature of the particular language. So, for instance, Diver justified the grammatical category Dual by showing that that category, defined as a set of signals bearing the meaning TWO, explains the deployment of various suffixes unique to Homeric Greek; but that category cannot be justified for English because there is no comparable class of suffixes for which that category is an explanation.

Sign-based theory does not posit the grammatical category subject for English because there is no linguistic problem in English for which that construct, however defined, is an optimal solution. The complex range of distributional, syntagmatic and semantic facts traditionally dealt with in terms of 'subject' can be explained in a more satisfactory way by partitioning them into several sets and accounting for each set by a different construct. Each is a grammatical system similar in structure to the Entity Number and Focus Number Systems. Drawing on Diver (1984), as summarized in Lattey (1980), we now provide brief sketches of these systems, together with the subset of facts each system is designed to explain.

5.3 The Control System

The first set of facts involves the sequential order of words or phrases referring to Participants in an Occurrence.

[4]   *The lion* killed *the tiger*.
[5]   *The tiger* killed *the lion*.

Both *the lion* and *the tiger* participate in the activity of 'killing' and their syntagmatic positions indicate which animal is the killer and which the victim. Diver accounts for these facts by treating their positions as word-order signals in a grammatical system whose semantic substance relates to the role each Participant plays in the Occurrence.

Examples [4] and [5] would support the meaning AGENT for

pre-position and the meaning PATIENT for post-position. But that hypothesis must be discarded in light of examples [6]–[9].

[6] *The key* opened *the door.*
[7] *The cows* milk *50 to 60 gallons of milk* a day. (said by a dairy farmer)
[8] *The shoes* dance *her* out into the street. (dialogue from *The Red Shoes*)
[9] *John* told *Mary.*
[10] *John* told *the story.*

In [6], [7] and [8] the initial Participants play the roles of 'instrument', 'patient' and 'causer' respectively, while in [8] and [9] the Participants following the Occurrence play the roles of 'agent' and 'addressee'. Clearly then 'agent', 'patient', 'instrument', 'causer' and 'addressee' cannot themselves be meanings in this system, since none is invariantly associated with either of the two positions.

While no semantic constant can be posited for each position independently, a consistency emerges when one looks at the power relation between the two Participants. In each case, the first Participant exercises *a greater degree of control* over the Occurrence than does the second Participant. In [4] *the lion* exercises a greater degree of active control in bringing about the killing than does *the tiger*, whose participation is surely unwilling. In [6] *the key*, by fitting the lock, controls the opening to a greater extent than does *the door*. In [7] *the cows*, while relatively passive, still control the milking to a greater extent than do *the gallons of milk* by virtue of producing the milk and co-operating in the activity. In [8] the magical *shoes* compel the unwilling dancer to dance to her death. Finally, both *Mary* in [9] and *the story* in [10], while playing different substantive roles, control the telling to a lesser degree than does *John*, the teller.

The Control System categorizes the two Participants (P) in terms of the semantic parameter along which they consistently contrast, namely, their degree of control over the Occurrence. Since their substantive control varies from Occurrence to Occurrence, the categorization is purely relational: HIGHER and LOWER.

As was the case with the *Entity -$\emptyset$* signal, both P_1 and P_2 are relationally defined. P_1 is the *first of two* Participants associated with a single Occurrence, and P_2 is the *second of two* Participants. So if only one Participant is mentioned (e.g., John left; the door opened), no Control meaning is being signalled. In

FIGURE 5.2   The Two-member System of Control

$$
\text{DEGREE OF CONTROL} \atop \text{OVER THE OCCURRENCE}
\left\{
\begin{array}{l}
\text{HIGHER} \;=\; P_1 \\[2ex]
\text{LOWER} \;=\; P_2
\end{array}
\right.
$$

view of this fact, the morphological correlates of the two meanings are more accurately defined as comprising a single, complex signal, $P_1 \ldots$ *Occurrence* $\ldots P_2$, which simultaneously designates P_1 as HIGHER and P_2 as LOWER.

English offers a communicative alternative to the Participant System. A preposition may also express the relation of a Participant to an Occurrence.

[11]   John spoke *to* Mary.
[12]   The book was written *by* John.

Since the principles that apply to the position of prepositional phrases may contravene the power relation defined by the Control System, its word-order signal must be circumscribed (by hypothesis) so as to *exclude* Participants in prepositional phrases. Thus neither [11] nor [12] count as instances of $P_1 \ldots$ *Occurrence* $\ldots P_2$.

The two meanings HIGHER and LOWER (CONTROL) are always interpreted contextually. They interact with both the Occurrence and the identity of the Participants before surfacing in the message in much the same way as the article and number meanings interact with the words *chicken* and *people* to push their interpretation in one direction or another. As a result of this interaction, the perceptible effect of the meanings HIGHER and LOWER (CONTROL) on any given occasion is more precise than the meanings themselves. This greater precision is reflected in the observational descriptors 'agent', 'patient', 'causer' 'instrument' and 'addressee'. But these notions are all pragmatic extrapolations by the hearer, products of language use, not semantic categories of the linguistic code itself.

English has a second Control System applicable in situations involving three Participants. This system employs the word-order signal $P_1 \ldots$ *Occurrence* $\ldots P_2 \ldots P_3$, which categorizes the three Participants as exercising HIGH, MID and LOW degrees of control respectively. The switch from HIGHER and LOWER (in the two-member system) to the more polarized values HIGH

MID and LOW reflects the greater precision of the ranking due
to the presence of an additional Participant.

[13] *John* told *Mary the secret.*
P_1 P_2 P_3
HIGH   MID   LOW

[14] *John* bought *Mary the book.*
P_1 P_2 P_3
HIGH   MID   LOW

[15] *John* envied *Mary her money.*
P_1 P_2 P_3
HIGH   MID   LOW

In [13], Mary exercises some control over the 'telling' by
attending to John and, presumably, inspiring his confidence;
while in [14] she has motivated the act of 'buying'; and in [15] she
has engendered the 'envying'. In all three cases, then, Mary's
degree of control is less than the first-mentioned Participant but
more than the third-mentioned Participant. Again, Participants in
prepositional phrases are excluded from the control ranking. So,
for example, [16]–[20] are instances of P_1 . . . *Occurrence* . . . P_2
not P_1 . . . *Occurrence* . . . P_2 . . . P_3.

[16] *John* told *the secret* to Mary.
[17] *John* told *Mary* about the secret.
[18] *John* bought *the book* for Mary.
[19] *John* envied *Mary* on account of her money.
[20] *John* opened *the door* with a key.

As was true of the terms Entity and Occurrence, the term
Participant designates the conceptual status of a word on an
individual occasion, not a fixed class of words. This means that a
hearer must first decide what expressions name distinct entities
critically participating in an Occurrence in order to identify the
word-order signals. Thus [7] counts as P_1 . . . *Occurrence* . . . P_2
rather than P_1 . . . *Occurrence* . . . P_2 . . . P_3 because *a day* does
not refer to an entity critically participating in the activity of
milking.

[7] *The cows* milk *50 to 60 gallons of milk* a day.

Similarly, [21] does not count as an instance of P_1 . . .

Occurrence . . . P₂ because *Mr Smith* and *my teacher*, being co-referential, are not two distinct Participants.

[21]   Mr Smith is my teacher.

5.4 The Focus System

When only one Participant is mentioned, as in [21], it is not categorized in terms of its degree of control. This makes the configuration *Participant . . . Occurrence* suitable for messages in which there is no appreciable activity, and hence no control exercised by the Participant (e.g., *be, seem, appear*). The absence of a control categorization also means that when the Participant does exercise control there is no restriction on its degree or nature.

[22]   *Sterling Moss* drives well.
[23]   *The car* drives well.
[24]   *The gasoline* drives well.
[25]   *The road* drives well.

The single Participant may play any role implied by the Occurrence itself so long as it is a contextually plausible one.

There remains, however, the problem of accounting for the syntagmatic position of a single-mentioned Participant. Since such Participants regularly follow the Occurrence in some other languages (e.g., Sp. *Salió la niña*) its pre-position in English cannot be attributed to general cognitive principles alone. Rather, it must be treated as an arbitrary structural feature.

This takes the form of a third grammatical system that categorizes a Participant according to the *amount of attention* concentrated upon it with respect to the Occurrence. This system has two values, MORE and LESS, borne by the signals *P . . . Occurrence* and *Occurrence . . . P* respectively, and is operable only when there is a single Participant.

[26]   A fly was swimming in my soup.
         P   Occurrence
      MORE FOCUS
[27]   There was   a fly in my soup.
              Occurrence P
                   LESS FOCUS

The meaning LESS FOCUS slightly reduces the amount of

attention concentrated on the single-mentioned Participant in comparison to the highlighting effect of its systemic opposite, MORE FOCUS. Typically, speakers choose to do this for Participants making their first appearance in the discourse (as in [28a]), entities whose thematic significance has yet to be established; and even then, only when they make their appearance in an unobtrusive way. The meaning LESS FOCUS thus favours state-like Occurrences such as *be*, *lie*, *stand*, and *remain*, which do not immediately command attention.

[28a]   On a small grassy knoll between the Lincoln Memorial and the Washington Monument there *lies a national memorial*.   (first mention)

[28b]   *This memorial is* unique because after years of neglect, soldiers killed in Vietnam finally got the overdue national recognition and honour they deserved. (second mention)
        (Alfonse D'Amato, US Senator, fundraising letter)

The Control-Focus interlock
Taken together, the Control and Focus Systems account for the syntagmatic position of a Participant in three different message types: one Participant messages, two Participant messages and three Participant messages. So long as the analytical focus remains sentence-bound, no additional constructs need be posited. However the introduction of discourse-level facts forces an elaboration of the Focus System.

It is a well-established fact that in extended discourse thematically important entities, main characters for example, regularly recur as P_1 in the Control Systems. (In sentence-based terms, thematically important entities favour subject position.) The meaning HIGH(ER) Control assigned to P_1 does not, by itself, seem to be an adequate explanation. For this reason, revised versions of the Focus System must be posited that apply to messages involving two and three Participants. In both versions, the meanings IN FOCUS and NOT IN FOCUS ride piggy-back on the Control System signal to produce a complex interlocking structure. Figure 5.3 shows this grammatical interlock between the two-member Control System and the two-member Focus System.

According to Figure 5.3, the word-order signal P_1 . . . *Occurrence* . . . P_2 simultaneously designates P_1 as exercising a HIGHER degree of control over the Occurrence than P_2, and, in addition, deserving of more attention than P_2 in the ongoing

FIGURE 5.3   Interlock of the Two-member Control and Focus Systems

$$\begin{array}{l} \text{DEGREE OF CONTROL} \\ \text{OVER THE OCCURRENCE} \end{array} \left\{ \begin{array}{l} \text{HIGHER} = P_1 = \text{IN FOCUS} \\ \\ \text{LOWER} = P_2 = \text{NOT IN FOCUS} \end{array} \right\} \begin{array}{l} \text{FOCUS ON} \\ \text{PARTICIPANTS} \end{array}$$

discourse. (The shift from the meanings MORE and LESS FOCUS to IN FOCUS and NOT IN FOCUS reflects the fact that the Focus opposition becomes more polarized when its two values overtly contrast with respect to a single Occurrence.) A similar interlock exists for the three-member Control System, differing in structure from the above only in that both P_2 and P_3 are designated as NOT IN FOCUS.

Exemplification of the Focus Systems

Single-sentence examples could serve to illustrate the Control System because its meanings relate to the role of a Participant in a single Occurrence. By contrast all three versions of the Focus System relate to the thematic status of Participants. This means single-sentence examples would prove ineffective because they provide no indication of the relative importance of the Partici-pants other than the Focus meanings themselves. The Focus meanings must be embedded in contexts which provide independ-ent evidence of the thematic status of the Participants. In this sketch a single passage must suffice. Example [29] is a newspaper report of the outcome of a footrace, quoted in its entirety. (Thanks go to Bonny Gildin for this example.)

[29]   Stu Mittleman, who says he does best on hot and dry days, yesterday won his third consecutive New York Road Runners Club 100-mile invitational run and bettered his American record in rainy, chilly weather at Shea Stadium.
'I was the one to beat out there and I felt a lot of pressure to finish,' said Mittleman, who was clocked in 11 hours 56 minutes 33.6 seconds.
Mittleman, who led throughout, added, 'I don't run too well in the rain and I run better when it's hot.'
The race, now recognized as a national championship by The Athletics Congress, had its four previous runnings around the lake at Flushing Meadows-Corona Park.

Mittleman, a 31-year-old who teaches the sociology of sport, psychology and history at Queens College and lives in Manhattan, had set the previous American record last year at 13 hours 11 seconds.

Dr. R. Lion Caldwell, also 31, of Cibecue, Ariz. finished second, two laps behind the winner. Dr. Caldwell was clocked in 13:19:11.8. Third was Chit Yeter, a 47-year-old native of Turkey who now lives in New York. He was followed by Park Barner, 38, of Camp Hill, Pa., who won the 100-mile run in 1979.

The competitors ran around the warming track at Shea Stadium and along the edge of the parking lot.

Mittleman, who ran bare-chested last year, wore a running shirt this time, a concession to the weather. He changed shirts about 40 times during the 100-lap run.

A total of 45 men and three women started the run, but only 20 men and one woman completed the race. Sue Medaglia, a 47-year-old secretary who lives in the Pelham Bay section of the Bronx, finished 18th, clocking 18:36:28.

(Al Harvin, *The New York Times*)

The Focus meanings are strikingly illustrated by the contrasting ways the four finalists in the race are initially introduced.

[29a] *Stu Mittleman*. . . .won his third consecutive (. . .)run and
       (Stu Mittleman). . .bettered   his American record

P_1	Occurrence	P_2	Word-order Signal
IN FOCUS		NOT IN FOCUS	Focus meanings
(HIGHER)		(LOWER)	Control meanings

[29b] *Dr. Caldwell*. . .finished second. . .
       P   Occurrence
       MORE FOCUS

[29c] Third   was   *Chit Yeter*. . .
       Occurrence   P
                  LESS FOCUS

[29d] He was followed by *Parker Barner*. . .
                     (no degree of focus specified)

In a straightforward report of a footrace, the thematic importance of the finalists should parallel their performance in the race. Most important is the winner, next the runner-up, and so on. Evidence that the writer sees things this way can be found in the order he has introduced the finalists into the discourse. Additional evidence comes from the amount of commentary each receives. Six of the thirteen sentences in the report are devoted to the winner; two sentences are devoted to the second-place finalist, and a single sentence each to the third and fourth-place runners. Two precise finishing times are given for the winner, one for the second-place runner, and none for the third and fourth-place runners. (Recall the connection between precision and cognitive salience seen in Chapter 4.)

This hierarchy of relative importance is reflected in the way the writer has deployed the Focus System meanings to introduce each finalist. Stu Mittleton, the winner, is initially introduced as a Participant in the Occurrences *won* and *bettered* in [29a]. The position of *Stu Mittleton* preceding *won* and *bettered* counts as two instances of P_1 in the word-order signal P_1 . . . *Occurrence* . . . P_2. This has the effect of twice according him maximal prominence with the meaning IN FOCUS, which explicitly ranks him above *his* . . . *run*, designated as NOT IN FOCUS, and above *his American record* also designated as NOT IN FOCUS.

The writer then subordinates the second-place finalist slightly by shifting to the non-polarized version of the Focus System and its meaning MORE FOCUS [29b]. The third-place finalist is further demoted in importance with the meaning LESS FOCUS [29c]. Finally, the fourth-place runner is not ranked at all for Focus. He is introduced in a prepositional phrase associated with an Occurrence in which the third-place finalist receives MORE FOCUS, thus implicitly ranking below the three who placed [29d]. (The third-place finalist is promoted from LESS FOCUS to MORE FOCUS with his second mention as in [28].[1])

A more refined exploitation of the Focus System can be detected in the treatment of the three entities that receive a second mention prior to the introduction of the runners-up, namely, the winner, the race and his record. All three are initially ranked for Focus in the first sentence [29a]. In the course of the first five paragraphs, attention is consistently kept on Mittleton, the winner, with the meanings IN FOCUS, MORE FOCUS and LESS FOCUS. Only once is a Participant other than Mittleton placed IN FOCUS.

[29e]   *The race. . .had*   its four previous runnings. . .
      P_1 Occurrence P_2
    IN FOCUS   NOT IN FOCUS

The race is roughly equivalent to *his third consecutive New York Road Runners Club 100-mile invitational run* in the first sentence. There the referent was categorized as NOT IN FOCUS, but with its second mention in the fourth paragraph it is promoted to IN FOCUS.

His American record is also categorized as NOT IN FOCUS in the first sentence but, in contrast to *the race*, retains that ranking in its referentially equivalent second mention in the fifth paragraph.

[29f]   Mittleton. . .had set *the previous American record.* . .
       P_1 Occurrence P_2
    IN FOCUS   NOT IN FOCUS

His American record does not merit promotion to IN FOCUS because it relates to background information about one runner. (Note the use of the past perfect tense *had set*, in contrast to the simple past *had* in [29e].)

The only other runner mentioned by name is Sue Medaglia, who appears IN FOCUS in the final paragraph along with her finishing time. Her momentary claim to Focus is that she is the only woman to complete the race.

5.5 The Probability System

The final set of facts involving the syntagmatic position of Participants was touched on briefly in Chapter 1. There we posited *Inversion* as the signal of the meaning DOUBT. This meaning figures in a complex multi-valued system, including both *do Verb* and the modal auxiliaries, which categorizes an Occurrence in terms of its *relative probability*. The meaning DOUBT is the least precise value in the system, merely indicating that the Occurrence is (or was) less than certain without assigning it any specific probability value. It is most frequently employed for questions.

[30]   Is the open, airy, multipurpose space adequate?
    Inversion
      DOUBT

The signal *Inversion* in the Probability System can, however, be formally identical to the *Occurrence* . . . *P* signal in the one-participant Focus System.

[31]   But in place of the drafty, back-house kitchen that was
       sagging on rotting sills and a mortarless stone foundation
       is the open, airy, multipurpose space that has become the
       new heart of the house.
                                    (Mike McClintock, *Country Journal*)

This structural homonymy creates the possibility of confusion for
the hearer. Speakers resolve the ambiguity by always including
additional contextual information that implies the presence of
one or the other word-order signal. When *Occurrence . . . P* is
intended, speakers include an initial locative word or phrase
which alerts the hearer that a new Participant is about to be
introduced (as in [28a], [29c] and [31]).[2] When *Inversion* is
intended, they categorize the Occurrence in terms of a specific
level of probability. This has the effect of introducing a second
morphological component whose inversion with the Entity in
Focus no longer has the appearance of *Occurrence . . . P.*[3]

[32]   *Did* he leave before three? (not: *Left he* before three?)
[33]   *Should* he leave before three?

As noted in Chapter 1, the meaning DOUBT has a wider
range of application than questions. It can be employed for a
message of pure uncertainty if (still more) contextual information
is added to steer the hearer away from the statistically favoured
interpretation of DOUBT as a question.

[34]   *Rarely* did he leave before three.
[35]   *Should* he leave before three, *Sarah will finish the
       project.*
[36]   *Should* he be there before three, *tell him to wait for me.*

Language-particular categories
The discussion of the Control, Focus and Probability Systems has
illustrated the analytical consequences of operating with language-
particular rather than universal categories. Sentence-based theory
assumes the existence of a single (universal) category – subject –
which in English occurs in various positions, each associated with
different semantic characteristics. The analyst thus shoulders the
responsibility of eventually providing a coherent definition of that
category from which the language-particular facts of English
follow in a principled way. Until such time, only description is
possible.
       By contrast, sign-based analysis (as exemplified by Diver) takes

the formal and semantic heterogeneity in English as evidence that multiple categories are involved. The various syntagmatic configurations of Participants are analysed as manifestations of different signals, each bearing a different complex of meanings drawn from different grammatical systems. The meanings in each system give rise to communicative strategies which are nothing more than creative exploitations of their systemic values: for example, the strategy illustrated by [29] where the Focus meanings are used to rank, and re-rank, Participants according to their evolving thematic status in the discourse. The practical advantage here is that the analyst now has a greater inventory of constructs with which to operate. More important, since the definition of these constructs has not been postponed, description and explanation can go hand in hand.

5.6 Revision of the Focus Number System

The Focus Number System presented in Figure 5.1 is illustrated by examples [37]–[40] in their two contrasting versions.

[37a]   The boy *walks* through the field.
[37b]   The boys *walk0* through the field.
[38a]   There *remains* one boy without a book.
[38b]   There *remain0* two boys without a book.
[39a]   The boy *waters* the lawn.
[39b]   The boys *water0* the lawn.
[40a]   The boy *teaches* his brother the game.
[40b]   The boys *teach0* their brother the game.

The word *boy(s)* is categorized as receiving slightly different degrees of Focus by the various Focus System signals. In [37], $P \ldots Occurrence$ accords *boy(s)* MORE FOCUS; in [38] $Occurrence \ldots P$ accords *boy(s)* LESS FOCUS; and in [39] and [40] the signals $P_1 \ldots Occurrence \ldots P_2$ and $P_1 \ldots Occurrence \ldots P_2 \ldots P_3$ both categorize *boy(s)* as IN FOCUS. In each case, *boy(s)* is the entity in Focus because no entity ranks higher in Focus than *boy(s)*.

In the four *a* sentences *Occurrence -s* categorizes the entity in Focus as ONE, and in the four *b* sentences *Occurrence -0* categorizes it as MORE THAN ONE. The independent contextual support for this categorization is the grammatical number of *boy* itself, provided by the Entity Number System. *Boy0* (= ONE) correlates with *Occurrence -s*, and *boys* (= MORE THAN ONE) correlates with *Occurrence -0*.

The need for revision
When linguistic signs are conceived as communicative tools, one
expects speakers to employ a linguistic signal whenever its
meaning fits the message. The deployment of *Occurrence -s* and
-∅ in [37]–[40] are simple and straightforward confirmations of
this expectation and thus serve as empirical evidence in favour of
the hypothesized signs. By the same token, whenever such
expectations are not confirmed, doubt is cast upon the hypothesis;
either it is fundamentally wrong, or it demands revision.

In its present form, the Focus Number System gives rise to
unconfirmed expectations of deployment that force revision. The
early revisions are entirely conventional and thoroughly familiar
to any speaker of English. We begin with them as a way of
illustrating the way sign-based theory deals with the three
traditional problems of morphological irregularity, portmanteau
morphology and grammatical homophony.

The first revision involves no more than an elaboration.

[41a]   The boy *is* tall.
[41b]   The boys *are* tall.
[42a]   The boy *has* three books.
[42b]   The boys *have* three books.
[43a]   The boy *does* his homework.
[43b]   The boys *do* their homework.

While the *a* and *b* sentences clearly contrast in Focus Number, it
is problematic whether the signals *Occurrence -s* and *-∅* are
present. The problem is easily resolved by positing additional
signals of the two Focus Number meanings in the form of the
is/are, *has/have* and *does/do* contrasts. These formatives function
as portmanteau signals bearing both lexical and grammatical
meanings. When this morphology functions in an auxiliary
capacity it retains its value in the Focus Number System.

The second revision is more in the way of a circumscription,
prompted by unattested but predicted forms. The signal *Occurrence -s* is anticipated whenever its meaning ONE (Entity in
Focus) fits the message. Thus [44a–c] are expected.

[44a]   The boy cans walk through the field.
[44b]   The boy musts walk through the field.
[44c]   The boy mays walk through the field.

Since *Occurrence -s* never occurs with the modals, and the
actually occurring *The boy can/may/must walk* could not be

instances of *Occurrence -0*, it appears that the entire Focus Number System is, for some reason, not being employed. Pending a satisfactory systemic explanation (Note 5 to come) the simplest provisional solution is to redefine the signals of the Focus Number System so that they include, as an additional component, the *absence* of the auxiliaries. This solution is perceptually viable from the hearer's standpoint because the modal auxiliaries comprise an easily recognizable set of forms numbering less than a dozen.

Interlock with the Time and Person Systems

Other unconfirmed predictions force further revision, this time on the meaning side. One would expect the Focus Number meanings ONE and MORE THAN ONE to be employed for all Occurrences regardless of their temporal location. The hypothesis thus predicts [45].

[45]   The boy walkeds through the field.

One possible revision would be a further modification of the Focus Number signals so that they included the absence of *-ed* (a signal of the temporal meaning PAST). This works well enough for [45] but does not solve the problem for those words which describe a past event without an *-ed* suffix.

[46]   John set out for Tibet.

The Focus Number System, even with the suggested revision, predicts [47].

[47]   John sets out for Tibet.

[47] occurs, to be sure, but it does not refer to an event located exclusively in the past.

Both these facts – the absence of the expected *walkeds* and the temporal reference to the present or future of *sets* – can be accounted for by according *Occurrence -s* an additional meaning, NON-PAST. With *Occurrence -s* bearing the meaning NON-PAST, it now becomes an inappropriate communicative tool for conveying a message about an Occurrence located exclusively in the past: while its Focus Number meaning fits such messages, its time meaning does not. As a consequence, the non-occurrence of *walkeds* (representing the contradictory collocation of the temporal meanings PAST and NON-PAST) becomes a non-

arbitrary fact of the distribution of *Occurrence -s* that follows
from its arbitrary time meaning NON-PAST. And the meaning
NON-PAST accounts for the restriction of [47] to reference to
the present or future as well.

Following a similar rationale, the meaning THIRD PERSON
(Entity in Focus) must be ascribed to *Occurrence -s* to account
for its absence when the entity in Focus is first or second person.

[48]   I walk through the woods.
[49]   You walk through the woods.

(The meanings NON-PAST and THIRD PERSON figure in
larger, multi-valued systems of Time and Person. These interlock
with the Focus Number System by virtue of the signal
morphology they share, to produce a structure resembling the
Control-Focus interlock in Figure 5.3.)

These various revisions of the original hypothesis have adhered
to the basic principle that the locus of rule-governed arbitrariness
in language is the linguistic sign. By confining all structural
arbitrariness to the sign level – prior to the introduction of
language users – the stage is then set for explaining the
collocation of linguistic signs in goal-directed terms. The intent of
each revision, then, has been to build into the sign structure of
English (arbitrary) morphological and semantic features which
can then provide systemic functional motivation for the way
language users employ linguistic signs in the communication of
messages.

Occurrence -$\emptyset_2$

A body of data still stands as counter-evidence to the Focus
Number hypothesis in its present form.

[50]   I recommend that he *begin* work next week.
[51]   I insist that he *leave* at once.
[52]   I urge that he *reconsider*.

The hypothesis predicts *Occurrence -s*, since its three meanings
ONE, NON-PAST, and THIRD all apply. Instead, an apparent
instance of *Occurrence -$\emptyset$* appears, whose meaning MORE
THAN ONE does not fit the message. Clearly, then, either the
Focus Number meaning assigned to *Occurrence -$\emptyset$* is wrong; or,
alternatively, *begin*, *leave* and *reconsider* are not, despite
appearances, instances of the Focus Number signal in Figure 5.1.

According to Diver, there exists in the Probability System a second *Occurrence -$\emptyset$* that bears the meaning DOUBT, HIGHER PROBABILITY. This signal interlocks with the Person and Focus Number Systems by virtue of bearing the meanings THIRD and ONE as well. This second zero signal will be called *Occurrence -$\emptyset_2$* and that in Figure 5.1 *Occurrence -$\emptyset_1$*. (*Occurrence -$\emptyset_2$* has one alternate, *be*, lacking Person and Number meanings.) The Person and Number meanings of *Occurrence -$\emptyset_2$* confine its use to just those contexts where it overtly contrasts with *Occurrence -s*, which carries no Probability information.

[53a] The supervisor has suggested that Miss Kittler *give$\emptyset$* more homework.

[53b] The supervisor has suggested that Miss Kittler *be* more strict.

DOUBT, HIGHER PROBABILITY

[54a] The supervisor has suggested that Miss Kittler *gives* too much homework.

[54b] The supervisor has suggested that Miss Kittler *is* too strict.

The meaning DOUBT, HIGHER PROBABILITY in [53] steers the interpretation of *give* and *be* towards the hypothetical, away from their straightforward factual interpretation in [54].

The existence of homonymous *Occurrence -$\emptyset$* signals bearing opposite Focus Number meanings clearly threatens the functional utility of both. In resolving the perceptual problem created by this homonymy, speakers have opted to maximize the expressive potential of *Occurrence -$\emptyset_1$* at the expense of *Occurrence -$\emptyset_2$* by limiting the use of the latter to just those contexts in which there is already reliable contextual indication that the Occurrence is in doubt. *Occurrence -$\emptyset_2$* is employed only in association with words such as *urge*, *advise* and *recommend* which strongly imply the realm of the hypothetical. Everywhere else speakers bypass *Occurrence -$\emptyset_2$* in favour of the morphologically unproblematic alternatives in the Probability System, which happen to be more precise semantically as well.[4]

[55] I recommend he *leave$\emptyset_2$* at three.

vs.

[56a] (I think) he *must leave* at three.

(not *He leave$\emptyset_2$* at three.)

[56b] (I think) he *may leave* at three.

[56c] (I think) he *might leave* at three.

[56d] (I think) he *can leave* at three.

[56e] (I think) he *could leave* at three.

As a result of its limited deployment in contexts that are highly redundant, *Occurrence* -$\emptyset_2$ has only marginal communicative value in English and, indeed, is not in the active repertoire of many speakers.[5]

5.7 Testing the Focus Number System

We can now move to tests of the Focus Number System in its revised form. Through qualitative and quantitative techniques of analysis it must be shown that language users employ *Occurrence* -*s* and *Occurrence* -$\emptyset_1$ (henceforth *Occurrence* -$\emptyset$) in ways that are predicted and explained by their hypothesized meanings. Since the effect of the Time and Person meanings is unproblematic, the validation will concentrate on the distributional consequences of the Focus Number meanings.

Examples [37]–[40] illustrated the two Focus Number meanings used in a straightforward descriptive capacity to reflect the objective referential number of the entity in Focus (as evidenced by the grammatical number of *boy*). While the point is hardly in doubt, it can be demonstrated that examples [37]–[40] are typical of normal language use by showing that the meanings in the Entity and Focus Number Systems correlate in the manner of the examples in actual running text.

TABLE 5.1   Co-occurrence of Entity Number (of P or P_1) and Focus Number[6]

	Entity -$\emptyset$	Entity -*s*
Occurrence -*s*	552 (100%)	0 (0%)
Occurrence -$\emptyset$	5 (8%)	61 (92%)
		$p < 0.001$

Source: Jane Smiley, 'Long Distance', *The Atlantic*, January 1987.

Table 5.1 presents the results of a count made on a short story of approximately 6500 words. *Occurrence* -*s* refers to an entity categorized as ONE (by the Entity Number System) 100 per cent of the time, and *Occurrence* -$\emptyset$ refers to an entity categorized as MORE THAN ONE 92 per cent of the time.

The procedure of moving from prototypical examples to quantitative testing was first illustrated in Chapter 1, where the use of *do Verb* for affirmative emphasis was demonstrated through its correlation with highlighting connectives like *but*. That demonstration was particularly effective in establishing the independent expressive value of *do Verb* because the correlation was high enough to establish statistical significance, but not so high as to suggest that *do Verb* was mechanical and automatic. One-seventh of the time *do Verb* functioned non-redundantly as the sole (intra-sentential) indication that a message of contrastive affirmation was intended.

By contrast, the correlation in Table 5.1 is so nearly categorical that it undermines the basic thesis being tested, namely, that *Occurrence -s* and *-∅* are meaning-bearing units with independent expressive value. Table 5.1 could be used to argue with equal force that *Occurrence -s* and *-∅* are semantically-empty formatives whose presence is mechanically determined by the grammatical number of the entity in Focus. In other words, it argues for the hypothesis of *verb agreement* in English.

5.8 The Hypothesis of Subject–Verb Agreement

We are confronted at this point with the classic dilemma of scientific theory-building, that of competing hypotheses for a given set of data. Such dilemmas are usually resolved by searching for places the two hypotheses differ in their predictions. In following this course we must first select some particular version of the competing hypothesis. The literature is full of references to a rule of verb agreement in English, but these are typically not formulated with sufficient precision for our purposes. Instead, verb agreement is treated perfunctorily as if it were already an established fact of the language.

> As is well-known, English has a rule of *person-number agreement* whereby a verb has to agree in person and number with the NP (Noun Phrase) immediately preceding it:[7]
>
> (Radford 1984:160)
>
> Many (perhaps most) languages have rules of agreement, by which a verb or adjective acquires an index or inflection indicating ('agreeing with') properties such as person, number, gender, etc. of some NP found elsewhere in the clause.
>
> (Anderson 1974:445)
>
> In general, verbs and auxiliaries in the present tense in English agree with the subject.
>
> (Bach 1974:76)
>
> The well-formedness condition which represents the agreement system of a particular language follows from the conjunction of language-particular agreement rules with universal laws governing agreement. For example, the verb agreement rule for English requires that a tensed verb agree only with its final subject.
>
> (Aissen and Ladusaw 1988:1)

Jacobs and Rosenbaum (1968) are more forthcoming. They present verb agreement as a two- (or three-) step process: copying the number and person features of the subject onto the auxiliary segment; copying these features onto the verbal from the auxiliary and deleting it (for sentences with no auxiliary); transforming the number and person features into a suffix. But even this is little more than a sketch. *The crocodiles are hungry* and *the ballerina laughs* are the only examples cited of the extent of coverage.

If, however, we are permitted to extrapolate from the remarks above, divergent predictions emerge. The conception of verb number held by those scholars appears to be essentially the same as that of Jespersen, who expressed it in a pithy statement more than half a century earlier.

[T]he plural form of *sing* (in *Birds sing*) . . . is only a meaningless grammatical contrivance showing the dependence of the verb on the subject.

(Jespersen 1933/1966:216)

If the inflection of the verb for subject number is a meaningless grammatical contrivance, then it should proceed in a purely mechanical and categorical fashion. The grammatical form of the verb should be 100 per cent predictable from the grammatical form of the subject so that the verb affix should never appear to have independent expressive value. Any apparent counter-examples to verb agreement should be readily attributable to extraneous considerations such as momentary confusion about the actual identity of the grammatical subject.

The Focus Number System, on the other hand, portrays the verbal affixes as fully-fledged meaning-bearing units. Like the Entity Number signals, they are chosen for their independent expressive value and need not mechanically echo other semantic choices. Thus, one should find instances where the Focus Number choice *differs* from the grammatical number of the entity in Focus. Furthermore, the hypothesis predicts under what circumstances this should occur. It will be when the entity in Focus *spans the opposition of number*; when, like a pair of scissors, it is simultaneously both one and two (or more) things.

Table 5.1 is clearly a vote in favour of verb agreement. The skewing between a singular subject and a singular verb is 100 per cent, and the five instances of a singular subject and a plural verb all involve a single word, *people*. Upon examination, however, the short story upon which the count was done contains scarcely any instances (other than *people*) of messages that span the opposition of number. As in most narratives, nearly all the entities in Focus are human beings, and human beings span the opposition of number only when they are described by lexical items such as *family*, *committee* and *audience* that treat them as a well-defined aggregate.

To find messages likely to provoke contrasting Entity and Focus Number meanings one must turn to non-narrative prose, both spoken and written, in which the entities in Focus tend to be conceptually more complex. Here many examples of the predicted collocations can be found.

Type A: Entity in Focus = ONE; Focus Number = MORE THAN ONE

[57] This afternoon our *panel are* three male singers.
(Edward Downes, Texaco Metropolitan Opera broadcast)

[58] The Parsons *family were* great letter writers, and the samples of Arch's wheedling, money-grubbing epistles included here are comic masterpieces, marvels of double talk and self-deception.
(Molly Haskell, *The New York Times Book Review*)

[59] At ADT (security systems) 98 years' *experience have* taught us that no one alarm device will foil a determined burglar.
(Advertisement)

[60] Five years ago 5 per cent of tax returns were subject to review. Today, only *one per cent are* subject to review.
(*Weekend Edition*, National Public Radio (NPR))

[61] I surmise that the *reason* why Mill's doctrine of denotation, without its safeguards, caught on, while his truths about connotation failed to do so, *were* two.
(Gilbert Ryle, 'The Theory of Meaning')

[62] *The whole process* of learning a first and second language *are* so completely different.
(Laura Holland)

[63] Rudolph is especially effective in crowd scenes like the opening, where *movement* of people and camera *are* delicately braided, where odd characters flutter through the background unemphasized.
(Stanley Kauffman, *The New Republic*)

Type B: Entity in Focus = MORE THAN ONE; Focus
Number = ONE

[64]   *The sex lives* of Roman Catholic nuns *does* not, at first
       blush, seem like promising material for a book.
                                                    (*Newsweek*)
[65]   *Two million dollars comes* from corporations and found-
       ations, but almost $400,000 from private gifts.
                                            (*The New York Times*)
[66]   *Cherry cokes is* the most popular drink here.
                                    (*All Things Considered*, NPR)
[67]   *Two drops deodorizes* anything in your house.
                                     (Air freshener advertisement)
[68]   *Little people's rights is* just as important as rich people's
       rights.
                                    (Roy Cohen, Tomorrow, NBC)
[69]   For one thing, the player is much closer to the
       instrument than the listener, and *the sounds* he hears *is*
       thus a different sound.
                                  (John Holt, *Instead of Education*)

Type C: Two Entities in Focus conjoined by *and*; Focus
Number = ONE

[70]   *Gas and excess acid* in your stomach *is* what we call
       Gasid Indigestion.
                                         (Alka-Seltzer commercial)
[71]   The plane was diverted to Utah where *four parachutes
       and half a million dollars was* delivered.
                                                  (WINS News)
[72]   The two things that most stood out are the present
       weakness and low level organization of ROAR [Restore
       Our Alienated Rights], and *the explicit racism and
       implicit fascism* that *gives* ROAR its reason for exist-
       ence.
                            (The Revolutionary Communist Newspaper)
[73]   We know that *the company's destiny and ours is* the
       same.
                                     (Bernard Krisher, *Newsweek*)
[74]   *Galloping horses and thousands of cattle is* not necessary
       to cinema; I call that photography.
                                  (Alfred Hitchcock, radio interview)
[75]   I just want you to know that *this whole Watergate*

> *situation and the other opportunities was* a concerted
> effort by a number of people.
>
> (Jeb Magruder, Newsweek)

Traditional treatments

At this point, a straw-man charge could well be made. Certainly
all reference grammars take cognizance of such well-known
exceptions to the rule of verb agreement in English. In some
cases, they simply note the deviations without commentary.

> *A number of* takes the plural, but *the number of* takes the
> singular.
>   A number of students have dropped that course.
> The number of students in this school is 2000.
>
> (Celce-Murcia & Larsen-Freeman 1983:38)

In other cases, they attempt to provide an explanation for why
the rule of verb agreement is being broken.

> Collective nouns . . . may take either a singular or plural
> inflection depending on the meaning.
>   The Gang of Four has been discredited. (= the gang as a
> whole) The Gang of Four have been discredited. (= the
> individual gang members)
>
> (Celce-Murcia and Larsen-Freeman 1983:38)
>
> (As for the use of the plural form where it is distinct from the
> singular, no difficulty is felt in most of the cases in which the
> subject is itself in the plural or consists of two or more words
> joined by means of *and* . . .) But when the two joined words
> *form one conception* [emphasis W.R.], the verb is put in the
> singular as in:
>   Accuracy and precision is a more important quality of
> language than abundance.
>
> (Jespersen 1933/1966:217)

In still other cases, the apparent counter-examples to verb
agreement are portrayed as actually supporting the hypothesis by
virtue of being instances of agreement at a deeper level.

> Two factors interfere with concord as presented in 7.18.
> 'Notional concord' is agreement of verb with subject according
> to the *idea* of number rather than the actual presence of the
> grammatical marker for that idea. Thus *the government* is

treated as plural in *The government have broken all their promises* (BrE), as is shown not only by the plural verb *have*, but also by the pronoun *their*.

(Quirk and Greenbaum 1973:176)

None of these apologies, we maintain, succeed in altering the fact that our data constitute legitimate counter-evidence to a rule of subject-verb agreement in English. This is clearly the case when nothing more is offered than the bald statement of the disconfirming observations: '*A number of* takes the plural, but *the number of* takes the singular.' As a purely descriptive statement, this generalization may serve as a useful guide to correct usage for the non-native speaker. But in the context of an account of verb number aspiring to theoretical coherence it is clearly an acknowledgement of empirical failure because the agreement rule does not anticipate any interaction between the article accompanying the grammatical subject and the number inflection of the verb. (Indeed, to the extent the grammar of English makes any prediction regarding articles, it would predict that grammatical agreement should break down with *the*, not *a*, since *the* is unmarked for number while *a* is explicitly marked as a singular.)

Semantic explanations

The appeal to meaning would seem to provide what was lacking above, namely, a principled rationale for the departure from grammatical agreement. Such appeals have a *prima facie* plausibility within the context of a traditional grammar because traditional grammar adopts an explicitly notional base. With respect to the operation of an agreement rule, however, such appeals to meaning are illicit and unmotivated. If, as Jespersen asserts, the verb inflection is 'a meaningless grammatical contrivance showing the dependence of the verb on the subject' then the departures from grammatical agreement should all involve some unusual kind of dependence relationship between subject and verb; whether the subject itself forms one or two conceptions in the mind of the speaker should be of no consequence.

To be sure, our own rationale in terms of a spanned opposition is close in spirit. But the notion of a spanned opposition, as developed in Chapter 2, applies to the relation between a message and contrasting meanings. So in an account claiming that the verbal inflection *always* reflects the relative appropriateness of the meanings ONE and MORE THAN ONE to the speaker's message, it can be legitimately argued that the choice would fluctuate in those situations where both meanings are equally appropriate.

The agreement rule, on the other hand, does not prepare the ground for such an argument. The verbal affixes themselves are devoid of semantic content; and the linguistic feature that supposedly determines their appearance is the *grammatical* number of the subject, not the speaker's communicative intent. Such appeals to meaning implicitly accord the verb inflection an independent expressive value that violates the essential claim of the rule in whose aid the appeals are made.

Notional concord

The term 'notional concord' attempts to portray the apparent counter-evidence to grammatical agreement not as deviations from the rule, but as adherence *at a deeper level*. As Quirk and Greenbaum put it, there is 'agreement of verb with subject according to the *idea* of number rather than the actual presence of the grammatical marker for that idea'. Thus, *people, family,* and *faculty* take a plural verb because these words, while unmistakably singular in form, designate a referential plurality.

The trouble with this proposal is that the explanatory power of 'notional concord' is *greater* than the basic rule of 'grammatical concord' of which it is supposedly a particular instance. That is, it subsumes most of the data covered by the rule of grammatical agreement. For Jespersen's example *Birds sing*, it could be said that *sing* is agreeing with 'the idea of number' of *birds*, not with its morphological plurality. If the modern principles of grammatical argumentation were applied, the rule of grammatical agreement and the rule of notional agreement should, by all rights, switch places. Notional agreement should become the basic 'rule', and grammatical agreement should be reserved for those few cases that could not be handled by the former (say, *guts* and *remains*).

The consequence of such a revision is that it dramatically alters one's conception of the nature of the phenomena. Verb number becomes essentially a fact of semantic coherence, not a fact of rule-governed formal determination. That being the case, one might as well dispense with the notion of 'agreement' altogether and invoke, in its stead, some general Gricean-like maxim of good communicative behaviour: make your linguistic choices so as to best reflect what you have to say. But then it makes more sense to accord the verb affixes inherent semantic content to which general principles of thematic coherence most obviously apply, as the Focus Number System does.

Within the context of a modern formal grammar, on the other hand, notional concord has no place. The proposal that a verb may 'agree with an idea' is just the kind of poorly-constrained escape hatch that led Chomsky to reject the notional basis of traditional grammar in favour of an axiomatic approach, in which such notions were either expressed formally or abandoned as unscientific.

Chomsky himself has made only programmatic suggestions as to the proper formal treatment of verb number. In Chomsky (1965) verb number is not dealt with specifically, but in a general discussion of inflectional processes rules of agreement are likened to phonological rules of assimilation (p. 175). In Chomsky (1981) an abstract 'inflectional' element INFL (initially outside the VP) bears the feature [+Tense]; and if [+Tense] then it bears the additional features of person, gender and number, forming the complex AGR ('agreement'). This element AGR is 'basically nominal in character' (p. 52). The elements in INFL are assigned to the initial verbal element of VP by a rule (R) of Affix-movement (p. 256). So far, so good. But the issue crucial to the success of such a treatment is the determination of the number feature of AGR. Examples [57]–[75] show it cannot be by a simple copy mechanism that transfers the grammatical number of the head noun of the subject phrase to the verb.

Lapointe (1980/1986) proposes an alternative generative treatment in which verb agreement is the result of a filter mechanism rather than a grammatical rule *per se*. The full inflectional paradigm of a verb appears in the lexicon (*sing*, *sings*) and is allowed to co-occur freely with (subject) noun phrases by the Phrase Structure rules. But the rules for translating surface syntactic structures into their corresponding logical forms only yield well-formed logical forms for SSs that contain no unbound variables, namely, those which exhibit subject-verb agreement.

Lapointe circumscribes his study as addressing only 'unequivocal cases of *formal* agreement'. He excludes *sense* agreement 'in which agreement is determined by the actual gender or cardinality that the referents of a NP have in the real world', sentences with conjoined noun phrases as subject, and 'agreement which is not governed by rules of grammar in the strict sense at all' (1980:328). In one deft stroke here, Lapointe excludes all the data that would call the existence of formal agreement into question. At the same time, he fails to provide any guidelines, formal or otherwise, by which to distinguish formal agreement from sense agreement. This is a serious omission because once one concedes the existence of sense agreement, one cannot fail to recognize that most sentences which agree in form *agree in sense as well*. Lapointe thus begs the question of the existence of formal agreement as a distinct linguistic phenomenon, rather than as one falling within the scope of a more comprehensive theory of sense agreement.

If, on the other hand, one grants the existence of formal agreement and accords it analytical primacy, as Lapointe clearly does, this means that [76], exhibiting both formal and sense agreement, should count as the former and be handled in the same way as *The birds sing*.

[76]   Seven million *people* out on the street *was* thought of as a social catastrophe.
(Michael Harrington, *Morning Edition*)

But this means that [76] will have a different treatment from [77], with which it seems to have much in common.

[77]   Even though it doesn't seem like a lot, in a small room that thirty or forty *children seems* like quite a few.
(interview, *Morning Edition*)

Alternatively, if [76] and [77] both count as sense agreement, then in what category does [78] fall?

[78]   More than 3.3 million *people were* out of work.
(*Newsweek*)

Furthermore, whether or not a distributional fact is 'governed by rules of grammar in the strict sense' is largely a question of the ingenuity of the analyst in devising such rules, not a pre-analytical fact that can be established by mere inspection. For example, [79a] appears to contain the requisite morphological material for analysis in terms of formal agreement and moreover, cannot be set aside as a stylistic variant of [79b] which is surely unacceptable.

[79a]   The following list of *plants* and *animals are* typical New York swamp dwellers.
(printed display placard, The Bronx Zoo)
[79b]   The following list of plants and animals *is* typical New York swamp dwellers.

Lapointe's silence on the grammatical status of sentences

[57]–[69] and [76]–[79] means that the only structural types his treatment can be said to cover unproblematically are those with personal pronouns and proper names as subjects. (All his examples are, in fact, of these two types; and in French, not English.) Thus the real crux of the problem is left entirely unaddressed. Yet Lapointe concludes his discussion of English verb number with the blithe assertion 'and this is essentially all that has to be said about person/number agreement in English' (1980:317).

The great virtue of modern formal linguistics has been its explicitness. But this virtue can be realized only if all relevant components of a formal analysis are in place. When components critical to its empirical testing are left for the sympathetic reader to infer, then there has been no methodological advance, practically speaking, over the procedures of traditional grammar. Programmatic proposals and fledgling theories (Lapointe's apt phrase) are certainly in order during the heady days of paradigm formulation. But at some point progress must be measured in terms of demonstrated empirical success (Gross 1979). Lapointe's treatment, appearing more than twenty years after *Syntactic Structures*, makes one wonder when, if ever, generative theory will advance to the stage Thomas Kuhn (1962) calls normal science.

Morgan (1972) is an early noteworthy exception to the generally complacent attitude toward verb number in English. He takes a hard look at data similar to our own and, recognizing their seriousness, considers the damage they do to a number of common assumptions about verb agreement. He concludes that the assumption that probably must be abandoned is that of verb agreement as a single process. On the basis of the wide variation in speaker judgements regarding verb number Morgan proposes the following:

> The most likely explanation for these facts was alluded to earlier: that the speaker learns a relatively simple principle of agreement which somehow fails to extend to complex cases. This sometimes leads to patching the principle by adding subsidiary principles and [verb agreement] ends up as a (possibly hierarchical) set of principles. The details of the patch vary considerably from speaker to speaker and some speakers apparently fail to patch at all for certain cases.
>
> (Morgan 1972:285)

While Morgan deserves credit for recognizing so early on the serious implications of such data for the view of verb agreement as a single process, he does not go so far as to question the legitimacy of the notion itself. Indeed, Morgan seems to argue that so long as *any* data exist in which the number of the verb corresponds to that of the grammatical subject, verb agreement in some form stands.

> For instance . . . to show that assumption 4 is wrong [i.e., at the point where Verb Agreement applies the verb and the NP it agrees with are clause-mates W.R.] is to show that there are cases where the verb agrees with a non-clause-mate subject. *It obviously does not follow from this that the verb never agrees with a clause-mate subject* [emphasis W.R.]. Surely there is something right somewhere with these assumptions.
>
> (Morgan 1972:284)

Since a purely random association between subject and verb number would support verb agreement 50 per cent of the time, it is hard to see how the notion could ever be challenged on empirical grounds if one consented to Morgan's methodological ground rules.

In the end, though, Morgan is right. Arguing against verb agreement in principle by pointing out the empirical inadequacy of particular proposals amounts to trying to prove a negative. Whatever the difficulties, it could always be maintained that some yet-to-be-discovered formulation will one day prove successful.

The point at which an analyst decides it is time to abandon an initially promising hypothesis is a matter of personal judgement, and we cannot fault continued efforts to account for verb number in formal terms. But at the risk of sounding churlish, we do object to the promotion of verb agreement from a tentative hypothesis to an established fact of English *in advance* of the formal success that promotion demands. This promotion is all the more objectionable when the 'fact' of verb agreement is then cited as evidence (e.g., Newmeyer 1983, Smith and Wilson 1980) of the correctness and viability of the very theoretical framework in which it has *yet to earn* a legitimate place.

While the notion of subject-verb agreement has not received the kind of critical scrutiny we believe it deserves, the possibility that agreement rules might be serving some legitimate communicative function has been entertained. In his work on verb prefixes in Achenese, Lawler (1975) searches for an explanation beyond a formal one, and clearly sees verb number and person as something more than 'a meaningless grammatical contrivance'. In Achenese the verb agrees with its overt subject in active sentences and with its underlying logical subject (normally not expressed) in passive sentences. Furthermore, although the verb in relative clauses (whose head noun can only be the grammatical subject) is usually left unmarked, it bears agreement morphology when the verb is passive. Lawler proposes that both these distributional facts have a functional explanation in terms of the information contributed by the 'agreement' morphology to the comprehension process. The verb prefixes supply information not overtly available to the hearer in the surface morphology of the sentence. Lawler concludes that the distribution of the verbal morphology in Achenese is best understood in terms of a cognitive model of language.

> In a cognitive model, the hearer continually makes 'guesses' as to the meaning of the sentence as it is being processed, and revises these guesses when further information is presented that changes the initial guesses. This has the benefit of taking into account real-time processing, and putting a premium on the signals that allow the hearer to decode the sentence properly.
>
> (Lawler 1975:406).

Langacker (1988) provides a sketch of what such a cognitive model might look like. Against the Chomskian thesis of an autonomous syntax, Langacker proposes a symbolic alternative in which all morphological units bear semantic content. Though Langacker makes only one passing reference to English verb number, he recognizes its occasionally distinctive value and argues, as we will in Chapter 8, that the redundant use of grammatical morphology does not rob it of its meaning.

While many significant points of agreement exist between cognitive grammar and sign-based theory, they differ on one important issue. Cognitive grammar preserves the Chomskian equation between the structure of language and the structure of the mind (diverging, to be sure, on the essential nature of that structure). Sign-based theory, on the other hand, sees language as a facilitating communicative instrument rather than an all-encompassing cognitive system in its own right. This means it does not initially assume a perfect match – cognitive isomorphism – between the categories of language and the categories of thought (as perceived through introspection). Discrepancies, such as those inherent in spanned oppositions, will naturally arise because of the competing evolutionary pressures on an instrument that must be at once versatile and learnable.

A treatment of verb number more congenial with our own is that of Pollard and Sag (1988). Pollard and Sag propose an information-based (rather than derivation-based) approach to grammatical agreement. They too reject verb number as purely syntactic in nature and see the referential parameter associated with the subject phrase as the critical determining factor. In their view 'two elements which participate in an agreement relation specify partial information about a single linguistic object' (p. 237). Collective nouns, for example, 'are lexically marked to introduce parameters unspecified for number' (p. 250). The verb then assigns an agreement value to the subject.

This proposal goes a long way in explaining examples [54]–[75]. But as in Lapointe, the crux of the problem has again been shifted to the grammatical characterization of the noun phrase functioning as subject, and collective nouns constitute only a fraction of the problem. Since Pollard and Sag apparently still entertain the feasibility of a formal treatment of verb number, it seems fair to adopt a wait-and-see attitude until their formal machinery is firmly in place.

5.9 Speaker Error

One legitimate basis for setting aside some of the apparent counter-evidence to verb agreement is that of 'performance' error. Under conditions of actual language use speakers and writers are attending to a multiplicity of factors, only one of which is grammatical correctness. Thus occasional mistakes would be expected in the exercise of an arbitrary convention like verb agreement. By the same token, this phenomenon should be confined to contexts that evidence some kind of formal complexity which would trigger such mistakes.

[80]   Over at RCA, there has been admirable sensitivity to matters of repertory and program length in Compact Disc reissues, and the firm's *promise* of 12 CDs a month from the Red Seal vault *are causing* a lot of mouths to water.

(Theodore Libbey, *High Fidelity*)

[81]   A study committee of the Southern Association of Colleges and Schools said new *requirements* of belief in biblical inerrancy *appears* to have been arbitrarily imposed and responsibility of faculty curtailed.

(The Associated Press)

For [80] and [81], it would appear that the writers were simply losing track of the identity of the grammatical subject and making the verb 'agree' with an intervening noun. The Speaker Error hypothesis predicts, then, that speakers will tend to err where intervening material separates the head noun of the subject phrase from its verb.

Prediction 1:   There will be more agreement failures when intervening material separates the head noun of the subject phrase from its verb than in the absence of intervening material.

In testing this prediction, one must take care that the Focus Number hypothesis could not also explain the results. For if the intervening material has the semantic effect of making the entity in Focus span the opposition of number, then the present analysis would predict occasional 'disagreement' as well, as in [82].

[82]   The remainder of the paintings *were* to be lent to the Los Angeles County Museum.
(*Morning Edition*, National Public Radio)

Since the words *remainder* and *paintings* both describe what is in Focus, and are categorized with contrasting Entity Number meanings, the Focus Number hypothesis also predicts occasional 'disagreement'. Thus the Speaker-Error hypothesis must be construed as applying to formal complexity that does not also entail semantic complexity of a kind that creates a spanned opposition.

Since *of* often links words in a quasi-coreferential relation as in [82], all sentences with subject phrases of the structural types *N(sg) + of + N(pl)* and *N(pl) + of + N(sg)* will be excluded from the test of Prediction 1. While this eliminates [80] and [81], which are undoubtedly errors, it does not unduly handicap the Speaker Error hypothesis because if it is merely a question of the language user's losing track of the head noun of the subject phrase, then *any* intervening material should occasionally provoke such lapses. Prediction 1 thus predicts occasional agreement failure in sentences like [83] but not in [84].

[83]   *The group* involved in these reports came and went from my house in broad daylight, at least twice, on Saturday afternoon, and apparently *were* not observed by the press organization in question.
(Gary Hart, *The New York Times*)

[84]   *The group was* afraid of retribution from local authorities if it went to the state attorney general's office.
(Janet Baker and Howard Mann, *Newsweek*)

Prediction 1 will be tested on a body of data drawn from natural language use. A description of the procedure by which it was gathered appears in Chapter 7. For the moment, we note only that the procedure involved mechanically selecting structurally matched pairs of sentences from the same source. Tables 5.2, 5.3 and 5.4 show the results of the test on sentences with singular subjects, plural subjects and subject phrases comprised of two singular nouns conjoined by *and*.

TABLE 5.2   Morphologically singular noun subject: relation between intervening material and agreement failure

	– *Intervening material*	+ *Intervening material*	
+ Agreement	(56%) 105	(44%) 81	
– Agreement	(50%) 51	(50%) 50	$X^2 = 0.94$
			non-significant

TABLE 5.3   Morphologically plural noun subject: relation between intervening material and agreement failure

	– *Intervening material*	+ *Intervening material*	
+ Agreement	(69%) 59	(31%) 27	
– Agreement	(65%) 51	(35%) 27	$X^2 = 0.19$
			non-significant

TABLE 5.4   Singular nouns conjoined with *and* as subject: relation between intervening material and agreement failure

	– *Intervening material*	+ *Intervening material*	
+ Agreement	(73%) 86	(27%) 32	
– Agreement	(43%) 51	(57%) 67	$X^2 = 21.32$
			$p < 0.001$

The Speaker Error hypothesis receives support only from compound subject sentences, where double (57 per cent vs. 27 per cent) the agreement failures occurred where there was intervening material separating the subject phrase from its verb. The small favouring in Tables 5.2 and 5.3 proves to be statistically insignificant.

If intervening material makes people lose track of the identity of the grammatical subject, then the more intervening material there is, the more likely it is that mistakes should occur.

Prediction 2:   The amount of intervening material should, on
                 average, be greater when the verb disagrees
                 with its grammatical subject than when it
                 agrees.

Tables 5.5, 5.6 and 5.7 present the results of the test of
Prediction 2 on the examples in the right-hand column of Tables
5.2, 5.3 and 5.4.

TABLE 5.5 Morphologically singular subjects: mean number of words
           between head noun of subject and its verb.

Mean number of words when verb disagrees:	5.72	(N = 50)
Mean number of words when verb agrees:	3.89	(N = 81)
Mean difference:	+ 1.83	non-significant

TABLE 5.6 Morphologically plural subjects: mean number of words
           between head noun of subject and its verb: (N = 54)

Mean number of words when verb disagrees:	5.33	(N = 27)
Mean number of words when verb agrees:	4.67	(N = 27)
Mean difference:	+ 0.66	non-significant

TABLE 5.7 Singular nouns conjoined with *and* as subject: mean number
           of words between second noun and the verb:

Mean number of word when verb disagrees:	4 10	(N = 67)
Mean number of words when verb agrees:	4.09	(N = 32)
Mean difference:	+ 0.01	non-significant

While the differences in means are all in the predicted directions,
none attain the level of statistical significance. Chance would
produce the results in Table 5.5 one time in four, and the results
of Tables 5.6 and 5.7 are considerably closer to chance levels.

The Speaker-Error hypothesis might take a more sophisticated
form in which intervening material would show the strongest
effect in contexts where the subject phrase itself contains both a
singular and a plural noun. Now the sentences excluded from the
test of Prediction 1 are the most suitable testing ground, namely,
those with subjects of the structural type *Noun (sg) + of + Noun
(pl)*. (The basis for excluding these data from the earlier test no
longer holds since the spanned opposition factor is now a
constant.)

TABLE 5.8   *Noun(sg)* + *of* + *noun(pl)* subjects: mean number of words between the noun(sg) of the subject phrase and the verb:[8]

Mean number of words when verb disagrees:	4.72	(N = 92)
Mean number of words when verb agrees:	5.11	(N = 92)
Mean difference:	− 0.39	non-significant

Table 5.8 shows that when the verb disagrees with the grammatical head of the subject phrase, the mean number of words separating the two is actually slightly *less* than when the verb agrees, though again at a chance level.

We conclude from these data that while individual examples such as [80] and [81] clearly show that speakers do occasionally err in their choice of verb number (just as they occasionally err in all other linguistic choices), the statistical support for the Speaker-Error hypothesis is too weak to permit the body of examples [57]–[75] to be excluded from the scope of responsibility of any proposed rule of subject-verb agreement in English.

Furthermore, in Tables 5.2 and 5.3 the majority of agreement failures do not involve syntagmatic complexity. In [57] and [58] no intervening material separates the verb from its subject, and *panel* and *family* are just as clearly morphological singulars as *boy*.

Note that when the Speaker-Error hypothesis is construed so as to differentiate it from the Focus Number hypothesis, no appeal can be made to the referential or cognitive plurality of *panel* and *family*. Given the view of the verb affixes as semantically empty, and an agreement rule stated in terms of the grammatical number of the subject, there should be no correlation between agreement errors and semantic factors. Yet, as is well known, words like *family*, *panel* and *faculty* often occur with a plural verb while *boy* never does.

Notes

1. The article also provides an example of the Focus opposition for Occurrences that introduce direct quotations.

   'I was the one to beat out there and I felt a lot of pressure to finish,' *said Mittleman*, who was clocked in 12 hours 56 minutes 33.6 seconds.

   Mittleman, who led throughout, *added*, 'I don't run too well in the rain. . .

   While Mittleton is in Focus with respect to both 'saying' and 'adding', here he is being mentioned simply to identify the quotation. Diver (personal communication) reports there is considerable variation among writers as to the principle of choice in this circumscribed situation. Some use the Focus opposition to imply the relative importance of the quotation to the discourse. It is hard to argue such a contrast in this case. But one can point to the fact that *Middleton . . . added* (= MORE FOCUS) occurs before the quotation in sentence initial position, a place of natural discourse prominence, while *said Mittleton* (= LESS FOCUS) does not.

2. When *Occurrence . . . P* is used with direct quotations the quotation itself serves to disambiguate the word-order signal. Moreover, a locative would usually not suit the message since a new Participant is not being introduced.

3. The one exception is *be*, whose extreme imprecision, as noted in Section 1.6, is often not compatible with the implication of cognitive salience that accompanies this more precise categorization.

4. This also represents a generalization to the third person of the communicative strategies that must be employed in the first and second person, where *Occurrence -$\emptyset_2$* is not available due to its meaning THIRD PERSON (in Focus).

5. In Diver's analysis *Occurrence -$\emptyset_2$* stands in direct opposition to *Occurrence -ed$_2$* (homonymous with *Occurrence -ed$_1$* = PAST) which bears the meaning DOUBT, LOWER PROBABILITY (e.g., If I *had* the time, I would go). The grammatical opposition between HIGHER PROBABILITY (*Occurrence -$\emptyset_2$*) and LOWER PROBABILITY (*Occurrence -ed$_2$*) is always exploited with the modals: He *can go* vs. he *could go*. If *can go* is an instance of *Occurrence -$\emptyset_2$*, as Diver proposes, this provides the systemic explanation for the lack of exploitation of the Focus Number System with the modals: the Focus Number opposition is not exploited with the modals because *another* grammatical opposition is being exploited, and their signalling structure is such that the values in the two systems cannot be combined. This is a better solution to the problem of [44] than the provisional, stop-gap one we offered.

6. In this calculation seven instances of *Occurrence -$\emptyset$* whose entities in Focus were described by lexical items conjoined by *and* were omitted.

7. Radford later calls this an informal rule and appeals to its inadequacy as support for an abstract level of structure underlying sentences whose grammatical subject does not precede the verb. Our point here is that Radford assumes that an agreement rule of some type exists in English, the only issue being its form.

8. A separate body of such sentences in which the verb agrees was gathered for this test since the original corpus contained too few instances.

Chapter 6

The Focus Number opposition

The data presented in Chapter 5 stand as strong *prima facie* evidence against a rule of subject-verb agreement in English because: (1) the verbal inflection is not in accord with the grammatical number of the subject; (2) there are insufficient grounds to exclude such data as instances of speaker error; and (3) the examples do not exhibit any unique structural characteristics by which they could be *excluded* from the rule's legitimate domain of application. At the same time, such usage is no more than suggestive evidence in favour of the present analysis. For while the examples illustrate the combinatory freedom of *Occurrence -s* and *-0* that is the hallmark of freely-chosen expressive units, they fall short of establishing that the Focus Number meanings ONE and MORE THAN ONE actually motivate the choice. To establish that fact, a different kind of datum is required.

An important conclusion reached in Chapter 3 (and underscored in Chapter 4) was that the two meanings of the Entity Number System function in terms of their relational opposition. The Focus Number meanings function in the same relational way. The methodological consequence is that in testing the Focus Number System one must test the opposition between its two meanings, not each meaning in turn. The Chapter 5 data are less than ideal in this respect because the entities in Focus are too disparate to illustrate the Focus Number opposition clearly. The hypothesis demands demonstration through contrasts like those on the animal questionnaire: pairs of examples produced by the *same* speaker or writer and which involve the *same* entity in Focus, but which exhibit *contrasting* Focus Number meanings.

The present chapter is devoted to an examination of such data. In each pair of examples the entities in Focus are expressed with closely comparable phrases, all having the same word as grammatical head. In each case the contrast between *Occurrence* *-s* and *-∅* reflects a difference in the message regarding the relative 'oneness' of the entity in Focus. This systemic consistency is intended to become repetitious to the reader. Our aim is to illustrate the open-ended range of substantive message contrasts that manifest this relational consistency. Since each example pair is produced by the same person and drawn from the same text, the language user's idiolect and stylistic register are eliminated as possible variables.

6.1 Exploitation of the Focus Number Opposition

[1a]   My *family have been* prominent, well-to-do people in this Middle Western city for three generations.

[1b]   Her *family is* one aunt about a thousand years old.

(F. Scott Fitzgerald, *The Great Gatsby*)

Family is a word whose meaning contains conceptual components of singularity and plurality in equal measure. Like *people*, it designates a referential plurality of human beings which is conceived as a single social unit. Spanning the opposition of number as it does, *family* is a word with which speakers might be expected to exploit the Focus Number opposition for expressive effect.

In both [1a] and [1b] only a single 'family' is being referred to, so the stem *family* is categorized as ONE by the Entity Number System in both. However in [1a] the 'family' is being equated with a referential plurality ('well-to-do people') whereas in [1b] it is being equated with a single person ('one aunt'). Since the grammatical substance of the Focus Number System is the number of the entity in Focus *with respect to the Occurrence* – which in [1] involves states of being that differ numerically – Focus Number reflects this difference of predication; in [1a] *have been* categorizes the entity in Focus as MORE THAN ONE and in [1b] *is* categorizes it as ONE.

[2]   Superficially they were opposites. Shi Peipu's *family was* aristocratic; Bernard's, from a small town in Brittany, *were* merchants.   (Joyce Wadler, *People*)

In [2] 'family' is again characterized in two ways: as 'aristocratic' and as 'merchants'. The word *aristocratic* being unmarked for grammatical number, downplays the referential plurality and allows the social-unit component of *family* to predominate; accordingly, the entity in Focus is categorized as ONE. The word *merchants*, on the other hand, highlights the referential plurality of *family*, and the entity in Focus is categorized as MORE THAN ONE.

In both [1] and [2] the entity in Focus is explicitly recharacterized lexically in contrasting ways. The contrast in [3] is more subtle, but still involves Occurrences that differ in the degree to which they underscore the referential plurality of *family*.

[3a] The Kent *family* of Bountiful, Utah, *have chosen* to remind themselves – and the world – of the death of their daughter Debi every hour of every day; their porch light has never been turned off since Nov 8, 1974, when Debi vanished. 'In our house,' says Debi's mother, Belva, 52, 'the last person home always turned off the light'.

[3b] Her *family* still *looks back* fondly at the little girl who once dreamed of a career in ballet, and those memories shine as brightly as the porch light.
                    (Pete Axthelm and Michael Ryan, *People*)

In [3a] the Kent family are involved in the activity of 'choosing to remind themselves' whereas in [3b] they are involved in the activity of 'looking back fondly'. The referents of the word *family* are, in reality, acting as independent agents in both cases. But [3a] underscores this fact linguistically with the word *themselves* whereas [3b] does not. The Focus Number contrast registers this difference in the momentary cognitive salience of referential number in the respective Occurrences.

The word *faculty* spans the opposition of number in a way similar to *family*, referring to an aggregate of individuals who share a common professional identity.

[4a] Hence, departments on different campuses associated with particular disciplines often resemble one another in the way the *faculty organizes* its work, the methods of training students, and the curriculum.

[4b] Some believe that *faculty have* less reason for involvement in university business because they play very different roles on campus, have different sets of interests, and are more preoccupied by individual professional pursuits.
                    (Richard Levinson, *Academe*)

In [4a] the categorization of 'faculty' as ONE (*organizes*) is echoed in the phrase *its work*, while in [4b] its categorization as MORE THAN ONE (*have*) is echoed in the following clause *because they play* . . . However an appeal to pronominal number is at best only a partial justification for the Focus Number choice because it simply shifts the locus of the problem to another word. The ultimate explanation for both sets of choices is to be found in the fact that the notion 'faculty' is categorized as ONE (by both *organizes* and *its*) as part of a message about the way whole departments resemble each other, while categorized as MORE THAN ONE (by both *have* and *they*) as part of a message about the way individual faculty members differ from each other.

The same confluence of structural and thematic factors is evident in [5].

[5]   There are a number of other new faculty members who have been appointed as State of New Jersey professors, with special funds to encourage excellence provided by the state. Other long-time Rutgers professors of similar distinction are heading new units or chairing special projects. Together through their teaching and research, all the Rutgers *faculty create* the university's reputation.

The university can provide the physical setting and encourage a climate of innovation but the *faculty shapes* its own research and teaching tasks. In this regard, mention should be made of the creation in 1985 of an Academic Forum to rethink the character and content of a liberal arts education.

(Edward Bloustein, foreword to a university report)

Immediate support for the Focus Number contrast comes from the contrasting pronominal number within the same clause: *their teaching and research* vs. *its own research and teaching tasks*. But again, those choices were themselves made in response to the contrasting discourse focus of the paragraphs in which they appear. The first paragraph of [5] focuses on individual faculty members, while the second paragraph shifts its focus to the institution in which a faculty is an organizational unit.

Example [5] should recall examples [23] and [24] in Chapter 2, where *persons* was employed in a paragraph dealing with the legal status of individuals while *people* was employed in a passage about retirement communities. The fact that global expressive intent would affect lexical choice is hardly surprising. So too for grammatical categories such as Entity Number that have acknowledged semantic value. The analytical bridge between those two relatively transparent instances of expressive choice and the more subtle deployment of the Focus Number System was provided in Chapter 4. Chapter 4 established that some people categorize aggregates of animals as either ONE or MORE THAN ONE simply to reflect the relative cognitive salience of the animals as separate individuals, as in A vs. B contrast below.

[A] Just as the sun set, three *rabbits* cautiously entered the garden and began to nibble the lettuce.

[B] Returning to the woody undergrowth, Jake found his traps had caught a half dozen *rabbit0*, enough for his hungry companions back at the house.

The descriptive precision and vividness of *cautiously entered* and *nibbled* in A imply a greater interest in the animals as separate individuals than do the two predications about the animals in B of 'being caught in a trap' and 'being enough'. With the referential plurality of *rabbit* firmly established by *three* and *a half dozen*, the choice of Entity Number is free to comment upon its differing cognitive salience.

Examples [1–5] show the same expressive parameter at work, but now it is the Focus Number System that assumes responsibility. In [4b] the inherently collective nature of the word *faculty* makes the Entity Number System an inappropriate tool for distinguishing between degrees of cognitive salience; (*faculties* would suggest that multiple groups were involved). So the Focus Number opposition was employed in its stead, to the same communicative effect.

[6a] and [6b], produced by the same speaker on different occasions, explicitly recharacterize the entity in Focus in contrasting ways.

[6a] This afternoon our *panel are* three male singers.

[6b] Our *panel* of opera experts today *is* certainly a lively one.
       (Edward Downes, Texaco Metropolitan Opera Quiz)

Again, the Focus Number choice reflects the contrasting predications made about the entity in Focus, not the grammatical number of the word *panel*.

Examples [7a–d] are drawn from an article about the success enjoyed by the British musical *Les Miserables* on foreign stages.

[7a]   Hugo's novel has a large readership in Japan, which is
         one reason Toho is spending 1 billion yen to do the
         show. The 55-member *cast*, chosen by Caird, Schonberg
         and Boublil from an initial 11,000 applicants, *ranges*
         from experienced actors like Sakae Takita and Takeshi
         Kaga (alternating in the roles of Jean Valjean and
         Javert) to students and secretaries.

[7b]   Colm Wilkinson, the forceful Irishman who plays
         Hugo's central character, ex-convict Jean Valjean,
         remembers that when the English *cast was* first
         assembled by Nunn and Caird, the directors gave the
         performers research projects relating to France in the
         period of Hugo's story – the 1830s.

[7c]   In many senses the American *cast* of 'Les Miserables'
         are more truly the children of Victor Hugo than the
         English cast.

[7d]   The American *cast* (only Wilkinson and the adorable
         Frances Ruffelle are from the original London com-
         pany) – youthful and young veteran performers like
         Terrence Mann as the fanatical manhunter Inspector
         Javert, Randy Graff as the wretched prostitute Fantine,
         Leo Burmester and Jennifer Butt as the viciously
         clownish Thenardiers, David Bryant and Judy Kuhn as
         the young lovers Marius and Cosette, Michael Maguire
         as the rebel leader Enjolras, Braden Danner as the
         intrepid street kid Gavroche – *perform* with the fierce
         gusto of the children of Victor Hugo (mixed with the
         euphoria of actors who've made it into the cast of a
         superhit).

                                        (Jack Kroll, *Newsweek*)

In [7a] and [7b] the Occurrences in which *cast* is the entity in
Focus both underscore its conceptual status as a single body.
Only the cast as an aggregate can 'range'; no single member
individually 'ranges from an experienced actor to a student or
secretary'. Similarly, no single member is individually 'assembled',
only the cast as a whole. Accordingly the Focus Number System
categorizes the Occurrences of 'ranging' and 'being assembled' as
involving only ONE entity in Focus.

Both [7c] and [7d], on the other hand, make predications of
cast that highlight its conceptual status as a grouping of separate
individuals. 'Being . . . the child(ren) of Victor Hugo' and
'performing with the fierce gusto of the children of Victor Hugo'
are true of each member of the cast considered individually.

Accordingly, the Focus Number System categorizes these two Occurrences as involving MORE THAN ONE entity in Focus.

[8a]   For 12 years, the *couple has refused* to pay federal income taxes to protest US military policy. But now the Internal Revenue Service wants the $23,478.31 they say the *couple owes* the government.

[8b]   The *couple* stopped paying federal income taxes in 1977, and *have remained* self-employed so they would not have taxes withheld by an employer. Corner works as a landscape architect and Kehler is a public policy researcher and consultant.

(B. J. Roche, *The Boston Sunday Globe*)

In [8a] the couple is involved in the Occurrences of 'refusing (to pay federal income taxes)' and 'owing (the government)'. Presumably the couple files a joint return, so the 'refusing' and 'owing' are done as a collective act. These two Occurrences, then, highlight the 'couple' as a single conjugal unit and so are categorized as having only ONE entity in Focus.

In [8b] on the other hand, 'remaining self-employed' is a predication that applies to the husband and wife individually. The following sentence specifying the self-employment of each underscores their status as separate individuals with respect to employment. Accordingly, the entity in Focus in the Occurrence of 'remaining (self-employed)' is categorized as MORE THAN ONE.

[9a]   There *was* a *couple* who yearned for a baby but disappointment seemed their lot. The wife suffered two early-pregnancy miscarriages followed by three barren years.

[9b]   The *couple*, who *were* in their early 30's, contacted adoption agencies, which declined to interview them.

(Ilene Barth, *The Recorder*)

In [9a] the categorization of *couple* as ONE has no contextual support within the clause *there was a couple*; but in the following clause the pair is described as sharing an emotion that underscores their status as a conjugal unit: 'yearning for a baby'. In [9b] a predication unrelated to their conjugal status is made about the two people: 'being in their thirties'. The MORE THAN ONE of *were* reflects the introduction of a message component that now underscores their individuality.

6.2 Category Shift

The systemic reason the Entity Number and Focus Number choices can diverge in this fashion without producing incoherence is that the two systems are actually talking about slightly different things. The grammatical substance of the Entity Number System is NUMBER OF ENTITIES described by the attached lexical stem; its meanings relate directly to the expressive potential of the word to which they are attached. The grammatical substance of the Focus Number System, on the other hand, is NUMBER OF ENTITIES IN FOCUS with respect to the Occurrence described by the attached lexical stem. Its meanings concern the entity in Focus *as it relates to the Occurrence*, not the idiosyncratic expressive potential of the particular word describing that entity. This means the Focus Number System offers speakers the opportunity for a fresh assessment. And this time it is the lexical stem inflected for Entity Number (together with any associated material) whose interpretation is pushed one way or another so as to bring it into line with its evolving status within the larger communication.

The phenomenon of category shift was established early in Chapter 2. Because Entity Number is assessed in terms of the conceptual category imposed by the attached lexical stem, the counting category shifts from word to word e.g., *player* vs. *team*; *person* vs. *people*. (It was this shift of categories along a *paradigmatic* axis that stymied Bloomfield's attempt to abstract across the class of plural nouns and come up with a single notional constant as a 'class meaning'.)

When the Entity and Focus Number Systems are deployed jointly, there exists the possibility for a *syntagmatic* category shift. In choosing Focus Number, speakers are building upon that part of the message already established by the expression identified as $P_{(1)}$, further refining it rather than simply echoing it. In example [1], the notion of 'family' is reshaped by the Focus meanings MORE THAN ONE and ONE as part of its conceptual metamorphosis into 'well-to-do people' and 'one aunt'. Since the expressive range of the lexical stem has already been partitioned once by the Entity Number System, the range within which the Focus Number opposition can operate is smaller and the effect is usually more subtle.

The systemically-mandated role of the Occurrence in the choice of Focus Number is strikingly illustrated by the word *number* itself.

[10a]   The *number* of professional women who have access to Sigourney Weaver's wardrobe *is* nil.

[10b]   But an increasing *number* of professionals *seem* to be going the way of Tess McGill, ravamping their hair, makeup and wardrobe, hoping to be taken more seriously in the business world.

(Patricia Leigh Brown, *The New York Times*)

The phrases describing the entities in Focus are closely comparable in a conventional structural parsing. More to the point, they both span the opposition of number conceptually by virtue of containing distinct components categorized with contrasting Entity Number meanings: *number0*; *women* and *professionals*; just the situation where the Focus Number System might be expected to reveal its independent expressive value.

[10a] and [10b] differ markedly, though, with respect to the nature of the Occurrence. 'Being nil' is arithmetic in nature and clearly applies to a number, while 'seeming to be going the way of Tess McGill' (i.e., revamping hair, make-up and wardrobe) puts a human being in Focus. Each demands a different kind of counting category, and the writer has signalled this category shift in the choice of Focus Number. The ONE of *is* highlights the notional component to which its predication most directly applies ('number') and the MORE THAN ONE of *seem0* highlights the component to which it most directly applies ('professionals').

To be sure, a formal sentence-based treatment might well choose to posit a covert structural difference between the two subject phrases to which the verb inflection could then be portrayed as a mechanical response: *number* functions as logical head in *the number of professional women* and as a kind of quantifier in *a number of professionals*. But the conceptual status of the word *number* is something a reader realizes only in retrospect, well into the sentence. And the grammatical number of *is* and *seem0* play a significant role in hastening that realization. Sign-based analysis aims at capturing the real-time functional role of linguistic signs in the actual communicative process, not an after-the-fact logical analysis of the communication as a whole. As for the differing logical status of *number* itself, both are encompassed by the word's inherent semantic value so long as the word is treated as a single linguistic sign designating an arithmetic figure.

[11a]   But the *number* of people making real changes *seems*

slight, even in places where information about AIDS is readily available.

[11b]   A growing *number* of sexually active heterosexuals, especially in cities with a substantial caseload of AIDS patients, *are considering* taking the test.

(Katie Leishman, *The Atlantic*)

Again the Occurrences contrast with respect to the kind of entities they place in Focus; 'seeming slight' applies to a number and 'considering taking a test' applies to people. Accordingly, Focus Number is reckoned in terms of 'number' in [11a] and 'heterosexuals' in [11b].

Departing momentarily from our format, example [12] parallels [11] except for the fact that the lexical heads of the P phrases are not identical.

[12]   But the larger demographic picture suggests a compensating trend. Even though a growing *fraction* of males in the crime-prone years *are* minorities and low income, the total *number* of males in those years *is dropping*.

(David Bloom and Neil Bennett, *The New Republic*)

The Occurrence of 'being minorities' directly involves 'males', not a 'fraction', while the Occurrence of 'dropping' directly involves a 'number', not 'males'.

This same difference in the nature of the Occurrence is evident in the *number* examples from Celce-Murcia and Larson-Freeman (C-M and L-F) cited in Chapter 5. Yet they make no mention of it. The factor they see as critical reveals the way one's theoretical commitments guide one's observations.

A *number of* takes the plural, but *the number of* takes the singular.
A number of students have dropped that course.
The number of students in this school is 2,000.

(Celce-Murcia and Larsen-Freeman 1983:38)

Confronted by clear evidence against a rule of subject-verb agreement, C-M and L-F seize on the one overt structural difference between the two subject phrases, the difference in article. Apparently the damage done to the notion of subject-verb agreement is mitigated, in their eyes, if the verbal inflection can at least be linked to some other element within the subject phrase, if not to the grammatical number of its overt lexical head.

In fairness to C-M and L-F, the difference in article does relate
in a principled way to the verb inflection indirectly; (definite) *the*
reflects the status of the word *number* as 'logical head', while
(indefinite) *a* reflects its status as an indefinite quantifier. But in
order to draw that connection, C-M and L-F would have to
concede that the phrases *a number of* and *the number of* are
grammatically analysable into their component linguistic parts:
that is, that *the*, *a*, *number*, and *of* are all functioning just the way
they do everywhere else. C-M and L-F's treatment, on the other
hand, suggests the two phrases are best regarded as fixed
expressions. But then the correlation of each with the inflection
of the verb should hold 100 per cent of the time, which is not the
case.

[13a] Most startling was the fact that *the increased number of
       cancers were* occurring at radiation exposure levels well
       below the official limit of 5 rads per year.
                                   (Brian Jacobs, *Greenpeace*)
[13b] Male attitudes also differ markedly by generation.
       According to sociologist Fujiwara, *an increasing num-
       ber of men* under 30 now *approves* of women working
       in a 'non-traditional' job, 'if only because the second
       income has become so important in urban, expensive
       Japan.'
                                    (Bill Powell, *Newsweek*)

In [13a] the MORE THAN ONE of *were occurring* follows the
earlier rationale because it is an Occurrence that most directly
involves individual 'cancers', not a single 'number'. That same
rationale would predict MORE THAN ONE for [13b] as well.
But in [13b] there is a competing factor. While the Occurrence of
'approving' applies most directly to *men*, the larger context
reflects a sociological perspective. The ONE of *approves*
underscores that fact that the larger discourse is concerned with
the behaviour of the 'men' as a group.
     Example [14] involves a similer competition among principles
of choice.

[14a] The *majority* of early elementary teachers *are* women.
[14b] The *majority* of mathematics taught in the elementary
       grades *is* of the ritual type because the concrete
       concepts of addition, subtraction and multiplication
       formulate the curriculum.
            (Audrey Fleming, term paper, Rutgers University)

The two Occurrences of 'being (women)' and 'being (of the ritual type)' apply most directly to 'teachers' and 'mathematics' respectively, and the word *majority* functions logically to quantify the scope of the two predications.

While *mathematics* and *teachers* are both categorized as MORE THAN ONE, the communicative purpose is different. The *Entity -s* of *teachers* is a straightforward indication of referential plurality, whereas the *Entity -s* of *mathematics* (as proposed in Chapter 2) is simply there to steer the hearer toward an entity interpretation of the stem *mathematic*.

Though mathematics does involve several branches, the cognitive salience of its individual components is less than that of *women*, which refers to a plurality of physically discrete human beings. The Focus Number contrast registers this difference in the relative 'oneness' of the entity in Focus.

Examples [13] and [14] show that neither the article nor the distinction between structural head and quantifier can be raised to the level of governing principle because neither proves to be categorically decisive.

Example [15] is the transcribed text of a political commentary. It contains three instances of *a majority* and one of *a plurality*, all functioning as structural head of the phrase describing the entity in Focus. Yet two are categorized as ONE and two as MORE THAN ONE by the Focus Number System.

[15]   By now, Dukakis is a familiar figure to four out of every five voters. That makes him quite a well-known figure indeed. One supposedly big negative, that he's too liberal, that's rejected by fifty-two to thirty-four per cent among a cross-section of likely voters nationwide.

In fact, a polling reveals that he has a number of strong positives going for him. For example, by three to one, voters of all parties admire the job he's done in Massachusetts on the economy and on controlling government spending. By two-to-one, most voters view him as a firm and resolute executive who would know how to get things done in the White House. By three-to-one, a *majority admire* him as the first generation son of Greek immigrants who worked hard to be a success.

There is one major negative about Dukakis. A fifty-nine to thirty-four per cent *majority worries* that he's lacking in foreign policy experience that a candidate for president should have. But the bottom line with the voters is impressive. By fifty-eight to twenty-seven per cent, a *majority agree* with the claim that Dukakis has the personality and leadership qualities that a president should have.

Even most Republicans feel that way about him. When the same cross-section of all voters is asked an identical question about Vice President Bush, a much closer fifty to forty-seven per cent *plurality thinks* he has the same qualifications. In short, Dukakis appears to have deeply impressed the American electorate, and he seems to be electable, at least for now. The politicians endorsing him are just now beginning to catch up with the voters.

(Lou Harris, *Morning Edition*, National Public Radio [henceforth NPR], 2 March 1988)

The Occurrences of 'admiring' 'worrying' 'agreeing' and 'thinking' all put human beings in Focus; but they are described by the words *majority* and *plurality* that characterize them as singular arithmetic quantities. Conceptually, then, the entities in Focus span the opposition of number.

The decisive factor in the choice of Focus Number is the presence of information within the P_1 phrase bolstering the numerical aspect of the entity in Focus. In two instances, *majority* and *plurality* are modified by phrases that specify their precise arithmetic values: *a fifty-nine to thirty-four per cent majority*; *a much closer fifty to forty-seven per cent plurality*. This contextual elaboration serves to increase the cognitive salience of the semantic categories 'majority' and 'plurality' in the evolving message. Without such specifying information, the balance tips in favour of the conceptualization implied by the Occurrences themselves, 'human being'. The Focus Number meanings reflect this shift in counting categories by reckoning the first two instances as ONE and the latter two as MORE THAN ONE.

Example [15] recalls the Salinger passage from Chapter 4 in which Holden Caulfield briefly describes a museum exhibit as containing *deer∅*, but later switches to *deers* when he elaborates his description: *with their pretty antlers and their pretty skinny legs*. In [15] the contextual contrast is more subtle, for it actually involves the weighting of information rather than the amount; in the case of both *a majority admire∅* and *a majority agree∅*, their arithmetic values are specified elsewhere in the sentence. But that information is conveyed in an initial adverbial phrase, not as a linguistic component of the P_1 phrase itself.

6.3 Generality of Application

Examples [1]–[15] have involved a handful of collective nouns and expressions acknowledged as problematic by traditional treatments of verb number. If the deviations from grammatical agreement were confined to a fixed set of words and phrases, as some reference grammars suggest, then our uncompromising rejection of the apologies they offer might seem unduly hardnosed. The most effective data in favour of the present analysis, then, will be examples showing the Focus Number meanings employed in a free and productive way with words and expressions which cannot be circumscribed structurally or semantically.

Just such a circumscription is, needless to say, an absolute necessity if formal determination were to be claimed. A formal rule of subject-verb agreement must embody a statement of both (1) the formal relation itself (i.e., the matching subject and verb number morphology), and (2) its domain of application (i.e., a structural description of the class of sentences over which it operates). Without the latter one does not have a formal rule, merely an empirical generalization of a distributional skewing observable in running text (Gross 1979:863).

[16]   Although Hoy and Lortie's *work indicate* that student teaching is a period of socialization, Sack and Harrington's (1982) *work indicates* that it is likely that student teachers will vary in the stage of socialization they have reached by the end of their student teaching experience.
                                        (Michele W. Hummel, Rutgers University
                                         EdD dissertation)

Work can refer to a body of scholarly research as well as individual exemplars. The ONE of *work0* suggests that both instances of the word should be interpreted in a collective way here. However the first instance is categorized for Focus Number as MORE THAN ONE and the second as ONE.

No linguistic support for this shift can be found in the immediate context. But Hummel's bibliography lists two books by Hoy and Lortie, and only one by Sack and Harrington. In the pages preceding [16] the two books by Hoy and Lortie are discussed separately. The MORE THAN ONE of *indicate0* reflects the plurality of the actual published form of Hoy and Lortie's work while ONE of *indicates* reflects the singular published form of Sack and Harrington's work.

Example [17] comes from a first-hand account of a couple undergoing fertility counselling.

[17a] I join her at the microscope. 'Want to see?' she asks. I bend my head, adjust the eyepiece and the focus and Jeff's *sperm come* into view, exactly the way they look in films about reproduction, only I'm looking at *his* [original emphasis] sperm this time, wiggling around in my mucus.

[17b] Jeff goes in early in the morning, and leaves his contribution in a little jar. From there his *sperm is* washed, and supercharged with my estrogen.
(Paulette Bates Alden, *The New York Times Magazine*)

Following Wierzbicka's rationale for *rice* in 2.7, *sperm* is counted as ONE by the Entity Number System in both [17a] and [17b] because the components of the aggregate are identical in appearance and too small to have separate cognitive significance on their own. Nevertheless, when viewed under a microscope their status as separate mobile creatures is unmistakable, for they are seen 'wiggling around'; hence *come∅*. With unaided vision, on the other hand, the microscopic reality is no longer apparent and they become an indistinguishable mass, merely 'a contribution'; hence *is washed*.

Example [18] is from an article on drug use by professional athletes.

[18a] Anabolic *steroids are* synthetic hormones that increase muscle strength, bulk and stamina.

[18b] The language of steroids is indeed nonpejorative. They are not 'street' but 'prescription.' They are not 'mood altering' but 'performance enhancing.' Addressed in such terms, many athletes decide to bargain with their bodies, trading vague longterm risks for a few extra years of high income in their short careers. Crack is a cop-out, this reasoning goes; *steroids is* a business decision.
(Pete Axthelm, *Newsweek*)

The notion 'anabolic steroids' would seem to span the opposition of number all on its own since endocrinologically speaking steroids are a class of hormones while from an athlete's viewpoint they are administered as a single drug. In the course of the article the writer categorizes 'steroids' first as MORE THAN ONE (*are*) and then as ONE (*is*) in anticipation of their recharacterization as 'hormones' and 'a business decision' respectively.

Example [19], from a small-town newspaper article about a community survey, parallels [18].

[19a]   Interviews and observations have determined that the major religious *concerns* in this city *are* youth, senior citizens and housing.

[19b]   But the study shows that the major *concerns* of parents *is* drug and alcohol abuse by students.

(*The Summit Independent*)

In both [19a] and [19b] the entity in Focus is described by the lexical stem *concern*, categorized as MORE THAN ONE because each 'concern' has discrete components in the minds of those surveyed. But these conceptual components differ in their relative heterogeneity: the use of drugs and alcohol both fall within the category of 'substance abuse', whereas 'youth', 'senior citizens' and 'housing' are a more disparate collection. The writer has reckoned Focus Number in terms of the counting categories introduced as the messages evolve, thus highlighting the differing heterogeneity of the two sets of 'concerns'.

Example [20] comes from an article reporting the conclusions of a scientific investigation into the composition and origin of dust.

[20]   Those who study dust estimate that 43 million *tons* of it *settle* over the U.S. every year. About 31 million *tons* of this *is* natural and the other twelve million man-made.

(Penny Ward Moser, *Discover*)

In [20] the first communicative point is the large amount of dust settling yearly over the US, and the meaning MORE THAN ONE of *settleØ* reflects the quantification of the dust into a plurality of tons by the phrase *43 million tons*. Then the point shifts to the origin of the dust, and this requires dividing the initial quantity according to its source. Now the counting category shifts from 'tons' to 'natural' (and 'man-made'), and the meaning ONE of *is* reflects this new grouping.

[21a]   Chester Langway's laboratory holds six *miles* of ice that *reveal* volumes about Earth's past and, perhaps its future.

[21b]   One problem is a shortage of ice. Greenland's ice sheet

is the size of the United States east of the Mississippi, and Antarctica is 10 times larger; even six *miles* of cores in storage *is* 'like putting a teacup in Boston and one in Florida and trying to figure out what's been going on in between,' he said.

(Darren Dopp, Associated Press)

The phrases functioning as P_1 in [21a] and P in [21b] are both expressions of measured quantities. But they relate in different ways to their respective Occurrences. In [21a], each mile of ice independently reveals a certain amount of information to the scientists. Accordingly, the Occurrence of 'revealing (volumes)' is categorized as having MORE THAN ONE entity in Focus.

In [21b], on the other hand, the phrase *six miles of cores* relates as a single quantity to the Occurrence of 'being like putting a teacup in Boston. . .'. The counting category implied by the Occurrence is actually 'the *enterprise* of investigating the Earth's history through examination of a quantity of ice'. This notion receives no overt linguistic expression but can be inferred from the passage as a whole. The ONE of *is* facilitates this inference by muting the plurality inherent in the words *six*, *miles* and *cores*.

[22]   The only *music* not recorded *are* a few utility arrange-
       ments (used for scene changes and character exits) –
       which are in any case verbatim repeats of music
       recorded herein, and a few brief incidentals (specifi-
       cally, the moment in Act One, Scene Three when Ellie
       discusses Magnolia with Ravenal, while the strings play
       'Make Believe,' and the famous 'letter scene' in which
       Ellie reads Magnolia Ravenal's farewell letter to a slow
       accompaniment of 'Why Do I Love You'). I have
       omitted these sequences for the following reasons: a)
       they are very brief. . .; b) the *music* played *is heard*
       elsewhere throughout the play.

       (John McGlinn, notes on *Show Boat*, EMI Records
       Ltd)

The Occurrence of 'being (a few utility arrangements)' effects a reconceptualization of 'music' as a plurality of entities, while the Occurrence of 'being heard' effects no such reconceptualization. The Focus Number meanings anticipate the differing directions in which the two passages develop.

Example [23] is drawn from a radio interview with an art

dealer who has organized an art exhibit designed to encourage the purchase of art works as financial investments.

[23]   We're here to prove *Old Masters don't bite*. There's this popular conception that *Old Masters is* something esoteric and remote and hard to understand.
          (Penelope Hunter Steeple, *Morning Edition*, NPR)

The phrase *Old Masters* evokes both a number of prestigious painters and the art works they produced. The Occurrence of 'biting' implies an animate entity in Focus, and the MORE THAN ONE of *don't bite* pushes one to construe *Old Masters* as referring, on one level at least, to human beings. The Occurrence of 'being (something esoteric and remote and hard to under-stand)' on the other hand, involves a predication that applies to the painters' work taken collectively, and the ONE of *is* facilitates this reconceptualization of their work as a single body.

Note that *Old Masters* cannot be analysed as a polysemous phrase with two separate and distinct senses, only one of which is triggered on any individual occasion. For in *Old Masters don't bite* both putative senses are present simultaneously; the word *bite* evokes the painters themselves, while the larger communicat-ive import is that their paintings do not intimidate.

The following example concerns the growing popularity of astrology as a national pastime.

[24]   A 1986 Gallop poll showed that *52 per cent* of American teenagers *subscribe* to [astrology], as *does* at least *50 per cent* of the nation's departing First Couple.
          (John Allen Paulos, *New York Times Book Review*)

The MORE THAN ONE of *subscribe∅* reflects the fact that what is in Focus with respect to 'subscribing to astrology' is a plurality of teenagers. The ONE of *does (subscribe)* reflects the fact that what is in Focus, while linguistically described as *50 per cent*, is actually a single individual, Nancy Reagan.

Example [24] would suggest that simple referential number is the critical factor when the entity in Focus is a per cent, but [25] shows it to be referential number *as it relates to the Occurrence*.

[25]   Accordingly, in the text that follows, I shall use the word *creole* to refer to languages which:
          (1) Arose out of a prior pidgin which had not existed for more than a generation,

(2)   Arose in a population where not more than *20 per cent were* native speakers of the dominant language and where the remaining *80 per cent was composed* of diverse language groups.

(Derek Bickerton, *Roots of Language*)

In [25] the Occurrence of 'being native speakers' applies to each member of the '20 per cent' individually, whereas the Occurrence of 'being composed of diverse language groups' applies to 'the remaining 80 per cent' as a whole.

Example [26], while departing again from our format of lexically identical entities in Focus, otherwise parallels [25].

[26]   The sheer number of controllable parameters made it impossible to verify all of them. Well over 1,200 different *settings* of individual controls *are* available, and the possible *combinations* of settings *runs* into the millions.

(Julian Hirsch, *Stereo Review*)

The Occurrence of 'being available' applies to each of the '1,200 different settings' individually, while the Occurrence of 'running into the millions' applies to the 'combinations of settings' taken as an aggregate.

In [27] the word *politics* describes the entity in Focus. For a word like *politics* (as argued in 2.11), MORE THAN ONE is being employed merely to suggest entityhood, because the lexical stem *politic* would suggest otherwise. With the Entity Number System responding to this local morphological problem, the Focus Number System assumes full responsibility for indicating the number of what is in Focus.

[27]   Moreover, the hunger issue is certainly influenced by politics – *politics* that *oversimplify* the problem and *mask* the difficulty of achieving solutions. Advocates for aiding the poor, as well as their conservative opponents, are obscuring the fundamental problems of who isn't getting enough to eat and why.

The *politics* of hunger in America *has begun* to follow a predictable and historical pattern: first comes 'the anecdotal stuff' – shocking stories in papers and on TV about brain-damaged babies. . . .

(Nick Kotz, *The New Republic*)

When *politics* is a cover term for a complicated and unclear range of activities of two opposing factions, the two Occurrences of 'oversimplifying' and 'masking' characterize this feature of the message as MORE THAN ONE. But when the writer abstracts away from this confusing hubbub of political activity and claims to perceive a single underlying pattern, then *politics* is characterized as ONE: *has begun.*

Dual motivation

The meanings of the Focus Number System relate (by hypothesis) equally to the description of the entity in Focus and to the Occurrence in which it plays a role. This means that both are germane to the Focus Number choice, and example pairs [1] – [27] have illustrated different language users deploying the number opposition to reflect either one factor or the other. Example pairs [28] and [29] again illustrate each factor in turn, but now both pairs are drawn from the *same* text and have the *same* P phrase: *a set of assumptions.*

[28a] When *a set of assumptions is placed* in the memory of the deductive device, all the deductive rules in the logical entries attached to their consituent parts are accessed.

[28b] *A set of assumptions* which will constitute the axioms, or initial theses, of the deduction *are placed* in the memory of the device.

(Sperber and Wilson, *Relevance*)

In [28] the entity in Focus spans the opposition of number because *set* and *assumptions* bear opposite Entity Number meanings. However *of* subordinates *assumptions* slightly to *set*, and in [28a] the ONE of *is placed* reflects the greater cognitive prominence of *set* with respect to *assumptions*. In [28b], on the other hand, the prominence of *assumptions* is bolstered by its relative clause *which will constitute the axioms* (itself a reiteration of plurality), and the Focus Number switches to MORE THAN ONE.

Consider now [29] by the same authors.

[29a] With a formal system, it is decided in advance what assumptions are to be used as premises; *a set of assumptions are provided* which, for the purposes of this deduction at least, are to constitute the axioms or initial theses of the system (hence such systems are often

called axiomatic deduction systems).

[29b] *A set of assumptions* [P] analytically *implies* an assumption Q if and only if Q is one of the final theses in a
deduction in which the initial theses are [P], and in
which only analytical rules have applied.

(Sperber and Wilson, *Relevance*)

In [29a] each assumption is individually 'provided', hence *are*.
The greater salience of 'assumptions' over 'set' is evident as the
passage continues to recharacterize the things provided as
'axioms or initial theses'. By contrast, the assumptions in [29b]
must function as an integral 'set' with respect to the Occurrence
of 'implying an assumption Q'. The authors make clear that the
set of assumptions is now functioning as a single unit by
introducing the singular symbol [P] to represent it.

Thematic considerations
Examples [28] and [29] showed the effect of sentence-internal
factors. Examples [30] and [31] illustrate the effect of sentence-
external factors. Recall that the footrace passage in Chapter 5
illustrated how the (word-order) Focus Systems function at the
inter-sentential level to reflect the thematic status of entities
in the evolving discourse. The Focus Number System can
function in a similar capacity. Example [30] shows the Focus
Number opposition responding to the heightened prominence
of the lexical head of the P_1 phrase due to its second
mention.

[30] Womanless History, in other words, is about 'winning'
and has been written by the 'winners'. Feminist analysts
of that version of reality have come to realize that a
privileged *class* of men in western culture *have defined*
what is power and what constitutes knowledge. Excluded
from these definitions and hence from consideration in
the traditional History curriculum are types of power
and versions of knowledge which this privileged *class* of
men *does not share*.

(Peggy McIntosh, 'Interactive Phases of Curricular
Revision: A Feminist Perspective')

The MORE THAN ONE of *have defined* reflects the composition
of the 'privileged class' as a plurality of 'men' (who have acted
individually as 'definers'). But with its second mention the
discourse prominence of 'privileged class' increases, and this is

registered both in the switch from *a* to *this* and in the switch from
MORE THAN ONE to ONE (*does not share*).

Traditional explanations of agreement failures (e.g., Jespersen
1933/1966:217) sometimes claim that the language user is
conceiving of the subject in a different way numerically from its
overt expression, a line of analysis that preserves verb number as
a sentence-internal phenomenon. But that rationale leaves
unanswered the question of why the user did not then express the
subject in a way indicative of his or her *actual* conception in the
first place. (For instance, if McIntosh were conceiving of the
subject of the verb *have defined* as a conceptual plurality, why
then did she write *a privileged class of men* rather than, say,
certain privileged men?) An answer involving competing discourse factors is possible once the expression of the P phrase and
Focus Number are treated as independent choices, each potentially responsive to a different set of considerations.

Example [31] shows the Focus Number opposition in use
following a different thematic rationale because the constellation
of competing contextual factors is now slightly different.

[31]   Precisely this kind of trouble can be seen nowadays in
        the field of education. As one evidence, several
        universities have recently described themselves – in
        private communications – as having divided faculties:
        one *group* of faculty members *teaches* a great deal, and
        is paid very little; the other *group teach* very little, but
        are paid considerably more.

                    (Robert Davis, *Journal of Mathematical Behavior*)

'Teaching' is an Occurrence that puts human beings in Focus.
So semantically it relates more directly to *faculty members* than
to *group* (which can refer to inanimates as well). One might then
have expected Davis to write *one group of faculty members teach*.
But the point of the larger passage is the division of university
faculties into two opposing *groups*, and the conceptual affinity
between the notions of 'teaching' and the immediately adjacent
'faculty members' threatens to blunt the thematic thrust of the
passage as a whole. The ONE of *teaches* serves to maintain the
reader's attention on the word *group*.

By contrast, there is no overt linguistic competition for the
reader's attention in *the other group teach a great deal*. Here,
then, the counting category for Focus Number may safely revert
to that implied by the word *teach* itself (i.e., 'teachers').

6.4 Lexical Phrases Conjoined with *And*

The following examples employ lexical phrases conjoined with *and* to describe what is in Focus.

[32]   Wide pine *flooring and paneling give* any New England home its final touch of character and tradition. It's [*sic*] durability in 17th and 18th century homes, where it still exists, speaks for itself.

  Our *flooring and paneling is cut* from trees over a century old which measures [*sic*] 16″ to 40″ at the base.

(Professionally prepared advertising brochure for Carlisle Restoration Lumber)

'Flooring' and 'panelling' are functioning as separate architectural features in their capacity of 'giving any New England home its final touch of character and tradition'; hence *give∅*. Prior to their installation on the other hand, when they are still 'being cut from trees', they are indistinguishable; hence *is cut*. Note that this collapse to unity is forshadowed by the pronouns *it's* and *it* (both referring to 'flooring and panelling') in the previous sentence, which also concerns an inherent property of the wood itself, its durability. Note, too, the presence and absence of descriptive specification (*wide pine*) associated with the switch in Focus Number (cf. example [15]).

[33]   '*Heaven and hell is* not about ending up in two different places,' says moral theologian James Burtchaell of the University of Notre Dame. 'It's about ending up in this life, and forever in the next, being two very different kinds of persons. It's about character, not context.' In other words, *heaven and hell are* no longer thought of as different locations, with separate ZIP codes, but radically opposed states of intimacy with and alienation from God.

(Kenneth Woodward, *Newsweek*)

Heaven and hell are conventionally thought of as two different locations, with separate ZIP codes as Woodward puts it. But these two notions can also be taken as jointly defining a complex construct that has a single theological significance. In [33], Burtchaell denies the first conceptualization and affirms the second. In speaking of their theological significance – what they are collectively 'about' – he unifies them with the Focus Number

meaning ONE; but when Woodward elaborates the conception
Burtchaell is rejecting – that of being different locations – he
individualizes them with the meaning MORE THAN ONE.

[34]   *A highly potent plastic explosive and a miniature*
       detonation device apparently similar to those used by a
       Palestinian terrorist group *were* components of the
       bomb that exploded last week aboard a Trans World
       Airlines jet over Greece, investigators said today.
            Detailed examinations of the airplane and debris by
       Greek and American bomb specialists this morning
       produced the first physical evidence that this might
       point to the involvement of a specific terrorist group,
       T.W.A. officials here said.
            'The evidence is beginning to point to a certain type
       of very, very sophisticated bomb and to a particular
       modus operandi,' a senior T.W.A. official said.
            The examination has also shown that *a combined*
       miniature timer and detonator device was used to
       explode the bomb, the investigators added.
                                   (Robert Suro, *The New York Times*)

   In this account of a terrorist bombing the first clause merely
describes the internal structure of the bomb; mention of its actual
explosion is delayed to the following clause. The meaning MORE
THAN ONE of *were* prepares the way for the characterization of
'a highly potent plastic explosive' and 'a miniature detonation
device' as separate structural 'components'.
   In the last sentence, the Occurrence in terms of which Focus
Number is assessed involves an explosion (*was used to explode
the bomb*); the bomb's components, *a miniature timer* and *a
detonator device*, are now being regarded as a single functional
unit, as evidenced by the word *combined*. The meaning ONE of
was reflects this new conceptualization.
   Compound lexical phrases describing what is in Focus favour
mixed grammatical number most strongly because, as Chapter 7
will explain, they always span the opposition of number.
However the chance that the same compound lexical phrase will
recur (in the same text) as $P_{(1)}$ is exponentially smaller than the
chance of a single lexical item recurring as $P_{(1)}$. Yet clearly the
same contextual correlates are in evidence with compound
phrases.

[35a]   But if [Jean Kirkpatrick's] *article and its reception was*

the zenith of the neocon permeation of the 'ideological atmosphere,' it was also to prove her nadir.

[35b]   *Arms control and detente were* illusions, no substitute for military strength.

(Christopher Hitchens, *Mother Jones*)

The Occurrence in [35a] is that of 'being the zenith. . .' while in [35b] it is that of 'being illusions'. The Focus Number meanings of *was* and *were* reflect the grammatical number of the words *zenith* and *illusions* that recharacterize the entities in Focus. [36] parallels [35].

[36a]   *Dating and getting to know other people is* a normal part of life.

[36b]   But the good news is, as long as *sexual activity and sharing drug needles are* avoided, it doesn't matter.

(C. Everett Koop, *Understanding AIDS*)

In [36a] the Occurrence is that of 'being a normal part of life' while in [36b] the Occurrence is that of 'being avoided'. The Focus Number meanings of *is* and *are* reflect the numerical recharacterization of what is in Focus in [36a], and the absence of such recharacterization in [36b].

The Focus Number choice in the following examples is more subtle in that it reflects a logical distinction having no overt morphological correlate.

[37a]   Front end combustion system with tight firebox burns wood slowly and completely. *Adjustable draft in door and unique baffle system transfers* heat into room – not up chimney.

[37b]   *Rain fly and floor are* urethane-coated to prevent moisture penetration.

(L. L. Bean Catalogue)

With respect to the Occurrence of 'transferring heat into the room' the adjustable draft and baffle system of the stove function together as a single structural feature; hence they are categorized as ONE. With respect to the Occurrence of 'being urethane-coated' the rain fly and floor of the tent remain separate entities, hence MORE THAN ONE.

[38a]   *The small size and high price* of housing [in Japan] *exceeds* even my apprehensive expectations.

[38b]   *Food and rent are* very expensive but once you've taken
        care of them there's not much else to spend your money
        on.

                                    (James Fallows, *The Atlantic*)

The price of housing is always a function of size. A small
apartment may seem expensive and a large apartment may seem
cheap even though the rent for both may be the same. Price and
size are thus logically related. On the other hand, the price of
food and rent may vary independently. Fallows registers the
intimate relation between the price and size of an apartment with
the meaning ONE, and the logical independence of the price of
food and rent with the meaning MORE THAN ONE.

[39a]   *Buying and using* hi-fi equipment *tends* to be confusing
        and intimidating, not the least because of the technical
        jargon in brochures and sales talk.
[39b]   *Digital tape recording and the digital compact disc are*
        now common place; why not digital broadcasting?
                                    (Peter Mitchell, *Opus*)

Setting aside the possibility of acquisition by theft, the use of hi-fi
equipment implies prior purchase; so 'buying and using hi-fi
equipment' are related in a quasi-logical, implicatory fashion
similar to 'the small size and high price of housing' in [38a]. On
the other hand, digital tape recording and the compact disc are
logically-distinct technological innovations. The Focus Number
contrast reflects the different degrees of conceptual independence
of these collocated pairs.

[40a]   This superb new presentation. . .notably surpasses
        Berglund's earlier effort. *The greater clarity and impact*
        of digital sound *has* a lot to do with this, but Berglund
        has, in addition, completely rethought the piece.
[40b]   *Wagner and his interpreters are* at last completely in
        focus.
                                    (Bill Zakariasen, *High Fidelity*)

In [40] both collocated pairs are now linked in an implicatory
relation. But 'clarity and impact' are abstractions whereas
'Wagner and his interpreters' are discrete human beings. The
Focus Number choice reflects the natural cognitive salience of
human beings over non-discrete abstractions. The same contrast
is present in [41].

[41a]   *The modern art and cult* of conducting *was invented* by Richard Wagner for the express purpose of performing the Beethoven symphonies.

[41b]   *Bernard Haitink and the Concertgebouw*, in their new complete set of the nine symphonies for Philips, *represent* the modern view of Classical Beethoven in high estate.

(Eric Salzman, *Stereo Review*)

Relational opposition

The striking thing about examples [1]–[41] is the difficulty they pose for a treatment attempting to account for verb number in terms of formal determination, and the simplicity of statement that can be achieved once one is willing to concede that they are instances of expressively motivated choice. What remains constant and predictable across speakers (regardless of the structural configuration of the context) is the *direction of exploitation* of the grammatical opposition: MORE THAN ONE always reflects a greater individuality of the entities in Focus than does ONE. Only in this sense is the grammatical behaviour of these two units 'rule-governed'. How speakers choose to adhere to this 'rule' is up to them.

Recall this was the same systemic consistency demonstrated in Chapter 4 for the Entity Number System. With both systems, the meanings ONE and MORE THAN ONE reflect their relational opposition at the inter-sentential level, not the structural configuration of the particular sentence in which they appear.[1] One final example drives this point home.

[42a]   *But the alarmingly high rate of teenage pregnancy and the fear of AIDS and other sexually transmitted diseases have opened up* the debate over what to do about the precocious sexual activity of young people.

(Barbara Kantrowitz, *Newsweek*)

An editor at *Newsweek* lifted this sentence from the text of the article and revised it to produce the following bold-faced headline.

[42b]   *The alarming rate of teenage pregnancy and the inexorable spread of AIDS has raised* troubling moral questions and given new urgency to the debate over how best to protect our children.

Since [42a] and [42b] were produced by different writers one cannot be sure how either would have crafted the contrasting sentence. But the fact remains that the relational opposition between the Focus Number meanings is preserved. The switch from MORE THAN ONE (*have opened up*) to ONE (*has raised*) is accompanied by a reduction in the lexical specification (= precision) of what is in Focus.

6.5 The Variationist Alternative

Examples [1]–[42] support the analysis of *Occurrence -s* and *-∅* as independently chosen, meaning-bearing units because (1) the signals do not consistently correlate with the overt grammatical number of any single constituent within the $P_{(1)}$ phrase, and (2) they do correlate with various contextual features supporting the relational contrast between the meanings ONE and MORE THAN ONE. For the analyst committed to the notion of subject-verb agreement, however, these data might be seen as arguing for one of two syntactic alternatives, discussed briefly in turn.

Examples [1]–[42] might be interpreted as support for a full-blown variationist treatment. But our data constitute variation only in the context of a sentence-based structuralist conception of language, wherein certain sentence-internal, structural features supposedly stand in fixed determining relations to others. Faced with the evidence above that no single structural feature has a categorical effect, the variationist concludes that their determining effect must be couched in terms of statistical probability; hence 'variable rules'.[2]

In the context of sign-based theory, on the other hand, examples [1]–[42] do not constitute 'variation' because, to repeat, the systemic opposition between ONE and MORE THAN ONE is always maintained and always exploited along the same cognitive parameter. What might be said to 'vary' is merely the crossover point at which speakers switch from ONE to MORE THAN ONE. But that kind of variation is of a benign and familiar variety that has never, to our knowledge, been cited as evidence for the variationist position. The cross-over point between *big* and *small*, for example, is substantively different depending on whether one is talking about a mouse or an elephant. With such purely relational contrasts like *big* and *small*, *tall* and *short*, *new* and *old*, the crossover point is always adjusted so as to make the distinction maximally informative for the given topic of discourse. So, too, with the Focus Number distinction. Formal treatments of verb number aiming at explanation in terms of a syntactic rule (whether of the categorical or variable variety) treat the substantive structural features associated with the contrast as causal rather than merely corroborative. Chapter 7 will develop this point in more detail.

6.6 Covert Subject Number

Examples [1]–[42] might be seen as arguing for a second syntactic alternative, namely, for the existence of a covert grammatical distinction between the apparently identical subject phrases. A covert, subject-number feature might be posited whose scope encompasses the subject phrase as a whole. This, then, would be the feature of subject number with which the verb (mechanically) agrees (cf. Weinreich, 1980).

This proposal recalls the joke about the scholar who claimed the Homeric poems were not written by Homer himself but by a contemporary Greek poet of the same name. For the linguistic feature determining verb number would still be freely chosen, independently of the grammatical number of any lexical item within the subject phrase itself. It is simply a way of preserving the shibboleth of subject-verb agreement by a formal trick, while conceding the central empirical claims of the Focus Number System.[3]

Admittedly this stratagem would maintain the formal locus of the determining feature of verb number in the grammatical subject. But that is a plus only in the context of sentence-based theory, with its *a priori* commitment to the subject-predicate distinction. Sign-based theory favours tying grammatical categories to the morphological formatives they directly control.

We hesitate to counter such a proposal with the practical problems of its execution since the ingenuity of a skilled practitioner of formal linguistics is certainly greater than our own. But one problem is worth noting.

Within modern syntactic theory, deletion is a formal device that allows a constituent to be posited in the underlying representation of a sentence even though it has no overt morphological realization. Such a constituent is deleted when it is grammatically identical to another constituent which does survive into the terminal representation. (This allows the absent constituent to be deduced according to the same structurally-defined principles that permitted its deletion.) So, for instance, *Angus* is the underlying subject of the verb *bought* in [43], but it is grammatically identical to the subject of *walked*, and so is deleted.

[43]   Angus walked to the toy store and bought a Nintendo
        game.

The identity condition for deletion predicts, then, that in a
sentence containing two finite verbs the subject of the second can
only be deleted when it is grammatically identical to the subject
of the first.

Consider now [44], which contains two verbs inflected for
contrasting verb number but only one overt grammatical subject.

[44]   *The Copenhagen school*, and particularly Hjelmslev's
        glossematics, *is* generally very poorly known in this
        country, and thus, no doubt, *deserve* a volume of their
        own.

                        (Valerie Becker Makkai, *Phonological Theory*)

In [44] the underlying subject of the verb *deserve* is presumably
the Copenhagen school. Since this phrase serves as the grammatical subject of the verb *is* as well, it may be deleted following
the identity condition.

So far, so good. But in order to account for the shift in verb
number one must claim that in the first clause *the Copenhagen
school* is categorized as singular by the covert feature of subject
number (hence *is*), while in the second clause it is categorized as
plural (hence *deserve∅*). But then the underlying subjects of the
two verbs are no longer grammatically identical, in which case
the condition for deletion has been violated!

No such impasse is encountered by the Focus Number System
hypothesis, since it says the P phrase and the Focus Number
signals make independent semantic contributions to how we
construe the entity in Focus. The word *school*, construed as a
scholarly faction, spans the opposition of number conceptually
since it refers to a number of scholars who form a single group.
But within this group is a prominent subgroup, Hjelmslev's
glossematics.

The message the writer wishes to convey touches first on the
unitary and then on the composite nature of the 'school'. Part of
one's ignorance of the Copenhagen school lies in not knowing
about the diversity within it. With respect to 'being poorly
known' then, it is appropriately characterized as ONE. On the
other hand, the diversity within the school argues for the merits
of a volume devoted to it. With respect to 'deserving a volume of
their own', it is appropriately characterized as MORE THAN
ONE. Here, then, the notion 'school' undergoes a transformation

as the Occurrence shifts from one that highlights its unitary aspect to one that highlights its collective aspect.

In [44] the contrasting Focus Number meanings highlighted different facets of the meaning of *school* itself. In [45] the lexical item serving as the head noun of the apparent grammatical subject of the two verbs is not semantically complex in the manner of *school*, so giving the analyst attempting a formal treatment less to work with.

[45]   According to university officials *the average salary* of the striking employees *is* $16,500 and *range* from $10,896 for the beginning employees to $25,110 for those at the top of the line.

(Alfonso Narvaez, *The New York Times*)

The entity in Focus with respect to 'being $16,500' is 'the average salary'. Since 'the average salary' is being equated with a single monetary figure, it is categorized as ONE by the Focus Number System. With respect to 'ranging from $16,500 to $25,110', on the other hand, the entity in Focus is clearly the various salaries of the striking employees, not a single 'average salary'.

Yet the individual salaries and the average are related mathematically in a familiar way, and, for Narvaez at any rate, the existence of individual salaries is so strongly implied by the notion of 'average salary' that the individual salaries themselves do not require explicit mention. The meaning MORE THAN ONE, together with the semantic value of *range* itself, push the reader to infer these new (unexpressed) entities.

6.7 Grammaticality Judgements

The trump card held by the proponent of subject-verb agreement, of course, is the fact that Focus Number is not 'freely chosen' in the sense that both options will always produce equally successful communications. In most contexts, one option produces a result recognized to be perfectly comprehensible, normal and acceptable, while the other option produces something judged to be strange, queer, far-fetched, puzzling, unlikely, or incomprehensible; in a word, *wrong*. The question arises, then, as to the weight this fact carries in the present context. Do such 'grammaticality' judgements constitute a bedrock body of primary data against which linguistic analyses of all stripes must be measured? Or are they merely the parochial favourite of one particular way of doing linguistics?

From the beginning, generative theory has aimed to account for the grammaticality of sentences. This is to be accomplished by a theory of linguistic competence which will predict, by means of a rigorously formal algorithm, whether a given sequence of words counts as a grammatical or ungrammatical sentence in the language. The notion of grammaticality is critical here because that term figures in the statement of one central goal of the enterprise.[4]

On the other hand, sign-based theory aims to explain the use of linguistic signs in the communication of messages. The notion of grammaticality figures not at all in this formulation. Speaker judgements provide, to be sure, an indication of the extent to which the communicative potential of a meaning should be exploited. But such judgements are not, in themselves, the object of explanation.

Nevertheless, the present analysis ought to be able to offer something in the way of explanation of such judgements, for they presumably relate to the semantic structure of the two Number Systems. They do so by way of the communicative strategies the two systems motivate and which guide their joint deployment.

The Entity and Focus Number Systems in English provide the language user two opportunities to categorize the entity in Focus numerically. In all those cases where the message falls exclusively on one side or the other of the grammatical opposition, speakers will choose the same way both times (since they have no communicative motivation to do otherwise). Only when the message spans the opposition of number conceptually will the two choices sometimes diverge.

In such cases of numerical divergence, there is always some independent evidence of the spanned opposition. Often the meaning of the lexical stem describing the entity in Focus is numerically complex (e.g., *family*, *couple*, *panel*, *majority*). On other occasions the Occurrence itself clarifies why the entity in Focus must be understood in a manner that contrasts with the Entity Number categorization of the word describing it (e.g., *Steroids is a business decision*).

Such contextual elaboration is necessary because the two Number Systems can only indicate *that* the message spans the opposition of number; they cannot by themselves indicate *how*. On the other hand, the contextual elaboration that explains *how* it is spanned cannot say *to what extent* it is spanned. This the Focus Number choice provides, by marking an implicit paradigmatic contrast between the intended message and other unintended alternatives.

The quasi-minimal pair examples examined in this chapter have illustrated such simultaneous contrasts on the syntagmatic and paradigmatic axes. Those cases where Focus Number differed from Entity Number (e.g., *the family are* . . .) illustrated a syntagmatic contrast within a single sentence: the grammatical encoding of the spanned opposition by the two systems in tandem. But that contrast, then taken as a unit, distinguished the message from other possible messages on a paradigmatic axis, one exemplar of which the writer fortuitously happened to have supplied in the same text (e.g., *the family is* . . .).

The introduction of the paradigmatic axis of contrast means that even when the Entity and Focus Number meanings 'agree', the combination is still functioning contrastively to distinguish the message from paradigmatic alternatives which would call for them to 'disagree'. Chapters 7 and 8 develop this point in more detail.

The communicative strategy invoked here is not idiosyncratic to the Number Systems, for at its most general level it amounts to the familiar rule of thumb that a good writer prepares the reader for the ideas to come, and then adequately develops them. Chapter 1 illustrated how this principle applies in a way resembling its application to grammatical number. Both *do Verb* and highlighting connectives such as *but* were shown to indicate the presence of thematic contrast. Yet these, by themselves, did not specify the nature of the contrast. On the other hand, the surrounding context, which supplied the nature of the contrast, did not by itself say whether the extent of the contrast was sufficiently great to merit explicit comment; that was marked by the writer's decision whether or not to employ *do Verb* (with or without a highlighting connective).

Grammatical correctness

Returning now to the issue of grammatical correctness, the reason why the mechanical permutation of Focus Number usually produces a negative reaction is that the surrounding context does not provide sufficient explanation for what the Focus Number meaning says.

[46]   *The boys walks* through the field.

Nothing in [46] explains the ONE of *walks*. (Of course if *walks* is taken as given, then it could equally well be said that nothing in [46] explains the MORE THAN ONE of *boys*.) Putting this in the problem-solving terms of 3.2, [46] does not provide sufficient information for the hearer to invent a plausible communicative intent that would have motivated any speaker to construct the particular sequence of linguistic signs occurring in [46].

The important point here is that the anomaly of [46] involves a breach of a communicative strategy, not a breach of some structural feature or pattern inherent in the language itself. As illustrated in this chapter, the collocation of the meanings ONE and MORE THAN ONE (both relating to the Entity in Focus) is a well-established structural pattern.

[47]   My *specialty are* mice and silverfish.
                          (Woody Allen, *The Purple Rose of Cairo*)

Obstacles to formalization
The obstacle to formalizing this communicative strategy – as a rule of verb agreement attempts to do – is that it may be adhered to in so many different ways they would seem to defy enumeration. The root problem here is that communicative strategies bring us squarely into the arena of linguistic *creativity*. This creativity can be of two kinds. There is sometimes a cognitive creativity involving the creation of a novel message. And there is always a rhetorical creativity involving the ingenuity with which the expressive resources of the language are deployed.

Critical to this latter kind of creativity is the element of human judgement. What one language user may regard as adequate contextual explanation for the choice of Focus Number, another may not. Consider again example [45].

[45]   According to university officials *the average salary* of the striking employees is $16,500 and *range* from $10,896 for the beginning employees to $25,110 for those at the top of the line.
                          (Alfonso Narvaez, *The New York Times*)

There is nothing novel in the idea of a salary range. But the way this writer has chosen to express it, forcing the reader to infer the notion of a plurality of salaries from the phrase *the average salary* alone, may well strike more discriminating English writers as awkward or momentarily confusing. But even if there is consensus on this point, and one could devise an adequate formal statement for it, one should hesitate to build the tyranny of the majority into the structure of a communicative system employed by all.

The obstacles to formalization increase when the two kinds of linguistic creativity combine, for then one is confronted by a novel message communicated in a novel fashion.

[48]   Everyone seems to be having fun at Coca-Cola's expense. The wise cracks proliferated when the company felt obliged to restore old ('Classic') Coke to the market along with its new cola, introduced just last April. 'Coke are it,' some people gibed . . .

If Coca-Cola had it to do over again, it might have added New Coke without abandoning the old. Re-creating Classic was expensive. But the new product appears to be a notable success in some markets, like Los Angeles, and the expense will soon be forgotten if the combined gains persist. The bottom line remains the bottom line, and at least for the moment, Coke *are* it. [original emphasis]

(The New York Times)

If readers do not get the joke of *Coke are it* in the first paragraph they certainly get it by the end of the second paragraph, for the entire article appears to have been constructed so as to prepare the reader for that punch line.

[48] warns that the distinction between novel message and novel expression cannot be pressed too far, for in this case the novelty of the message lies precisely in the allusion by its linguistic expression to the company's advertising slogan *Coke is it*, a paradigmatic alternative already familiar to the reader.

A better candidate for message-level creativity is example [49].

[49]   Yes, Virginia, there *are a Santa Claus*.
                              (Paul Froiland, *TWA Ambassador*)

Out of context [49] is well-nigh uninterpretable, for it contains two apparent anomalies: the indefinite article with a name, and the grammatical number of *are*. *Are* indicates *that* the message spans the opposition of number, but the linguistic context provides no explanation of *how*.

The contextual elaboration in this case is extra-linguistic. [49] is the caption to a picture introducing an article entitled *Santa 101*. The picture shows typical grammar school paraphernalia: books tied with a strap, a lunchbox, pencils, a report card and a red apple.

But the picture is hardly enough. In order to create a coherent message for [49] the reader must possess two items of cultural knowledge. In American universities the academic level of a course is typically indicated by its catalogue number; a beginning French course is numbered 101 (and 102 is its second-semester continuation); *French 201* is second-year level, and so on. In constructing an interpretation for [49], then, the reader must recognize *Santa 101* as a beginning-level academic course. Yet the grammar school artefacts suggest it does not involve anything scholarly in the usual sense.

More critical is the recognition of a literary allusion. In 1897 the editor of the now-defunct *New York Sun* received a letter.

Dear Editor:
  I am eight years old. Some of my little friends say there is no Santa Claus. Papa says, 'If you see it in the Sun, it's so.' Please tell me the truth. Is there a Santa Claus?

                                                       Virginia O'Hanlon

In reply, Francis P. Church wrote (in part):

Dear Virginia:
  Your little friends are wrong. They have been affected by the skepticism of a skeptical age. They do not believe except what they see. . .
  In this great universe of ours, man is a mere insect, an ant, in his intellect, as compared with the boundless world about him, as measured by the intelligence capable of grasping the whole of truth and knowledge.
  Yes, Virginia, there is a Santa Claus. He exists as certainly as love and generosity and devotion exist, and they abound and give to your life its highest beauty and joy. Alas! How dreary would be the world if there were no Santa Claus. It would be as dreary as if there were no Virginias. . .

For many years, this exchange was republished at Christmastime by newspapers throughout the United States and is familiar to at least an older generation of Americans.

Putting these various clues together – linguistic, pictorial and cultural – many American readers are able to arrive at a message that spans the opposition of number in a way that explains the MORE THAN ONE of *are*. The article will be about a school for people learning to be department store Santas (who listen to children's requests about what they want for Christmas). This conclusion is confirmed by the article that follows.

Two communicative functions

Example [49] illustrates two points central to sign-based theory: the individual semantic contribution of each linguistic sign to the message; and the role of signs as distinguishing tools. The numerical contrast in [49] is not simply a response to different aspects of a single referent as in many previous examples. The MORE THAN ONE of *are* implies the numerous students of the Santa role, while the ONE of *Santa Claus∅* (and *a*) relates to the mythic figure of Father Christmas. Each number meaning independently helps to shape a different component of the message.

The role of linguistic meanings as tools for *distinguishing* messages (rather than conceptual *components*) is also clear. The number meaning of *are* distinguishes the intended message from its paradigmatic alternative (Yes Virginia, there *is* a Santa Clause). Yet [49] cannot be said to *encode* the intended message; that is, the idea of a Santa Claus school, or students of a role, cannot be ascribed to any component word or phrase.

[49] is an effective example because it is not open to several popular analytical stratagems of sentence-based theory. There are, for instance, no other words with which *are* could be said to 'agree'. Nor is it possible to hypothesize deleted (or 'understood') words or phrases to serve in that capacity. [49] is unusual on this score, for it is completely resistant to paraphrase; any alteration, such as changing *are* back to *is*, or supplying putatively deleted words, destroys the effect the writer intended.

Claiming that [49] involves a change in selectional restrictions of *Santa Claus* is difficult in view of the indefinite article *a*, which supposedly always takes a singular count noun. Neither does any word in [49] reflect a newly-acquired 'sense'.

On the other hand, [49] does not seem open to explanation in terms of pragmatic inference. The conventional approach to pragmatic inference requires, as its point of departure, literal sentence meaning, and in the case of [49] it is hard to imagine what that could be. With [49], at any rate, the step from text to message is a single unmediated leap, not an extrapolation from a 'literal' interpretation.

Another tack, borrowed from stylistic theory, might be to say *are* is an arbitrary attention-grabbing device whose only purpose is to suggest that an interpretation deviating from the original is intended (i.e., rule-breaking for stylistic effect). But if that were all that was involved, substituting *be* for *is* (i.e. Yes Virginia, there *be* a Santa Claus) should be equally effective. Clearly something more than mere formal deviation was desired in the choice of *are*. Its grammatical meaning MORE THAN ONE serves as a *substantive semantic clue* that the intended message spans the opposition of number in a way that contrasts with the paradigmatic alternative of the original wording: multiple Santa Clauses are involved in some way.

6.8 Linguistic Creativity

In the context of the present analysis, there is no reason to devise a basis to set [49] aside. For upon examination, [49] does not prove to be grammatically or structurally deviant in any way. To begin with, the co-occurrence of the indefinite article *a* with a name is commonplace.

[50]   I find myself in agreement with many people in the Republican party: *a* Hatfield, *a* Case, *a* McCloskey, *a* Javits sometimes.

(Charles Goodell, interview on radio station WBAI)

[51]   *A* Rockefeller kills himself.

(Headline, *The New York Post*)

Precedent can even be found for the use of the indefinite article with a (singular) lexical stem categorized as MORE THAN ONE by the Focus Number System.

[52]   But when *a* people *are* pounded night after night with that kind of hysterical reporting, it naturally shakes their confidence.

(Richard Nixon, press conference)

Furthermore, the message motivating the collocation of ONE and MORE THAN ONE in [49] is the familiar one in which attention is focused on people who comprise a culturally-defined composite entity.

[1a]   My *family have been* prominent, well-to-do people in this Middle Western city for three generations.

(F. Scott Fitzgerald, *The Great Gatsby*)

[6a]   This afternoon *our panel are* three male singers.

(Edward Downes, Texaco Metropolitan Opera Quiz)

Family and *panel* differ from *Santa Claus*, of course, in that as inherent collectives they always designate a referential plurality whereas *Santa Claus* does not. But the use of a non-collective lexical stem (categorized as ONE) for both singular and plural reference is also well established.

[53]   The *buffalo∅* is grazing.
[54]   The *buffalo∅* are grazing.

One anomaly of [49] lies in the unusual nature of the plurality. In [54] the plurality is no more than the sum of its referential parts, while in [49] it is composed of multiple manifestations of a single mythical being that has an independent existence. That is, Santa Claus is something more than the set of everyone dressed up in Santa Claus suits.

The complex nature of the plurality in [49] is the key to the use of the indefinite article. The ONE of *a* points to a singularity of reference that exists above and beyond the group of people playing the role.

Speaker judgements
Speakers are right, to be sure, in reporting there is something unusual about [49], but they have no special expertise in determining the nature of its anomaly. That is the job of the linguist. Upon analysis, the anomaly of [49] involves *an unusual communication*. The recent cultural innovation of a school for department store Santas has inspired one writer to invent a novel message, and a novel mode of expression (namely, by way of literary allusion) to produce a striking conflation of originality of both means and end. It is this striking originality to which all English speakers respond. But so long as the grammatical and lexical resources of the language are being deployed in accordance with their regular systemic values, following established communicative strategies, one must conclude – despite speaker reports – that [49] conforms to the principles, patterns and values of English in every respect.[5]

This analysis of [49] reflects the recognition by sign-based theory that the greatest challenge to linguistic theory-building lies in the creative aspect of language. The idealization of a language as a discrete and self-contained object of knowledge is untenable if it requires modification every time speakers think of something new to say. For if every cultural and communicative innovation triggers a structural change in the language itself – diachronic change – then true synchronic creativity does not exist. Any linguistic framework that sees grammatical anomaly or linguistic innovation in [49] is guilty of both failing to come to terms with the creative aspect of language, and failing to adhere to the basic principle of idealization from which modern linguistics arose: namely, the distinction between language itself – a self-contained system of purely relational units – and the endlessly novel communicative purposes to which that system is put.

Notes

1. This is why the present analysis is not, in the final analysis, sentence-based. The term 'sentence' here is being construed in its theoretically relevant sense as the analytical construct which encompasses the relevant explanatory factors. The present account is non-sentence-based because the explanation for Focus Number lies in the relational contrasts between complexes of signals comprising instances of the Focus-Control interlock; the fact that these contrasting instances fall in stretches beginning with a capital letter and ending with a period has no particular theoretical significance.

2. Poplack and Tagliamonte's (1989) study of the *verb -s* inflection in early Black English is a recent example. P and T establish how frequently the *verb -s* occurs in a variety of contexts: person, number and definiteness of the subject; phonological environment; and verbal aspect. They then submit these results to a factor analysis which they say 'enables us to determine which environmental factors have a significant *effect* (emphasis W.R.) on *-s* insertion and deletion . . .' (p. 72). Yet they make no attempt to establish a conceptual or systemic connection between the *verb -s* and the environmental features that would explain why they (and not others) should have the effect they do. In the absence of any systemic connection (other than the variable rule itself), it is hard to see how one's understanding of the Black English *verb -s* would change in any meaningful way from what it presently is if all the environmental factors and calculated probability values had turned out to be substantially different.

    P and T's sole stab at explanation is the suggestion that their data reflect the remnants of 'an earlier variable system along with the constraints on its variability' (pp. 75–6). More baldly put, an earlier mess begat a later mess.

3. This line of analysis would become empirically distinguishable from the present one if rules could be written which stated the conditions under which the grammatical number of the subject phrase could diverge from that of its head noun. But in view of the critical relation between the Occurrence and Focus Number, the rules would often have to appeal to formal grammatical properties within the predicate, not the subject. This makes the verb ultimately 'agreeing' with the predicate itself – hardly a state of affairs that can be regarded as confirmation of subject-verb agreement.

4. Consider Katz on the centrality of this notion: 'A study that abandons the goal of explaining what makes strings of words well-

formed sentences of English can make no claim to be a study of English grammar' (Katz 1980:17). While generative theory recognized early on that speaker judgements could only be taken to reflect acceptability, and that 'grammaticality' was better conceived as a theory-defined notion, speaker judgements are still relied upon to provide a rough-and-ready delineation of the set of sentences for which structural descriptions must be generated.

5. Katz and Bever (1976), taking aim at generative semantics, argue the dangers of making grammatical theory proper account for all acceptability judgements. 'The generative semanticist's criterion of what calls for grammatical explanation makes every performance factor count as a legitimate part of grammar' (p. 59). This leads to the (futile) attempt to provide a homogeneous form of explanation for heterogeneous phenomena (p. 49). In a similar spirit, the present analysis argues for a still-more conservative definition of the 'grammatical'. The goal of an autonomous theory of purely grammatical knowledge, which we share with Chomsky, forces a return to a sign-based conception of linguistic structure.

Chapter 7

Testing the Focus Number opposition

Chapter 6 illustrated the Focus Number meanings functioning contrastively as fully-fledged expressive units. The question now arises as to the generality of the phenomenon. To what extent do English speakers and writers exploit the Focus Number opposition in the manner of the examples? The problem is that only rarely do language users supply the analyst with contrasting pairs like those in Chapter 6, where both the lexical stem and grammatical number of the entity in Focus remain constant.

The same problem arose early in Chapter 4 after Hirtle's *deer* and *buffalo* examples and our own self-reported usage. The generality of the precision strategy was demonstrated through an instrument that allowed subjects to replicate the anecdotal examples in a controlled fashion many times over. This time, however, a questionnaire instrument has a serious defect. Unlike 'noun number', 'verb number' is regarded as a measure of grammatical correctness and is invariably an important topic in any prescriptive grammar of English. As a result, it is a grammatical point about which a fair number of speakers (even speakers of Standard English) have considerable anxiety. Investigating Focus Number through a questionnaire, which would unavoidably direct subjects' attention to the choice, runs the risk of revealing only what people think they *ought* to do, hazily recalled from grammar school days, rather than what they actually do. So instead of the experimental route of Chapter 4, we opt now for a demonstration relying entirely on naturalistic data drawn from a variety of sources, both spoken and written. At the same time, we wish to preserve the virtues of the closely controlled questionnaire instrument.

7.1 Method of Data Collection

Over a period of two years this writer compiled a corpus of examples falling into six structural types defined in terms of the permutations of the signals from the Entity and Focus Number Systems. In three types the Entity and Focus Number meanings concur and in three they contrast.

FIGURE 7.1   Structurally-defined example types

Lexical Head of P or P$_1$ Phrase	Focus Number		Reference Code
Entity -0	+ *Occurrence -s*	=	1A
Entity -0	+ *Occurrence -0*	=	1B
Entity -s	+ *Occurrence -0*	=	2A
Entity -s	+ *Occurrence -s*	=	2B
Entity -0 and *Entity -0*	+ *Occurrence -0*	=	3A
Entity -0 and *Entity -0*	+ *Occurrence -s*	=	3B

Readers are advised to master the system of reference in Figure 7.1 because it will be employed throughout this chapter. Figure 7.1a defines the reference code in traditional syntactic terms to facilitate its mastery.

FIGURE 7.1a   Explication of reference code

Type 1	=	morphologically *singular* subject
Type 2	=	morphologically *plural* subject
Type 3	=	singular *conjoined* nouns as subject
Subtypes A	=	subject and verb *agree* in number
Subtypes B	=	subject and verb *disagree* in number

Since the present objective is to demonstrate the generality of the usage illustrated in Chapter 6, the statistical comparisons will all be between sets of examples where the Entity Number of the 'subject' (i.e. the grammatical head of the P or the P$_1$ phrase in the Focus-Control interlock) is a constant but the Focus Number meanings differ. That is to say, all the comparisons will be between the A and B versions of each basic type, never across Types 1, 2 and 3. This is because in all the example pairs in Chapter 6 the grammatical number of the 'subject' was held constant.

These data were collected from a variety of sources that represented the writer's normal reading patterns. As for the spoken data, some came from conversations in which the writer was either a participant or observer. (No data from the writer's own speech were included.) The majority, however, were drawn from two daily radio news programmes of one and one half and two hours' duration. These consisted of both written text read aloud and interview features, the latter comprising a significant portion of the programmes.[1]

Initially the written and spoken data were kept separate in the belief they might require separate analysis. However as data collection progressed it became clear that with respect to the strategies of deployment of the two number systems there was no difference between the examples drawn from these two sources, and in the end the two were pooled.

Representativeness
The integrity of the quantitative procedures to be employed depends upon the data being statistically representative of the source materials. This was achieved in different ways for the frequently occurring Types 1A, 2A and 3A and the relatively rare Types 1B, 2B and 3B. During the initial stages of data collection all instances of the latter (in which Entity and Focus Number 'disagreed') were gathered. But the task soon became too onerous, and an alternative procedure was adopted. Certain periods of reading and listening were designated in advance, during which we collected all examples of 'subject-verb dis-agreement' (Subtypes B) and we refrained from collecting examples encountered during periods not so designated. This method assured that we did not inadvertently prejudice the data base by selecting just those examples that favoured the Focus Number hypothesis.[2]

For those data exhibiting 'subject-verb agreement' (Subtypes A), the *embarras de richesse* available made it impractical to gather all instances, and representativeness was achieved in a different way. Upon finding an example of Types 1B, 2B or 3B, (exhibiting contrasting grammatical number), we continued searching for the next instance of its structural counterpart exhibiting concurring grammatical number (1A, 2A or 3A respectively). If no such example was found in the same written or spoken text, the first available instance was taken from a comparable source. This method assured that the corpus of concurring examples (A) was assembled in a purely mechanical manner.[3]

Heterogeneity of source materials
This procedure had the effect of controlling for the heterogeneity

of source materials by assuring that the A-type examples were drawn from the same sources, in the same proportions, as the B-type examples. Whatever subtle undetected differences of exploitation that might exist between spoken and written English, informal conversation and formal news-reporting, narrative and non-narrative prose, magazine and newspaper style, academic and non-academic writing, these would all be equally represented in the two bodies of data that would later be compared and balance each other out. Thus the heterogeneity of source material could only have a detrimental effect on the hypothesis (i.e., diluting statistical tendencies that might prove more robust if each genre were to receive separate analysis). It could never produce spurious support.[4]

The distortion of frequency ratio
One distributional fact that is obviously obscured by our procedure is the relative frequency of the A and B versions of Types 1, 2 and 3. For the outcome is sets of A and B examples of equal size when, in fact, instances of concurring grammatical number (A) greatly exceed those of contrasting grammatical number (B) in natural discourse.

The striking statistical favouring of like number meanings (Types 1A and 2A) in the two number systems was the first empirical evidence offered in support of the Focus Number hypothesis in Chapter 5, repeated below as Table 7.1.

TABLE 7.1   Co-occurrence of Entity Number (of P) and focus number

	Entity -$\emptyset$	*Entity -s*	
Occurrence -s	552 (100%) Type 1A	0 (0%) Type 2B	
Occurrence -$\emptyset$	5 (8%) Type 1B	61 (92%) Type 2A	p < 0.001

Source: Jane Smiley, 'Long Distance', *The Atlantic*, January 1987.

Were we writing for readers whose minds were *tabulae rasae* with respect to both the facts and structure of English, we would doubtless have adopted a procedure of data collection that would allow us to offer multiple demonstrations of this favouring since it strongly supports the present hypothesis. The drawback is that this favouring supports the notion of subject-verb agreement as well; little would thus be gained by its repeated demonstration.

For the same reason, Chapter 6 focused on data that, while admittedly rare, favoured one hypothesis over the other, due to the fact that the contrasts in message usually involved aspects of the Occurrence. The discussion scrupulously avoided appealing to the grammatical number of the 'subject' alone as support for the choice because that was a constant in all the example pairs. Since the present chapter aims to test for the generality of such usage, it too will make no appeal to the greater frequency of the A versions of Types 1, 2 and 3 in running text. Instead, it will examine how numerically-balanced classes of A and B examples differ in composition.

7.2 The Relation of Distributional Skewings to Grammatical Hypotheses

While the correlations between 'subject number' and 'verb number' in Table 7.1 support both hypotheses, they do so in different ways, and before proceeding further it will be useful to explain how this is so. According to the hypothesis of subject-verb agreement, the grammatical number of the subject stands in a relation of formal determination to the grammatical number of its verb. Since that relation is (in the syntactic account) hard-wired into the structure of the language itself, subject number becomes a *causal* variable of verb number (and in a quantitative demonstration it becomes a statistical variable as well). In the context of the agreement hypothesis, then, Table 7.1 is a demonstration of the relation between cause and effect.

According to the Focus Number hypothesis, on the other hand, the causal variable with respect to Focus Number is always the message being communicated (i.e., *constructio ad sensum*). Other syntagmatic elements serve for the analyst as corroborating evidence of that message since they, too, were chosen as part of the same communicative act; and they become statistical variables in the context of a quantitative demonstration. But they are never elevated from statistical variable to causal variable.

Statistical vs linguistic norm

This means that no combination of number signals – no structural pattern – enjoys any favoured theoretical status at the systemic level. While certain combinations greatly outnumber others, all permutations occur, and each, examined in context, seems equally well suited to the message being communicated. No combination of number signals, then, is a linguistic deviation, or linguistic exception to anything, only a statistical one.

The price paid for this position is that now instances of numerical concurrence are as much a problem for the analyst as those of numerical contrast. Structural Types 1A, 2A and 3A cannot be passed off as instances of the 'norm', *for there is no linguistic norm*, only a statistical norm. Such statistical affinities merit no additional codification since they are already apparent for all to see. What they call for is an explanation.

Linguistic redundancy

This returns us to the question of how Table 7.1 supports the Focus Number hypothesis. Since the two number systems allow all possible syntagmatic combinations, none enjoying any special theoretical status, the only recourse would seem to be an appeal to a preference for redundancy. The preponderance of structural Types 1A and 2A in running text would then be a specific instance of this preference by virtue of the fact that they represent the collocation of the number meanings ONE with ONE, and MORE THAN ONE with MORE THAN ONE respectively.

To be sure, other manifestations of linguistic redundancy could easily be cited. But if a preference for redundancy were to function in a truly explanatory capacity, then this psychological predilection would have to be established entirely independent of language itself. That is, redundancy in language would have to be portrayed as the linguistic manifestation of some more general psychological characteristic in evidence *outside* language as well. We did, in fact, follow that analytical line in Chapter 3 where we argued that the relation of communicative efficacy holding between a meaning and a message was merely the linguistic manifestion of people's goal-directed deployment of tools in general. In the present case, however, redundancy seems too exclusively linguistic a phenomenon to be open to such external motivation.[5]

Systemic explanation

A more promising line of reasoning, we believe, is to relate Table 7.1 to the Focus Number System by way of language-internal factors that have already been established, namely, the communicative strategies motivated by the Entity Number, Focus Number, Focus and Control Systems.

According to the presentation in Chapter 5, the meanings in all three versions of the word-order Focus System relate primarily to the status of entities in the evolving discourse, not to their status within the sentence itself. (Recall the passage about the outcome of a footrace.) Only the meanings in the two Control Systems relate entities at a purely local level, by categorizing them in terms of their control of a particular Occurrence.

Since both the Focus and the Control meanings are borne by the same word-order signal, there is a constellation of (potentially conflicting) factors that bear on the way a language user describes the entity in Focus. To repeat, this is because the entity in Focus relates both to the thematic structure of the discourse as a whole (via the Focus System) and to one particular Occurrence (via the Control System). Naturally language users try to reconcile these competing factors in a harmonious way, but for present purposes it is necessary to idealize the situation in its simplest and most extreme form, as follows.

Sometimes language users describe the entity in Focus lexically and grammatically solely with an eye to its role in the subsequent Occurrence. In all these cases the Entity Number of the first-mentioned Participant (henceforth P) will concur with Focus Number because both number choices are being made in response *to the same feature of the message*. This yields the combinations ONE + ONE and MORE THAN ONE + MORE THAN ONE.

[1] In the sequel, the *group is* allowed back in Manhattan, director Ivan Reitman hints, 'because the city needs their services in a bigger and better way'.

(*Newsweek*)

[2] When the *brakes were* wet, you'd step on the pedal, it'd feel hard, but the car wouldn't stop.

(*Car Talk*, NPR)

On other occasions, language users will be guided in their description of the entity in Focus by considerations *other* than how it relates to the subsequent Occurrence. As illustrated by example [31] in Chapter 6 (repeated below as [3]), they may choose to capture the thematic status of the entity in Focus in the evolving discourse by describing it so as best to reflect its relation to previously mentioned entities in Focus.

[3] Precisely this kind of trouble can be seen nowadays in the field of education. As one evidence, several universities have recently described themselves – in private communications – as having divided faculties: *one group* of faculty members *teaches* a great deal, and is paid very little; *the*

> *other group teach* very little, but are paid considerably
> more.
> (Robert Davis, *Journal of Mathematical Behavior*)

In *the other group teach*, the 'teachers' are described as *the other group* so as to maintain the parallelism with the previous entity in Focus *one group*, not in response to their role as 'teachers' (which would have favoured, say, *other faculty members*, since 'teaching' is not a group activity). And in that previous clause the 'teachers' were described as *one group* (and categorized as ONE by the Focus Number System) so as to underscore the notion of 'divided faculties' in the previous sentence. Both the choice of *one group* and *the other group*, then, were actually made in response to clause-external factors rather than to the two Occurrences of 'teaching'.

Chapter 2 showed that similar considerations are responsible for the choice between *persons* and *people0* (the latter often provoking contrasting Focus Number). And Chapter 4 showed that speakers usually describe a plurality of animals as either ONE or MORE THAN ONE in response to their cognitive salience on a generic basis (see Table 4.49), not exclusively according to the way the animals relate to a particular Occurrence. Various local factors unrelated to the following Occurrence may play a role as well: the interpretive problem posed by the stems *mathematic*, *acoustic*, and *politic*; and lexical gaps, such as the absence in English of a word that refers to heaven and hell collectively (see [33] in Chapter 6).

Within this subset of situations taken together, the collocation of Entity and Focus Number will be statistically symmetrical since each is chosen on different grounds; sometimes the Entity Number choice will be the same as the Focus Number choice (e.g., *one group0 of faculty members teaches*; *the buffaloes graze0*), creating the spurious appearance of intra-sentential 'agreement'; and sometimes it will be different (e.g.,*the other group0 teach0*; *the buffalo0 graze0*).

When speakers describe the entity in Focus solely in response to any of these latter factors, then *no statistical skewing* results between the signals of the two number systems; they will occur in combinations whose ratios reflect the frequency of the various number signals occurring in the text as a whole. On the other hand, describing the entity in Focus solely with an eye to its role in the subsequent Occurrence will yield the combinations *Entity -0 + Occurrence -s* and *Entity -s + Occurrence -0* one hundred per cent of the time.[6]

The confirmation of a communicative strategy

On an individual occasion one can never be certain which strategy the language user is following. But overall one can. The skewing in Table 7.1 stands as evidence that some of the time language users do, indeed, choose both Entity Number (of P) and Focus Number in response to the *same* notional feature of the message. And the extent of that favouring reflects how often they do so.

The existence of this communicative strategy supports, in turn, the hypothesized Entity Number, Focus Number, Focus and Control Systems because it is the meanings in those four systems that have shaped the strategy. (Bear in mind that a communicative strategy is a way people employ linguistic meanings to communicate messages, not co-occurrence patterns of signals; those are merely the empirical consequences of the strategy.)

According to this logic, the existence of a statistical skewing is what serves as evidence of a communicative strategy. But its strength – over and above that necessary to establish statistical significance – provides *no additional support* for either the strategy itself or for the grammatical system(s) that engendered it. This is because we have at this point no reason to predict, say, that the local strategy evidenced in Table 7.1 should predominate so markedly over, say, the discourse strategy of example [3], which presumably has equally solid systemic motivation. Far from inspiring complacency, the nearly categorical skewing of Table 7.1 raises a problem of its own. Why should this one communicative strategy enjoy such hegemony in view of the fact that the competing ones have apparently equally firm systemic support?

An answer to this question is the topic of Chapter 8. Its presentation is being postponed because it will critically involve the structure of the Focus Number System as it relates to that of the Entity Number System, and until the former has been firmly established, an answer now would amount to building on sand. The remainder of this chapter is devoted to a quantitative testing of the communicative strategies illustrated briefly in Chapter 5 and extensively in Chapter 6. The statistical skewings created by these strategies constitute the most persuasive empirical evidence possible in favour of the Focus Number System.

7.3 Contrasting Grammatical Number in a Spanned Opposition

Chapter 5 argued that the Focus System hypothesis differs from the Verb Agreement hypothesis in that the former predicts contrasting number choices when the entity in Focus spans the opposition of number all by itself. In such situations the conceptualization of the entity in Focus hangs in the balance between a singularity and a plurality, open to resolution by the Focus Number System.

The Type 1 corpus

In the Type 1 corpus (having 'singular subjects') there are a number of morphological correlates to a spanned opposition. Some lexical stems traditionally known as collectives have it built into their meanings (e.g., *panel, family*). Another correlate is the construction *Entity -0 of Entity -s*, in which the same referents are described with contrasting number meanings (e.g., *the remainder of the paintings*). The initial prediction of the Focus System hypothesis, then, is that instances of contrasting Entity and Focus Number (Subtype B) will tend to occur when the entity in Focus is expressed in either of these two ways. Table 7.2 demonstrates this favouring by showing how the P phrases (which describe the entity in Focus) in the Type 1A and Type 1B sentences differ statistically.

TABLE 7.2   A comparison of Type 1A and Type 1B P phrases[7]

	1 Name	2 Person	3 Quasi- Collective	4 Collective	5 Entity -0 of Entity -s	6 Other	
Occurrence -s	26	27	19	5	7	109	
Type 1A	(13%)	(14%)	(10%)	(3%)	(4%)	(56%)	
Occurrence 0	1	0	14	81	106	11	$\chi^2 = 282.00$
Type 1B	(0%)	(0%)	(7%)	(38%)	(50%)	(5%)	$p < 0.001$

Eighty-eight per cent of Type 1B sentences have their entities in Focus described by either a collective (Category 4) or an *Entity -0 of Entity -s* phrase (Category 5), in contrast to seven per cent for Type 1A sentences.

In attempting to classify lexical stems as collective on a purely notional basis (i.e., without regard to Focus Number) we encountered a grey area. Words like *element, flower, youth* and *experience*, while not inherently collective (like *panel* and *family*), are susceptible to collective reference in the proper context: *an insurgent element, the flower of British youth, 98 year's experience*. For present purposes a borderline class was established (Category 3). The six categories of Table 7.2 are defined below:

Category 1: Names of persons: *Hedda, Arthur Kennedy, Santa Claus*.

Category 2: Words that describe a person: *man, woman, daughter, friend, director, singer, president, partner*.

Category 3: Words whose meanings do not inherently designate aggregates but which are susceptible to use for collective reference: *youth, work, element, school, system, relation, relationship, breed, species, literature, adminstration, government*.

Category 4: Words whose meanings inherently designate aggregates: *group, staff, audience, team, pair, crowd, majority, couple, faculty, family, folk, cast, clergy, crew, panel, committee*; all percentages (e.g., *one per cent, 20 per cent*); (*people* omitted.)[8]

Category 5: *Entity -∅ of Entity -s: the rest of the pregnancies, a handful of American Jews, a row of horns, a change of presidents, an increasing number of men.*[9]

Category 6: Other than Categories 1–5: *annoyance, reason, reaction, age*.

Table 7.2 shows that Type 1A and Type 1B sentences also differ with respect to the personhood of their entities in Focus. Twenty-seven per cent of the Type 1A sentences have P phrases which are names of persons (Category 1) or lexical stems describing a person (Category 2), whereas only one such instance occurred in the Type 1B corpus (the Santa Claus example). A person, of course, constitutes a cognitive unity *par excellence*. Falling at one polar extreme of the number opposition, a person is least susceptible to being conceptualized as spanning the opposition of number.[10]

The Type 2 corpus
The Type 2 corpus (having 'plural subjects') exhibits the same differences between the entities in Focus categorized with concurring (A) and contrasting (B) Focus Number meanings.
Table 7.3 shows that Type 2B sentences, like Type 1B sen-

TABLE 7.3   A comparison of Type 2A and Type 2B P phrases

	Person	Entity -s of Entity -∅	Other	
Occurrence -∅ Type 2A	23 (25%)	3 (3%)	65 (71%)	
Occurrence -s Type 2B	5 (5%)	11 (12%)	75 (82%)	$\chi^2 = 16.83$ $p < 0.001$

tences, disfavour entities in Focus that are persons (e.g., *lenders*, *viewers*, *critics*) in comparison to the Type 2A sentences. Similarly, Type 2B sentences favour (in relative terms) entities in Focus expressed with a phrase that is the formal converse of the favoured Category 5 in Table 7.2, namely, *Entity -s of Entity -∅*.

[4]   *Seventy years of Marxist doctrine* now *seems* headed for the dust heap.

(Dan Rather, CBS News)

Note, however, that this latter favouring is much less pronounced in the Type 2 corpus than in the Type 1 corpus; Category 5 accounted for 50 per cent of the Type 1B sentences whereas its formal converse accounts for only 12 per cent of the Type 2B sentences. Table 7.3 is clearly less successful in differentiating the concurring (Type 2A) sentences from the contrasting (Type 2B) sentences than was Table 7.2.

The category of lexical collective was not included in Table 7.3 because *panels*, *families* and *faculties* do not fall between the opposition of number as do their singular counterparts. However Type 2B sentences do favour a structural type that proves upon examination to be roughly comparable in its cognitive effect to that of a lexical collective. That structural type is a P phrase quantified by a numeral e.g., *ten bears, eight rounds of ringwork, two kids*.

The way numerical quantification implies a message spanning the opposition of number is not apparent until one takes into consideration the reason speakers bother to specify the exact number of entities in Focus. The message they wish to communicate is often about the arithmetic size of the aggregate.

[5]   With only two hundred bears roaming the park lands, *ten bears is* a significant number.

(*All Things Considered*, NPR)

TABLE 7.4   Type 2: numerical quantification of the P phrase

	+ Numerical quantification	− Numerical quantification	
Occurrence -∅ Type 2A	7 (8%)	84 (92%)	
Occurrence -s Type 2B	34 (37%)	57 (63%)	$\chi^2 = 22.95$ $p < 0.001$

[6]   New York model Colleen Kaehr estimates that *eight rounds* of ring work (moving constantly and shooting punches at a trainer's padded mitts) *is* the equivalent of three aerobics classes, 'in terms of the sweat level'.
(Charles Leerhsen, *Newsweek*)

[7]   I mean, *two kids is* really more like having four kids, especially if they're both still in diapers.
(*thirtysomething*, ABC)

Numerical quantification of the entity in Focus is frequent in the Type 2B corpus just as lexical collectives are frequent in the Type 1B corpus because the communicative motivation for both is frequently the same: the message is one that involves the individual components of an aggregate as well as the aggregate as a unitary whole.

As [4], [6] and [7] show, the category of numerical quantification can combine with those of Person and *Entity -s of Entity -∅*. When numerical quantification is allowed to supercede the latter two categories in the tabulation, the independent statistical effect of *Entity -s of Entity -∅* disappears. Type 2A entities in Focus now differ from those of Type 2B only with respect to personhood and numerical quantification.

TABLE 7.5   Integration of Tables 7.3 and 7.4, with numerical quantification superseding Person and *Entity -s of Entity -∅*

	Person	Entity -s of Entity -∅	Numerical quantification	Other	
Occurrence -∅ Type 2A	22 (24%)	3 (3%)	7 (8%)	59 (65%)	
Occurrence -s Type 2B	2 (2%)	2 (2%)	34 (37%)	53 (58%)	$\chi^2 = 34.98$ $p < 0.001$

While the descriptive categories for the Type 1 and Type 2 sentences are now no longer identical, the subsumption of *Entity -s of Entity -∅* by the category of numerical quantification, and its cognitive equivalence to lexical collectives, argues that all three are, at a higher level of abstraction, indicative of the same thing: namely, a message involving an aggregate as a unitary whole as well as its individual components.

The Type 3 corpus
This chapter began with the caveat that we would not be concerned with the relative frequency of the A and B versions of the three basic sentence types. An exception must be made in the case of Type 3. While our corpus does not allow a statistical demonstration, it is a well-recognized fact that sentences with conjoined nouns as subject exhibit agreement failure far more frequently than do Types 1 and 2. (Lapointe [1980/1986], excludes such sentences altogether from his theory of grammatical agreement, presumably because they would seem to require separate treatment.)

The relative frequency of Type 3B sentences, we now argue, is due to the fact that Type 3 sentences *inherently* span the opposition of number in a way that Types 1 and 2 typically do not. To see why this is so we must consider the communicative motivation for a speaker opting for a Type 3 over a Type 2 sentence.

[8]   That buzzword ('mission') has lost its currency; in the national competitions, graduate *teaching* and pure *research* win the prestigious prizes, and everyone's 'mission' is the same.

(Mary Burgan, *Academe*)

[9]   But ranchers complain that too many wild *horses* roam the plains.

(Howard Birkus, *Morning Edition*, NPR)

In [8] the writer has opted to express what is in Focus with two lexical stems conjoined by *and* (Type 3) because no single lexical stem in English encompasses what she is talking about while still maintaining the desired precision of reference. In [9], by contrast, the speaker has opted for Type 2 because the entities in Focus are similar enough to be described by a single lexical stem, *horse*.

The conceptual heterogeneity inherent in a Type 3 sentence often makes counting difficult. (Recall Frege's point quoted in

Chapter 2 that before counting can proceed the entities must be reduced to a common genus.) It is frequently unclear whether a ONE and a ONE (i.e., *Entity -∅* and *Entity -∅*) amount to MORE THAN ONE, or simply two instances of ONE. For when entities are reduced to a common genus – as required for the purposes of assessing Focus Number – they often collapse into an undifferentiated unity.

[10] That is what we do, for example with Walter Gieseking's haunting Mozart performances, pretending that *the crystalline delicacy* and *penetrating insight belongs* to a realm unsullied by Nazi alliances.

(Edward Rothstein, *The New Republic*)

In reducing *crystalline delicacy* and *penetrating insight* to a common genus, (say, 'artistic sensitivity'), the two seem to merge into a single thing, hence *belongs*.

While this explains the relative frequency of Type 3B sentences, it remains to be shown that Type 3B entities in Focus incline towards the ONE pole of the Focus Number opposition to a greater extent than do the Type 3A entities in Focus. The most straightforward route would appear to be a categorization of the conjoined lexical stems in terms of their relative synonymy. Following that line of analysis *delicacy* and *insight* in [10] would be rated as closer conceptually than *teaching* and *research* in [8].

Unfortunately such judgements introduce a subjectivity that would raise a doubt about the significance of the results. For this reason we opted for an analysis that, while only indirectly getting at what we are after, has the advantage of being less dependent upon subjective judgement.

The categories of names and (lexically described) persons can be retained since they are objectively applicable and should both favour Type 3A; two human beings already comprise a common genus, and the natural cognitive salience of separately mentioned human beings is hard to suppress.

[11] Ironically, both *Lewis* and *Presley were* alike in more ways than not.

(J. D. Considine, *The Baltimore Sun*)

For present purposes, however, names and persons will be collapsed into the single category *human being* to which we add (singular) lexical collectives. All three occur too infrequently in the Type 3 corpus to merit separate tabulation; moreover their mixed pairing, as in [12], would require still more subclassification.

[12]   I know that the world shares the grief that *Mrs Kennedy*
        and her *family* bear.
                (impromptu address to the press, Lyndon Johnson)

Cognitive rapprochement

Still required is a category that will serve as an analogue to those
of numerical quantification, *Entity -0 of Entity -s* and lexical
collective that figured in the analyses of sentence Types 1 and 2.
What we are looking for are structural features that, in one way
or another, effect a *cognitive rapprochement* of the entities in
Focus, thus favouring their conceptualization as a ONE when
reduced to a common genus.

A possessive pronoun is one such feature.

[13]   *Her* ability as an instructor and *her* love of the field was
        clearly evident.
                (Ruth Venning, letter of recommendation)

In [13] the words *ability* and *love* are drawn together conceptually
by the word *her* which relates both to a single person. A genitival
relation can, however, be expressed by other means as well.

[14]   The amount and the nature *of the resins* determines
        how much control the mousse allows.
                (*Consumer Reports*)

The phrase *of the resins* applies to both *amount* and *nature* and so
draws the two words together conceptually by associating both to
another entity.

[15]   Living one's illness *without meaning* and facing one's
        death *without meaning* requires us, therefore, to live
        ironically in relation to the Western metaphors of
        selfhood and its ideals of responsibility and self
        mastery.
                (Michael Ignatieff, *The New Republic*)

In [15] the repeated phrase *without meaning* links *living* and
facing by underscoring their common experiential core.

[16]   Prices are so high now that student *attendance* and

regular *attendance* by people who are not wealthy is impossible.

(Terence McNally, *New York Times*)

In [16] the conjoined entities in Focus are both expressed by the same word, *attendance*, thus favouring their conceptual merger. (Recall Wierzbicka's point that when referents are too similar – e.g., *rice* – they are counted as ONE.)

[17]   Neither conductor recognizes that the trio must be played at the same tempo as the scherzo if Beethoven's transformation, and the joke *that goes with it*, is to signify anything.

(William Malloch, *Musical America*)

In [17], the conjoined entities in Focus, *Beethoven's transformation* and *the joke*, are drawn together conceptually by *that goes with it*, which underscores the close association of the latter with the former.

[18]   Normally, seeing and caressing *one's partner* plays an important part in sexual intercourse.

(translated quotation, Simone de Beauvoir, *Age of Sexuality*)

Seeing and *caressing* are drawn together conceptually in the message because both activities directly involve *one's partner*.

The P phrases of examples [13]–[18] are quite diverse structurally: possessive pronoun applicable to both conjuncts; prepositional phrase applicable to both conjuncts; lexically identical conjuncts; relative clause relating one conjunct to the other; shared grammatical complement. Yet all these structural features have the common cognitive effect of drawing together the two lexical phrases conjoined with *and* in a tighter conceptual relation than is found elsewhere (e.g., [19]).

[19]   Both simple innumeracy and ignorance of higher mathematics (the latter quite an excusable condition) contribute to this limiting of literary possibilities.

(John Allen Paulos, *The New York Review of Books*)

In other words, they push the conceptualization of the entities in Focus toward the 'singular' pole of the grammatical opposition of Focus Number.

While the various morphological realizations of our cover-category cognitive *rapprochement* are less problematic than the criterion of relative synonymy, they are not entirely free of subjectivity since several require the analyst's assessment of constituent relations. For example, we judged *of higher mathematics* in [19] as applying only to *ignorance*, and so did not count [19] as an instance of cognitive *rapprochement*. On the other hand, we judged *of the resins* in [14] as applying to both *amount* and *nature*, and so did count it. Nevertheless we strove for consistency in applying our criteria to both the Type 3A and 3B sentences, always deciding clearly comparable cases in the same way and resolving less clear cases in disfavour of the predicted skewing. Table 7.6 contrasts Type 3A and Type 3B P phrases with respect to human beings and cognitive *rapprochement*, the latter comprised of the structural features illustrated by examples [13]–[18].

TABLE 7.6   Comparison of Type 3A and Type 3B P phrases with respect to human being and cognitive *rapprochement*

	Human being	Cognitive Rapprochement	Other	
Occurrence -∅ Type 3A	16 (13%)	28 (24%)	74 (63%)	
Occurrence -s Type 3B	3 (3%)	63 (53%)	52 (44%)	$\chi^2 = 26.30$ $p < 0.001$

Table 7.6 shows that the *Occurrence -s* favours the cover-category cognitive *rapprochement* by a ratio of two to one (i.e., 53 per cent to 24 per cent). And, as before, *Occurrence -s* disfavours human beings more strongly than *Occurrence -∅*.

7.4 Extent of the Spanned Opposition

Chapter 6 argued that the Focus Number opposition is exploited by speakers to indicate the *extent* to which the entity in Focus spans the opposition of number, not merely the (categorical) fact that it does. Table 7.6 supports this claim because the disfavouring of cognitive *rapprochement* by the Type 3A corpus is far from categorical; 24 per cent of the Type 3A sentences fall into that category. This argues that Focus Number is still making an independent expressive comment rather than being mechanically determined by structural features of the P phrase, as is shown

in the following contrast. ([20A] = + cognitive *rapprochement*;
[20B] = − cognitive *rapprochement*.)

[20A]   *My life* as a critic and *my life* as a teacher *are* essentially
        inseparable.
                        (Wayne Booth, *New York Times Book Review*)
[20B]   And I'm certain *my life* and *my son's life doesn't mean* a
        thing to them [= townspeople vampires].
                        (Movie dialogue, *A Return to Salem's Lot*)

At the same time, the relational opposition of the Focus Number
meanings is preserved in Table 7.6 because the (non-categorical)
favourings are in the directions predicted by the hypothesis.

We return now to the Type 1 corpus for a demonstration of
this same point. The earlier analysis, to recall, did not establish
the independent expressive value of Focus Number. Table 7.2
(repeated below) made it appear that speakers almost always opt
for MORE THAN ONE whenever the P phrase is a lexical
collective or an *Entity -0 of Entity -s* phrase.

TABLE 7.2   A comparison of Type 1A and Type 1B P phrases

	1 Name	2 Person	3 Quasi-Collective	4 Collective	5 Entity -0 of Entity -s	6 Other
Occurrence -s Type 1A	26 (13%)	27 (14%)	19 (10%)	5 (3%)	7 (4%)	109 (56%)
Occurrence 0 Type 1B	1 (0%)	0 (0%)	14 (7%)	81 (38%)	106 (50%)	11 (5%)

Table 7.2 does not suggest that speakers manipulate Focus
Number for expressive purposes in Type 1 sentences as they
clearly do in Type 3 sentences.

Such subtle exploitation of the System cannot, however, be
demonstrated on the original Type 1 data because the Type 1A
corpus contains only twelve examples of Categories 4 and 5, too
few for comparison with the Type 1B corpus (containing 187
examples falling into these two categories).

For this reason a *second* corpus of Type 1A examples was
created whose P phrases fall just in Categories 4 and 5. These
were collected in the same mechanical manner, at the same time,
as the Type 1, 2 and 3 examples and will serve as the Type 1A
corpus in Tables 7.7–7.9 in lieu of the original Type 1A corpus
examined in Table 7.2.

Semantic weight

First to be examined are sentences with their P phrase of the structural type *Entity -∅ of Entity -s* (i.e., Category 5 in Table 7.2). The factor that tips the balance in favour of ONE or MORE THAN ONE is the relative semantic 'weight' of the lexical stems categorized as *Entity -∅* and *Entity -s*. When *Entity -∅* and *Entity -s* are of equal semantic 'weight', the balance tips in favour of ONE because the preposition *of* subordinates *Entity -s* to *Entity -∅* slightly in the message. But when *Entity -s* outweighs *Entity -∅* semantically, this can counteract the subordinating effect of *of*, and the balance tips in favour of MORE THAN ONE.

For present purposes, semantic 'weight' is defined as the amount of semantic specification supplied by *Entity -∅ beyond that of pure numerical quantification*. To the extent *Entity -∅* functions as a quantifier, it merges conceptually with what it quantifies (i.e., the *of Entity -s* phrase). Conversely, to the extent it has semantic content beyond pure quantification it can command attention on its own.

Words that express a numerical fraction fall at the 'light' end of this continuum. *One fifth* expresses nothing more than a fraction of a whole. Decimal fractions will also be counted in this class despite the admittedly problematic decision to treat *per cent* as an instance of *Entity -∅* (e.g., *59 per cent*). Decimal fractions are expressively equivalent to numerical fractions and *per cent* is not, at any rate, an instance of *Entity -s*.

Next on the continuum of semantic weight are lexical stems that name an arithmetic fraction of a plurality: *majority, minority, portion, remainder, bulk*. Referentially they are equivalent to numerical and decimal fractions, but the paradigmatic contrasts among these words argue they have slightly more lexical content (beyond simple plurality) than the former.

Next on the continuum are words that designate an aggregate imprecisely: *group, handful, host, spate*. These no longer imply an arithmetic fraction yet are unspecific about the kind of aggregate designated. (They can, for example, refer to both animate and inanimate collectives.)

Next come words that contain precise specifying content. This class includes both traditional collectives like *team, band, jury* and *panel*, and words that merely imply plural reference: *list, breed, concentration, pattern, web, crazy quilt*.[11] The lexical content of these words now includes precise information about the nature of the aggregate; *team* and *band* both imply a group of human beings, and *jury* and *panel* are even more specific.

Finally come words that do not contain in their meanings any hint of referential plurality: *presence, process, retrieval, problem, weight*.

Summarized below are the definitions of these five classes, along with examples. Bear in mind these are all subdivisions of just the *first* component of *Entity -∅ of Entity -s*. All are followed by an *of* phrase with a lexical stem (categorized as MORE THAN ONE) that clearly designates a plurality of referents: *of women, of opera experts, of cartridges*.

1. decimals, and fractions with *one* as numerator (e.g., *59 per cent of Americans; one fifth of Australian men*),
2. words naming or implying a fraction of a whole: *majority, minority, portion, remainder, bulk, rest, (a great) deal, (a) percentage*.
3. imprecise aggregate: *group, handful, host, spate,*
4. precise aggregate: *team, band, audience, jury, delegation, generation, population, pattern, distribution, proliferation, row, series, sequence* (the word *number* [e.g., *a number of students*] while falling into this category, is excluded here and reserved for separate examination),
5. semantically specific words that do not imply a referential plurality: *presence, process, retrieval, weight, shortage, cloud, circle, study*.

Table 7.7 compares Type 1A and Type 1B P phrases of the structural configuration *Entity -∅ of Entity -s*, with their *Entity -∅* component classified in terms of classes 1–5.

TABLE 7.7   Type 1 P phrase = *Entity -∅ of Entity -s*; Sub-classification of *Entity -∅* according to semantic weight

	1	2	3	4	5	
Occurrence -s Type 1A	0 (0%)	5 (5%)	10 (11%)	43 (47%)	34 (37%)	
Occurrence -∅ Type 1B	15 (16%)	36 (39%)	11 (12%)	21 (23%)	9 (10%)	$\chi^2 = 60.46$ $p < 0.001$

Table 7.7 shows a nearly perfect percentage increase in the top row as the first component of the *Entity -∅ of Entity -s* phrase acquires more semantic content. This increasing semantic content gradually shifts *Entity -∅* from being construed as merely a quantifier of the *of Entity -s* phrase (another form of cognitive *rapprochement*) to one that commands attention in its own right.

The result is that as the cognitive prominence of *Entity -∅* increases, the *of Entity -s* phrase is less able to wrest attention away from *Entity -∅* when it comes to Focus Number.

The progression is less than perfect because our procedure conflates the effect of semantic weight with the effect of the varying frequency of the five message types in natural discourse. And unfortunately this conflation entirely destroys the predicted reverse progression in the bottom row.

What is needed now is a manner of presentation that will capture the effect of semantic weight in the top and bottom rows simultaneously while at the same time *suppressing* information about the differing frequencies of classes 1–5 in the corpus as a whole. A presentation in terms of the ratio of the percentages in the five columns does this.

TABLE 7.7a   Percentage ratio of classes 1–5 in Type 1A to Type 1B

	1	2	3	4	5
Type 1A / Type 1B	0	.13	.92	2.04	3.70

Table 7.7a now shows a perfectly regular progression for classes 1–5.

The of phrase
In Table 7.7 the first component of the *Entity -∅ of Entity -s* phrase varied while the second component was effectively a constant. We will now hold the *Entity -∅* absolutely constant and demonstrate the effect of the *of* phrase on the Focus Number choice. Drawing again on the specially selected corpus of Type 1A examples, we offer a demonstration involving examples in which the first component is the word *majority*. However the *of* phrases, while all referring to a real-world plurality, will contrast in Entity Number, as in [21A] and [21B].

[21A] The majority of the *audience* here *was* in their teens and twenties.
                                   (*All Things Considered*, NPR)
[21B] The majority of multisyllabic *words get* shortened in popular usage, and nymphomaniac is usually curtailed to 'nymphy' or just plain 'nymph' from which it derived in the first place.
                                   (Karl Steiner, *Club*)

Table 7.8 compares the Focus Number choice for *majority of Entity -0* with the choice for *majority of Entity -s*. (In Table 7.2, the former was counted as a lexical collective, Category 4, and the latter was counted as *Entity -0 of Entity -s*, Category 5.)

TABLE 7.8   P phrase = *Majority of Entity*: *of Entity -0* vs. *of Entity -s*

	Majority of Entity -0	Majority of Entity -s	
Occurrence -s Type 1A	10 (83%)	2 (17%)	
Occurrence -0 Type 1B	5 (16%)	27 (84%)	$\chi^2 = 17.81$ $p < 0.001$

Table 7.8 shows that when the entity in Focus is expressed by the phrase *majority of Entity -0* the Focus Number choice is ONE 83 per cent of the time, and when it is expressed by the phrase *majority of Entity -s* the choice is MORE THAN ONE 84 per cent of the time.

Collectives
We turn now to an examination of lexical collectives, Category 4 in Table 7.2. Chapter 6 began with examples involving the words *family*, *faculty* and *couple* in which there was a pronominal reference to the entity in Focus in either the predicate or in a following clause. The grammatical number of the (personal or possessive) pronoun was then appealed to as support for the Focus Number choice, as in [22A] and [22B].

[22A]   And this fall the couple *expects its* first child.
                                    (*The Greenfield Recorder*)
[22B]   Robert Mays of Lakeland, Florida got an early birthday present this week when a Florida court ruled against a Pennsylvania couple who *contend* May's 10-year-old daughter is actually *their* child.
                                    (*USA Today*)

Table 7.9 tests for the generality of such usage. Since the original Type 1 corpus had only five Type A examples of lexical collectives (see Table 7.2), Table 7.9 draws again on the specially gathered corpus of Type 1A examples, this time examining those with a lexical collective. Table 7.9 shows the relation between Focus Number and the grammatical number of a personal or possessive pronoun that refers to the entity in Focus.

TABLE 7.9 Type 1 P phrase = lexical collective; singular vs. plural pronouns referring to the entity in Focus

	it/its	*they/them/their*	
Occurrence -s Type 1A	10 (63%)	6 (37%)	
Occurrence -0 Type 1B	0 (0%)	19 (100%)	$\chi^2 = 13.70$ $p < 0.001$

Lexical collective = *family, faculty, couple, team, group, jury, cabinet, audience, staff, clergy, congregation, commission.*

Table 7.9 shows that singular pronouns outside the P phrase favour *Occurrence -s* and plural pronouns favour *Occurrence -0*.

Table 7.9 includes just those examples of lexical collectives containing overt pronominal reference. The majority of lexical collective examples do not, however, contain pronominal reference, and in those we were unable to find any consistent morphological feature corroborating the Focus Number choice. Yet upon examination there often appears to be some idiosyncratic support. Consider for instance the following Focus Number contrast involving the word *crew*, both appearing in the same text.

[23] Each week 'Pirate TV's' scruffy *crew*, supposedly transmitting from a barge off Manhattan, *take* aim at the deadliest forms of airwave pollution. . . A spoof of ESPN introduced the Extra-Sensory Perception Network (Filmed highlights of tomorrow's games! Lists of players who are *going* [original emphasis] to be injured!) Semiregular features include 'Rastapiece Theater,' which presents dreadlock versions of the classics and 'The Above Sea World of Jacques Cousteau,' wherein the *crew* of the Calypso *invades* dry land to liberate the fish in pet stores.

(Harry Waters, Newsweek)

The base meaning of the word *crew* is the complement of deck hands on a ship, referents who, in their professional capacity, are a homogeneous aggregate. In the second instance of *crew* in [23], *the crew of the Calypso*, the meaning of *crew* applies literally. In the first instance, *'Pirate TV's' scruffy crew*, *crew* applies metaphorically to five people who are actually comedians in a TV series, each with his own comic personality. This difference in the applicability of the word *crew* (literal vs. metaphorical) is then reflected in the contrasting Focus Number of *invades* and *take∅*.

Note that the Focus Number choice in [23] cannot be said to be due to considerations of 'referential number' in any strict sense because in both cases the word *crew* is actually referring to the same five people. Instead, it reflects an inherently linguistic contrast, namely, the degree to which the five referents constitute a prototypical 'crew'.

While a rationale for the Focus Number choice in [23] can be mustered here, the choice is clearly not the result of a mechanical play of contextual features, but a (non-redundant) instance of expressively-motivated choice.

7.5 Recharacterization of Entity in Focus

While Tables 7.1–7.9 all confirm predictions drawn from the Focus Number hypothesis, they are not totally at odds with the notion of subject-verb agreement because the statistical correlates of 'verb number' still involve semantic or structural characteristics of the grammatical subject. More telling support for the Focus Number hypothesis will be demonstrations that semantic and structural features *directly related to the Occurrence* play a critical role, as was the case in many of the example pairs examined in Chapter 6. To this evidence we now turn.

One such feature is a predicate noun. In a predicate noun construction the entity in Focus is recharacterized by a lexical stem inflected for Entity Number. Since Focus Number indicates the number of entities in Focus *with respect to the Occurrence* – which is now one of recharacterization (e.g., *be, seem, appear*) – one would expect the Focus Number choice to be influenced by the *same* considerations that influence the grammatical number of the word recharacterizing the entity in Focus.

The Type 3 corpus contains the largest number of such examples. In the example pairs below, the Focus Number meanings reflect the grammatical number of the italicised predicate noun rather than the somewhat problematic grammatical number of the closely comparable P phrases.

[24A] Racism and sexism *are* not *problems* in the soap [opera] world.
(Brent Staples, *New York Times Book Review*)
[24B] If liberal Judaism and Christianity *is a way* of having God without an afterlife, reincarnation is an option for

those who want an afterlife without God.

(Kenneth L. Woodward, *Newsweek*)

[25A] Japanese coherence and harmony *are* relatively new *phenomena* in a century marked by bitter struggles between the military and the large industrial groups, between tenant farmers and landlords, between industrial workers and employers.

(Robert Reich, *The New Republic*)

[25B] And without laboring the point, Herbert Lottman, in this stylishly crafted biography, makes us appreciate the extent to which Flaubert's life and work *was a staggeringly successful exercise* in sublimation.

(Jay Tolson, *USA Today*)

[26A] We are the only nation where giving and volunteering *are* pervasive *characteristics* of the entire population.

(Brian O'Connell, *The New York Times*)

[26B] Brushing and flossing regularly *is the best way* to fight tooth decay.

(*New York and Company*, WNYC)

Table 7.10 shows the statistical generality of this principle of choice illustrated by examples [24]–[26].

TABLE 7.10   Type 3 with predicate nouns; predicate noun = *Entity -s* vs. *Entity -0*

	Entity *-s*	Entity *-0*	
Occurrence -0 Type 3A	13 (65%)	7 (35%)	
Occurrence -s Type 3B	0 (0%)	17 (100%)	$\chi^2 = 14.30$ $p < 0.001$

There is a 65 per cent to 0 per cent favouring of the Focus Number meaning MORE THAN ONE when the Occurrence equates the P phrase with a lexical stem also marked as MORE THAN ONE (by the Entity Number System); and a 100 per cent to 35 per cent favouring of the Focus Number meaning ONE when the Occurrence equates the P phrase with a lexical stem marked as ONE.

This principle of choice is also evident in the Type 2 corpus.

[27A] Anniversaries all too easily *become rackets*, with

hustlers looking to squeeze every event for a last drop of profit.

(John Schwartz, *Newsweek*)

[27B] 'Private psychiatric beds for teenagers *is* the fastest growing *segment* of the hospital industry' says Dr. Jerry M. Wiener, president of the American Academy of Child and Adolescent Psychiatry.

(*Newsweek*)

Table 7.11 shows this tendency for the subclass of Type 2 predicate noun examples.

TABLE 7.11   Type 2 with predicate nouns; predicate noun = *Entity -s* vs. *Entity -0*

	Entity -s	*Entity -0*	
Occurrence -0 Type 2A	4 (36%)	7 (64%)	
Occurrence -s Type 2B	2 (7%)	34 (94%)	$\chi^2 = 7.18$ $p < 0.01$

Table 7.11 shows that plural predicate nouns are disfavoured in absolute terms by both 2A and 2B (36 per cent and 7 per cent). But the disfavouring of a plural predicate noun by Type B is greater, by 29 percentage points, than that by Type A. Thus, the *relational value* of the Focus Number meanings manifested in absolute terms in Table 7.10 is still in evidence.

7.6 The Non-Categoricalness of Statistical Skewings

Table 7.11 provides an opportunity to address the question of the non-categorical nature of the skewings in our tables. According to the rationale presented earlier, the various contextual features associated with Focus Number are not its direct cause. The true causal variable of Focus Number is always the message being communicated; the contextual features are merely indirect evidence of that message. But that contextual evidence, because it is indirect, is sometimes imperfect and inexact. For example, the two instances in the lower left-hand cell of Table 7.11 going against the prediction were the following:

[28]   According to one industry consultant, Marc Finer, 1988 sales of CD players *was 4.4 million units*, an increase of

about a million from the previous year.
(Gerald Gold, The New York Times)

[29]   . . .the average faculty and staff rates at colleges and
universities in the Northeast was $183 [read dollars
W.R.] a year, considerably higher even than the current
Rutgers rate, which averages $25 per faculty and staff
registration.
(Rutgers University Parking Report)

In [28] and [29] the Entity Number categorization of the predicate
noun phrases 4.4 million units and $183 (dollars) is MORE
THAN ONE due to the measurement category employed. Yet
the actual conceptual status of these phrases in the message is still
that of a unitary aggregate, as in [27B]. Had we allowed
ourselves to categorize messages on a purely notional basis, the
skewing in the bottom row of Table 7.11 would have been 100
per cent since [28] and [29] still conform in spirit to the principle
being tested. The fact that it was not 100 per cent is simply the
consequence of our having adopted a testing procedure that
avoids reliance on the subjective judgement of the analyst. But
the price of this objectivity is an inexactness of measurement.

7.7 Messages of Size or Sufficiency

Qualitative examination of the disconfirming examples in a table
is analytically useful because it can suggest new parameters of
measurement in which the disconfirming examples can become
confirming examples.[12] Both [28] and [29] involved Occurrences
in which the size of an aggregate is in some way critical (as
evidenced by the numerical quantification of the predicate
nouns). If one is willing to relinquish this objective evidence in
favour of the analyst's subjective judgement that a message of
quantity or sufficiency is intended, [28] and [29] now become part
of a larger pattern that can be tested outside the circumscribed
structural domain of predicate nouns.

[30]   Even though it doesn't seem like a lot, in a small room
that 30 or 40 children seems like quite a few.
(Interview, Morning Edition, NPR)

[31]   One hundred calls is not too much to ask for.
(Fund raising pitch for radio station WNYC)

[32]   Well, I got some nice presents; I think you did. And
anyway, some presents is better than no presents at all.
(Cornelia Reid)

While morphologically diverse, examples [30], [31] and [32] all express messages relating in some way to the arithmetic size of an aggregate, just like [28] and [29].

The examples above did not appear in Table 7.11 because they are predicate adjective constructions not predicate nouns. This body of Type 2B examples will now be examined and contrasted with a comparable body of predicate adjective Type 2A examples such as [33], in which the message is typically not about the arithmetic size of an aggregate.

[33]	Just because they made the cosmetics OK doesn't mean that all four wheels *are where they should be*.

(*Cartalk*, NPR)

Table 7.12 demonstrates that Type 2 predicate adjective constructions favour the Focus Number meaning ONE (2B) over MORE THAN ONE (2A) when the predication is about the arithmetic size or sufficiency of an aggregate.

TABLE 7.12	Type 2 predicate adjective constructions; predicate adjective phrase = +/− message of size or sufficiency

	+ *Size/sufficiency*	− *Size/sufficiency*	
Occurrence -∅ Type 2A	1 (5%)	18 (95%)	
Occurrence -s Type 2B	10 (53%)	9 (47%)	$\chi^2 = 8.91$ $p < 0.01$

The favouring of ONE for messages about size or sufficiency also holds for Type 2 sentences that would be classified syntactically as transitive and intransitive, as illustrated by [34]–[38].

[34]	Twenty-five dollars *brings* you six months of this program schedule.

(Fundraising promotional, Channel 13, New York)

[35]	Two drops *deodorizes* anything in your house.

(Air freshener advertisement)

[36]	Two thousand troops in Panama *doesn't put* too much strain on the Pentagon.

(CBS News)

[37]	I sat down and said, 'Look, only eight seconds of the

President's speech *is going to wind up* on the air'.

(Peggy Noonan, *Ms*)

[38] The first three records you save *pays* for the cartridge timer.

[Advertisement, *High Fidelity*)

Tables 7.13 and 7.14 show the statistical generality of this strategy in the Type 2 corpus for transitive and intransitive constructions respectively.

TABLE 7.13 Type 2 transitive constructions; predication = +/− size or sufficiency

	+ *Size/sufficiency*	− *Size/sufficiency*	
Occurrence -∅ Type 2A	2 (6%)	31 (94%)	
Occurrence -s Type 2B	6 (33%)	12 (67%)	$\chi^2 = 6.55$ $p < 0.02$

TABLE 7.14 Type 2 intransitive constructions; predication = +/− size or sufficiency

	+ *Size/sufficiency*	− *Size/sufficiency*	
Occurrence -∅ Type 2A	2 (10%)	19 (90%)	
Occurrence -s Type 2B	6 (67%)	3 (33%)	$\chi^2 = 7.80$ $p < 0.01$

Both Tables 7.13 and 7.14 show a tendency to choose the Focus Number meaning ONE (2B) rather than MORE THAN ONE (2A) when the predications involve size or sufficiency. The fact that such messages comprise a lower per cent of the Type 2B corpus in Table 7.13 than in Table 7.14 (33 per cent vs. 67 per cent) is not germane here. What is germane is the left-hand column ratios, which are closely comparable: $\frac{6\%}{33\%} = 0.18$; $\frac{10\%}{67\%} = 0.15$.

While subjective judgement could not be avoided in deciding whether or not the examples in Tables 7.12–7.14 were about size or sufficiency, more objective evidence exists in the form of the numerical quantification of the P phrase itself (e.g., *two kids*, *twenty-five dollars*, *eight seconds*). Recall that the statistical favouring of numerically quantified Type 2 P phrases for *Occurrence -s* was demonstrated earlier in Table 7.4. But again, that evidence is not a completely reliable indication of a message of size or sufficiency. Example [33], whose P phrase is numerically quantified (*all four wheels*), is not about size or sufficiency; it is simply about the location of each of the four wheels (*are where they should be*).

7.8 The Word *Number*

Tables 7.12–7.14 involved the Type 2 corpus. The effect of a message of quantity or sufficiency on Focus Number can also be demonstrated for the Type 1 corpus. As illustrated in Chapter 6, the affinity of the meaning ONE for a message about a numerical quantity is most strikingly seen when the word *number* is itself the grammatical head of the P phrase.

[39A] For instance, in the past 20 years the *number* of French journalists who happen to be women *has risen* from 15 per cent to 25, although they're still paid 25 per cent less than men.

(John Leonard, *Ms*)

[39B] A *number* of members, such as Rep. Ben Jones of Georgia, *have acknowledged* they are recovering alcoholics.

(Steven Waldman, *Newsweek*)

In [39A] and [39B] the P phrases are both morphologically and conceptually complex. The different Occurrences affect the prominence of their conceptual components in the message as a whole. The Occurrence of *has risen* relates most directly to the arithmetic 'number' component, whereas the Occurrence of *have acknowledged* relates most directly to the 'members' component.

We will now demonstrate the generality of this parameter of contrast by showing that the lexical stem expressing the Occurrence is the critical variable. In Table 7.15 the P phrases are all of the structural type *number0 of Entity -s* (i.e., Category 5 in Table 7.2). The Type 1B examples are drawn from the original corpus of Type 1 data while the Type 1A examples are drawn from the specially-selected corpus originally gathered for Table 7.7. However both bodies of data were omitted from that table for separate examination here. Counted as + *Quantity* in Table 7.15 are the following lexical stems, all clearly designating Occurrences particularly suitable for predications about numerical quantities: *increase, decrease, decline, rise, soar, double, grow (eightfold/ at the present rate), fluctuate, shrink,* and *be nil/small/ high/ down/slight/ a small part/rated high.*

TABLE 7.15 P phrase = *number0 of Entity -s*; Occurrence = +/− quantity

	+ *Quantity*	− *Quantity*	
Occurrence -s Type 1A	23 (79%)	6 (21%)	
Occurrence -0 Type 1B	1 (7%)	14 (93%)	$\chi^2 = 21.04$ $p < 0.001$

Table 7.15 shows that when the P phrase is *number of Entity-s*, Occurrences specifically applicable to an arithmetic 'number' strongly favour the Focus Number meaning ONE, and Occurrences that are not specifically applicable to a 'number' strongly favour the Focus Number meaning MORE THAN ONE.

Chapter 5 cited the claim by Celce-Murcia and Larsen-Freeman (1983:38) that *a number of* takes a plural verb and *the number of* takes a singular verb. Table 7.16 below shows there is indeed a strong statistical favouring of such collocations, though it falls short of the categoricality implied by Celce-Murcia and Larsen-Freeman.

TABLE 7.16 P phrase = *The number of (Entity -s)* vs. *A number of (Entity -s)*

	The number of	*A number of*	
Occurrence -s Type 1A	24 (83%)	5 (17%)	
Occurrence -0 Type 1B	3 (20%)	12 (80%)	$\chi^2 = 16.42$ $p < 0.001$

Tables 7.15 and 7.16 show statistical skewings of nearly equal strength. Moreover, the population of the four cells in the two tables is nearly identical; that is, the same examples fall into the same cells. Clearly the article accompanying *number* is as good a predictor of Focus Number as the semantic content of the lexical stem designating the Occurrence. Tables 7.15 and 7.16 are, then, equally accurate *descriptions* of the collocational behaviour of the word *number*.

Nevertheless, we maintain that Table 7.15 is the correct characterization of the collocational behaviour of *number* because Table 7.15 employs a descriptive category that integrates that behaviour into a larger pattern in the language, namely the one evidenced in Tables 7.12, 7.13 and 7.14. And that pattern is, in turn, a specific instance of the more general pattern evidenced in Tables 7.9, 7.10 and 7.11.

Moreover, this larger pattern is itself motivated *deductively* by the Focus Number System hypothesis. The hypothesis says that Focus Number reflects the number of the entity in Focus *as it relates to the Occurrence*. Naturally, then, one would predict statistical affinities between the Focus Number meanings and Occurrences of different kinds. The hypothesis does not, on the other hand, make any directly derivable prediction about the relation between articles and Focus Number. Any such statistical relation must be dealt with on an *ad hoc* basis, in terms of how the articles affect the interpretation of one particular lexical stem.

The fact that a larger principle lies behind Table 7.15 but not Table 7.16 also means that something can now be said in the way of explanation of the disconfirming examples. For instance, the one example falling in the lower left-hand cell of Table 7.15 is the following.

[40]   A smaller number of steps suggests a growing ability to
        organize.
                            (Angela Bodino, Rutgers Ed D dissertation)

The lexical stem *suggest* is not one that by itself implies an arithmetic figure (as does *increase* and *decrease*), and so [40] was counted as going against the prediction in Table 7.15. Yet the message as a whole is about the inverse relation between two quantities: decreasing steps and increasing ability. Thus when examined directly in light of the larger principle, the disconfirming evidence proves to be confirming evidence after all.

On the other hand, when purely *inductive* descriptive categories (e.g., *the* and *a*) are employed, exceptions to the 'rule' must remain exceptions because there exists no general principle that can integrate the exceptions into a larger pattern.[13]

The contrasting insightfulness of Tables 7.15 and 7.16 shows how an approach to linguistic analysis based on initial syntactic description (coupled with a focus on grammatical 'correctness') is likely to close the door to later functional explanation. For the contextual feature critical to our functional explanation, namely, the nature of the Occurrence, never earned a place in Celce-Murcia and Larsen-Freeman's syntactic description (presumably because the article seemed more general than an open list of lexical stems). In its absence, the collocational behaviour of the word *number* becomes yet another example of the essential arbitrariness of 'syntax'. The methodological bias of syntactic analysis towards purely formal description makes the centrality of 'arbitrary syntax' in language self-fulfilling.

7.9 Occurrences Implying More-Than-One Entity in Focus

Tables 7.11–7.15 showed that an Occurrence that is part of a predication about the size or sufficiency of a referential plurality favours the Focus Number meaning ONE because ONE forces the plurality to be reconceptualized as a unitary aggregate. By the same token, we now argue, an Occurrence contributing to a predication that forces a referential plurality to be conceived as *separate entities* strongly favours the Focus Number meaning MORE THAN ONE, as illustrated by examples [41]–[43].

[41] Never before has the Vatican said so directly that faith and prejudice *are incompatible*.
(Kenneth Woodward, *Newsweek*)

[42] In Japan, a booming economy and full employment *have combined* to require a new import, foreign workers.
(Bob Edwards, *Morning Edition*, NPR)

[43] Oberlin College and the Smithsonian Institution *join forces* to publish – in score form – transcriptions of classic jazz music.
(*Oberlin Alumni Magazine*)

The Occurrences of 'being incompatible', 'combining' and 'joining forces' all imply the involvement of more-than-one entity in Focus. (Others in the corpus are 'being alike', 'being synonymous', 'being mutually supportive', 'teaming up', 'blending', 'meeting', 'sharing' and 'naming different roles'.)

While such Occurrences are relatively rare, they favour the Focus Number meaning MORE THAN ONE strongly enough to attain statistical significance in the Type 3 corpus.

TABLE 7.17　Type 3 P phrase; +/− plurality implied by Occurrence

	+Implied plurality	−Implied plurality	
Occurrence -∅ Type 3A	17 (17%)	81 (83%)	
Occurrence -s Type 3B	2　(2%)	99 (98%)	$\chi^2 = 13.60$ $p < 0.001$

In Table 7.17, 17 per cent of the Occurrences categorized as MORE THAN ONE (3A) imply a plurality of entities in Focus, while only 2 per cent of the Occurrences categorized as ONE imply a plurality of entities in Focus (3B).

Since the Occurrences implying a plurality of entities in Focus could not be specified in objective formal terms, we counted all problematic cases as going against the predicted skewing. Yet again they do not, upon examination, appear to violate the basic principle being tested. For example, the two instances in the lower left-hand cell of Table 7.17 were the following.

[44]　We know that the company's destiny and ours *is* the same.

(Bernard Krisher, *Newsweek*)

[45]　Heaven and hell *is* not about ending up in two different places; it's about ending up in this life, and forever in the next, being two very different kinds of persons.

(James Bertchaell, *Newsweek*)

The Occurrence of 'being the same' in [44], while necessarily implying two entities, asserts their actual identity (in contrast to 'being alike' and 'being synonymous'). As for [45] ([33] in Chapter 6), the Occurrence of 'being about ending up in two different places' is, in fact, being denied.

This concludes the statistical tests of the Focus Number System. There remain two areas where the Focus Number hypothesis should be tested, but our data base does not contain enough instances to carry out the requisite tests. We offer instead a qualitative discussion.

7.10　*Occurrence . . . P*

One context in which Entity and Focus Number frequently contrast is so-called *there*- insertion sentences.

[46]   There isn't any more clean areas.

> (Major Donald Amin, interview
> *All Things Considered*, NPR)

[47]   There's no undershirts there.

> (Colin Reid)

In informal speech a good number of such collocations are quite likely 'performance errors' arising from the fact that the speaker must choose Focus Number before having decided how to describe the entity in Focus. But they occur in written English as well. And here we find the same contextual elements associated with contrasting Entity and Focus Number that proved to be statistically significant elsewhere.

[48]   Colleges must begin to touch the sacred territory of departmental offerings. . . . There is a need to deal not only with the Western tradition but with non-Western materials, whether derived from feminism or literary theory. There *is enough* time and *enough* room in four years of college.

> (Leon Botstein, *The New York Times*)

[49]   Since there *are a large number* of pizza places, it soon becomes clear they cannot make much more than $15,000 each because of the competition.

> (*The Recorder*, Greenfield MA)

[50]   Nine hundred feet below the surface *are a unique combination* of metals.

> (Television documentary, 'Planet Earth: Gifts from the Sea')

Green (1984) offers evidence that something more than a temporal factor is involved. She reports that when nineteen native speakers were asked what agreement they accepted for a series of seven permutations of the sentence *There --- a man and a woman in the garden* (effected by substituting *two women* for *a woman*, reversal of noun phrases, and verb inversion) no two informants accepted the exact same set of sentences. Furthermore, some of them vacillated from moment to moment or day to day about whether certain examples were acceptable or not.

Green argues that this kind of inter- and intra-speaker variation suggests that the rules which speakers have internalized for subject-verb agreement don't extend naturally to *there*-insertion cases.

As Morgan (1972) [quoted in Chapter 5, W.R.] suggested, many speakers may have grammars which simply do not predict any agreement at all for *there-* insertion sentences. Other speakers may have added 'patches' to ensure coverage of *there-* insertion cases. The evidence for this is that some consistently chose a plural verb whenever the closest conjunct was plural, and some did so when either conjunct was plural. Some chose a singular subject whenever the subject did not immediately precede the verb, and so on.

(Green 1984:30)

The present analysis offers a different explanation, one that sees purely systemic factors operating rather than a systemic breakdown that then calls for 'patches'. According to the One Participant Focus System sketched in Chapter 5, the signal *Occurrence . . . P* bears the meaning LESS FOCUS. This linguistic sign is often employed, along with *there*, to introduce previously unmentioned entities into a discourse, to get them on the scene as it were, before anything more is said about them. A grammatical device that withholds maximum attention is ideal for such a purpose. Note that the meaning LESS FOCUS of *Occurrence . . . P* helps to explain why [51] is anomalous but [52] is not.

[51] ?There grazed a deer in the middle of the field.
　　　LESS FOCUS
[52] There was a deer in the middle of the field.
　　　LESS FOCUS

The lexical precision of *graze* is out of place in a context in which one's attention is being diverted from the agent. One only sees that a deer is 'grazing' (as opposed to merely 'being') after focusing one's full attention upon it.

Turning now to the Focus Number choice, Chapter 4 argued that in the context of a referential plurality the meaning MORE THAN ONE represents greater precision than ONE; and the questionnaire established that speakers exploit the Entity Number opposition to reflect different degrees of cognitively salient individuality as implied by the surrounding context.

It is reasonable to see the occasional choice of ONE for a referential plurality in '*there-* insertion' sentences as an instance of the same thing. Speakers are implying lessened discourse salience both by the choice of the meaning LESS FOCUS (signaled by *Occurrence . . . P*) and by the descriptive imprecision implicit in the Focus Number meaning ONE. The variation among informants found by Green parallels that of the subjects on the questionnaire. Unfortunately our corpus of such examples is not sufficient to test for the textual correlates that would support this rationale.

7.11 *Each* and *Every*

Although prescriptive grammars mandate a singular verb with the words *each* and *every*, both words may occur with *Occurrence -∅* when the context underscores the plurality of reference.

[53]   Unless *every* one of you *want* to be sent down to the principal's office, this must stop right now.
                    (dialogue, *The Boy in the Plastic Bubble*)

[54]   *Every* one of the more than 4000 political appointees *have gotten* similar letters.
                    (Linda Chavez, *Morning Edition*, NPR)

[55]   *Each* of those (radio) programmes *run* back to back.
                    (on-air caller to WNYC)

[56]   Well, that's where *each* of us *come* in.
                    (Liz Carpenter, address to The National Press Club)

But again, our corpus does not allow this apparent tendency to be tested.

7.12 The Relation Between Hypothesis and Testing Procedure

It is useful now to examine in more detail how the various analytical procedures employed in Chapters 4–7 relate to the grammatical hypotheses they were designed to test. The grammatical systems of sign-based theory are composed of linguistic signs whose meanings categorize a single semantic substance (e.g., ENTITY NUMBER, FOCUS NUMBER, DIFFEREN-TIATION, DEGREE OF CONTROL). If the meanings in such systems were employed in a purely objective manner, it would be possible to test each meaning in turn, on the basis of its substantive semantic value alone. That is, each meaning would be tested by showing that it was descriptively *true* of all the messages for which it was employed (the usual procedure in semantic analysis).

However grammatical meanings are not employed in such a straightforward way. Instead, speakers exploit their relational opposition, adjusting the cross-over point between them to make the choice maximally informative for the given context. As a consequence, a grammatical meaning must be seen as relating to a message both *substantively* and *differentially*. It characterizes the message semantically in some way while at the same time differentiating it from some unintended alternative lying in its penumbra.

What must be tested, then, is the relational opposition between the meanings. But since the semantic opposition may apply to a given message in more than one way (and even along a single parameter of contrast different speakers may be operating with different cross-over points), many messages can legitimately be judged to incline towards *opposite* poles of the opposition by different speakers. This means that both speaker and context must be controlled for. One needs to see a *single* speaker deploying *both* poles of the opposition to distinguish closely related messages that contrast along the semantic parameter of the grammatical system.

The questionnaire in Chapter 4 was designed to do this. Thirty-two of Tables 4.5–4.43 showed individual speakers exploiting both poles of the grammatical opposition of Entity Number to distinguish messages about a referential plurality of animals whose individuality differed in cognitive salience. Since the predicted behaviour was a bi-directional act of differentiation, the unit of analysis was response pairs, not individual responses.

The Chapter 6 data were also in the form of response pairs. The pairs showed individual speakers exploiting both poles of the Focus Number opposition to distinguish closely related messages which differed with respect to the relative 'oneness' of the entity in Focus. Yet those example pairs were essentially a series of case studies. Still required was statistical evidence that the example pairs reflected general tendencies of use.

The practical problem blocking such a demonstration was that usually no single speaker provides examples of contrasting Focus Number like the closely comparable example pairs in Chapter 6. And unlike Entity Number, the prescriptive pressures associated with Focus Number made a questionnaire impractical.

The solution has been to compare groups of speakers, each employing only *one* pole of the Focus Number opposition. If the groups are sufficiently large, each speaker in one group should have a *doppelgänger* in the other group who, selecting the same parameter of contrast and operating with the same cross-over point, has produced the *differentiated alternative* of the first speaker. In other words, each *doppelgänger* has made overt the implicit paradigmatic message contrast underlying the Focus Number choice of the first. Each is doing what his alter ego *would* do, *if only he had a chance*, namely, choosing the contrasting Focus Number meaning for a message (type) lying on the opposite side of the shared cross-over point.

By comparing the two groups statistically, one is pairing up each speaker with his *doppelgänger*, with the result that one has now created sets of structurally-matched example pairs each produced, in effect, by a single speaker, comparable to those examined in Chapter 6.[14]

The testing procedure went as follows. A particular message type was chosen which had consistent morphological correlates; for example, a message about multiple entities which were then recharacterized as some other kind of entity (i.e., Type 2 or 3 with a predicate noun). This basic message type was then divided into two contrasting sub-types which, according to Chapter 6, speakers sometimes distinguish by means of the Focus Number opposition. This message contrast should ideally have an overt morphological correlate; here the grammatical number of the predicate noun served in that capacity.

If speakers are, in fact, sometimes choosing Focus Number on the basis of the *same* feature of the message as the one responsible for the grammatical number of the predicate noun, then there should be a skewing of the Focus meaning ONE toward predicate nouns also categorized as ONE, and a skewing of the Focus meaning MORE THAN ONE toward predicate nouns categorized as MORE THAN ONE. This prediction was confirmed by Tables 7.10 and 7.11.

Note that we have no basis to predict *how often* a speaker will actually do this, so we cannot anticipate the strength of the skewing. Any speaker could just as well have chosen Focus Number according to the grammatical number of the P phrase, a parameter of contrast equally relevant to the opposition. (In the case of the Type 2 corpus, speakers would be underscoring the difference between a Type 2A and a Type 1A message, which they in fact regularly do, as shown by Table 7.1.) But in all those cases in which speakers choose Focus Number on the basis of the P phrase, their output will be distributed symmetrically with respect to the grammatical number of the predicate noun. So the predicted skewing *vis-à-vis* the predicate noun, however weak, will never be effaced.

Since we cannot say how often a speaker will operate on this or that strategy, we can have no expectation about the substantive (percentage) values in the upper or lower rows of a table considered independently, only an expectation about their column relations. Each communicative strategy predicts a purely relative skewing of *more* and *less* (cf., Table 7.11).

That relation is borne out in the predicted direction by each and every table for each and every context in which it was tested. There is, then, no variation at the systemic level. The relational opposition between the Focus Number meanings holds *100 per cent of the time*; what varies is merely its morphological manifestation. Here we have in actuality what, for Chomsky, has only been a counter-factual idealization, namely, a speech community *perfectly homogeneous at the systemic level of grammatical structure.*

7.13 The Axis of Systemic Grammatical Structure

This grammatical homogeneity within the speech community is an actuality within sign-based theory because in a sign-based conception of linguistic structure the basic and fundamental grammatical relations are defined on the *paradigmatic* axis, not the syntagmatic axis. These are the relations existing in language itself, idealized as a self-contained system. The syntagmatic relations among signs in language use (with which sentence-based theory is concerned) are but imperfect and derivative reflections of their true paradigmatic values.[15] The associated syntagmatic elements will reflect, at best, only the message being expressed, not its paradigmatic alternative, which, for the casual observer, is always eclipsed.

Since different speakers will naturally be influenced by different unspoken alternatives, the syntagmatic statistical affinities will rarely hold 100 per cent of the time. This is why the enterprise of writing rules for the syntagmatic combination of signs so often falls short of empirical success. Their sequential combination is not ultimately controlled by relations of determination on the syntagmatic axis, but by value relations to unchosen alternatives on the paradigmatic axis, as each of those paradigmatic oppositions applies in turn to the message being expressed.[16]

7.14 The Choice of Communicative Strategy

While Tables 7.1–7.17 show no true variation at the level of paradigmatic grammatical structure they clearly show a high degree of collocational variation. This arises from the fact that any given message is usually of a complexity that allows a grammatical opposition to apply to it in more than one place. Consider example [57].

[57]   A variety of snow and weather conditions *are* part of
       skiing's challenges.
                (Placard on Yankee Clipper ski lift, Mount Snow)

As justification for the choice of MORE THAN ONE (*are*) one
can point to the Entity Number of either *conditions* or *challenges*,
claiming that the cognitive salience of *variety* and *part* is
diminished in the message because of their semantic imprecision.
But had the verb been *is*, one could then point to the Entity
Number of either *variety* or *part* as support for the choice, saying
that *of* subordinates *conditions* and *challenges* slightly in the
message.

As example [57] illustrates, the Focus Number opposition
cannot be applied to most messages as unitary wholes; it must be
applied to some particular fraction. This means a speaker must
first single out some notional fraction and make the grammatical
choice on that basis alone. We call this the selection of a
communicative strategy.

Statistical weightings

Since speakers clearly favour certain communicative strategies
over others, the next stage of analysis would seem to be an
investigation of the relative favouring of communicative strategies
in those contexts where more than one strategy legitimately
applies. Statistical techniques of analysis are readily available to
carry out such investigation. Each of the syntagmatic contextual
correlates of Focus Number that were examined individually in
our tables would be treated as a statistical predictor of Focus
Number. One would then calculate the statistical weight that
must be assigned to each of these variables to achieve optimal
predictive success. These statistical weightings would then serve
as indirect evidence of the favouring of certain communicative
strategies over others. The final stage of analysis would then
address the question of why speakers favour certain strategies
over others.[17]

Unfortunately this line of analysis is not possible with the
present data base due to the way it was assembled. Recall that
each pair of A and B examples comprising Types 2 and 3 was
produced by a different speaker/writer. And in the case of the
Type 1 corpus, all of the tables except Table 7.2 involved a
specially selected corpus of Type 1A sentences produced, in
many cases, by different speakers/writers than those responsible
for the Type 1B sentences.

This procedure was a practical necessity due to the infrequency of Types 1B, 2B and 3B in normal discourse. But it deprives us of critical information. It means that we are unable to say what any statistical weighting of strategies implies about individual speakers. For example, suppose that when Strategies X and Y are both applicable, Strategy X is favoured 70 per cent of the time and Strategy Y is favoured 30 per cent of the time. We would not know whether this 70/30 favouring consistently held for each speaker individually or, alternatively, whether 70 per cent of the speakers opted for Strategy X 100 per cent of the time and 30 per cent of the speakers opted for Strategy Y 100 per cent of the time. That is to say, one would not know whether the 70/30 favouring was a fact of intra-speaker variation or a fact of inter-speaker variation; both would produce the same statistical result for the corpus as a whole.

Yet it is critically important to know what kind of fact is involved because that determines the kind of explanation that would then be sought. If it is a fact of intra-speaker variation, the explanation will be psycho-linguistic. It will be rooted in structural features of the linguistic code common to the speech community as a whole and will invoke cognitive and communicative principles that apply equally to all speakers. On the other hand, if it is a fact of inter-speaker variation, then the explanation will be socio-linguistic, in that it must appeal to differences among speakers (or differences of social context). This would open the door to all the socio-linguistic variables that differentiate sub-groups of speakers or social context from each other.

Because we would not know in which direction to turn in search of an explanation for such statistical weightings, no particular purpose would be served in calculating them. They would be no more than a statistical description of our corpus, and, as such, would be of little interest.

The Table 7.1 skewing
There is one communicative strategy, however, for which we do have the requisite information. That is the communicative strategy evidenced in Table 7.1. Table 7.1 shows one writer choosing Focus Number on the basis of the *same* notional fraction of the message as that motivating her choice of Entity Number for the grammatical head of the P phrase (i.e., she makes her subjects and verbs 'agree' in number).

The nearly categorical favouring of this one communicative strategy in the Table 7.1 corpus is due, in part, to the fact that in narrative prose the opportunity to choose many of the competing strategies examined in this chapter does not arise. But as speakers of English we know that Table 7.1 could be replicated within a few percentage points on any non-narrative text of any chosen genre, both spoken and written. Whatever the weighting differences among the other strategies affecting Focus Number may be, they pale in comparison to the clear and unmistakable hegemony of this first and most basic strategy.

We can, then, proceed with confidence to address the question of why this one communicative strategy so strongly outweighs all others, for we know without a doubt that it does for all speakers of Standard English. This certainty means that we know the kind of explanation that must be sought. The explanation will be psycho-linguistic not socio-linguistic. That is to say, it will be rooted in structural features of the linguistic code common to the speech community as a whole and will invoke universal cognitive and communicative principles that apply equally to all speakers. This explanation is presented in Chapter 8.

Notes
1. The programmes were *All Things Considered* and *Morning Edition*, produced by National Public Radio and broadcast on local affiliates. Both programmes were re-broadcast at a later hour, allowing examples noted during the first broadcast to be taped and transcribed.
2. Further assurance, to ourself at any rate, comes from the fact that during the period of data collection (nearly complete before Chapter 6 was written) we had not yet settled on the actual statistical predictions we would later be testing. Only during the close-grained analysis carried out in Chapter 6 did we come to understand in detail the communicative strategies underlying the Focus Number choice (especially those relating to the Occurrence).
3. Often the sentence directly following the B sentence lacked Focus Number or had its P phrase of a different grammatical number. This meant that the matching A and B sentences were separated by several intervening sentences. This was almost always the case for Types 2 and 3. So the comparisons between the A and B sentences of Types 2 and 3 should not be affected by their sequential order in the source texts. For the Type 1 sentences, most of the comparisons will (for a reason to be explained) be between subclasses of the 1B sentences and specially selected, matching subclasses of 1A sentences, sometimes drawn from different sources.
4. The one difference noted among the various source materials was that Types 1B, 2B and 3B occur less frequently in narrative than in non-narrative prose (both spoken and written). As suggested in Chapter 5, we believe this is because in narrative prose the entities in Focus tend to be human beings, and the natural cognitive

salience they enjoy makes their referential number almost always relevant to the associated Occurrence. The difference between narrative and non-narrative prose is thus due to a global difference in *content* (rather than of communicative strategy or style), similar to the global difference in content between legal and journalistic prose noted in Chapter 2 that resulted in different favourings of *persons* and *people*.

5. Recall Newmeyer's critique, cited in Chapter 1, of functional accounts that 'attribute whatever structural property is being discussed to informally described human states, drives, needs, abilities and such that have no basis in any existing formalized theory of human behaviour or cognition'. Erica Garcia (personal communication) alerted me to the dangers of relating quantitative data to grammatical hypotheses in terms of a generalized preference for redundancy (or coherence). She deserves credit for first pointing out the conceptual shortcomings in all previous Form-Content work (e.g., Diver 1969 and Reid 1977) that implicitly argued in such a fashion and is responsible for our attempt here to offer an alternative line of reasoning.

6. One context in which this 100 per cent skewing can be observed is where the entity in Focus is expressed with a third-person personal pronoun. During the ten years of anecdotal and subsequent systematic data collection, we have found no instances of types 1B or 2B in which the entity in Focus is described with a personal pronoun. In such cases there is no lexical stem whose interpretation need be manipulated by the Entity Number meanings (often the motivation for contrasting grammatical number), and the Entity Number choice always reflects the relation of what is in Focus to the subsequent Occurrence, as in the following example.

    The jury is appointed to be the finder of facts and yet attorneys don't always bring out everything *they need* to know.
                                                    (Mark Frankel, *Newsweek*)

    Note the grammatical number of *they* reflects its role in the Occurrence of 'needing to know', not the grammatical number of its antecedent, *jury*. We infer from this that language users often follow this local strategy when a lexical stem *is* involved, producing the skewing in Table 7.1.

7. Omitted from this and subsequent counts are all instances of *people* with a plural verb, the *United States* and *news* with a singular verb, grammatically plural titles (e.g., *Aliens*), and words such as *data* and *media* whose Entity Number categorization is in flux. This was to assure that the statistical support for the Focus Number hypothesis was not due to a small number of words whose grammatical status is problematic or whose use might be regarded as entirely conventionalized. Also omitted from the corpus of 1A

and 2A examples were those whose entity in Focus was expressed with a personal pronoun, since no comparable examples of 1B, 2B and 3B were found, for the reason offered in note 6. Names describing the entity in Focus were, however, included in the 1A and 3A corpora because of the Santa Claus example in Chapter 6. Examples with a relative pronoun expressing the entity in Focus were included so long as there was no doubt about its antecedent (e.g., The *couple*, who *were* in their thirties . . .).

8. As noted in 7 above, *people* was omitted entirely from the study because its high frequency would have made Table 7.2 and several others largely a reflection of the distribution of that word alone.

9. Category 5 supersedes Category 4. Thus *a group* and *a group of people* both count as 4 but *a group of scholars* counts as 5.

10. It is now apparent why we had no interest in excluding from consideration the Santa Claus example discussed in Chapter 6 (*Yes, Virginia, there are a Santa Claus*). When the data for grammatical analysis are statistical facts of language use rather than 'grammaticality judgements', it makes little difference whether a disfavouring is categorical or just short of categorical.

11. We initially attempted to distinguish between explicit and implicit collectives but found it was impossible and so grouped them into a single class. Especially problematic were words like *population*, *generation* and *variety*.

12. This entire chapter is, in fact, devoted to an examination of the (competing) principles of choice responsible for sentences that would fall into the disconfirming cells of Table 7.1.

13. Because there is, at heart, only a single basic principle underlying the deployment of the Focus Number System, the various contextual correlates of Focus Number examined in this chapter will not be subjected to multivariate analysis. Multivariate analysis is an appropriate statistical tool in an exploratory study in which the causal variable(s) are not yet known. In the present case, however, the causal variables are known: the meanings in the Focus Number System and the message being conveyed. Whether or not the various structural correlates of the message are statistically independent is immaterial since the structural correlates are not being regarded as causal, merely corroborative. Each table is a demonstration of the systemic value relation between the two Focus Number meanings as their opposition applies to different message contrasts, a relation which, despite the variety of its morphological manifestations, *is everywhere the same*; each offers a different way to look at essentially the same linguistic fact. (Thus the structural correlates should all be, in theory, statistically dependent.) Recall the case study in Chapter 2 of *persons* vs. *people0* that demonstrated that the various correlates at the genre, paragraph, sentence, and word level were all essentially instances of the same linguistic fact (and thus would presumably all prove to

be statistically dependent).

14. The discussions in 1.14 and 4.14 of idealization in linguistic theory implied that sentence-based theory requires a more extreme idealization than does sign-based theory. The present discussion shows that at the stage of hypothesis testing (i.e., quantitative analysis), sign-based analyses may require a more complex abstraction from observation and idealization of speakers than does sentence-based theory.

15. The only case when systemic relations are directly manifested syntagmatically is when both paradigmatic values in a grammatical system are signalled simultaneously. For example, in the case of the Focus-Control interlock the word-order signal P_1 . . . *Occurrence* . . . P_2 simultaneously designates P_1 as both HIGHER CONTROLLER and IN FOCUS and P_2 as both LOWER CONTROLLER and NOT IN FOCUS.

16. This makes syntax – the investigation of syntagmatic relations – the study of (idealized) linguistic 'performance'. Katz and Bever (1976) argue the dangers of conflating performance and competence phenomena within a generative framework. 'If we attempt to account for such hybrid phenomena within the grammar itself, we will obstruct the development of a simple and revealing theory of the grammatical structure of the language, since the demand to integrate principles unrelated to the explication of grammatical properties and relations will prevent the rules of grammar from properly rendering genuine grammatical generalizations about the sound/meaning correlation in language' (p. 49). Our restriction of purely grammatical facts to paradigmatic structural relations follows Katz and Bever's reasoning precisely.

17. We would not accord such statistical weightings any psychological reality because that would turn speakers into mathematical automatons mindlessly calculating contextual factors so as to conform to some external 'norm'. Such a view is inconsistent with our basically instrumental view of language, in which the psychological motivation for linguistic behaviour is the attainment of a personally meaningful goal.

Following the same reasoning, when an Irish Catholic voter pulls the Democratic lever in an American election he or she does not do so so as to adhere to the statistical norm that Irish Catholics vote Democratic, but on the basis of some personal judgement. That personal judgement is, to be sure, strongly affected by the political opinions of the voter's family and friends, who are probably, among other things, also Irish Catholics. But it is not influenced, we maintain, by the demographer's abstraction 'Irish Catholic voters'.

We believe this position is consistent with Durkheim's justification of sociology as a discipline separate from psychology on the grounds that the behaviour of groups of people cannot be accounted for in terms of the psychology of its individual members (Dinneen 1989). Conversely, we argue here, the behaviour of individuals cannot be accounted for in exactly the same terms (i.e., rules and norms) as those applicable to group behaviour.

Chapter 8

Textual resonance

Chapter 7 tested for communicative strategies that support the Focus Number System as a fully-fledged expressive device. Yet the fact remains Focus Number usually simply echoes the grammatical number of the P phrase. This raises two questions: why is this manner of deployment favoured so strongly over others? Secondly, in what meaningful way is this a *communicative* strategy at all? For while *Occurrence -s* and *-0* are being used, to be sure, in ways consistent with their systemic semantic values, communication would scarcely break down in their absence.

As a quick rejoinder to that line of argument, the fact that one can do without a tool at a pinch does not vitiate a claim for its functional utility when available. We can all eat with our hands at a picnic, but still find forks, knives and spoons useful at home. This chapter makes a case similar in spirit. The Focus Number System facilitates the task at hand without, in the final analysis, being crucial.

A more telling analogy here involves the difference between a conventional photographic negative and a holographic negative. Each small point on a conventional negative encodes information relevant to a particular feature of the image being represented; if a fraction of the negative is removed, a corresponding fraction of the image is lost. On a holographic negative however, there is no analogue correspondence between points of the negative and features of the image; the image is simultaneously encoded at all points, though at lower degrees of resolution. Excising a portion of the negative reduces the resolution but leaves the image as a whole intact. In the case of holography, then, trying to partition a negative into those fractions that are functionally critical and those that are superfluous is entirely to misunderstand the basic principle upon which that system of representation operates.

So too with language. To try to partition its components into the semantically critical and the semantically redundant is to miss the peculiar genius of its design; and with it, an understanding of its internal system of checks and balances that have evolved in response to the exigencies of human communication. In short, it is to miss the answer to the question of why language is the way it is.

8.1 The Perceptual Problem of Signal Identification

The perceptual problem of signal identification is not usually taken into account in semantic analysis. Instead, consideration is restricted to the semantic values of signals as they relate to a completed interpretation. This makes traditional semantic analysis entirely *product*-oriented, focusing exclusively on the endpoint of a successful communicative act. And naturally, when informational value is assessed from that vantage point, the Focus Number meanings do indeed prove to be redundant most of the time.

What is being overlooked is the communicative *process* itself; in particular, the process by which a hearer identifies the signals. It is all too easy, then, to begin thinking of the semantic interpretation of signals *already identified* as the major problem of comprehension.

But linguistic signals of the kind we have posited do not present themselves for interpretation at the outset. The -*s* and -$\emptyset$ suffixes, to recall, are not by themselves linguistic signals, merely the morphological components of signals. Until the lexical stem associated with -*s* or -$\emptyset$ has been understood as describing an Entity or Occurrence, no linguistic signal has been perceived, and hence no meaning has been signalled.

This simple fact has a profound consequence for an understanding of the real functional value of the Focus Number System. The information it provides, though often superfluous with respect to the completed interpretation, is far from superfluous for the language user in the process of arriving at that interpretation from the stream of sound that initially confronts him. The Focus Number System, in conjunction with the Entity Number System, facilitates this move from pure sound to linguistic signals, making the comprehension process more nearly linear than it would otherwise be.

TEXTUAL RESONANCE

8.2 Systemic Distinctiveness

This case for the functional value of the Focus Number System would appear to be along the lines of 'structural marker'. In a sense, this is correct. The difference is that the structure the Focus Number System marks is semantic, not syntactic, because the linguistic means by which it operates are the same as those illustrated in Chapter 6.

Our case begins with the systemic semantic difference between the two number systems. The meanings in each system, to recall, categorize slightly different semantic substances: those of the Entity Number System directly relate to the expressive potential of a particular lexical stem, while those of the Focus Number System reflect how the P phrase relates to the larger communication. Thus no combination of number meanings is redundant in strictly systemic terms.

The pragmatic consequence of this can be illustrated by re-examining the deployment of the two systems in schematized fashion. The two systems contain four signals that can be combined in basically four ways (discounting their sequential order). As illustrated in Chapter 6, speakers employ these four pairings in the communication of four basic types of messages.

FIGURE 8.1   Message types

	Message type	Example
A.	focus on one entity conceived as an unarticulated whole;	(Her family is one aunt about a thousand years old.)
B.	focus on the component parts of an articulated entity;	(My family have been prominent well-to-do people.)
C.	focus on one entity but with discrete parts or manifestations;	(Steroids is a business decision.)
D.	focus on multiple separate entities.	(Anabolic steroids are synthetic hormones.)

The actual alignment between the signals and the message types is shown in Figure 8.2. (For the purposes of this demonstration the more complex permutations involving conjoined phrases have been set aside.) Figure 8.2 reveals the unique communicative value of each signal. The *Entity -0* indicates the intended message is of either type A or B while excluding types C and D; and the *Entity -s* does just the reverse. Similarly, the *Occurrence -s* narrows the intended message type to either A or C while excluding types B and D; and the *Occurrence -0* the

FIGURE 8.2 Alignment between signal combinations and message types

1.	*Entity -0 + Occurrence -s* →	A.	focus on one entity conceived as an unarticulated whole
2.	*Entity -0 + Occurrence -0* →	B.	focus on the component parts of an articulated entity
3.	*Entity -s + Occurrence -s* →	C.	focus on one entity but with discrete parts or manifestations
4.	*Entity -s + Occurrence -0* →	D.	focus on multiple separate entities

reverse. In short, the distinctive potential of each signal is *equal* when assessed in isolation.

8.3 Contextual Non-distinctiveness

Of course the number signals are never assessed out of context in this manner. Focus Number is always understood in light of what can be gathered about the intended message from the rest of the utterance. In many contexts, message types B and C can be eliminated as real possibilities; no message involving a spanned opposition could be intended.

[1]   The boy0 walks through the field.
[2]   The boys walk0 through the field.

With types B and C eliminated, the number marking of *boy* alone distinguishes types A and D, and the information signalled by the Focus Number System appears to be contributing nothing at all.

Meaning vs. information
But diminished informational value does not set the Focus Number signals apart from other meaning-bearing units. A lexical item can appear uninformative as well, when assessed in light of the other lexical choices.

[3]   He took a pack of Marlboros, drew out a _____, and lit up.

There would seem to be no doubt about the identity of the omitted lexical item; taking the context as given, the word *cigarette* is as predictable as the Focus Number meanings often appear to be. But predictability of this kind does not rob a signal of its meaning, merely its informative value. Weinreich articulates this point, and its consequence for semantic theory, in a particularly forceful way.

> The second stimulus for this work was a realization that the information-theoretical doctrine, 'obligatory = meaningless,' has been seriously misused in linguistics. The inverse proportion between redundancy and information applies only to elements of the signal, i.e., to the surface structure. It is on that level – the phonological – that the notion was so fruitful in linguistics, and it is on the level of signals that it was again productive in information theory. . . But if we are to have a semantic theory within linguistics, *it must be clearly established that what a signal loses through redundancy is not its meaning, but merely its informativeness* (emphasis W.R.), its power autonomously to identify an element of the deep structure.
>
> (Weinreich 1980:189)

Furthermore, the informative value of a meaning never drops to zero because predictability is never absolute for either lexical or grammatical signs. *He* in [3] could be a small boy who withdraws a *chocolate drop* placed in the pack by his father, and lights up *with pleasure*. Similarly, most speakers of English would regard the Focus Number decision in [4] as a foregone conclusion.

[4]   Yes Virginia, there is a Santa Claus.

Yet Chapter 6 included the example *Yes Virginia, there are a Santa Claus*. In short, nothing is 100 per cent predictable from the hearer's standpoint. There is, to be sure, a high degree of statistical predictability. But that says nothing about what will occur on an individual occasion. The appearance of complete predictability can only be achieved through an idealization of the data which excludes novel utterances from consideration for no other reason than that they mar the picture of complete predictability.

8.4 Overlapping Message Partials

A more accurate picture of the status of Focus Number is to see it as near one end of a continuum, with 100 per cent information value at one pole and zero per cent at the other. Rarely, though, is the 100 per cent pole attained, because any given feature of the message will typically play a part in determining the choice of more than one linguistic sign. As a result, the listener perceives that the various aspects of the message to which each meaning individually contributes *overlap* and *reinforce* each other in a variety of ways. Consider the multiple ways this happens in [5].

[5]   Those students feel indignation.

The word *student* indicates the involvement of a 'scholar' who is both 'animate' and 'human'. (For present purposes the word *student* is glossed HUMAN SCHOLAR.) Once we move beyond *student*, the semantic overlapping begins. The meaning MORE THAN ONE is signalled twice, once by *those* and again by the *Entity -s* of *students*; each instance contributes to the same feature of 'plurality' in the message. But since the notion of 'plurality' is inextricably linked to what is being counted, it encompasses that portion of the message to which *student* contributes as well.

This kind of semantic reinforcement is to be found throughout the rest of the sentence. The word *feel* designates a kind of 'experiencing', something only an animate being can do; and this feature of animacy implicit in *feel* reinforces the animacy intrinsic to the word *student*. Similarly the word *indignation*, designating a peculiarly human feeling (glossed here as RIGHTEOUS ANGER), elaborates what the word *feel* implies, while at the same time echoing the humanity of *students*. Finally, the meaning MORE THAN ONE of *feel0* contributes to the same portion of the message as do the number meanings of both *those* and *students*; but in addition it contributes to the same portion as does *feel*, since the meanings of the Focus Number System apply to what is in Focus with respect to the Occurrence itself.

Figure 8.3 illustrates these mutual, overlapping contributions described above. The arrow from each meaning points to a circle which encompasses those message features signalled or implied by the meaning. The overlapping of the circles represents the semantic reinforcement that results when two or more meanings contribute to the same conceptual fragment of the message. (Note the deictic meaning of *those* as well as the Focus and Control meanings of P_1 . . . Occurrence . . . P_2 have been omitted in this illustration.)

Redundancy, the multiple signalling of the same information, is a particular instance of what we are talking about. Strict redundancy exists between the Entity Number meanings of *those* and *students*. But elsewhere redundancy is too narrow for our purposes. No strict identity of meaning holds between the *Entity*

FIGURE 8.3   The contribution of meanings to message features

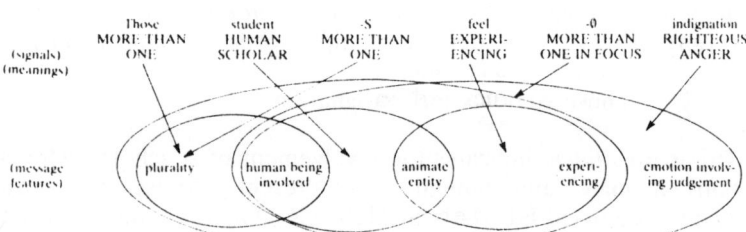

-s of *students* and the *Occurrence -∅* of *feel∅* in [5], for, to repeat, the semantic substances of the Entity and Focus Number Systems are not identical. And certainly no strict identity of meaning exists between *feel* and *students*.

8.5 Textual Resonance

We are speaking instead of the amplification and confirmation of facets of the message by the meanings of various signals. We have chosen to call this linguistic phenomenon *textual resonance*. *Resonance* is a term borrowed from acoustics and the metaphor here seems particularly apt. When the air in a simple cylinder is excited, it vibrates loudest (and lowest) at a frequency called its fundamental. In addition, it vibrates at higher frequencies whose wave lengths are odd-integer multiples of the fundamental frequency, producing a resonance series (Shriberg and Kent, 1982:377).

Of importance here is the musical value of the early resonances in this series. The third and fifth resonances represent, in harmonic terms, the dominant and the mediant. Sounding together with the first resonance, they form a major triad, the basic signature chord of the musical key represented by the fundamental. The idea of meanings being *in harmony* with some feature of the message, yet nevertheless semantically distinct from it, is behind our choice of the word resonance.

Textual resonance is created when two meanings jointly contribute to the communication of *the same feature of the message* (i.e., are in harmony). While two meanings may contribute to the same feature of the message by virtue of their identity, identity is not required. The essence of textual resonance lies in an identity of communicative *goal*, not in an identity of the semantic means employed to achieve that goal. Distinct semantic means can contribute to the same communicative end.

The function of textual resonance

Why is language structured in such a way that we end up signalling (or implying) the same feature of the message more than once? What role does such textual resonance play in language use?

The key to the answer lies in the signalling apparatus that language users must rely on. The lexical and grammatical signals in any language are, to a significant degree, perceptually indeterminate. Pike's example of perfect lexical, grammatical and structural homonymy, *the sun's rays meet/ the sons raise meat*, comes to mind here. Similar examples can be easily constructed. (Thanks go to Jack Abramowitz for these examples.)

[a]   The morning sun shone in.
[b]   The mourning son shown in. . .
[a]   Wood ant chews the stake.
[b]   Would aunt choose the steak?
[a]   The miner tied suede bows.
[b]   The minor tide swayed beaux.
[a]   The baron peers through the cellar.
[b]   The barren piers threw the seller.
[a]   Mail sent to plane.
[b]   Male scent too plain.
[a]   Hoarse cantors buy hymn.
[b]   Horse canters by him.

These examples are effective in illustrating the widespread homonymy of lexical and grammatical signs in English because their orthographic representation makes clear that different linguistic signs are involved, while our ear tells us they sound exactly the same. But their very perfection obscures the implication such homonymy has for linguistic theory. More instructive are the everyday examples in which the homonymy is only partial, for such examples illustrate both the perceptual problem it creates – morphological and interpretive indeterminacy – and its solution, *textual resonance*. Consider the following example.

[6]   *Those books* seem interesting.

Here 'plurality' is indicated by both *those* and *books*. But notice that the hearer can recognize this multiple marking of Entity Number only after interpreting the phrase *those books* as invoking 'distal bookish entityhood' and identifying in which number system the *-s* on *books* falls. In other words, a part of the message had to be arrived at before one could recognize that 'plurality' was being indicated twice. The *Entity -s* signal cannot be identified on morphological grounds alone, for many words end in /s/, and *-s* as a suffix serves as (part of) a signal in both number systems.

The real functional value for the hearer of such multiple signalling emerges more clearly when we consider the interpretation of the alternative phrase *that books* in the context of a discussion of a computer at an airline terminal.

[7]   *That books* all our reservations.

It can be seen in retrospect that the plurality of *those* in [6] helped resolve the identity of the *-s* on *books* (i.e., which number system it is in), as well as the conceptual status of *book* (i.e., whether it designates an Entity or an Occurrence), both of which, in turn, helped us infer the message. Moreover, the particular aspect of the message which the MORE THAN ONE of *those* helped resolve (i.e., that *book* is to be taken as an *Entity*) is precisely the aspect that must first be established before one can speak of multiple marking of plurality.

The value of partial exclusion
We have argued for the functional value of the multiple signalling of 'plurality' in the phrase *those books* by showing how the extra number information on *those* blocks the identification of the *-s* on *books* as *Occurrence -s*. This multiple signalling of number does not, however, block all possible parsings of the phrase in its spoken form.

[8]   *Those books'* covers are soiled.

The *-s* on /bʊks/ in [6] is still provisionally open to identification as the genitive *-s* in its oral version as is shown by [8]. But the *-s* on /bʊks/ in [6] and [8] does block still another interpretation of the lexical stem *book*, namely, that of a modifier of some word following it.

[9]   *Those book* covers are soiled.

Thus, although the multiple signalling of number by the phrase *those books* in [6] does not completely determine its ultimate interpretation for the hearer (in its oral version at any rate), it does serve to eliminate two interpretive possibilities of the lexical stem *book*, those of [7] and [9].

Granted, most sentences, including these, can only be construed in one way taken as a whole. But without such multiple signalling of number information, the collective signal indeterminacy of short sequences that comprise whole sentences would present too many possibilities for all to be juggled simultaneously, even though they may ultimately have only a single resolution.

And in speech at any rate, word and sentence boundaries are not givens; they are themselves part of the hearer's problem, not aids to its solution. Hearers must begin somewhere to gain a foothold, and the multiple signalling of number in *those books* allows them to make a provisional interpretation of that sequence right from the start, upon which they can build. Once started, additional textual resonance (e.g., the MORE THAN ONE of *seem0* in [6]) serves in the way of early *confirmation* for hearers that they are on the right interpretive track.

8.6 Semantic Cohesion

The idea of linguistic elements in a discourse being in harmony semantically is hardly new. Halliday and Hasan, in *Cohesion in English* (1976), present a careful analysis and typology of the phenomenon. Most instances of Halliday and Hasan's *cohesion* are instances of what we are here calling textual resonance. But their central concern is different, and it is worthwhile to develop both the similarity of insight and the difference in application.

The nature of *text* is the basic problem addressed by Halliday and Hasan (H and H). 'What are the properties of texts in English, and what is it that distinguishes a text from a disconnected sequence of sentences?' (p. 1). *Cohesion* is their answer, and their study investigates the various ways cohesion is achieved. Cohesion occurs wherever the interpretation of one element in the discourse is dependent on that of another. Such dependence relations create what H and H call a *tie*.

Their archetypical example of a cohesive tie is the relation between a pronoun and its antecedent. They then extend this notion to quasi-pronoun words like *one* and *the same*, pro-verb forms like lexical *do*, ellipsis, conjunctions, and finally to pairs of words that stand 'in some kind of recognizable lexicosemantic [word meaning] relation' (p. 285). This includes near synonyms

(*climb . . . ascent*); superordinates (*elm . . . tree*); opposites (*wet
. . . dry*); ordered series (*Tuesday . . . Thursday*), unordered
series (*basement . . . roof*) and so on. But a cohesive effect can
derive from words in proximity whose meaning relation is not
easy to classify in systemic semantic terms: *laugh . . . joke*; *blade
. . . sharp*; *king . . . crown*; *boat . . . row*; *sunshine . . . cloud*;
garden . . . dig.

Throughout their study H and H stress that cohesion is a
purely semantic phenomenon, not a formal one (presumably
because many of the semantic relations that create it do not lend
themselves to formalization). A text is not a higher level of
linguistic structure, one composed of a structured sequence of
sentences; 'a text is best regarded as a *semantic* unit: a unit not of
form but of meaning' (p. 2).

How, then, do the notions of cohesive tie and textual
resonance differ? H and H see the interpretation of words as
necessary steps in moving from the text to the message. From this
comes the notion of a *tie*, defined as a dependency relation
between words alone; for them, the message can be idealized as
evolving in discrete incremental steps through the integration of
words interpreted in context.

In our conception, the message itself must be treated as a
gestalt rather than a structured entity analysable into conceptual
fractions uniquely associated with individual words. As a
consequence, the move from text to message, although proceeding incrementally in real time, cannot be broken down into
discrete steps. Analytically it must be treated as a single leap
(recall the discussion of *Yes Virginia, there are a Santa Claus* in
Chapter 6). Textual resonance, then, involves a diadic pair of
means-ends relations, not a relation between means (i.e., word
meanings) alone.

While the nature of textuality is H and H's chief concern, they
do touch on the functional role of cohesive ties in comprehension. In the following passage H and H underscore the active
participation of the reader in bringing 'meaning' to a text.

> One of the major problems in understanding linguistic interaction . . .
> is that of knowing how the listener fills in the missing information. The
> listener assigns meanings and interprets what is said to him; but in
> doing so *he is himself supplying a great deal of the interpretation*. The
> sentences and clauses and words that he hears, however perfectly
> formed lexicogrammatically . . . are semantically full of holes. Or
> rather this is the wrong metaphor. . . It would be more appropriate to
> describe it in terms of focus. *What the lexicogrammar of the text*

presents is more like a picture that is complete but out of focus, with the outlines blurred and the details imperceptible [emphasis W.R.].
(Halliday and Hasan 1976:299–300)

And later:

Our intention in this book has been to survey the lexicogrammatical resources in question, and show their place in the linguistic system. But the cohesive relations themselves are relations in meaning, and the continuity which they bring about is a semantic continuity. *This is what makes it possible for cohesive patterns to play the part they do in the processing of text by a listener or a reader, not merely signalling the presence and extent of text but actually enabling him to interpret it and determining how he does so* [emphasis W.R.].
(Halliday and Hasan 1976:303)

The present analysis of Focus Number attempts to extend the explanatory potential of semantic cohesion to the intra-sentential relation of subject-verb number so as to *supplant* the traditional (still-programmatic) formal treatment.

8.7 Interpretive Bootstrapping

Chapter 3 characterized the interpretive process as creative problem-solving. The problem confronting the hearer is to invent a communicative motivation responsible for the speaker's juxtaposing the particular signs he did. With the recognition that the identity of the linguistic signs is not a given, a second dimension is added to the problem. In comprehension, the hearer is simultaneously solving for unknowns of *two* kinds – both the message and the signs – using as a point of departure whatever seems more certain, solving for the others and incorporating them into the growing beachhead.

This is why our case for the functional value of Focus Number is not reducible to the more conventional notion of 'structural marker'. The Entity and Focus Number signals cannot be identified on the basis of purely structural principles – templates of possible sentence types – for in terms of abstract structural patterns *any* combination of number signals is possible.

The crucial guiding principle is contextual plausibility. The hearer is weighing the relative plausibility of different message types (cf., Figure 8.2) that result from different possible signal identifications, and opting for whatever makes more sense. H and H provide an amusing example that brings this process to consciousness precisely because it goes awry.

As another example [of cohesion], consider the old piece of schoolboy humour:
   Time flies.
   – You can't; they fly too quickly.
The first sentence gives no indication of not being a complete text; in fact it usually is, and the humour lies in the misinterpretation that is required if the presupposition from the second sentence is to be satisfied.

                                               (Halliday and Hasan 1976:4–5)

Here the misinterpretation includes the mis-identification of the -s on *flies* as *Entity* -s rather than *Occurrence* -s.

The fact that considerations of pragmatic plausibility play a crucial mediating role in the move from sound to signals makes semantic interpretation essentially a bootstrap operation. As more of the message is provisionally arrived at more signals can be identified, each cycle gradually expanding the message. H and H's insistence that cohesion is a semantic phenomenon, not a formal one, underscores this point.

8.8 A Second Illustration

A more extensive illustration of the interpretive help that textual resonance supplies is provided by variants of the sequence *demonstrative* + *book* + *cover* of [8] and [9] created by permuting -s endings. With the addition of the genitive -s the interpretive possibilities of the three word sequence expand considerably. Combining -s endings with *book* and *cover* (along with the *that/those* contrast) yields eight overtly distinct sequences. Setting aside the possibility of the word *cover* occurring as part of a neologism like *cover-reservation*, and restricting the appearance of the genitive -s to *book*, the eight phonological sequences are open to nine interpretations. These possibilities are illustrated below with full sentences. Since our point will be that most of the sequences can be provisionally interpreted without reliance on what follows, the first three words are in capitals and separated from the rest of the sentence. (Note that in their spoken form the first three words of [13] and [14] are non-distinct.)

[10]	THAT BOOK COVER	seems dirty.
[11]	THOSE BOOK COVER	boxes are too small.
[12]	THAT BOOK'S COVER	seems dirty.
[13]	THOSE BOOKS' COVER	seems unattractive.
[14]	THOSE BOOKS COVER	American history from the Revolution to the Civil War.

[15]	THAT BOOK COVERS	American history from the Revolution to the Civil War.
[16]	THOSE BOOK COVERS	seem dirty.
[17]	THAT BOOK'S COVERS	seem dirty.
[18]	THOSE BOOKS' COVERS	seem unattractive.

Relevant here is the fact that six of these nine interpretations can be (tentatively) arrived at on the basis of the three word sequence *alone*.

[10']	THAT BOOK COVERØ
[12']	THAT BOOK'S COVERØ
[15']	THAT BOOKØ COVERS
[16']	THOSE BOOK COVERS
[17']	THAT BOOK'S COVERS
[18']	THOSE BOOKS' COVERS

The hearer may make provisional interpretations of these three word sequences, upon which he or she can build as the utterance continues.

Nothing much can be made of the first three words of [11]. But while a positive interpretation requires the next word *boxes*, the three word sequence does function negatively by blocking its interpretation in the manner of [10'], [12'], and [15']–[18']. Similarly, the interpretations of [13'] and [14'] require additional information since they are phonologically identical. But again, each functions negatively to block its interpretation in the manner of the remaining seven. And the interpretive indeterminacy of [13']/[14'] is resolved by the very next word, significantly, through the presence or absence of a signal from the Focus Number System.

[13']	THOSE BOOKS' COVERØ *seems* . . .
[14']	THOSE BOOKS COVERØ *American* . . . .

Written and spoken English

This demonstration, like the first, employed a carefully constructed phrase. While effective in illustrating a wide range of parsing options, it is bound to seem contrived. A second shortcoming is the fact that the demonstration had to appear in written form, whereas the communicative value of the Focus Number System is realized most strongly, we believe, in speech. Consider now a non-fabricated example. Despite the advantage of word and sentence boundaries, readers may find themselves pausing momentarily at the same place we did, then to be steered back on course by the absence of an expected signal of Focus Number, and reassured by its later appearance.

[19]   These are happy sounds, joys to find. Similarly many pregnant women develop murmurs as the torrential blood flow to the gravid uterus places an extra work load on the working heart.

(John Stone, *New York Times Magazine*)

If English lacked the Focus Number System, the sequence *the torrential blood flow* would surely be interpreted as an instance of the word-order signal *P . . . Occurrence*, an interpretation consistent with the following material *to the gravid uterus*. Moreover, without the Focus Number System the word following *uterus* would be *place*, yielding a garden-path interpretation equivalent to 'The torrential blood flows to the gravid uterus place'. Only upon encountering the final material would one realize one had taken a wrong turn, far too late to do anything but return to the beginning for a fresh start.

Imprecision of lexical meanings
The discussion so far has focused on the morphological indeterminacy of linguistic signs. A similar kind of interpretive indeterminacy exists on the meaning side, and in solving that problem for the hearer the speaker often creates textual resonance.

We have argued in several places that lexical meanings are *less precise* than their ultimate interpretation in particular contexts. Chapter 2 posited a single base meaning for *people* which was then further narrowed by contextual information before emerging in the message. Similarly the mass vs. count distinction was attributed to the effect of articles and number meanings, not to separate 'mass' and 'count' senses of the words themselves.

This imprecision in lexical meaning is clearly the rule. Consider the word *feel* in [5]. *Feel* designates a kind of 'experiencing' that differs in subtle ways from *sense, perceive, be aware of,* and in grosser ways from *touch, hear, think,* and *believe*. But *feel* encompasses experience of a disparate variety: tactile (*feel a breeze*); physiological (*feel a chill*; *feel hungry*) and psychological, both active (*I feel angry*) and passive (*I feel their anger*).

Typically, speakers narrow down the interpretive potential of

feel with further information, usually in the form of a specification of what is being felt. But when this is done, a second
indication of a message of 'experiencing' is often introduced
because certain things only exist in the experiencing, e.g., *chills*,
hunger, *anger* (and *indignation* cf. [5]).

8.9 The Functional Indeterminacy of Lexical Stems

The signals from the two number systems pose the perceptual
problem they do because (1) both systems employ the same
morphological material (i.e., *-s* and *-∅*) and (2) the associated
lexical stems are not recognizably different. That is to say, in
English 'nouns' and 'verbs' do not, by and large, comprise
formally distinct morpheme classes. Words that describe entities,
such as *book* and *cover*, can describe occurrences as well.

The repercussions of this fact extend beyond the Entity and
Focus Number Systems themselves. The status of a lexical stem
as an entity or occurrence in the message is critical to the
recognition of the various word-order signals of the Focus-
Control interlock: P_1 . . . *Occurrence* . . . P_2; P_1 . . . *Occurrence*
. . . P_2 . . . P_3; P . . . *Occurrence*; *Occurrence* . . . P (cf.
discussion of [19]).

The extent of this functional indeterminacy in English has been
calculated by Joe E. Pierce (1985). Pierce made a study of 30,000
words of running text from which all verbs and all nouns were
taken and listed. In the end, 90 per cent of the two lists were
identical. Ten similar studies, Pierce reports, show a range from
59 per cent to 93 per cent, averaging 80 per cent. All these
calculations were based on actual texts published in 1959 in
popular magazines. The figures are somewhat higher than what a
dictionary count would yield. But according to Pierce, many of
the words that are used only as nouns or verbs rarely occur.

Pierce concludes that the facts of English do not support the
establishment of distinct grammatical classes of nouns and verbs,
but, rather, a single 'verb-noun' word class. Pierce argues in
terms of the practical consequences in the language classroom.

The importance of this fact for second-language teachers is that with
this situation any rule given for nouns or verbs will be valid only about
half the time, but rules given for the class VERB-NOUN can be made
to be nearly 100 per cent accurate. In second-language classes, we
often teach *hand* as a noun early in the course, but the first time the
students hear the word in a sentence, the teacher says 'Hand me the

book'. If the student speaks a language such a Turkish, which has a
clear class of NOUN as opposed to a class VERB, he is completely
confused by this.

(Pierce 1985:2)

Our interest, though, is the implication for the native speaker,
who still must decide for each instance of *hand* whether to
construe it as an Entity or an Occurrence. The Focus Number
System often facilitates this move from pure morphology to
semantic interpretation. (See [19].)

8.10 Communication vs. Representation

As we noted earlier, the initial step of signal identification is
usually overlooked in assessing the semantic value of linguistic
units. This oversight is traceable to differing conceptions of the
essential nature of language. Language is usually conceived as a
representational system existing independent of its human users.
This leads to an idealizational framework in which low-level
perceptual difficulties are set aside, with the result that representational considerations *alone* govern the analysis of linguistic
meaning. Morphological formatives are accorded semantic content only when they can be portrayed as uniquely representing
some feature of the semantic interpretation of a sentence.
Assessed in those terms, multiple signalling of the same semantic
feature seems as pointless as duplicate pieces in a jigsaw puzzle.
Better to consolidate the second with the first and account for it
in terms of a relation of formal determination (e.g., a rule of
subject-verb agreement).

When language is conceived as a *communicative* system,
however, a wider range of considerations can play a role in the
analysis of linguistic meaning. The use of a meaning can be
justified in communicative terms whenever it helps the hearer, in
some way, to infer the speaker's intended message. Naturally this
would include cases where the meaning uniquely represents some
feature of the intended message. But the hearer may also need
help due to the nature of the associated linguistic signs. Either
the identification of their signals requires establishing certain
features of the message as a prerequisite, or their meanings can
suggest various kinds of messages in different contexts. In such
cases 'repetition' will be of help to hearers because *it is not
repetition for them at the point they encounter it.*

8.11 Factors Favouring the Resonating Mode

Two facts about the Focus Number System would seem to argue against its real functional value. The first is its use in a predominantly resonating mode; the second is its use when there appears to be no perceptual problem involving signal identification.

The consequences of availability
The Focus System is employed in a resonating fashion to a greater extent than might be expected of fully-fledged meaning-bearing units. Speakers do not, for example, exploit the possibility of contrasting Entity and Focus Number meanings in all cases of spanned oppositions (e.g., *the combination are*). Why are the Focus Number meanings employed predominantly in a resonating capacity?

This under-exploitation of the expressive potential of the Focus Number System stems from its *limited availability*, which has disfavoured the development of expressive strategies that would be critically dependent upon it. Consider first the inherent structural restrictions on its use. The system is only suitable for supplying information about the entity in Focus; with any other entity the system cannot be used. Moreover, even with respect to the entity in Focus the system is often not available. The Focus Number System interlocks with only certain tenses; it cannot, therefore, be used with any of the modal auxiliaries, the simple past (except with *be*) and the past perfect (see 5.6).

Consider now the expressive problem for the language user when the Focus Number System is unavailable. When entities in the message clearly fall on one side or the other of the number opposition, *Entity -∅* and *-s* alone are adequate. But when the message spans the opposition of number the Entity Number System cannot reflect this greater complexity. Either it must be ignored, or it must be captured by other means. This has led to the development of various stratagems – none involving the Focus Number System – for distinguishing straightforward 'singularity' and 'plurality' on the one hand, from more complex messages that span the opposition of number on the other. Lexical contrasts have developed: *people* vs. *persons*; *information* vs. *facts*; *research* vs. *studies*; *aircraft* vs. *airplanes*; and phrasal contrasts such as *choices* vs. *a series of choices*, *factors* vs. *a combination of factors*.

Having developed these alternative ways of dealing with spanned oppositions when the Focus Number System is *un*available, speakers continue to employ them when it *is* available (since not doing so would introduce a shift of communicative strategy and hence a complication). As a result, these alternative strategies have encroached upon the expressive area where the two number systems could jointly be exploited most effectively. The upshot is that speakers reserve the Focus Number System as an ancillary expressive device, to be used for subtle nuances when available, but not to be depended on.

Absence of perceptual problem
Turning now to the second problem, why do speakers not occasionally abandon the Focus Number System when there is no need for it even in its resonating capacity? For example, the sentence *The tree grows tall* does not seem to present any perceptual problem of the sort in the *book cover* example. Why, then, don't speakers simply abandon the Focus Number System and say:

[20]   The tree grow tall.

Here we argue, (as in the case of 'mass' reference) that the presence of a *-0* as a component of one of its signals makes abandonment of the system impractical. The omission of *Occurrence -s* is open to the interpretation by the hearer as *Occurrence -0*, whose meaning, MORE THAN ONE, would then be a positive *impediment* to comprehension. A speaker, then, could not abandon the system merely because he/she personally believes the message did not call for the information it conveys. It would have to be a strategic abandonment, one requiring a judicious weighing of whether the hearer will recognize the absence of *Occurrence -s* as abandonment of the system, or as *Occurrence -0*. Whatever minor saving in articulatory effort accrued by not pronouncing an *-s* would thus have to be paid for by a constant attendance to factors requiring additional expertise and considerable calculation. Easier for both parties involved simply to employ the Focus Number System without reflection, even in cases where the information may not seem to be particularly useful.[1]

An additional factor disfavours the abandonment of the Focus Number System. With the items *be* and *have* the signals of the Focus Number meanings are incorporated into the lexical stem itself (*is* vs. *are*; *has* vs. *have*). In language use these items comprise a significant percentage of the instances of the Focus Number System. For example, a tabulation of all instances of the Focus Number System in the Jane Smiley text examined in Table 5.1 and Table 7.1 yielded the following figures.

TABLE 8.1   Frequency of use of the Focus Number System with *have* and *be*

Number of instances of forms of *have* and *be* marked for Focus Number:	246
Remaining instances of Focus Number:	380
Percentage of *have* and *be*:	39.3%

The high frequency of *have* and *be* (where 'omission' of Focus Number is morphologically impossible) reinforces the general strategy of employing the Focus Number meanings across the board without calculation.[2]

While conceding an element of automaticity in the use of the Focus Number System, the rationale offered above is still essentially functional since it involves a *means-end* relationship, but now developed at the level of communicative strategy. The complexity of means by which the Focus Number System could be intermittently abandoned is not worth the end achieved – a minimal saving of articulatory effort.

Absence in the past tense
In attributing the predominantly resonating use of the Focus Number System to its limited availability we may seem to have undermined the case for its functional utility in even that capacity. For if speakers can do quite well without it (in the simple past tense), how can it make any significant contribution in the simple present?

This objection overlooks the fact that the perceptual problem the Focus Number System helps to solve does not exist elsewhere in quite so severe a form. When the tense is other than the simple present, the lexical stem designating the Occurrence almost always bears overt unproblematic morphology. In both the simple and compound past tenses the *-ed* suffix unambiguously identifies the associated lexical stem as an Occurrence rather than an Entity, (e.g., he *studied*; he *had studied*.) The auxiliaries (*be*, *have* and the modals) provide similar help.

This point can be illustrated by re-examining the examples already discussed, putting them now in the past.

[7]   THAT BOOKS   a lot of reservations.
[7a]   THAT BOOKED   a lot of reservations.

The *-ed* of *booked* in [7a] favours the interpretation of *book* as an Occurrence (concomitantly favouring *that* to be understood as P_1 of $P_1 \ldots Occurrence \ldots P_2$) just as does the *-s* of *books* in

[7], despite the fact -*ed* bears no number information.

Similarly, when [10]–[18] are put in the past tense the net interpretive indeterminacy of the first three words does not increase, because the -*ed* (without Focus Number information) is still as reliable a clue to which lexical item expresses the Occurrence as are the Focus Number signals (which do bear such information). Relevant here are the past tense versions of [14] and [15], which are the only two of the nine whose initial three words include an Occurrence.

[14a] THOSE BOOKS COVERED American history from the Revolution to the Civil War.

[15a] THAT BOOK COVERED American history from the Revolution to the Civil War.

The first three words are no less provisionally interpretable than their simple present analogs [14'] and [15'].[3]

In summary, the absence of Focus Number information in the past tense is counter-balanced by the greater morphological distinctiveness of the *Occurrence* -*ed* signal (i.e., its non-identity with either signal in the Entity Number System and the genitive -*s*). Conversely, the extra number information the hearer receives from the Focus Number System in the simple present is offset by the morphological identity of its signals with those of the Entity Number System and the genitive -*s*. In short, the joint use of the Entity and Focus Number Systems more or less *maintains* (rather than increases) the amount of interpretive help the hearer receives in the past tenses, where the signals are more reliably identified on purely morphological grounds.

8.12 The Complementation of Communicative Strategies

Chapter 7 ended with a question about the hegemony of a communicative strategy. Why do English speakers choose Focus Number most of the time on the basis of the *same* feature of the message as that responsible for the number of the grammatical head of the P phrase (cf. Tables 5.1 and 7.1)?

This chapter has argued for the functional utility of such usage in terms of the role of textual resonance in the comprehension process. But Chapters 6 and 7 established that speakers employ other strategies as well, ones that we maintain are equally well-motivated semantically and often have greater expressive value.

The tendency to make Focus Number reflect the Entity

Number of the grammatical head of the P phrase is due, in part, to the fact that on many occasions the other strategies are inapplicable. Yet it seems safe to say that English users do favour this one strategy to a greater extent than can be attributed solely to the inapplicablity of the alternatives. We can now return to the question of this favouring for an answer.

This communicative strategy is favoured over all others because it complements two sets of associated strategies, one set on the speaker's side and the other set on the hearer's side. Recapitulating the rationales developed in this chapter for the predominantly resonating use of the Focus Number System, we argue as follows.

For speakers, this strategy allows them to express messages spanning the opposition of number by means of the *same* communicative strategies that they employ everywhere else, where the Focus Number System is unavailable (i.e., in the simple past, the past perfect and all the modal auxiliary tenses). That is, they employ lexical contrasts (*leaves* vs. *foliage*) and constructions such as *Entity -∅ of Entity -s* to indicate that the entity in Focus spans the opposition of number rather than forsaking those established expressive routines and switching to a manipulation of Focus Number alone.

For hearers, this strategy has the effect of maintaining the same *amount* of interpretive help, located in the same *place*, as exists when the Focus Number System is unavailable. This enables them to identify the word-order signals of the Focus-Control interlock on the basis of the *same* perceptual strategies as they rely upon everywhere else. That is to say, it allows them to disambiguate which lexical stem should be construed as a *Participant*, and which an *Occurrence*, according to the same perceptual strategies applicable to the simple past and to all the tenses that employ an auxiliary.

At the heart of this rationale is the psychological principle that, all things being equal, people prefer simplicity and consistency. But note that we are not applying this principle directly to the Focus Number System. That is, we are not simply arguing that a general preference for consistency leads speakers to choose Focus Number following the same strategy every time. This cannot be argued because elsewhere we have seen much strategic diversity in the deployment of a grammatical system. Chapters 3 and 4 showed the Entity Number System being deployed in ways that amount to a slightly different strategy for every word. So long as there are no larger repercussions, language users can cope with a high degree of strategic diversity. In fact, they favour diversity whenever it increases the expressive capacity of a linguistic sign.

In the case of the Focus Number System however, uncon-
strained divergence from the basic principle of choice would have
far-reaching repercussions, for it would force both speaker and
hearer to switch over to different expressive and perceptual
strategies associated with many different grammatical systems
(and the entire lexicon as well). The argument, then, is that
speakers exploit the expressive potential of a grammatical system
to the extent that it does not undermine and interfere with the
other expressive and perceptual strategies upon which they also
rely.[4]

When speakers do depart from this basic strategy of choosing
Focus Number, it is usually in contexts that contain some element
that alerts the hearer to the possibility of a shift in communicative
strategy: a collective, an *Entity -∅ of Entity -s* phrase, an animal
name, numerical quantification, a finite form of *be* (foreshadow-
ing a recharacterization of the entity in Focus), lexical stems
conjoined with *and*. In the absence of such contextual alerts, the
hearer is likely to be thrown off course. When speakers
occasionally misjudge the sufficiency of the contextual alert it
amounts to a kind of linguistic sabotage, and hearers react with a
strongly normative protest.

8.13 The Locus of Arbitrariness in Language

This chapter has argued that textual resonance of the type
created by the Focus Number System has its explanatory roots in
inherent characteristics of the communicative process. By building in a high degree of resonance, a speaker mitigates the
problems of:

1. the perceptual indeterminacy of linguistic signals;
2. the imprecision of the linguistic meanings borne by those
   signals; and
3. hearers' need for early reassurance that they are on the
   right interpretive track.

The analysis thus achieves *explanation* in the accepted sense of
tying the presence and behaviour of a language-particular feature
to universal characteristics of linguistic structure and human
psychology.[5]

Causal vs. systemic explanation
Yet it is clear our account stops short of claiming that these same

considerations compelled English to develop a Focus Number System at the particular time it did.[6] That is, the account does not address the question of the original causal factors driving the historical evolution of the system, only the question of its *deployment* once in place. Its predominant manner of deployment is explained in terms of the functional role in the communicative process of the textual resonance that deployment helps to create. By what linguistic means a particular language achieves that resonance is a part of its arbitrary structure, and that is the status we have accorded the Focus Number System.

The divergence between the present analysis and the traditional one in terms of an agreement rule is not, then, on the issue of arbitrariness *per se*. Both accounts see the 'verb -*s*' as a manifestation of language-particular arbitrariness. The issue is the locus and extent of the arbitrariness. In the present analysis only the existence of *Occurrence -s* as *a signal of a meaning* is arbitrary; its deployment by speakers in language use is not. Given the existence of *Occurrence -s* and *-0* in the inventory of linguistic signs that is English, their syntagmatic deployment by speakers follows general principles underlying the deployment of both lexical and grammatical signs in the communication of messages. And their contribution to textual resonance supports and maintains their *continued* presence in the language, for the structural characteristics of language make textual resonance necessary for successful communication. Absolute synchronic arbitrariness in language is thus seen to reside in the linguistic sign.

8.14 The Demands of Synchronic Explanation

Perhaps the present analysis requires an additional demonstration before explanation can be claimed. What is lacking at this point is a metatheory that would tell us exactly how much textual resonance a language requires. Such a theory would:

1. quantify the amount of signal and meaning indeterminacy existing in any given language, and
2. quantify the amount of interpretive help any particular linguistic sign provides.

Broad application of such a theory would presumably lead to a conclusion about how explicit a language must be in order to remain a viable communicative instrument. It could then be demonstrated that the Focus Number System fills the critical gap.

Repeated application to other linguistic features would yield an explanation for why some (like the Focus Number System) have remained in English to the present, while others, say, the *thou-thee* distinction, fell by the wayside hundreds of years ago.

The synchronic idealization

Without denying that such a theory is a highly desirable and legitimate goal, we maintain it goes beyond the requirements of synchronic explanation. Indeed, to insist upon it is to deny the legitimacy of the idealization of a language as a synchronic system, wherein questions of historical change can be set aside as outside its immediate scope of responsibility.

Let us examine more carefully the ramifications of such a requirement. Once introduced, it would apply across the board to any linguistic sign whose informational value in discourse were ever observed to drop below 100 per cent. This would mean, for instance, that an analysis of the English possessive pronouns *his* and *her*, which dealt with them in terms of the sex of their referents, would require, *in addition*, an explanation (in terms of quantified functional yield) for why successive generations of English speakers have continued to maintain this grammatical distinction in view of the fact that (a) it is sometimes redundant (e.g., *She brushed her teeth*), and (b) other languages, like French, get along quite well without it.

Similarly, a semantic analysis of the lexical signs *ser* and *estar* in Spanish that successfully accounted for the use of each would still not be complete until it could demonstrate why Spanish speakers continue to preserve both words in their language when English speakers manage to get along quite well with only a single word, *be*.

Cast in this way, such a requirement becomes a demand for a quantified functional theory of linguistic change. For any explanation of why structural features of a language do not change (e.g., why English has preserved the *his-her* distinction) will necessarily explain why they do change (e.g., why English lost the *thou-thee* distinction).

It can be seen, then, that insisting that all synchronic analyses be accompanied by a theory that predicts systemic stasis and change amounts to a rejection of purely synchronic explanation. We believe the idealization of a language as a structure amenable to purely synchronic analysis and explanation has proved too fruitful in modern linguistics to be cast aside. One is free to regard synchronic explanation of the kind offered here as a modest achievement when measured against the larger questions that remain unanswered. But that is not to deny the success it can legitimately claim.

This is more than a simple appeal to conventional wisdom. For Saussure, synchronic analysis held a logical primacy over historical analysis because it is the units and values yielded by synchronic analysis that provide the terms in which the historical problem can then be posed. One can scarcely speak of linguistic change in the absence of discrete units of which change can be predicated, which is what a synchronic analysis provides. If, on the other hand, the units, values and functions yielded by synchronic analysis were all to be regarded as provisional, one would have no secure framework in terms of which to pursue the larger historical question; nor, indeed, any established functional principles to which one could appeal in accounting for the historical evolution of a language.[7]

Notes
1. This rationale for Standard English suggests that non-standard dialects (e.g., Black English) in which the 'verb -s' is frequently 'omitted' be analysed as *not* having the signal *Occurrence -0*, which, as we have argued, is the systemic reason Focus Number is an 'obligatory' category in Standard English. In a dialect lacking *Occurrence -0* the 'omission' of *Occurrence -s* poses no problem of possible mis-identification.
2. Note that Table 8.1 only argues for the obligatoriness of the *use* of the Focus Number System, not the actual choice, which remains as free for expressive manipulation with *be* and *have* as elsewhere.
3. Actually, the past tense analogues of [10]–[18] are marginally more differentiated morphologically because the *-ed* in [14a] distinguishes its first three words from those of [15a] (*Those books' cover* seemed unattractive) whereas the present tense versions are homophonous.
4. Note the parallelism here with the treatment in Chapter 3 of the extension of the words *pig*, *cow* and *chicken*. In both cases the 'constraints' on the use of a linguistic sign are being attributed to systemic pressure rather than by formalizing them as arbitrary features of its grammatical description.
5. This functional justification for textual resonance differs from that for *redundancy* in communication theory (Shannon and Weaver 1971). As defined in communication theory, redundancy serves to compensate for channel noise, changes in the transmitted signal that can impede reception of the intended symbols. Redundancy makes it possible for a communication system to function under less than ideal conditions. For S and W there is no intrinsic need for redundancy; in an ideal (i.e., noiseless) system redundancy is not necessary.

   Channel noise has its analogue in the speech situation, and textual resonance does indeed serve to compensate for it. But our case for textual resonance involves the structure of the communicative system itself, and holds even when language is used under *ideal* conditions. Morphological and semantic indeterminacy are inherent structural features, not external, pragmatic considerations like channel noise.

6. According to Poplack and Tagliamonte's (1989) brief summary of the historical literature, *Occurrence -s* did not acquire its present value as a third person singular marker until the early seventeenth century. In Middle English there was considerable regional and stylistic variation. There is, moreover, still disagreement on the etymology of the -s suffix. Modern English -s is generally considered a descendant of Old English -þ, which marked present indicative in all forms save the first and second person singular (e.g., Jespersen, 1909/1949: 15). The -s suffix would then have acquired its present person and number meanings when it ceased to be used with plural subjects. On the other hand, Curme (1977:52) identifies Modern English -s as the reflex of the Old English second person singular -s, which spread first to second person plural, then to all plurals, and finally to third person singular.

7. Garcia (1985) maintains that a synchronic analysis must have the explanatory principles relevant to diachronic change built into it, a position with which we agree but would rephrase so it does not imply the obligation of doing synchronic and diachronic analysis simultaneously. To wit, in order for a diachronic analysis to be truly explanatory its causal factors must receive independent support through a demonstration that they are in evidence, and have (synchronic) systemic motivation, prior to the actual change.

Chapter 9

The complementarity principle

In an insightful exegesis of the Saussurean legacy Jonathan Culler [1976] credits Saussure with giving clear expression to an important feature of Modernist thought: modern thinkers no longer aspire to the goal of all-encompassing understanding.

> How does one cope, systematically, with the apparent chaos of the modern world? This question was being asked in a variety of fields, and the replies which Saussure gives – that you cannot hope to attain an absolute or Godlike view of things but must choose a perspective, and that within this perspective objects are defined by their relations with one another, rather than by essences of some kind – are exemplary. Saussure enables us to grasp with unusual clarity the strategies of Modernist thought.
>
> (Culler 1976:XV)

Because scientific inquiry requires choosing a perspective, some aspects of one's object of study will be in clear view while others will either be out of focus or not visible at all. No linguistic theory, then, can be comprehensive in the sense of capturing all those aspects that make up a layperson's conception of language, for that conception incorporates heterogeneous perspectives. It was Saussure's insight that this limitation is not a defect, but an inherent characteristic of human understanding.

The present analysis exemplifies this point in a striking way. Chapter 8 illustrated the importance of conceiving of a language as a communicative system if functional explanation is the goal. This conception, we now argue, *precludes* treating language as a representational system. Functional explanation of the kind offered in Chapters 5–8 is purchased at the price of relinquishing the longstanding view of language as a representational system of 'sentence meaning'.

While this case goes well beyond the subject of grammatical number we believe our treatment mandates it because the analysis has clearly made no attempt at integration with an explicit representation of 'sentence meaning'. Unless it can be shown that there exist principled reasons for setting that goal aside, the absence of a level of 'sentence meaning' in the present framework remains legitimate grounds for criticism.

9.1 Different Basic Units

The absence of a linguistic level of 'sentence meaning' can, of course, be attributed to the initial choice of the linguistic sign as the basic unit in language. From that choice it follows that 'meaning', as a well-defined linguistic object, exists only at the sign level. Notional content arising from the collocation of signs is roughly equivalent to what is usually termed 'utterance meaning', and so falls outside language proper.

But all this amounts to begging the question, for the Saussurean conception of *langue* as an inventory of signs, with the relegation of everything beyond the sign to *parole*, has long been regarded as a major shortcoming (Chomsky 1964:23; Culler 1976:87–9). Where, exactly, is the conflict between sign-based functional explanation and an explicit account of 'sentence meaning'? What blocks a grand synthesis?

The best way to demonstrate the trade-off is to explore the obstacles to analysing language as a representational system while preserving our functional account of Focus Number. Since any such synthesis would require revising our account in the direction of a formal, rule-based treatment, we will begin by examining two forms such revision might take. The first would merely append our account to a prior syntactic account; the second would modify the present account by partitioning the expressive and the resonating use of the Focus Number System for separate treatment.

9.2 The Modular Revision

Chapter 8 portrayed the Focus Number System as compensating for the widespread morphological and semantic indeterminacy of English. One might grant that the system is fulfilling a useful communicative function but maintain it belongs in a separate theoretical component. The following arrangement would ensue: there would be a formal, sentence-based, account of linguistic structure which included a rule of verb agreement; then a separate psycho-linguistic component, incorporating the notion of textual resonance as an aid to processing, would 'explain' the rule of verb agreement in terms of its contribution to textual resonance. The syntactic component could then still serve as the basis for the analysis of language as a representational system of 'sentence meaning'. Newmeyer (1983:2) advocates this 'modular' approach to theory-building in linguistics and claims it to be a central defining feature of the generative framework.

The first step in such a modular account would be a successful syntactic treatment of verb number. This account would have to be considerably more comprehensive than is usually attempted in that it could not restrict itself to 'normal usage'. It would be required to encompass all the data that are critical to the success of our functional account, namely, those of Chapters 6 and 7. No such syntactic account, to our knowledge, exists to date. Although programmatic outlines for syntactic treatments of verb number are available, fully formalized, comprehensive versions remain an elusive goal.

Until such observational adequacy is achieved, it is perhaps premature to speculate about the obstacles to synthesis that would then arise. But one such obstacle surfaces again in a more extreme form in the second revision to be examined and so may as well be introduced here.

As argued in Chapter 1, the categories and constructs of syntactic analysis are designed to facilitate a purely formal, axiomatic account of language. Consequently, they often do not lend themselves to later functional explanation; some alternative characterization is required. But that alternative characterization introduces a contradictory conception of the same linguistic unit. In the case at hand, an agreement rule would portray the verb -*s* as a meaningless morphological formative standing in a relation of formal determination, while the psycho-linguistic account must portray it as a fully-fledged, meaning-bearing sign in all contexts.

Another point of conflict lies in the contradictory conceptions of word meaning. Sentence-based semantic analysis takes the relation between word 'meaning' and sentence 'meaning' to be *compositional*. This view is so widespread it is somewhat inaccurate to attribute it to any single individual. For example, Fodor (1977) prefaces her comprehensive discussion of approaches to the study of semantics by a statement of their common ground: 'the meaning of a sentence is a function of the morphemes it contains and the way in which those morphemes are syntactically combined' (p. 4). The 'literal' meaning of a sentence then, resides *in* its parts, independent of the interpretive capacities of speakers and hearers. As a consequence the senses of words are designed to correspond to different paraphrases a word has in different sentences. Precision here is a virtue, for the more precise the various senses are, the easier it is to treat 'sentence meaning' compositionally.

> 'Sentence meaning' is arrived at mechanically through the amalgamation of word meaning along with grammatical information.
>
> (Katz 1972:xxiv)

In sign-based analysis, on the other hand, semantic analysis is based on the means-end relation. Linguistic meanings are merely hints and clues to the message; much is left for language users to flesh out. As a consequence, lexical (and grammatical) meanings tend to be imprecise.

Even Weinreich's deviation from the compositional view in favour of sentence meaning as a calculation still sees it as mechanically determined by its semantic parts.

> The goal of a semantic theory of a language, as we conceive it, is to explicate the way in which the meaning of a sentence of specified structure is derivable from the fully specified meanings of its parts.
>
> (Weinreich 1980:125)

But this precision at the level of word meaning eliminates the gap between the collective 'sum' of the meanings and the message. Yet it is precisely this gap between the semantic parts and the communicative whole which has provided one important functional justification for structural features such as Focus Number. So the psycho-linguistic component, operating on a different set of analytical principles, would have to *restore* the imprecision and indeterminacy the sentence-based component had striven to eliminate. In short, the psycho-linguistic component could not simply offer a higher-level explanation for the formal and semantic constructs within the syntactic component. It would have to offer a fully-articulated, shadow version of linguistic structure, one that contradicts, rather than complements, the version it is supposed to explain.

9.3 Partitioning the Expressive and the Resonating Modes

We turn now to a second possible revision, one more in keeping with the spirit of the present analysis. This time the Focus Number System would be retained as the sole characterization of the verb morphology, but its expressive mode and its resonating mode would be partitioned. Since Focus Number functions sometimes distinctively and sometimes redundantly, an explicit representation of 'sentence meaning' would seem to demand that the two modes receive different formal treatment.

This tack, we argue, proves unfeasible in practice. The framework required for distinguishing the expressive from the resonating use of linguistic signs is one in which the functional *raison d'être* for textual resonance is no longer rooted in inherent properties of linguistic structure. On the other hand, the framework which preserves the systemic motivation for textual resonance is one in which the expressive and the resonating use of linguistic signs *cannot be reliably distinguished*. We begin with a brief look at the problem of formalizing the expressive vs. resonating distinction before moving to the more important analytical and theoretical considerations.

The formal problem

Formalizing the expressive vs. resonating dichotomy is a problem because the signs in a language cannot be neatly partitioned into two corresponding classes. For example, the four signs functioning in a resonating fashion with respect to *students* in *Those students feel0 indignation* (see 8.4) function purely expressively (i.e., non-redundantly) on other occasions, as in the following examples:

[1]   *Those* antelope appeared frightened. (also: *Those* appeared frightened.)

[2]   Ham and eggs *are* popular.   (cf., Ham and eggs *is* popular.)

[3]   It *felt* good.

[4]   *Indignation* spread through the room.

Thus building the resonating vs. expressive distinction into linguistic theory would have to be done at a higher level, where the relative informational value of linguistic signs could be assessed in terms of an explicit representation of 'sentence meaning'. This would presumably lead to a calculus of linguistic representation which factored out the resonating value of linguistic signs, leaving only their expressive value i.e., their unique semantic contribution to the message being communicated.

This goal has a decidedly familiar ring, as does the problem of its execution. The formal machinery would resemble in many respects that required by Chomsky's (1965) theory of selectional restrictions and semantic features. But the continued program-matic status of the notion of selectional restrictions within generative theory after more than twenty-five years shakes one's confidence in the possibility of a successful solution in the purely formal terms the problem demands.

9.4 The Structural Indeterminacy of Messages

The most intractable problem, however, is not the formal one but the initial analytical one of deciding when a linguistic sign is, in fact, functioning in an expressive or a resonating capacity. The resonating mode, to recall, does not involve a direct relation between the meanings themselves (i.e., shared semantic features) but the indirect relation of jointly contributing to the same aspect of the message. In practice, as meanings approach identity it becomes increasingly difficult to determine whether they con-tribute to the same, or slightly different, aspects of the message.

This is a common problem when discrete units are imposed on a phenomenological continuum, one encountered a generation ago with the advent of the sound spectograph. At that time it was recognized that phonemes overlap in the acoustic stream in ways that defeat its exhaustive partitioning into segments that can be uniquely assigned to individual phonological units. Just this kind of indeterminacy exists in attempting to map directly between discrete semantic units and a notional continuum.

A visual analogy conveys the gist of the difficulty. Each meaning employed in the communication of a message serves for the analyst as a kind of spotlight that illuminates a particular portion (that portion to which the meaning contributes). But these spotlights can be turned on *only one at a time*, which means that at no time is the message ever illuminated in its totality (for analytical purposes, at any rate). As a result, the analyst cannot establish how the various portions he has successively glimpsed relate to each other in a precise enough way to allow him to piece together a structured conceptual analysis of the totality.

Consider now a specific example. When Focus Number and Entity Number contrast, each meaning is functioning expressively since each is clearly contributing to a different aspect of the message. Figure 9.1 illustrates the distinct notional components of the message to which the Number meanings ONE and MORE THAN ONE contribute in the sentence *The family disagree*. The ONE of *family∅* indicates that only a single 'family' is involved, while the MORE THAN ONE of *disagree∅* indicates that with respect to the event of 'disagreeing' the component parts of the

FIGURE 9.1   Expressive use

[5]   The *family0*   *disagree0*.

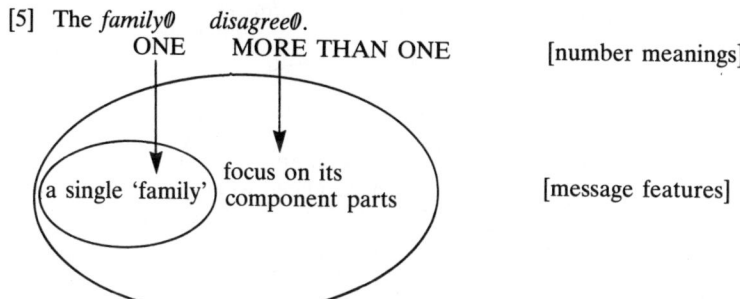

[number meanings]

[message features]

'family' are in Focus. In [5], then, each number meaning is contributing to clearly different aspects of the message.

On the other hand, when the Focus Number and the Entity Number are both ONE (or both MORE THAN ONE), they would appear to be contributing to partials of the message that are perfectly congruent conceptually. (Figure 9.2 is the picture implicit in the notion of verb agreement.)

FIGURE 9.2   Apparent resonating use

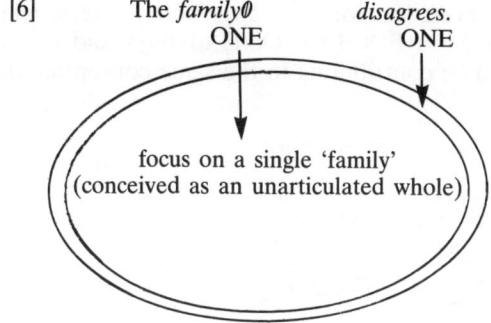

That, at any rate, is the conclusion when [6] is considered in isolation. But when [6] is considered in relation to [5], the contrast can be used to argue that the Focus Number meaning of *disagrees* contributes to a *different* partial, with the result that the two Number meanings ONE and ONE are again functioning *expressively*. This re-analysis is shown in Figure 9.3.

The ONE of *family0* contributes to the semantic partial of the message which [6] and [5] have in common (only a single 'family' is involved), while the ONE of *disagrees* contributes to the partial

FIGURE 9.3   Expressive use

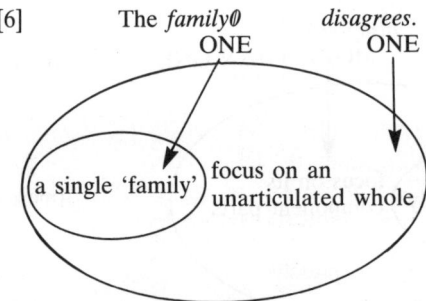

[6]   The *family0*   *disagrees.*
                    ONE   ONE

a single 'family'   focus on an
                    unarticulated whole

which distinguishes [6] from [5], namely, that the entity in Focus
is conceived on this occasion as an unarticulated whole. The
ONE of *disagrees* in [6] thus retains a measure of expressive
value, distinguishing the interpretation of *family0* from that of [5]
which highlights its component parts. (Recall the expressive
contrasts with the words *family*, *faculty*, *panel* and *cast* in Chapter
6.)

Example [6] is susceptible to this alternative conceptual
analysis because [6] and [5] are minimal pairs. In the absence of a
minimal contrast this line of analysis may appear problematic.
Consider the sentence *Five boys count the money*. Since no
coherent interpretation for *Five boys counts the money* can be
imagined, the MORE THAN ONE of *boys* and *count0* would
both appear to be contributing to the same conceptual fraction of
the message.

FIGURE 9.4   Apparent resonating use

[7]   Five *boys*   *count0* the money.
               MORE THAN   MORE THAN
                    ONE   ONE

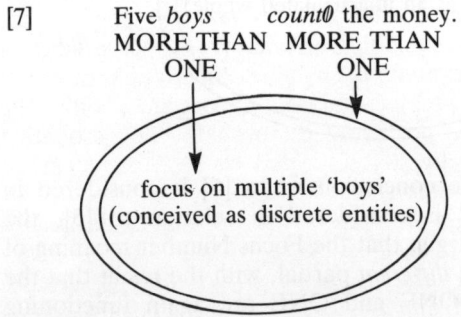

focus on multiple 'boys'
(conceived as discrete entities)

But the analysis in terms of contrast need not proceed strictly
by minimal pairs; for, to recall, the communicative problem the
number meanings help solve is to be found at the intra-sentential
level. And at that point the interpretation has not yet been

narrowed down to minimal pair alternatives. This means that [7] may be legitimately contrasted with [8].

[8]   Five boys counts as one team.

The MORE THAN ONE of *count∅* in [7] can now be seen as functioning to help steer the hearer away from the unintended 'middle voice' interpretation of *count* in [8], and toward its intended 'active voice' interpretation in [7].

FIGURE 9.5   Apparent expressive use

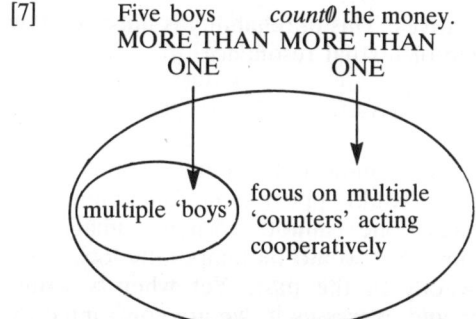

[7]   Five boys   *count∅* the money.

The question now arises: does Figure 9.4 or Figure 9.5 represent the correct conceptual analysis of the message? Or, are the two equivalent? Whether the Focus Number System is functioning in an expressive or a resonating capacity in [7] hinges on the answer to that question. Yet there seems to be no principled basis for providing an answer.

The point here is that there exists an *indeterminacy* in the semantic analysis of [7]. Depending on what [7] is compared to, a case can be made for the number meanings functioning in either a resonating or an expressive mode. In practice, only the expressive mode can be positively established; the resonating mode is the conclusion by default when the expressive mode cannot be convincingly demonstrated.

The boy walks through the field would appear to be such a default case. Yet *boy*, designating a young human male, resembles the semantic value of *Santa Claus*; and Chapter 6 provided an example of *Santa Claus* with the Focus meaning MORE THAN ONE:

[9]   Yes Virginia, there *are* a Santa Claus.

Thus, the possibility cannot be ruled out that one day, some speaker might find a suitable occasion for an utterance beginning *the boy walk. . .*, just as there arose the occasion for [9].

The role of creative imagination
The discussion above shows how within sign-based theory the conceptual analysis of a message into discrete fractions is critically affected by the alternative interpretive paths taken into consideration. Successful message analysis would thus seem to require fixing the number of relevant interpretive alternatives. Yet their number is largely a function of the imagination of the individual appraiser. The Santa Claus example in Chapter 6 illustrated the unreliability of people's judgements about coherent interpretive alternatives. This unreliability is illustrated by another apparent example of textual resonance.

[10]   He arrived a while ago.

In [10] the notion of past time is indicated by both *-ed* and *a while ago*. These two components would appear to be functioning in a resonating capacity because one cannot, off-hand, imagine a message involving past time that would be temporally located in any place other than wholly in the past. Yet when a writer envisions such a message and expresses it, we are confronted by an expressive possibility that had not occurred to us.

[11]   You read the latest polls every morning. . .You listen to the latest polls every evening. . . As a result, you know *President Reagan was re-elected next week* by a thumping majority. And you are puzzled, right?
        Waking up in the morning, tuning in to the world, hearing the hourly poll about *the great victory Mr. Reagan won next week*, you ask yourself "How come *I don't remember voting next week. . . .*
        Thanks to the amazingly scientific science of polling. . .*it is not necessary for you to have voted next week.*
                                    (Russell Baker, *The New York Times*)

In the light of example [11], *a while ago* in [10] could now be said to function expressively by ruling out the time perspective in the Russell Baker passage.

Distinguishing 'special effect' usage
The usual solution to the analytical difficulty created by such imaginative use of language is to distinguish between 'normal'

usage and usage for 'special effect'. But that would seem to be a criterion highly susceptible to subjective variation. Moreover, in the case of the Focus Number System it does not partition the data along the lines of 'agreement' vs. 'non-agreement'. No one could claim to perceive a special effect produced by the contrasting Entity and Focus Number meanings in such mundane sentences as *People0 want0 to leave by 10 o'clock*, and *The buffalo0 are grazing*. On the other hand, simple 'agreement' can, on occasion, create a special effect.

[12]   After nine years of bumps and grinds, Miss Doda and her silicone-inflated bosom *are* still packing them in . . . at the Condor, birthplace of topless entertainment.
(*The New York Post*)

The MORE THAN ONE of *are* forces Miss Doda and her bosom to be understood as an incidental grouping of entities, each an independent cause of the Occurrence *are packing in*. This would seem to count as a 'special effect'. Note this interpretation stands in contrast to that of [13], in which the Focus Number meaning of *has* tells the reader to understand *Barry's brother* and *fellow Bee Gee Maurice Gibb* as the same person without, it seems, producing any additional 'special effect'.

[13]   Barry's brother and fellow Bee Gee Maurice Gibb *has* never seen Andy's ghost, although he claims to have heard it while standing near the backyard dock of his Miami home.
(Cutler Durkee and Jonathan Cooper, *People*)

Others may find no special effect in [12] and a special effect in [13]; but that only underscores the shakiness of the distinction between 'normal' usage and 'special effect' usage.

The status of messages
The analytical indeterminacy illustrated above is due to the fact that in sign-based theory messages are treated as mere fragments of personal psychological experience, not reified linguistic objects. At the experiential level a message often seems to be an unstructured conceptual gestalt (e.g., *I'm hungry*). Some aspects of its internal structure emerge when it is considered in relation to the discrete linguistic meanings employed in its expression (e.g., Figures 9.1 and 9.2). And additional aspects emerge when the message is contrasted with related messages those meanings serve to block (Figure 9.3). During this blocking stage, however,

a meaning distinguishes a message not only from its fraternal twin, but from a hazy, open-ended range of disparate messages as well, alternatives that hover on the edge of consciousness as dimly-lit paths not taken (e.g., [8]). Depending on how far along the hearer is in the interpretive process, *one person's expressive differentiation is another's textual resonance.*

9.5 Generality of Explanation

Although the practical problems inherent in distinguishing the expressive from the resonating use of a linguistic meaning remain daunting, our reason for not pursuing that line of analysis is theoretical. Such a dualistic treatment would partition a body of data that is clearly susceptible to a single unified account and so would fail to attain the highest level of generality. Consider the structure of the present account.

The account of the Focus Number System in its expressive capacity has a descriptive and an explanatory component. Figure 8.2, repeated below as Figure 9.6, describes the joint use of the signals in the Entity Number and Focus Number Systems for four basic message types.

FIGURE 9.6   Signal combinations and message types

1.	*Entity -0 + Occurrence -s →*	A.	focus on one entity conceived as an unarticulated whole
2.	*Entity -0 + Occurrence -0 →*	B.	focus on the component parts of an articulated entity
3.	*Entity -s + Occurrence -s →*	C.	focus on one entity but with discrete parts or manifestations
4.	*Entity -s + Occurrence -0 →*	D.	focus on multiple separate entities

Figure 9.6 describes the relation between signal combinations and message types found in language use. But it provides no explanation for the particular alignment found. Any other alignment would accord the four signals equal distinctive value. Figure 9.6, then, does not go beyond description in theory-based terms.

The constructs that render the alignment non-arbitrary and motivated are the *meanings* assigned to each signal, shown in Figure 9.7. Each number meaning contributes semantically to distinguishable components of the message. These non-arbitrary connections between meanings and messages are instances of

FIGURE 9.7 Meaning combinations and message types

Entity Number		Focus Number		Message Types
1. ONE	+	ONE	A.	focus on one entity conceived as an unarticulated whole
2. ONE	+	MORE THAN ONE	B.	focus on the component parts of an articulated entity
3. MORE THAN ONE	+	ONE	C.	focus on one entity but with discrete parts or manifestations
4. MORE THAN ONE	+	MORE THAN ONE	D.	focus on multiple separate entities

means-end relationships; in each case, a particular signal is chosen because its associated meaning fits the speaker's message and distinguishes it from alternative interpretations at the inter-sentential level. (This allows the joint deployment of the Entity and Focus Number Systems to be treated as the sum of the parts – the collocation of independently chosen signs – rather than as a kind of discontinuous morpheme.)

Turning now to the use of the Focus Number System in its resonating capacity, a portion of Figure 9.6 describes the relation between signal combinations and message types observed in language use.

FIGURE 9.6a

1.	*Entity -∅ + Occurrence -s* →	A.	focus on one entity conceived as an unarticulated whole
4.	*Entity -s + Occurrence -∅* →	D.	focus on multiple separate entities

As before, a portion of Figure 9.7 provides the explanation for the alignment shown above.

FIGURE 9.7a

Entity Number		Focus Number		Message Types
1. ONE	+	ONE	A.	focus on one entity conceived as an unarticulated whole
4. MORE THAN ONE	+	MORE THAN ONE	D.	focus on multiple separate entities

Again the meanings fit the messages being conveyed, and the textual resonance they create at the intra-sentential level helps the hearer (in ways illustrated in Chapter 8) to arrive at the intended communication. The point, then, is that the *same* meanings responsible for the use of the Focus Number System in its expressive capacity account for its use in its resonating (or confirming) capacity as well.

Analytical advantage

More importantly, this generality of explanation provides a way around the analytical impasse concerning the structural indeterminacy of messages. The analyst is now freed from having to decide on each and every occasion whether the Focus Number System is functioning in an expressive or resonating capacity. For with respect to an individual example, the explanation of the Focus Number choice is always the same: the Focus Number meaning contributes semantically to a specific fraction of the message. The textual resonance that meaning may create is justified at a higher level; as argued in Chapter 8, textual resonance is a generalized strategic response to inherent structural characteristics of language that are always present.

Because the immediate means-end relation between meaning and message is the same in both the expressive and resonating modes, it is not surprising one has difficulty in deciding which it is on individual occasions. If the relation were different, that would no doubt provide the basis. But the difference between them actually hinges on the hearer's *degree of knowledge of the intended message* at the point he encounters the morphological components of the signals – to what extent he has already excluded alternative interpretive paths.

On the other hand, the speaker, from his perspective, is always doing the same thing: making a linguistic choice in response to some notional fraction of his intended message. Whether that fraction happens to be one the hearer has already deduced on some other basis is of no concern to him. Since the speaker need not analyse his intended message (structurally) in any greater detail than is required to make the succession of choices that confront him, there is no reason to expect the linguist to be able to do so. Attempting it amounts to over-analysis.

9.6 The Analysis of Messages

The analysis of messages clearly proceeds differently within sign-based and sentence-based theory. One aims at a structured conceptual analysis and the other does not. The following two sections retrace how this difference follows from the choice of different basic units and the subsequent analytical tasks each defines.

Sentence-based semantic analysis

As the basic unit of linguistic content, 'sentence meaning' requires both analysis and representation. Since this construct falls within the scope of language as a structured system, messages must be abstracted away from their communicative context and idealized as well-defined objects existing independently of speaker and hearer. (This step is fully justified in view of its initial idealization of sentences as abstract linguistic objects.)

Since the analysis of 'sentence meaning' is guided by a concern with propositional value, logical form and sentential relations, no simple one-to-one correspondence can exist; the analytical task becomes that of *mapping* between two independent levels of sentence representation, the semantic and the morphological.

An important feature of the mapping is its bi-directionality: starting at either end there is a rule-governed path to the other. The bi-directionality requirement provides a principled basis for imposing structure upon the message in two ways. First, it permits a conceptual partial to be analysed out of the message *only* when a minimal-pair contrast can be established. (For example, this would block ascribing the feature 'focus on multiple counters' to *Occurrence -∅* in *Five boys count∅ the money* because no minimal pair contrast exists to demonstrate its presence as a distinct message component to which it has a unique claim.)

Secondly, it forces a decision on each and every occasion as to whether two morphological units reflect the same, or different, features figuring in the semantic representation. (For example, it obliges the analyst to assign the feature 'focus on an unarticulated whole' to either *family* or *disagrees*, or both, in *The family disagrees*.)

Sign-based semantic analysis

In sign-based analysis, 'meaning' (as a linguistic object) exists only at the sign level. The semantic product of any sequence of signs is allowed to remain as personal psychological experience for both speaker and hearer. Messages are not idealized away from the communicative process because that process is where the communicative function of linguistic signs is to be found.

Since messages now fall *outside* language as a structured system, analysis cannot begin there. It must begin from the vantage point of constructs that reside within language proper. The analytical task involves working from the (hypothesized) meanings to features of the message that have motivated their choice.

At this point it may appear that things should proceed as they do within the sentence-based framework, yielding a bi-directional mapping between the meanings and the message. But now the analysis of a message is guided *only* by the meanings involved in its expression. And as meanings approach identity (as do the two sets of number meanings) the principled basis for analysing the message into distinct corresponding partials is lost.

This loss means that the structural relations among semantic partials of the message (i.e., their possible congruence) cannot always be determined. Sometimes a meaning is clearly serving as the sole linguistic clue to a particular fraction of the message; sometimes it clearly isn't; and elsewhere it is difficult to say. As a result, the message itself never emerges as a structured linguistic object from which one could trace one's steps back to the meanings. The 'mapping', such as it is, ends up *uni-directional*.

9.7 The Complementarity Principle

This chapter has argued that a complementarity principle obtains in the analysis of language. The idealizational and procedural framework that allows language to be analysed as a representational system *fails* to provide a functional explanation for many structural features posited along the way (e.g., a verb agreement rule). On the other hand, the framework that provides a functional explanation for such morphological features as verb number is one in which 'sentence meaning' *cannot* be posited as a structured linguistic object. To underscore the points of conflict between these two objectives we now recapitulate the steps in the present functional account of the Focus Number System as developed in Chapters 5–8.

A. The discussion in Chapter 8 of morphological and semantic indeterminacy highlighted the general problems that arise when linguistic signs are employed in the communication of messages: (1) *signals* can often not be identified on purely morphological grounds, their identification must rely on previously established parts of the message; (2) the *meanings* carried by the signals are usually not as precise as the corresponding features of the intended message that motivated their choice.

B. The systemic compensation for these two structural features of language is the maintenance within the linguistic code of multiple expressive devices for signalling the same feature of the message. Speakers have incorporated these into their strategies of communication so as to create textual resonance. Textual resonance is created whenever two or more meanings delineate, imply or suggest the *same* feature of the message (for the hearer). Both lexical and grammatical meanings are employed in this fashion.

C.   The Entity Number and Focus Number Systems exemplify both the problem and the solution. On the one hand, its four signals are morphologically ambiguous: an -*s* suffix figures in both systems and is identical to the genitive -*s* as well, while the two -*∅*'s pose an even greater problem for identification. The associated lexical stem often does not resolve the identity of the signal because most lexical stems in English are used to describe both entities and occurrences.

As for the content side, the meanings in the two systems are always less precise than the features of the message that motivate their selection because both Entity Number and Focus Number are inextricably tied conceptually to what is being counted, and the latter is tied to the Occurrence as well.

D.   On the other hand, the Focus Number inflection, in context, (1) can provide the critical clue that resolves the attendant morphological and interpretive indeterminacy of the adjacent signs; more often, it (2) serves to confirm aspects of interpretation already provisionally arrived at; and occasionally it (3) functions expressively as do other lexical and grammatical signs.

E.   The meanings posited for *Occurrence* -*s* and -*∅* are equally suited to function in all three capacities. Since the actual Focus Number choice can always be accounted for semantically (in the manner illustrated throughout Chapter 6), it is unnecessary, and often impossible, to identify which of these three functions it happens to be fulfilling for hearers on an individual occasion.

Internal functional explanation
The summary above reveals the cause of the analytical conflict. Our goal has been a *system-internal* explanation of Focus Number (Garvin 1984). This has required that the relevant explanatory factors be incorporated directly into the linguistic system itself.

We have aimed to describe grammatical and lexical structure so that it *inherently* confronts language users with problems of perceptual and interpretive indeterminacy. We have made sure that language is, in Halliday and Hasan's words, 'semantically full of holes'; that a text is like a picture 'complete but out of focus, with the outlines blurred and the details imperceptible'. That imprecision, in turn, has provided the systemic functional explanation for the existence of textual resonance, one specific instance of which is the multiple signalling of grammatical number.

This analytical tack is at cross purposes with an explicit representation of 'sentence meaning' because the latter requires just the reverse:

> Semantic theories can and should be so formulated as to guarantee that deep structures (including their lexical components) are specified as unambiguous in the first place and proceed from there to account for the interpretation of a complex expression from the known meanings of its components.
>
> (Weinreich 1980:104)

Adherence to this principle, along with the bi-directionality requirement, may eventually permit a structured conceptual analysis of 'sentence meaning'. But it would yield a picture of linguistic structure in which Focus Number has *no* appreciable role. All that is left of its clearly expressive function is a handful of minimal-pair examples of distinctiveness at the sentence level – *the family disagrees* vs. *the family disagree0* – scarcely enough material with which to build a convincing case for the Focus Number signals as independent meaning-bearing units.

As for the textual resonance the Focus Number System creates, its role in the communicative process would be lost sight of entirely because the idealizational framework of sentence-based theory bypasses the early stages of signal recognition and lexical interpretation to focus on two levels of linguistic representation where such problems *have already been resolved*.

The result is that Focus Number then appears to be a functionally-useless mechanical contrivance of arbitrary structure. Yet once the requisites for its functional explanation are incorporated into linguistic theory – perceptually ambiguous signals, semantically imprecise meanings indifferent to part-of-speech distinctions, and structurally indeterminate messages – it becomes impossible to treat language as an axiomatic representational system of 'sentence meaning'.

9.8 The Logical Independence of Communication and Representation

Sperber and Wilson (1986) help provide theoretical justification for why such a complementarity principle might exist in the analysis of language. Espousing the conventional view, Sperber and Wilson define language as essentially 'a grammar-governed representational system' that also happens to serve as an instrument of communication (p. 173). They then argue that there is no necessary logical connection between these two features of language. They are only necessarily linked if one arbitrarily defines them to be so.

> It would be possible to define a language even more restrictively: as a set of semantically interpreted formulas used for communication. It would then be true that language and communication were inextricably linked. However, the definition itself would then have to be motivated. In science, a definition is motivated when it groups together properties which are systematically linked in nature. Our point is precisely that the property of being a grammatically-governed representational system and the property of being used for communication *are not systematically linked* [emphasis W.R.]. They are found together in the odd case of human natural languages, just as the property of being an olfactory organ and the property of being a prehensile organ, though not systematically linked in nature, happen to be found together in the odd case of the elephant's trunk.
>
> (Sperber and Wilson 1986:173)

We are in agreement here with Sperber and Wilson. In fact, we are intent upon carrying this divorce of representation and communication one step further than do Sperber and Wilson by insisting that it goes *both ways*, just like the elephant's trunk. There is nothing, we argue, in the notion of communication that necessitates a representational system. Sperber and Wilson, committed as they are to the representational view, must argue the contrary.

> However language *is* a necessary attribute of communicating devices. Two devices capable of communicating with each other must also be capable of internally representing the information communicated, and must therefore have an internal language.
>
> (Sperber and Wilson 1986:174)

But a human being is not a 'device'! A human being is a sentient creature. The beguiling metaphor of man-as-machine has led Sperber and Wilson to overlook an important difference between the two: a human being *experiences*. It is thus a theoretical possibility that the messages motivating linguistic production exist as ongoing mental experience *without* necessarily being accompanied by ongoing representation of that experience, just as one can experience hunger and set about to make oneself a snack without constructing a (structured) mental representation of the proposition I AM HUNGRY. Representation only becomes a necessity when communicative objectives are idealized away from their experiential base as discrete abstract objects subject to logical analysis and manipulation.

9.9 Possible Relations Between Language and Thought

We hasten to clarify we are not ruling out the possibility that people may construct mental representations of their experience, or that a 'language of thought' may indeed exist; and that both may be crucial to an explanation of human cognitive abilities. We are simply insisting that one has no basis to make any assumption in advance about how such a 'language of thought' relates to natural language. Consider for a moment several of the possibilities.

Natural language could prove, upon investigation, to stand in a relation of perfect isomorphism to a language of thought. This would confirm the view of language as 'the window to the mind'. At the other extreme, natural language might prove to be no more than an imperfect, rough-and-ready, hit-or-miss, general-purpose communicative system that bears only a casual, tangential (and hence *unmappable*) relation to a language of thought. This would legitimate the popular lament 'my words don't seem to express what I want to say'. Language, as a communicative system, is successful only so long as the yardstick for success does not exceed everyday practical demands.

A third possibility is that the language of thought bears a close relation to natural language, but that the representations constructed with this language of thought are only *partial* representations of our actual mental experience. In this case, mental representations would bear the same relation to mental experience as a professor's lecture notes bear to his lecture: key words and phrases that recall for him the points he wants to make, but that would certainly not permit someone else to deliver his lecture unless that person had already heard it once before. Similarly, the language of thought would encode cognitively salient fragments of our mental experience (itself holistic and indeterminately structured) which would allow one to recall, examine and manipulate that experience to some extent; but it would not encode enough of the totality that the representations themselves would be directly subject to formal and universal 'laws of thought'.

On this view, mental representations would be idiosyncratic in that they would only be meaningful and interpretable to the person who actually had the experiences to which they relate. High-level abstract thought would not operate on mental representations themselves. Rather, it would proceed *in advance* of representation, intuitively darting here and there on the constantly unfurling scroll of polymorphous mental experience, constructing representations only after experiencing some insight worth probing and developing.

Yet another possibility is that mental experience is always accompanied by some kind of representation, but that its form (i.e., the categories employed and their degree of precision) would vary according to the immediate purpose for which it was constructed. The representation of one and the same mental experience could then range from the lecture-note variety if simple storage was desired, to the abstract analysis of formal logic if logical deduction was anticipated. When no larger purpose was immediately envisioned – often the case in normal communication – the mental experience triggered by a linguistic stimulus would be structured and represented only so far as is required to 'explain' that stimulus. (Recall Chapter 3 characterized comprehension as creative problem-solving, a process in which the message is the hearer's 'explanation' for the speaker's choice of linguistic signs.) On this view, all mental activity would be governed by means-end relationships of the kind found in natural language rather than by the algorithmic rules inspired by the mind-as-machine metaphor.

In view of all these logical possibilities (and surely others as well), we argue that no investigation of mental representation or the language of thought can serve as a reliable guide in the investigation of natural language because we do not know what can be legitimately inferred from the former about the latter. The actual relation between the two must be treated as a second-order problem that could only be properly addressed after one had completed independent analyses of the two.[1]

9.10 Formal vs. Functional Explanation

The practical consequence of this reciprocal divorce of representation and communication is that if either notion is adopted as

the essential and defining property of language, there is no
reason to believe that the linguistic theory engendered by one
will eventually intersect with the theory engendered by the other.
Indeed, one should be surprised if they did intersect since, as
Sperber and Wilson insist, the two properties 'are not systematic-
ally related'. Hence the complementarity principle.

The two theories are likely to diverge because they are
governed by different principles, each justified by their initial
conception of language. Most notably, they achieve explanation
by different mechanisms. Explanation within sentence-based
theory is dependent on the type-token relation defined by a
linguistic rule. The explanatory force of a rule-based account lies
in its axiomaticity, explicitness, and economy of statement.
Linguistic rules are deductively justified as the proper mode of
explanation by an initial (often implicit) language-as-machine
metaphor.[2]

Sign-based theory, on the other hand, proceeds from an
explicit instrumental metaphor.[3] As a consequence, the fundamental explanatory relation is the means-end relation (see 3.3).
Crucial here is the involvement of a human being. For only
human beings can envision goals and see linguistic objects as
suitable instruments to reach those goals. Yet it is precisely the
active presence of a mediating human mind that must be
excluded in an axiomatic system.[4]

9.11 Formalizing the Means-End Relation

The obstacle to formalizing the means-end relation is that the
goals guiding human behaviour can remain fuzzy and undetailed
at the time they are exercising their control. People pursue them
in a piecemeal fashion, altering their strategy as they take shape
and making minor corrections along the way. This creates a
Catch-22 situation for formalizing the means-end relation. If it
were to be reduced to an algorithmic mechanism, the communicative goal would have to be reified at the outset. Yet once that is
done, the end no longer justifies the means.

This insight into the essential nature of goal-directed activity
has already been incorporated into the study of creativity in a
related area, that of composition. The traditional approach to the
teaching of composition has been to instruct students to make a
thematic outline – the communicative goal in schematic form –
and then to move directly to drafting the final text. However
empirical investigation of the creative process has revealed a very
different picture (Emig 1971, Sommers 1980). Professional

writers report that they often begin *without* an outline and work through a series of drafts, each one a revision and expansion of the previous one. Through this process writers discover what they have to say, and how to say it.

From the standpoint of the final product, the trail of preceding drafts appears superfluous – a series of false starts. But from the standpoint of the creative process they are crucial. The final form of the text cannot be explained directly in terms of an original expressive intent because that itself is a product of its evolving linguistic expression.

The present analysis argues that if an explanation for the morphological particulars of a text is sought, this insight into linguistic creativity must be extended to the micro-level. The analogue to the series of drafts is the sequence of linguistic choices that collectively comprise a text.

Crucial here is a focus on process, not product. During the actual communicative process the message is undergoing continual metamorphosis in the course of its linguistic structuring by the succession of meanings chosen, each choice subtly altering the remaining communicative problem (recall here the phenomenon of category shift developed in Chapter 6). The communicative function of linguistic features like Focus Number lies in this moment-by-moment structuring process. Once that process is complete, their role is no longer apparent.

9.12 The Scope of Linguistic Theory

The role of 'meaning' in linguistic theory is a foundational one, and the status of messages in the present framework can be viewed as a resolution of two apparently conflicting recommendations regarding the idealization appropriate for fruitful linguistic analysis. Thirty-five years ago Chomsky warned against attempting to incorporate meaning within a theory of language.[5]

> Meaning is a notoriously difficult notion to pin down. If it can be shown that meaning and related notions do play a central role in linguistic analysis, then its results and conclusions become subject to all the doubts and obscurities that plague the study of meaning, and a serious blow is struck at the foundations of linguistic theory.
>
> (Chomsky 1955:141)

In their critique of Chomskian linguistics, Moore and Carling warn of the dangers of idealization in linguistic theory.

[A]ny theoretical framework in linguistics based on idealising away
from language users must lack both congruence with the object of
enquiry and relevance to the puzzles and mysteries of language in use.
(Moore and Carling, 1982:177)

The issue, as Moore and Carling clarify, is not actually the
importance of language users *per se*; most linguists grant their
importance in principle. The question is where to proceed from
there.

The real difficulty here is not with accepting the importance of
language users and their knowledge, beliefs and expectations to an
understanding of language functioning: it lies rather in defining an
investigable domain once these are accepted as central.
(Moore and Carling, 1982:177)

Sign-based theory offers an answer, one that heeds Moore and
Carling's warning not to idealize away from language users while,
at the same time, heeding Chomsky's early warning to beware of
attempting to integrate (sentence) meaning into linguistic theory.
Briefly, the answer is that messages are to be a part of the
explanans in linguistic theory rather than part of the *explanandum*.

Moore and Carling's investigable domain is defined here as
speakers' and writers' choice of linguistic signs in the communication of messages. By setting messages outside language proper, as
Chomsky originally proposed, the pitfalls he envisioned are
partially avoided.

Following Moore and Carling however (and departing from
Chomsky's original intent) messages have *not* been excluded
from linguistic explanation; for it is in terms of the message that
the language user's choices are justified. Messages are allowed to
reside in the minds of speakers and hearers in their non-discrete
and partially unstructured state, available for examination on a
piece-meal basis. Structure is imputed to them *only so far as
required to explain a speaker's choice of linguistic signs*. Handled
in this way, the ultimate intractability of messages is not an
obstacle in linguistic analysis so long as the investigation does not
become, in Chomsky's words, 'the study of meaning'.

Notes

1. Traditional grammar (and its modern rationalist descendants)
   proceeds on the assumption of a perfect isomorphism and allows a
   logical analysis of thought to inform its analysis of language. As a
   consequence, it effectively thwarts an unprejudiced investigation of

the actual relation between natural language and thought. Sign-based theory, on the other hand, maintains a studious neutrality on this issue. It thus provides the independent analysis of natural language which could then serve as the basis for later investigation of that more ambitious and significant question.

2. To their credit, Sperber and Wilson are explicit in their adoption of the machine metaphor.

> An informal system thus leaves an important part of the deductive process unspecified; it is left to the intelligent user of the system to decide how best to exploit it. In trying to construct a model of the mind . . . it is not legitimate to rely on informal systems of this type precisely because they leave an important part of the comprehension process unexplained. Formal systems (effective procedures, automata, algorithms) differ from informal systems in just this respect: their procedures can be carried out by an automaton whose decisions are predetermined at every stage. (pp. 94–5)

Our unwillingness to follow Sperber and Wilson's lead stems in part from the fact that they are attempting to construct a model of the mind whereas we are not. Yet it is surprising that an investigation of mind would resolve on essentially methodological and philosophical grounds the very question that sparked the investigation in the first place: to wit, the essential nature of cognitive processes. Specifically, Sperber and Wilson have decided on the basis of a general belief about the proper form of scientific explanation (presumably based on the physical sciences) that comprehension is essentially deductive and rule-based rather than, say, a process bearing important similarities to hypothesis creation, a possibility they discount at the outset as unlikely (pp. 66–7).

Sperber and Wilson's decision might be justified as merely a research strategy, an exploration of the hypothesis that the mind is an automaton. But then the hypothesis must be formulated with a clear conception of what analytical results would count as its falsification. Practically speaking, the most telling falsification would consist in an inability to construct a 'model of mind' that conforms to the demanding standards of complete automaticity, explicitness and determination they have set for themselves.

3. I owe the idea of 'guiding metaphors' in theory-building to Lakoff and Johnson (1980) and Janet Emig (1983). Ricardo Otheguy is responsible for the notion of the conflict between the language-as-machine and the language-as-instrument metaphors.

4. Most notably, an active intelligent human mind is crucial when language use is explained in terms of systemic value relations. Chapter 3 dealt with the referential extensions of the words *people*, *chicken*, *pig* and *cow* in terms of their value within a semantic field. These relations 'pressure but do not compel'. A human mind is required to experience this pressure; an automaton can only be

compelled, not pressured.

To be sure, the observable effects of this pressure on the user can be modelled in terms of statistical probability. But then the value relations themselves can be dispensed with. And in any event, probability is not the same thing as pressure, it is a qualitatively different kind of explanation. The availability of an attractive modelling mechanism cannot be allowed to determine one's conclusion about the intrinsic nature of one's object of investigation.

5. See Katz (1980) for a detailed analysis and critique of Chomsky's position on the status of 'sentence meaning' within generative theory.

Chapter 10

The phenomena of linguistics

Chapter 9 argued the fundamentally irreconcilable goals of sign-based and sentence-based linguistic theory. Why, then, would one opt for the former rather than the latter? Chapter 1 presented the choice as involving the linguist's initial guess about the essential nature of language. But on that issue there can be a legitimate difference of opinion. Can sign-based theory be supported in terms of more general principles underlying scientific inquiry? Or does it ultimately depend, as Chapter 9 left it, on an *a priori* commitment to functional explanation?

A period of uncommitted naturalistic observation has preceded the development of many theoretical sciences: modern astronomy is ultimately traceable to the observations of the heavens by ancient mariners. The present chapter argues that sign-based theory addresses a range of phenomena available prior to any particular conception of language, and independent of the judgements and reports with which sentence-based theory begins. Sign-based theory is thus empirically *grounded* in a way that sentence-based theory is not.

This case can best be made Socratically by inquiring what the initial impetus to linguistic theory-building could be. What gets the procedure on the road? The answer cannot be one's guess about the nature of language, because that should enter the picture only when theory-building begins. The question is, what are the pre-theoretical phenomena about which that guess is made? In short, what creates the need for a theory of language?

To clarify the kind of empirical grounding being sought for linguistics, let us take a closer look at the original phenomenological impetus to theory-building in one of the exact sciences by returning to our analogy with chemistry.

10.1 The Phenomena of Chemistry

Chemistry began as an attempt to bring order and sense to the experiential reality of the material world. The material world in which the chemist perceives himself to be living exhibits various kinds of asymmetries. Substances differ from one another in immediately perceptible ways: some maintain a fixed shape; others conform to the shape of their container; and still others fill all available space. Matter differs in weight, colour, texture, and hardness. And it behaves differently: substances often change their appearance, diminish or increase over time; some react violently when brought into contact while others do not. For anyone who asks questions at all, the material world presents a puzzle. And this puzzle exists quite independently of a commitment to any particular explanatory framework for its understanding.

As in many advanced sciences, the connection between molecular theory and the experiential reality to which it is a response has become indirect and at times tenuous. Chemists long since abandoned the pre-theoretical, observational categories of description that the layman might employ in favour of theory-defined categories: elements, compounds, acids, bases, oxidation, neutralization, and so on. But enough of a connection exists, manifested through the success of its predictions, that the chemist remains confident his work is still contributing to an explanation of (selected features of) a brute experiential reality.

10.2 Candidates for the Phenomena of Linguistics

The question now arises, What are the phenomena of linguistics? What, in linguistics, corresponds to the immediately perceptible asymmetry of the material world that lies behind chemistry? Before proposing an answer, let us examine four popular conceptions of the ultimate object of linguistic explanation to see why they do not provide the firm empirical grounding we believe a scientific theory demands.

The sentence
The sentence has long served as the starting point for linguistic theory (e.g., Chomsky 1957:13–14). Indeed, mainstream linguistic theory can with some justification be characterized as an attempt to define the nature of the sentence on both a language-particular and a universal level (Katz and Bever 1976:28). And with the sentence come, of course, all the traditional categories for its analysis (subject, object, comple-

ment, noun, verb, adjective), syntactic rules, and the associated concerns of sentence meaning and inter-sentential relations (e.g., synonymy) as well.

Surely it would be hard to argue that sentences constitute tangible features of experiential reality on a par with the perceptible asymmetry of the physical world. To begin with, one must possess specialized cultural knowledge to recognize them at all, knowledge intertwined with that of the written tradition and tutored to an unknown degree by early school-grammar training. Furthermore, even among the grammatical *cognoscenti* the frequent lack of consensus in speaker judgements scarcely needs elaboration. All this would seem to be clear proof that 'sentences' involve more than raw phenomena.

It appears, then, that 'sentence' is either a theory-internal construct or an *a priori* notion. Neither, we argue, makes it a suitable starting point for a scientific theory. For if it is a theory-internal construct, then the problem of its definition and analysis is a theory-generated one at best, and the question of the pre-theoretical problem that gave rise to the theory remains. On the other hand, if 'sentence' is an *a priori* notion, then that turns what purports to be an empirical science into a Platonistic philosophical investigation.

Lest this critique be dismissed as unreconstructed empiricism, we hasten to acknowledge that scientific theory-building does indeed require a leap beyond observation, a leap guided by one's initial guess about the nature of the phenomena. But the leap must be *from* something, something which would hold firm even if all one's beliefs were to prove false. The trouble with the notion 'sentence' is that it is a leap from a phenomenological void.

Permissibility

Another version of the pre-theoretical phenomena of linguistics is speakers' reactions to utterances, reactions characterized in terms of 'permissibility' (see note 4 in Chapter 6). This at least puts things on firmer empirical grounds. But while avoiding a language-related *a priori* notion it invokes a more general one. 'Permissibility' is a notion that only makes sense when a language is conceived as something of which it is appropriate to predicate utterances as being either 'in' or 'out'. It already anticipates a particular *kind* of linguistic theory, a formal one inspired by set theory, and thus embodies an implicit assumption about the nature of language; namely, that it is a quasi-mathematical, combinatory system amenable to treatment in axiomatic terms.

Furthermore, in view of the plethora of language phenomena surrounding us already, why would one fall back on introspection and subjective report if one were not fishing for empirical support for the notion 'sentence' to begin with? Such a deliberate ferreting out of data bears all the hallmarks of the search for support of a pre-established construct.

To be sure, searching for data to support a construct is quite legitimate once theory-construction is under way. But here we are turning back the clock to the purely observational stage and attempting to determine what gets linguistic theory started in the first place.

The relation between sound and sense

A third version of the pre-theoretical phenomena of linguistics is the relation between sound and 'sense' (Katz and Bever 1976:47). This has a greater common-sense legitimacy than the others. But by making the pre-theoretical object of study a *relationship* between disparate phenomena, it, too, embodies a covert assumption of a more general nature, namely, that there *exists* a (rule-governed) link between sound and 'sense'. Yet at the observational level one is confronted only by what pragmatics calls communicative *force*, something that varies erratically with the individual and the situation.

Actually, 'sense' in this formulation is generally taken to be the idealized object '(literal) sentence meaning', propositional value at the very least. It thus incorporates the long-standing view of language as a vehicle for the expression of *truth*, an inheritance from traditional grammar and logic.

The communicative process

How, then, does sign-based theory fare when subjected to the same critical scrutiny? Decidedly *worse* than the other three. Sign-based theory, as developed to date, pursues two analytical objectives: establishing the morphological and semantic identity of the linguistic signs that comprise a language; and then accounting for the choice of signs in terms of their semantic contribution to the communication of messages. Both goals are clearly theory-dependent, for they are couched in theory-internal terms (i.e., linguistic signs) and directly arise from its communicative orientation.

To be sure, a communicative approach to language is eminently reasonable. One can point to the fact that (1) language is employed by people for the purpose of communication a significant per cent of the time, and (2) things that evolve through time often come to reflect in their structure the function they serve. But these considerations fall short of establishing the communicative orientation (and its accompanying code metaphor) as deductively correct. As often noted (e.g., Newmeyer 1983), language is employed for a variety of purposes other than communication, each having a certain *prima facie* claim to being the key to its structure; and, moreover, communication is possible in the absence of a code (Sperber and Wilson 1986); finally, things are often employed for purposes which leave no mark on them. Thus the communicative orientation only has the virtue of plausibility, not necessity.

In short, all four versions of the ultimate phenomena of linguistics have moved beyond the purely observational stage because they all require idealizations that incorporate definite commitments to the nature of language. Such commitments are legitimate and necessary once theory-construction begins; but they are premature, we argue, if relied upon in the initial, rough delineation of the phenomena of the discipline at the pre-theoretical level. They are dangerous because they introduce at the very outset notions, conceptions and concerns that may actually be no more than a cultural inheritance. And if so, then linguistics has embraced problems for which there are no solutions.

10.3 Acoustic Asymmetry

What, then, is left at the observational level if sentence, sentence meaning, inter-sentential relations, permissibility, sound-sense relations, syntactic rules, thought, truth, linguistic signs, and the communicative process are all discarded as tainted starting points for linguistic theory?

In the context of the present framework, the ultimate phenomena of linguistics are to be found in the immediately perceptible acoustic asymmetry of vocal sound. The acoustic asymmetry of vocal sound is the linguistic analogue to the material asymmetry of the physical world that lies behind chemistry.

We are aiming here at something very simple. Vocal sound, in a naturalistic setting, can be recognized as departing from the acoustic symmetry of white noise. It is by and large periodic, for a start. Furthermore, vocal sound departs from acoustic symmetry in ways that go beyond what could be attributed to the varying vocal tract physiology of different individuals. This is evidenced by the fact that the vocal sound in different parts of the world can be recognized as acoustically different in consistent ways. For instance, most people with no knowledge of either Russian or Japanese could, with some practice, separate a collection of vocal samples recorded in Moscow and Tokyo into roughly the same two groups *purely* on the basis of consistently different acoustic characteristics. They could not do this if the vocal sounds produced by Russians and Japanese were either equally similar or equally different along all acoustic parameters.[1]

The same goes for the graphic configurations produced by people on paper. Samples of paper with graphic configuration from Moscow and Tokyo (consisting mainly of writing if randomly selected) can be distinguished and grouped by people with no knowledge of the writing systems employed.

All this goes in the way of showing that the acoustic and graphic output of people poses a legitimate problem independent of its notional value, and prior to any principled description or commitment to what its ultimate explanation may be. No *a priori* notion such as 'sentence', nor any relation to a second range of phenomena, nor even the notion of communication, need be initially introduced in order to give the analyst something to do. This departure from acoustic and graphic symmetry demands, all on its own, some kind of explanation. It must be due to *something*.[2]

10.4 From Phenomena to Theory

The analyst confronting the asymmetry of vocal sound proceeds to choose some promising orientation from which to construct an explanatory theory. Here the analyst's initial *guess* about the essential nature of the phenomena plays a critical role. The Columbia School adopts a communicative orientation. This choice, as noted, is not a logical necessity, but it is more than a stab in the dark because we know that among the various functions vocal sounds serve in society, communication is one.

The communicative orientation transforms the original pre-theoretical problem of acoustic asymmetry[3] into the theory-defined problem of explaining the sound (or graphic configurations) people produce as a consequence of trying to communicate. Since the vast preponderance of the world's vocal sound conveys little or nothing to us we can assume that a culture-particular arbitrary component is critically involved: a set of socially shared conventions.

Communicative structure

The basic structure of this set of conventions is taken to be a code system composed of paired signals and meanings. As support for this step one can point, with Saussure, to the fact that other systems of communication are known to embody this structure: musical notation, semaphore signalling and Morse code. The existence of such extra-linguistic sign systems establishes an initial psychological plausibility for language being structured along these lines as well; we know in advance that human beings are capable of learning and employing them.[4] So while the nature of linguistic structure must, in the final analysis, be regarded as innately determined – in that human beings are born with the capacity to acquire and manipulate sign systems – we have evidence external to language itself supporting the general nature of this genetic endowment.[5]

The introduction of messages

The communicative orientation also establishes the relevance to the enterprise of the notional content of the particular communication associated with a particular utterance. Concomitantly, it provides a principled basis for excluding from the theory's area of responsibility vocal sound deemed, in the course of analysis, to be non-code-based (e.g., humming, coughs, groans, whistles and the like). This has the effect of refining and delimiting a problem whose scope is narrower than the original, pre-theoretical problem which initiated the investigation (i.e., vocal sound in general).

Theory-based description

On the basis of an extensive examination of language use provisional signal-meaning hypotheses are developed. The hypothesized linguistic signals now serve as the principled categories of description of features of the theory-delimited phenomena (i.e. speech and writing), whose asymmetry has until now been perceived but not described. At this point the asymmetry is regarded as the collective product of the phonological and graphic shapes of the signals chosen by speakers and writers in attempting to communicate. The initial pre-theoretical problem of acoustic and graphic asymmetry has now advanced to the theory-defined problem of explaining the choice of linguistic signals.

The choice of linguistic signals is accounted for formally by the rule-governed link posited between signals and meanings. Signals are mechanically selected according to the meanings they bear in the hypothesized linguistic code. (Here lies the rule-governed domain of language.)

This step immediately raises the closely related problem of the choice of the hypothesized linguistic meanings. But it also provides the framework for its solution. The meanings establish the point of view from which the notional content of the associated message is described; as exemplified by the discussion of the examples in Chapter 6, messages are described in ways that highlight those aspects which the meanings help to characterize and distinguish.

The means-end relation
It is necessary to explore the possibility that the way meanings relate to messages is rule-governed as well. If so, the principles governing the construction of utterances could be treated as a self-contained axiomatic system. But investigation reveals that the qualitative message distinctions motivating a speaker's choice of meanings are continuously novel. This makes the phenomenon unsuitable for rule-governed treatment because the defining characteristic of rule-governed phenomena is that the number of relevant variables be finite.

Instead, the explanatory framework must be one into which new variables can be continually introduced, while still constraining their introduction in a principled way so they do not become *ad hoc*. This framework is based upon the means-end relationship that is known to underlie human behaviour in other domains. (See 3.3.)

The defining characteristic of a means-end relationship is that of *facilitation*: the means contribute to the accomplishment of the end. In language, the means are the hypothesized meanings of linguistic signs, and the end is the communication of a particular message. The means-end relationship is thus tested by examining whether a linguistic meaning facilitates in some statable way the communication of the particular message for which its signal is employed. (Here lies the goal-directed domain of language.)

The avoidance of *a priori* notions
Our intent here has not been to introduce a neo-empiricism to linguistics. Clearly once theory-construction begins, abstract theoretical constructs are freely posited. Neither have we ruled out of bounds a concern with a speaker's knowledge of his language; for while our initial starting point was (the acoustic result of) a range of human *behaviour*, the theory of linguistic signs is as much a theory of speaker knowledge as its generative counterpart.

But while acknowledging that no science can or does proceed

in a rigorously inductive fashion, we have insisted that linguistics commit itself to an initial range of primary phenomena – phenomena free of metaphysical entanglements – to which its theoretical constructs must ultimately answer. This prevents the introduction of possibly inappropriate *a priori* notions for which account would then have to be provided. Notions and constructs are introduced because they help to explain (selected features of) the original phenomena that initiated the enterprise, not merely because the analyst happens to find them interesting or because they have figured prominently within the long tradition of speculative language study.

Most importantly, the analyst is not initially committed to accounting for a link between the acoustic phenomena and anything else. The communicative orientation assures that the messages associated with utterances will play *some* role in the explanatory chain, but it does not specify its degree or nature. Specifically, there is no initial assumption of a linguistic object 'sentence meaning' for which a theory of language must account. This means that messages are of interest to the analyst only to the extent that they help explain the speaker's choice of meanings; *they never become the object of explanation themselves*. By this principle, sign-based theory steers a course between the Scylla of psychology and the Charybdis of philosophy.[6]

10.5 From Theory Back to Phenomena

In view of the serious indictment levelled at sentence-based theory, the claim that sign-based theory actually succeeds in breaking through its web of theory-internal constructs to something outside itself demands greater scrutiny. What, exactly, is the connection between the two number systems and the directly perceptible asymmetry of vocal sound we claim they are addressing? What is called for is a demonstration that the two number systems are, in fact, responsible for features of the overall acoustic asymmetry of English.

The obstacle to such a demonstration is that we have as yet no observational description of the characteristic acoustic asymmetry of English. In the analytical procedure sketched above (and followed in Chapters 2–8) we bypassed that step and moved directly to a theory-based description in terms of our hypothesized signals. But if one now demands a demonstration that the two number systems do in fact help explain acoustic asymmetry, neither our hypothesized signals, nor even their phonemic manifestations, can serve as descriptive categories. For then sign-based theory, like sentence-based theory, would be justifying itself in theory-internal terms.

What we need at this point is not descriptive categories derived from a phonological or grammatical analysis of English, but rather the kind of rough-and-ready, observational categories such as 'guttural' that the layman often employs to describe the sound of a language he does not know. In other words, we need easily-applicable categories with consistent acoustic correlates that will capture features of the characteristic acoustic asymmetry that makes English sound different from, say, French.

Sibilants and nasals are two such categories. Sibilants encompass a perceptually prominent range of sounds and are so-named because they all seem to hiss. This subjective impression is due to an objective acoustic property, the presence of aperiodic noise variably beginning at from 2500 to 4000 Hz and ranging up to between 6000 and 8000 Hz (Ladefoged 1975), produced by the turbulence of air passing between the tongue and the front palate.

Likewise, nasals encompass a readily identifiable range of sounds and are so-named because they all seem to issue from the nose. Their unique quality is due to an objective acoustic property, namely, the emergence of the third formant as the predominant one, due to the weakening of the normally strong first and second formants (caused by the lowering of the velum) that characterize oral sound.

These two phonetic categories are ideal for present purposes precisely because they stand in a haphazard and orthogonal relation to the real phonological and morphological categories of English. Each is, at best, a cover category for a number of sounds that are actually separate phonemes, each occurring in thousands of different signals.

Our demonstration will take the form of an illustration of how the characteristic acoustic patterning of English would be *altered* in the absence of the two number systems. The difference between the acoustic patterning of English with and without the two number systems constitutes that portion of its overall acoustic asymmetry for which the two number systems are responsible.

As a representative sample of English we will employ once again the Jane Smiley short story that was mentioned in Chapter 5 (Table 5.1). The first step is to count the number of sibilant and nasal sounds.[7] This is done by reading the text aloud and counting each instance of a nasal and sibilant sound perceived. 2503 nasal sounds and 2424 sibilant sounds were tabulated by the counter (trained in clinical phonetics) while attending to her oral rendition of the text.[8]

The next step is to cast some aspect of overall acoustic asymmetry in terms of our twö rough-and-ready categories. Since the categories do not neatly mesh with any phonological or grammatical analysis of English, there is no basis to prefer one descriptive statement to another. All have equal claim to legitimacy, and for present purposes it makes no difference what form it takes so long as it manages to encompass instances of the signals of the two number systems.

The most straightforward statement of observational fact is the ratio between sibilant sounds and nasal sounds.

TABLE 10.1   Observed ratio of sibilant to nasal sounds in running text

Number of sibilant sounds:	2424
Number of nasal sounds:	2503
Ratio of sibilant to nasal sounds:	0.97

Source: Jane Smiley, 'Long Distance', *The Atlantic*, January 1987.

The ratio of sibilant to nasal sounds is 0.97, a departure from symmetrical distribution of 0.03.

Similar calculations by the same counter following the same procedure were conducted on 700-word texts of French, German, Spanish and Russian. The differing ratios reflect how these other languages sound different from English along one objectively measurable parameter.

TABLE 10.2   Ratio of sibilant to nasal sounds in French, German, Spanish and Russian

French	0.67
German	0.74
Spanish	0.94
Russian	1.01

The third step is to calculate what the ratio between sibilants and nasals would be if neither of our two number systems existed while everything else remained the same. This is done by recounting the number of sibilants and nasals in the oral text, this time *omitting* all instances that are manifestations of the signals in the two number systems. (The number of nasals falls slightly due to three instances of the word *children*.)

362 THE PHENOMENA OF LINGUISTICS

TABLE 10.3   Calculated ratio in the absence of the two number systems

Number of sibilant sounds:	1652
Number of nasal sounds:	2500
Ratio of sibilant to nasal sounds:	0.66

It can be seen that in the absence of the two number systems the overall ratio of sibilant to nasal sounds would drop from 0.97 to 0.66. Put another way, the directly observable consequence of the two hypothesized number systems is that the ratio of sibilants to nasals in one particular text is 0.97 rather than 0.66, a ratio which would make it sound, in one respect at least, more like the sample of French.

This initial calculation can be broken down so as to show the effect of the Entity Number System and the Focus Number System individually. This break-down reveals that in the absence of the Entity Number System the ratio would be 0.88, and in the absence of the Focus Number System the ratio would be 0.71. The earlier difference of 0.31 between the calculated and observed ratios 0.66 and 0.97, can now be seen to be due chiefly to the existence of the Focus Number System in English.[9]

It is not only the simple existence of the two number systems that contributes to the overall acoustic asymmetry of English, but their substantive structure as well. If their structure were different, their effect would be different. This can be illustrated by calculating what the ratio between sibilant and nasal sounds would be if, say, the signals and meanings in each system remained the same, but their pairings were reversed. (In this calculation all words that manifest our signal *Entity -0* would be *Entity -s* and all instances of *Entity -s* would be *Entity -0*.)

TABLE 10.4   Calculated ratio of sibilant to nasal sounds with *Entity -s* = ONE and *Entity -0* = MORE THAN ONE

Number of sibilant sounds:	3221
Number of nasal sounds:	2500
Ratio of sibilant to nasal sounds:	1.29

Table 10.4 reveals that if the structure of English were slightly different from what it actually is, the ratio between sibilant and nasal sounds in the text would rise from 0.97 to 1.29. A similar calculation with the pairing of the signals and meanings in the Focus Number System reversed reveals that the ratio would drop

from 0.97 to 0.74, making it sound more like the sample of German.

In summary, the calculations show that both the existence and structure of the two number systems contribute in demonstrable ways to the overall acoustic asymmetry of English. These two theoretical constructs are thus ultimately justified because they (help to) establish an explanatory link (via the analyses presented in Chapters 2–8) between general goal-directed principles of human behaviour applied to the messages people wish to communicate, and the acoustic asymmetry of English.

10.6 Theory-Based Description

A demonstration of this kind was omitted in our analytical chapters for obvious reasons. Aside from the narrow theoretical point it establishes, the demonstration is neither very compelling nor interesting. But then no scientific theory appears particularly compelling or interesting if forced to illustrate its empirical success in terms of purely observational categories.[10] With good reason, all scientific theories soon shift over to the description of empirical data in theory-based terms. Theory-based categories allow the analyst to isolate and abstract from the disparate range of heterogeneous phenomena that initially confronts him just those facts relevant to the theory he is attempting to construct.

As illustration, we now offer an alternative demonstration of statistical asymmetry to be found in the same text, but now characterized in terms of the signals from the two Number Systems. Table 10.5 (occurring as Table 5.1 and 7.1) presents the departure from symmetrical distribution of *Occurrence -s* and *-0* and those instances of *Entity -0* and *-s* associated with lexical items describing the entity in Focus. The distribution of the four

TABLE 10.5 Co-occurrence of Entity Number (of P or P_1) and Focus Number

	Entity -0	*Entity -s*	
Occurrence -s	+55 552 (100%)	−55 0 (0%)	
Occurrence -0	−55 5 (8%)	+55 61 (92%)	p < 0.001

Source: Jane Smiley, 'Long Distance', *The Atlantic*, January 1987.

signals departs by ± 55 from what would be expected if their distribution were symmetrical with respect to each other.

Casting things in this form allows for a tighter link between theory and distributional fact, for it isolates just those facts about which the two analyses have something to say. First, the type of descriptive category (signals) is now motivated by a general theory of language. Their specific identity is supported by the fact that their hypothesized meanings can be demonstrated to contribute, in various ways, to parts of the messages associated with their appearance. Secondly, their statistical skewing is an instance of textual resonance. The general functional need for textual resonance is due to the widespread morphological and semantic indeterminacy inherent in the signals and meanings that constitute the linguistic code. Thirdly, the structure of the Focus Number System favours its deployment by and large in a resonating capacity (with respect to the Entity Number System) because of (1) the practical equivalence of its meanings with those of the Entity Number System (thus motivating similar strategies of use); (2) its limited availabilty in comparison with the Entity Number System; and (3) language users' favouring of communicative strategies that do not undermine and interfere with other strategies upon which they also rely.

While the skewing in Table 10.5 does not affect the ratio of sibilant and nasal sounds, it does have a directly perceptible acoustic correlate. The skewing of signals has the effect of distributing the sibilant sounds at more regular intervals in the acoustic continuum. If the signals of the two number systems exhibited no skewing, there would be more combinations of *Entity -s + Occurrence -s* and *Entity -∅ + Occurrence -∅* (often in adjacent words), producing the impression of irregularly distributed sibilant clumps.

10.7 Mediational Explanation

Sign-based theory clearly aspires to explanation in linguistic analysis; but of a kind differing from that of generative-transformational theory. The generative conception is essentially reductionist. It attempts to reduce linguistic structure to an axiomatic system whose formal characteristics are a particular manifestation of human genetics, whose basic structure is, in turn, a particular manifestation of organic chemistry, and so on.

Sign-based theory is non-reductionist in that it is not attempting to construct a sequence of deductively-linked sub-theories leading from speech back, presumably, to particle physics.

Instead, it is mediational. The theory of linguistic signs functions as a link between the acoustic continuum and a range of disparate facts that do not currently fall within the explanatory scope of any existing scientific theory.

It is hard to fault the generative goal in conception, for reductionism has proved spectacularly successful in the physical sciences. But one can question its feasibility in any investigation in the sphere of human affairs. If one's ultimate commitment lies in coming to the best understanding of the phenomena presently possible, then this argues strongly for the wisdom of allowing many aspects of the human condition to be taken as givens.

This refusal to axiomatize has been a major sticking point in the acceptance of functionalist approaches to language. Recall Newmeyer's criticism of functionalist approaches that 'attribute whatever structural property is being discussed to informally described human states, drives, needs, abilities, and such that have no basis in any existing formalized theory of human behaviour or cognition' (Newmeyer 1983:112); (cf. Sperber and Wilson 1986:93).

Naturally such a procedure is defective if there is any doubt about the drives, needs and abilities appealed to. But if the characteristics themselves can be established as descriptively valid, then the absence of a psychological theory that recognizes and explains them does not make them illicit. For instance, the Chapter 4 questionnaire asked subjects to decide whether particular animals interested them or not. The ranking of the thirteen animals that resulted was no more than a descriptive fact because it did not follow from any general psychological theory. But that unexplained *psychological* fact could legitimately serve to explain a *linguistic* fact, namely, the ranking of the animals according to the percentage of subjects categorizing them as MORE THAN ONE.

One can hope that such general characteristics of people will one day be rooted in a comprehensive psychological theory. But to insist that the practising linguist await such a theory is to forego the understanding presently possible and essentially to counsel closing shop.

Messages as givens
By far the largest body of facts taken here as given are the messages that people communicate. No explanation is offered for why a language user wishes to convey the particular message he or she does. Yet the messages people wish to convey are collectively a crucial determining factor in the overall asymmetry

created by the distribution of signals.[11]

The communicative intent of language users is, of course, taken as a given by all linguists. In the present context, however, this step is open to challenge because messages are, to recall, treated as a part of the *explanans*, not the *explanandum*: messages are facts against which linguistic meanings are tested, but not part of the primary data to be accounted for. For sign-based theory, then, the absence of a general psychological theory that explains why language users wish to convey the particular messages they do makes their presence in the *explanans* a serious impediment to a reductionist account.

Their introduction is justified because a fair degree of consensus among speakers of the language can be achieved regarding messages. One can establish *what* the message is without being able to explain *why* the speaker or writer wished to convey it. But that is all that need be established for the immediate task of accounting for the choice of linguistic meanings.[12]

The meaning-message link

A more problematic reliance on unexplained facts involves the link between meaning and message. This link has been characterized as a means-ends relation, where the means suit the end in a non-arbitrary way. In language, this relation takes the form of a readily recognizable conceptual connection between meaning and message. That is what allows hearers to infer novel messages in novel contexts without prior agreement.

While illumination by psychological theory is always welcome support for a claimed link between meaning and message, linguistic analysis need not await such illumination so long as there is substantial inter-subjective agreement that a link exists. To justify the choice of a linguistic meaning, merely the fact *that* people perceive a semantic connection need be established, not *why* they see it (or what it tells us about human cognition).

This leads to a kind of kitchen psychology in which the means-end relation is open to straightforward empirical confirmation because the facts at issue are themselves ones of impression and appearance. If, say, a representative group of people agree that the meaning MORE THAN ONE (Entity in Focus) fits the message conveyed by *the people are leaving* better than the meaning ONE (Entity in Focus), *then it does*; there is no higher truth against which the judgement must be tested. One can find the degree of agreement unsatisfactory, question the good faith of the judges, or suspect they have misunderstood the task; but their individual decisions are unappealable.[13]

While the implicatory connections among concepts are in themselves purely descriptive facts, their introduction as the bridge between meaning and message constitutes an *explanatory* step (within the context of linguistic analysis) because they are facts *of a different order* from those between which they mediate. Meanings, messages (and the acoustic continuum) are all language-particular, while the implicatory connections among concepts are *universal* facts about the way human beings think; for they must be judged as plausible and reasonable even by analysts who are not members of the culture whose language is under analysis. And it is precisely this requirement that raises the link they establish above that of language-particular description.

In linguistics, we have argued, the mode of explanation should follow from an emerging understanding of the phenomena under investigation, not from an *a priori* commitment to a grand idealistic design for scientific inquiry in general. As Moore and Carling (1982) put it, the drawback to an initial commitment to axiomatic, reductionist explanation in linguistics is that it requires an idealizational framework so severe that it excludes the very factors crucial to an understanding of the phenomena being investigated.

10.8 The Explanatory Chain

In view of the numerous ranges of facts taken as unexplained givens, in what sense can sign-based theory claim to offer explanation? Its explanatory force lies in the revelation that people's linguistic behaviour is a particular manifestation of a number of more general human characteristics and facts not initially recognized to be at work. To illustrate this link-up we will articulate, first in summary form, and then in step-wise fashion, the explanatory chain constructed in the course of this analysis.

At one end stands the communicative/instrumental orientation comprised of a general theory of linguistic structure based on its communicative function, along with those human characteristics and abilities upon which people draw in pursuing goals in general. At the other end lies a range of phenomena, the immediately perceptible acoustic asymmetry of vocal sound.

Standing between these two ends is a set of theoretical constructs: the two number systems, as well as ancillary hypotheses about their strategies of use. Their general nature is informed by the orientation; their specific nature is fashioned so as to select features of vocal sound as manifestations of signals whose presence is justified by the meanings they bear and their contribution to the communication of messages. Messages comprise a body of facts introduced by the orientation as relevant to the explanation of (a portion of) vocal sound by virtue of being the *goal* motivating its production.

The language-particular constructs function to bridge the two ends of the chain, providing a principled description (in terms of signals) of speech and, at the other, effecting a link (in terms of meanings and the strategies they engender) to the *universal* characteristics of linguistic structure and facts of human psychology as both these relate to the communicative goal. An explanatory connection is thus established between the initial orientation and (features of) the vocal product of a particular group of speakers.

And now in more detail as developed in Chapters 2–8:

A.   The *formal structure* of the two number systems derives from the fundamental conception adopted here of a language as a communicative system composed of paired signals and meanings. Its deductive support stems from the fact that other communicative systems are known to manifest that structure.

B.   The *substantive structure* of the two systems is justified on empirical grounds: the hypothesized signals manifest themselves in sound (or letters) associated with messages which their hypothesized meanings fit.

C.   The *manner* of their fit (i.e., their strategies of use) follows general principles (e.g., the precision strategy) that have wide independent empirical support from diverse languages. Their deductive support stems from two sources: (1) characteristics of the communicative instrument, and (2) characteristics of its users.

    1.   The *discrepancy* between the finite semantic resources of the language and the infinite expressive goals of its users pressures language users to exploit the communicative potential of the available meanings to a maximum (i.e., to employ them in ways that depart from objective truth).

    2.   The *goal-directed nature* of language use leads people to bring to bear on the problem of maximum exploitation those general characteristics of intelligence,

resourcefulness, ingenuity and imagination that they draw on in using tools to pursue goals elsewhere; both speaker and hearer rely on the implicatory and associative connections among concepts to imply and infer messages.

D.   The specific *nature* of the contribution of meanings to the communicative process is (1) to characterize and distinguish the intended message, and (2) to create textual resonance.

E.   Textual resonance functions (a) to help resolve the morphological and semantic indeterminacy which is a *universal* structural feature of language, and (b) to provide immediate confirmation to hearers that they are on the right interpretive track.

F.   The primary *mode* of their contribution to the communicative process is influenced (in the present analysis, at any rate) by their availability. Availability decreases the need for alternative, back-up strategies and thus favours strategies of deployment in which the meanings function expressively.

G.   The Entity Number System is always available any time a word designating an entity is employed, and thus often functions *expressively*. By contrast, the Focus Number System is only available with certain tenses, and only for the entity in Focus; its limited availability favours its use in a non-crucial, *resonating* capacity.

H.   The use of the Focus Number System in a resonating capacity is, in large part, responsible for *the asymmetrical association* of its signals with those of the Entity Number System (Table 10.5) in language use.

I.   The asymmetrical association of the signals of the two number systems contributes to *the overall perceptible acoustic asymmetry* of English (e.g. Tables 10.1–10.2) that constitutes (a component of) the ultimate phenomena at the observational level.

10.9 An Independent Linguistics

This chapter began with a discussion seemingly aimed at establishing our own claim to science and impugning that of others. But our real interest is not in adjudicating scientific credentials but in reclaiming for linguistics its rightful place as an independent discipline. By this we mean a discipline that finds human language of legitimate interest in its own right, not just for what it can tell us about the nature of thought, cognition, or the mind. Such a linguistics must delimit its own object of study, decide what its proper mode of explanation should be, and determine for itself what constitutes success.

The real consequence of our return to acoustic asymmetry as the foremost thing palpably and measurably *there* is not to restrict the linguist in what he can study, but to free him from all obligations, save one, that are not of his own choosing. Sentences, grammaticality, syntactic rules, sound-sense relations, (literal) sentence meaning, truth value, and, yes, linguistic signs, are all constructs of the analyst, who may elaborate or discard them as he sees fit. Either these notions prove their worth by contributing to an understanding of something logically prior and external to themselves, or they deserve to go the way of phlogiston and aether.

The goal of an independent linguistics is, at heart, a conservative one; and the result is a linguistic theory of relatively modest aspiration. But a more ambitious, visionary definition of the discipline runs the risk of remaining perpetually in a programmatic state, making the actual empirical success of the practising linguist impossible to assess.

We believe that the interests of linguistics as a fruitful, self-standing discipline are best served by a theoretical framework in which linguistic analysis can be practised as normal science. In such a framework, linguistics is free to draw upon the achievements in other disciplines whenever available, without being hobbled by a critical dependence on achievements that lie far in the future. It can grow in scope and rigour, as did the exact sciences, but at a pace commensurate with its actual empirical success. In the long run, we believe such a linguistics holds the promise of providing a solid and unique foundation upon which inquiry beyond language can build.

Notes

1. This is not to say that languages and dialects can be properly distinguished and classified on a purely acoustic basis. Whether or not the grouping corresponds to any linguistically significant one is irrelevant in the present context. Any grouping, if it can be replicated by either the same person or by other people, serves to establish the immediate point, namely, that the vocal sound produced by different groups of people manifests characteristically different acoustic asymmetries.

   Such vocal samples would consist mainly of speech if randomly selected, so this means that human speech is acoustically asymmetrical as well, although at this point there is no principled basis for restricting the scope of the initial problem to speech.

2. It might be objected, following Popper, that the acoustic asymmetry of vocal sound can only be recognized by human beings who are attuned to it because they already speak one language. But this observer-dependent aspect is present in the initial phenomena underlying all sciences. For all we know, perceiving the physical world in terms of three-dimensional space, time and physical objects is also observer-dependent, and that ultimate, observer-independent reality is quite different. But while this possibility is philosophically intriguing, it is not normally a concern of practising scientists. Any science, whether it be linguistics or chemistry, is made *by* human beings *for* human beings, not for contemplation by a transcendent intelligence (this, as we understand it, is Popper's larger point). Our aim here is not to free linguistics from its human practitioners and their perceptual and cognitive dispositions (clearly an impossibility), but simply to free it from metaphysical preoccupations and biases that are quite within our power to abandon.

3. To repeat, we acknowledge that the problem of acoustic asymmetry is not theory-free in Popper's sense of being independent of human cognitive categories and expectations. But it is, we maintain, not critically dependent upon a particular conception of the nature of language, nor, indeed upon the notion of language at all.

4. In calling Morse code extra-linguistic we are focusing exclusively on the conventional pairing between sound and letters, setting aside the fact that letters, in turn, serve to encode linguistic signals. If one nevertheless insists that Morse code is, in spirit, language based, then one is granting the point for which we are attempting to offer external support, namely, that the structure of language is essentially that of a code system.

5. It may be that the structure of language has no external motivation; that language is unique, having a structure all to itself. Although this is certainly a logical possibility, it would seem unwise, on methodological grounds, to entertain it at the outset. Better to reserve it as a conclusion to turn to only after all attempts to find external motivation for linguistic structure had failed. For if one

initially assumes lack of external motivation, it is hard to see what would ever lead the analyst to reconsider that assumption. On the other hand, if language has no external motivation, then attempts to demonstrate that it does will surely fail, and the null hypothesis will prevail in the end.

6. Since neither messages nor communication are its object of explanation, sign-based theory is neither a theory of 'meaning' nor a theory of communication (comparable, say, to that proposed by Sperber and Wilson 1986). Rather, it is a theory of acoustic asymmetry, a theory in which linguistic meanings (as well as the notion of language itself) are explanatory constructs. The dilemma of modern linguistics, we believe, is that it has attempted to construct explanatory theories for notions that are already, in themselves, explanations. The recommendation of the present chapter is to reinstate into linguistics the publicly observable phenomena to which such notions as language, 'meaning' and communication stand in an explanatory relation.

7. In demonstrating the acoustic asymmetry to be found in a sample of oral English we have, for practical reasons, narrowed the scope of the initial problem, for the sample does not include a representative component of the non-linguistic sounds (e.g., grunts, coughs, humming, whistling) also produced by English speakers. However until we have evidence to the contrary, the contribution of such non-linguistic sounds to acoustic asymmetry can be assumed to be a constant from group to group and thus it factors out if one's starting point is the characteristic ways the vocal sounds produced by people *differ* from each other. If, as is probable, the non-linguistic sound of various groups of people proves to differ in characteristic ways as well, then that, too, demands an explanation.

8. The counter adhered strictly to the phonetic reality of her pronunciation. Counted as sibilants were all instances of what a phonemic analysis would characterize as the phonemes /s/, /z/, /ʃ/, /ʒ/, /č/, /ǰ/, as well as sounds whose phonemic status is uncertain, but which, in the pronunciation of the counter contained a sibilant component e.g., si*tu*ation. Counted as nasals were all instances of what would be the phonemes /n/, /m/ and /ŋ/).

9. A similar demonstration of the effect of the two Number Systems on graphic asymmetry could be offered by calculating the ratio of curved-line to straight-line figures in the text with and without the signals from the two Number Systems.

10. Recall the allusion in Chapter 1 to the consternation of a chemist if he were required to demonstrate the explanatory power of molecular theory while employing the descriptive categories of alchemy.

11. For example, the short story we chose for our demonstration was told almost exclusively in the present tense, thus assuring frequent use of the Focus Number System. This had the effect of increasing the ratio of sibilant to nasal sounds over what it presumably is when

calculated on a larger body of data that included a representative amount of past tense narrative.

12. When features of the message are too subtle to be reliably assessed through introspective examination alone, then more objective methods must be employed. The questionnaire in Chapter 4 is an example.

13. Other examples of meaning-message links requiring such inter-subjective agreement include: the suitability of the meaning DOUBT for questions; the suitability of the meaning DIFFEREN-TIATION NOT REQUIRED for mass reference; the suitability of the meaning of *dial*$_1$ (posited in 3.6) for referring to the face of a rotary telephone; the suitability of HIGHER CONTROLLER (rather than LOWER CONTROLLER) for *John* in *John opened the door*.

When inter-subjective agreement is not possible, then one must indeed turn to 'illumination by psychological theory'. The application of the notion of semantic prototype that has emerged from recent psychological research into the way people apply conceptual categories is a case in point. Chapter 2 invoked this notion to good advantage in its discussion of *fruit* and *vegetable*.

References

ABRAMOWITZ, J. (1986) term paper for Introductory Linguistics, Yeshiva College, instructor Alan Huffman.

AISSEN, J. and LADUSAW, W. (1988) 'Agreement and Multistratality'. In Brentari, D., Larson, G. and MacLeod. L. (eds) *Parasession on Agreement in Grammatical Theory*. Chicago Linguistic Society, Chicago.

ALLAN, K. (1980) 'Nouns and Countability'. *Language* 3:541–67.

ANDERSON, S. (1974) 'On Dis-Agreement Rules'. *Linguistic Inquiry* 3:449–51.

AOYAMA, T. (1983) 'The free-floating Focus system in Japanese: Form-content analysis of *wa* and *ga*'. *Gengo kenkyu: Journal of the Linguistic Society of Japan* 83:41–60.

BACH, E. (1974) *Syntactic Theory*. Holt, Rinehart & Winston, New York.

BEVER, T. (1975) 'Functional explanations require independently motivated functional theories'. In Grossman, R., Sam, L. and Vance, T. (eds) *Papers from the Parasession on Functionalism*. Chicago Linguistic Society, Chicago.

BLOOMFIELD, L. (1933) *Language*. Holt, Rinehart & Winston, New York.

BOLINGER, D. (1977) *Meaning and Form*. Longman, London.

BOLINGER, D. (1978) 'Free will and determinism in language: or, who does the choosing, the grammar or the speaker?'. In Suner, M. (ed.) *Contemporary Studies in Romance Linguistics*. Georgetown University Press, Georgetown DC.

BOUSON, J. (1988) *'Is you jog?' – The Interlanguage Verbal System of College ESL Students*. Rutgers University Ed D dissertation, University Microfilms Intl.

CELCE-MURCIA, M. and LARSEN-FREEMAN, D. (1983) *The Grammar book*. Newbury House, Rowley Massachusetts.

CHOMSKY, N. (1955) *Semantic considerations in grammar*. Monograph No. 8, Georgetown Monograph Series, Georgetown, DC.

CHOMSKY, N. (1957) *Syntactic structures*. Mouton, The Hague.

CHOMSKY, N. (1965) *Aspects of the theory of syntax*. The MIT Press, Cambridge, Mass.

CHOMSKY, N. (1981) *Lectures on Government and Binding*. Foris Publications, Dordrecht.

CLARK, H. (1979) 'When Nouns surface as verbs'. *Language* 4: 767–811.

COLLIN, F. (1985) *Theory and understanding*. Blackwell, Oxford.

COMRIE, B. (1976) *Aspect*. Cambridge University Press, Cambridge.

CONTINI-MORAVA, E. (1976) 'Statistical demonstration of a meaning: the Swahili locatives in existential assertions'. *Studies in African Linguistics* 7:137–56.

CONTINI-MORAVA, E. (1983) 'Relative tense in discourse: the inference of time orientation. In Klein-Andreu, F. (ed.) *Discourse Perspectives on Syntax*. Academic Press, New York.

CONTINI-MORAVA, E. (1989) *Discourse Pragmatics and Semantic Categorization: the case of Negation and Tense-Aspect with special reference to Swahili*. Mouton de Gruyter, Berlin.

CULLER, J. (1976) *Ferdinand de Saussure*. Penguin Modern Masters, Harmondsworth, and (1986) Cornell University Press, Ithaca.

CURME, G. (1977) *A Grammar of the English Language*. Verbatim, Essex CT.

DINNEEN, F. (1989) 'Ferdinand de Saussure'. *The Georgetown Journal of Languages and Linguistics* 1:31–53.

DIVER, W. (1963) 'The Chronological system of the English verb'. *Word* 19:141–81.

DIVER, W. (1964) 'The Modal system of the English verb'. *Word* 20:322–52.

DIVER, W. (1969) 'The System of Relevance of the Homeric verb'. *Acta Linguistica Hafniensia* 12:45–68.

DIVER, W. (1975) 'Introduction'. *Columbia University Working Papers in Linguistics* (CUWPL) 2:1–26.

DIVER, W. (1976) 'A Concise Grammar of modern English'. *CUWPL* 4:1–21.

DIVER, W. (1981) 'On Defining the Discipline'. *CUWPL* 6:59–116.

DIVER, W. (1984) *The Grammar of English*. Unpublished manuscript.

DIVER, W. (1987) 'The dual'. *CUWPL* 8:100–14.

DIVER, W., OTHEGUY, R., REID, W., ZUBIN, D. and KIRSNER, R. (1980) 'The Ecology of Language'. *CUWPL* 5. Articles on grammatical systems in Spanish, French, German and Dutch with an Introduction.

DIVER, W., HUFFMAN, A., GILDIN, B., MOORE, K. and AOYAMA, T. (1982) 'A Solution to the Problem Posed by the Notion 'Subject''. *CUWPL* 7. Articles on Latin, French, Finnish and Japanese with an Introduction.

DUBOIS, J. (1985) 'Competing motivations'. In Haiman, J. (ed.) *Iconicity in Syntax*. John Benjamins, Amsterdam.

EMIG, J. (1971) *The Composing Processes of Twelfth Graders: NCTE Research Report no. 13*. National Council on the Teaching of English, Urbana, Illinois.

EMIG, J. (1983) *The Web of Meaning*. Boynton/Cook, Upper Montclair, New Jersey.

FODOR, J. D. (1977) *Semantics: theories of meaning in generative grammar*. Harper and Row, New York.

FREGE, G. (1950/1984) *The Foundations of Arithmetic*. Blackwell, Oxford.

GARCIA, E. (1975) *The Role of Theory in Linguistic Analysis: the Spanish pronoun system*. North Holland, Amsterdam.

GARCIA, E. (1977) 'On the Practical Consequences of theoretical principles'. *Lingua* **43**:129–69.

GARCIA, E. (1979) 'Discourse without syntax'. In Givon, T., Li, C. (eds) *Discourse and Syntax*. Academic Press, New York.

GARCIA, E. (1983) 'Context dependence of language and of linguistic analysis'. In Klein-Andreu, F. (ed.) *Discourse Perspectives on Syntax*. Academic Press, New York.

GARCIA, E. (1985) 'Quantity into Quality: synchronic indeterminacy and language change'. *Lingua* **65**:275–306.

GARVIN, P. (1984) 'Functional Empiricism – an explicit epistemoloy for a behavioural approach to semiotics'. *Toronto Semiotic Circle* **1**:31–55.

GILDIN, B. (1979) 'Subject Inversion in French: Natural Word Order or *l'arbitraire du signe*'. In Nuessel, F. (ed.) *Essays in Contemporary Romance Linguistics*. Newbury House, Rowley, Mass.

GILDIN, B. (1985) *The Problem of Subject Order in French: A Semantic Analysis*. Columbia University PhD dissertation, University Microfilms Intl.

GIVON, T. (1979) *On Understanding Grammar*. Academic Press, New York.

GOROKHOVA, E. (1990) *Acquisition of English articles by native speakers of Spanish*. Rutgers University Ed D dissertation, University Microfilms Intl.

GORUP, R. (1987) 'Verbs of double government in Serbo-Croatian'. *Slovene Studies* **9/1–2**:93–9.

GREEN, G. (1984) 'Why Agreement must be stipulated for there – insertion'. In Alvarez, G., Brodie, B. and McCoy, T. (eds) *Proceedings of the First Eastern States Conference on Linguistics*. The Ohio State University, Columbus, Ohio.

GROSS, M. (1979) 'On the failure of generative grammar'. *Language* **4**:859–85.

HAIMAN, J. (1985) *Iconicity in Syntax*. John Benjamins, Amsterdam.

HALLIDAY, M. and HASAN, R. (1976) *Cohesion in English*. Longman, London.

HIRTLE, W. (1982) *Number and Inner Space: A study of grammatical number in English*. Les Presses de L'Universite Laval, Quebec.

HUFFMAN, A. (1983) ''Government of the Dative' in French'. *Lingua* **60**:283–309.

HUFFMAN, A. (1985) *The Semantic Organization of the French clitic pronouns: lui and le*. Columbia University PhD dissertation, Univerity Microfilms Intl.

JACOBS, R. and ROSENBAUM, P. (1968) *English Transformational Grammar*. Blaisdell, Waltham, Mass.

JENNESS, D. (1955) *The Indians of Canada*, 3rd edn. National Museum of Canada Bulletin **65** (Anthropological Series No. 15), Ottawa.

JESPERSEN, O. (1933/1966) *Essentials of English Grammar*. University of Alabama Press, University, Alabama.

JESPERSEN, O. (1909/1949) *A Modern English Grammar. Part VI: Morphology*. Carl Winter, Heidelberg.

KALDENBACH, R. (1990) 'Home/Garden'. *The Recorder* February 17, Greenfield, Massachusetts.

KATZ, J. (1972) *Semantic Theory*. Harper & Row, New York.

KATZ, J. (1980) 'Chomsky on meaning'. *Language* **1**:1–41.

KATZ, J. and FODOR, J. (1963) 'The Structure of semantic theory'. *Language* **2**:170–210.

KATZ, J. and BEVER, T. (1976) 'The Fall and rise of empiricism'. In Bever, T., Katz, J., and Langendoen, T. (eds) *An Integrated Theory of Linguistic Ability*. Thomas, Y. Crowell Company, New York.

KEENAN, E. (1976) 'Towards a Universal Definition of 'Subject''. In Li, C. (ed.) *Subject and Topic*. Academic Press, New York.

KEENAN, E. and COMRIE, B. (1977) 'Noun Phrase Accessibility and Universal Grammar'. *Linguistic Inquiry* **8**:63–99.

KEMPSON, R. (1977) *Semantic Theory*. Cambridge University Press, Cambridge, Mass.

KIRSNER, R. (1969) 'The Role of *zullen* in the grammar of Modern Standard Dutch'. *Lingua* **24**:101–54.

KIRSNER, R. (1979a) *The Problem of Presentative Sentences in Modern Dutch*. North Holland, Amsterdam.

KIRSNER, R. (1979b) 'Deixis in Discourse: An exploratory study of the Modern Dutch demonstrative adjectives'. In Givon, T. and Li, C. (eds) *Discourse and Syntax*. Academic Press, New York.

KIRSNER, R. (1985) 'Does Sign-Oriented Linguistics have a Future?: on Sign, Text, and the Falsifiability of Theoretical Constructs'. In Tobin, Y. (ed.) *From Sign to text: a semiotic view of communication*. John Benjamins, Amsterdam.

KLEIN-ANDREU, F. (1983) 'Grammar in Style: Spanish adjective placement'. In Klein-Andreu, F. (1983) (ed.) *Discourse Perspectives on Syntax*. Academic Press, New York.

KUHN, T. (1962) *The Structure of Scientific Revolutions*. The University of Chicago Press, Chicago.

LABOV, W. (1973) 'The boundaries of words and their meanings'. In Bailey, C. and Shuy, R. (eds) *New Ways of Analyzing Variation in English*. Georgetown University Press, Georgetown.

LADEFOGED, P. (1975) *A Course in Phonetics*. Harcourt Brace Jovanovich, New York.

LAKOFF, G. (1977) 'Linguistic gestalts'. In Beach, W., Fox, S. and Philosoph, S. (eds) *Papers from the 13th Regional Meeting*. Chicago Linguistic Society, Chicago.

LAKOFF, G. (1986) 'Classifiers as a reflection of mind'. In Craig, C. (ed.) *Noun Classes and Classification*. John Benjamins, Amsterdam.

LAKOFF, G. (1987) *Women, Fire, and Dangerous Things*. University of

Chicago Press, Chicago.

LAKOFF, G. and JOHNSON, M. (1980) *Metaphors We Live By*. University of Chicago Press, Chicago.

LANGACKER, R. (1988) 'Autonomy, agreement, and cognitive grammar'. In Brentari, D., Larson, G. and MacLeod, L. (eds) *Parasession on Agreement in Grammatical Theory*. Chicago Linguistic Society, Chicago.

LAPOINTE, S. (1980) *A Theory of Grammatical Agreement*. University of Massachusetts PhD dissertation. Also available as 1986 Garland, New York.

LATTEY, E. (1980) *Grammatical systems across languages: A study of Participation in English, German, and Spanish*. City University of New York Ph D dissertation, University Microfilms Intl.

LAWLER, J. (1975) 'On coming to terms with Achenese: The Function of Verbal Dis-Agreement'. In Grossman, R. E., Sam, L. J., Vance, T. J. (eds) *Papers from the Parasession on Functionalism*. Chicago Linguistic Society, Chicago.

LEECH, G. (1983) *Principles of Pragmatics*. Longman, London.

LEONARD, R. (1980) 'Swahili *e*, *ka* and *nge* as Signals of Meanings'. *Studies in African Linguistics* **11**:209–26.

LYONS, J. (1968) *Introduction to theoretical linguistics*. Cambridge University Press.

MCCAWLEY, J. (1975) 'Lexicography and the count-mass distinction'. *Berkeley Linguistics Society* **I**:314–21. Reprinted in McCawley, J. (1979) *Adverbs, Vowels, and Other Objects of Wonder*. The University of Chicago Press, Chicago.

MORGAN, J. (1972) 'Verb agreement as a rule of English'. In Peranteau, P., Levi, J., Phares, G. *Papers from the Eighth Regional Meeting*. Chicago Linguistics Society, Chicago.

MORGAN, J. (1984) 'Some Problems of Determination in English Number Agreement'. In Alvarez, G., Brodie, B., McCoy, T. (eds) *Proceedings of the First Eastern States Conference on Linguistics*. The Ohio State University, Columbus, Ohio.

MOORE, T. and CARLING, C. (1982) *Understanding Language: Towards a Post-Chomskyan Linguistics*. Macmillan Press, London.

NEWMEYER, F. (1983) *Grammatical Theory: Its Limits and its Possibilities*. University of Chicago Press, Chicago.

OTHEGUY, R. (1977a) *The meaning of Spanish el, la and lo*. The City University of New York Ph D dissertation, University Microfilms Intl.

OTHEGUY, R. (1977b) 'A Semantic Analysis of the Difference Between *el/la* and *lo*'. In Suner, M. (ed.) *Studies in Romance Linguistics*. Georgetown University Press, Washington, DC.

PALMER, F. (1978) *Grammar*. Penguin Books, Harmondsworth.

PENHALLURICK, J. (1975) 'Old English case and grammatical theory'. *Lingua* **36**:1–29.

PENHALLURICK, J. (1987) 'The Semantics of auxilliary inversion in English'. *Australian Journal of Linguistics* **7**:97–128.

PIERCE, J. E. (1985) 'The nature of English grammar'. *English Teaching*

Forum, July: 2–8.

PIERCE, J. E. (1979) *How English really works*. The HaPi Press, Portland, Oregon.

POPLACK, S. and TAGLIAMONTE, S. (1989) 'There's no tense like the present: Verbal -s inflection in early Black English. *Language Variation and Change* 1:47–84.

POLLARD, C. and SAG, I. (1988) 'An Information-based theory of agreement'. In Brentari, D., Larson, G., MacLeod, L. (eds) *Parasession on Agreement in Grammatical Theory*. Chicago Linguistic Society, Chicago.

POPPER, K. (1959) *The Logic of scientific discovery*. Hutchinson, London.

QUIRK, R. and GREENBAUM, S. (1973) *A concise grammar of contemporary English*. Longman, London.

RADFORD, A. (1984) *Transformational syntax*. Cambridge University Press, New York.

REDDY, M. (1979) 'The Conduit metaphor'. In Ortony, A. (ed.) *Metaphor and Thought*. Cambridge University Press, Cambridge.

REID, W. (1974) 'The Saussurian Sign as a control in linguistic analysis. *Semiotexte* 1:31–53.

REID, W. (1977) 'The quantitative validation of a grammatical hypothesis: the passe simple and the imparfait'. In Kegl, J., Nash, D. and Zaenen, A. (eds) *Proceedings of the Seventh Annual Meeting of the North Eastern Linguistic Society*, Cambridge, Massachusetts.

REID, W. (1979) *The Human Factor in linguistic analysis: the passe simple and the imparfait*. Columbia University PhD dissertation, University Microfilms Intl.

REID, W. and GILDIN, B. (1979) 'Semantic analysis without the sentence'. In Clyne, Hanks, Hofbauer (eds) *The Elements: A Parasession on Linguistic Units and Levels*. Chicago Linguistic Society, Chicago.

RODRIGUEZ-BACHILLER, B. (1985) *Learning the conceptual boundaries of difficult lexical pairs: CAI for intermediate ESL vocabulary*. Rutgers University Ed D dissertation, University Microfilms Intl.

ROSCH, E. (1977) 'Human categorization'. In Warren N. (ed.) *Advances in cross-cultural psychology* Vol. 1, Academic Press, New York.

ROSS, J. R. (1970), 'On declarative sentences', in Jacobs, R. A. and Rosenbaum, P. S. (eds) *Readings in English Transformational Grammar*, Blaisdell, Waltham, Mass. pp. 222–72.

RUHL, C. (1989) *On Monosemy*. State University of New York Press, Albany.

RYLE, G. (1949) *The Concept of Mind*. Hutchinson's University Library, London.

SALINGER, J. (1962) *The Catcher in the Rye*. Signet Books, New York.

SAUSSURE, F. de (1916) *Cours de linguistique generale*. Payot, Paris.

SEARLE, J. R. (1969) *Speech Acts: An essay in the philosophy of language*, Cambridge U.P., Cambridge.

SHANNON, C. and WEAVER, W. (1971) *The Mathematical Theory of Communication*. University of Illinois Press, Urbana.

SHRIBERG, L., and KENT, R. (1982) *Clinical Phonetics*. John Wiley and

Sons, New York.

SMITH, N. and WILSON, D. (1980) *Modern linguistics: the results of Chomsky's revolution*. Indiana University Press, Bloomington.

SPERBER, D. and WILSON, D. (1986) *Relevance: communication and cognition*. Blackwell, Oxford.

SOMMERS, N. (1980) 'Revision strategies of student writers and experienced adult writers'. *College Composition and Communication* **31**: 378–88.

TOBIN, Y. (1982) 'Asserting one's existence in modern Hebrew'. *Lingua* **58**:341–68.

TOBIN, Y. (1989) 'The *ayin-dalet* ('-D) System in Modern Hebrew: A sign-oriented approach'. In Weydt, H. (ed.) *Sprechen mit Partikeln*. de Gruyter, Berlin.

WARE, R. (1972) 'Some bits and pieces'. In Pelletier, F. (ed.) (1979) *Mass terms: some philosophical problems*. Reidel, Dordrecht.

WEINREICH, U. (1966) 'Explorations in semantic theory'. In *Current trends in linguistics, 3: theoretical foundations*. Mouton, The Hague. Reprinted in Weinreich, U. (1980) *On semantics*. University of Pennsylvania Press, Philadelphia.

WIERZBICKA, A. (1985) 'Oats and Wheat: The Fallacy of Arbitrariness'. In Haiman, J. (ed.) *Iconicity in Syntax*. John Benjamins, Amsterdam.

WHORF, B. L. (1962) *Language, thought and reality*. Carroll, J. (ed.) MIT Press, Cambridge, Mass.

ZUBIN, D. (1978) *Semantic substance and value relations: a grammatical analysis of case morphology in modern standard German*. Columbia University PhD dissertation, University Microfilms Intl.

ZUBIN, D. (1979) 'Discourse Function of Morphology: The Focus System in German'. In Givon, T. and Li, C. (eds) *Discourse and Syntax*. Academic Press, New York.

ZUBIN, D. (1984) 'Affect classification in the German gender system'. *Lingua* **63**:41–96.

ZUBIN, D. and KÖPCKE, K. (1986) 'Gender and folk taxonomy: the indexical relation between grammatical and lexical categorization'. In Craig, C. (ed.) *Noun Classes and Categorization*. John Benjamins, Amsterdam.

ZWICKY, A. (1968) 'Naturalness arguments in syntax'. In Darden, B., Bailey, C. and Davison, A. (eds) *Papers from the Fourth Regional Meeting*. Chicago Linguistic Society, Chicago.

Index